THE DIVINE PROGRAMMER

Creating Miracles

Aly McDonald
Ed Rychkun

www.edrychkun.com

ISBN 978-1-927066-10-2

There is no copyright to this book. If it helps you to understand life and choose the better one by allowing you to create miracles of health and wealth, go ahead and copy whatever you need. Please pass it on and credit the website below or the dedicated researchers mentioned in this book

www.edrychkun.com.

CONTENTS

PREFACE 7
  Ed's Story 7
  Aly's Story 10
INTRODUCTION 15
  The Divine Programmer 15
  The 7 Steps Of Manifesting Reality 17
  Our Goal Is Processes And Procedures 22

PART ONE: CREATING MIRACLES 25
CREATING MIRACLES INTRODUCTION 26

1 DIVINE PROGRAMMING: QUANTUM TOUCH 31

2 DIVINE PROGRAMMING: REGRESSION THERAPY 37

3 DIVINE PROGRAMMING: NATIVE MEDICINE 42

4 DIVINE PROGRAMMING: DIVINE CONNECTION 48

5 DIVINE PROGRAMMING: ADAM DREAMHEALER 55

6 DIVINE PROGRAMMING: ANCIENT HO'OPONOPONO 59

7 DIVINE PROGRAMMING: JOHN OF GOD 67

8 DIVINE PROGRAMMING: RELIGION & FAITH HEALING 72

9 DIVINE PROGRAMMING: ANCIENT PRAYER 79

10 DIVINE PROGRAMMING: MATRIX ENERGETICS 83

11 DIVINE PROGRAMMING: CREATOR-CREATRIX 93
  My Creator-Creatrix Process 94
  Insights Into Return Of The Divine Feminine 99

12 DIVINE PROGRAMMING: ENERGY UNBLOCKING 103

13 SUBCONSCIOUS MIND POWER 108
  Let US Summarize Health Processes 108
  The Common Denominators Of Healing Miracles 112
  The Subconscious Is The Missing Link 114
  The Importance Of Brainwaves 115

Is It Important To Be In An Altered State?	119
Is There A Biological Process To Belief?	125
Why Do We Need To Be In A State Of Well-Being?	127
What Is The Programmable System?	130

PART TWO: ATTRACTING MIRACLES 135
ATTRACTING MIRACLES INTRODUCTION 135

14 PROCESS OF CREATION IN THE REAL WORLD 140

15 PROCESS OF CREATION IN THE UNREAL WORLD 144
A New Look At Creating Reality 145
The Creation Of Perception 149

16 NAPOLEON HILL: THINK AND GROW RICH 150
The Law Of Success 151
Napoleon Hill Summarizes 154

17 WAYNE DYER: THE POWER OF INTENTION 157

18 JOE VITALE: THE ATTRACTOR FACTOR 162
Joe's 7 Ways To Attract Money 166

19 ESTER & JERRY HICKS: THE LAW OF ATTRACTION 169

20 JOHN KEHOE: MIND POWER 176

21 THE LAW OF CAUSE AND EFFECT 184
When The Law Does Not work 188

22 SUBCONSCIOUS MIND POWER AGAIN 191

23 MEASURING BELIEF 197
How Do You Test Belief? 201
Energy Focusing 207

24 CHANGING BELIEFS 209
Practice Will Change Your Beliefs 210
The 30 Day Mind plan Daily Routine 211
The Energy Investment Portfolio 212
The Paradigm Shift In Energy 215

25 SHIFTING THE ENVIRONMENT 217
...Well-Being at A Cellular Level 217
What Are Enzymes? 218

Why are Enzymes So Important?	219
How Are Enzymes Utilized In The Body?	223
Why Take Digestive Enzyme Supplements?	224
Typically Available Enzymes	225
The Importance Of Minerals	226
The 30 Day Body Plan	228

PART THREE: THE DIVINE COMPUTER — 231
THE DIVINE COMPUTER INTRODUCTION — 232

Now What?	233

26 WHAT IS CONSCIOUSNESS? — 234

Consciousness And Near Death Experiences	235
Consciousness - Separate Intelligent Energy Form	236
What does Near Dying Tell Us?	240
Important Conclusions About Near Dying	242

27 THE CHAKRA ENERGETIC SYSTEM — 244

The Chakra Energetic System	244
As Above So Below	246
The Chakra Antennae	247
The Dormant Higher Abilities	251
Important Conclusions About The Chakras	253

28 THE HEART ENERGETIC SYSTEM — 255

The Double Torus And Energy Vortexes	255
The Heart-Brain And Emotions	260
Being In The Heart Brain	266
The Love Center	267
Important Conclusions About The Heart	271

29 THE ENERGY BODY SYSTEM — 274

The Energy Body Planes And Bodies	275
What Is The Soul?	280
The Soul's Evolution	283
The Auric Bodies And Their Issues	284
The Physical To Causal Bodies	288
The Physical Body	289
The Etheric/Vital Body	290
The Astral/Emotional Body	293
The Mental/Intellectual Body	294
The Causal/Soul Body	295
The Manasic/Higher Mind Body	296

The Buddhic/Christic Body	**297**
The Atmic Body	**299**
The Monadic Aspect	**299**
The Logoic/God/Goddess/Solar Aspect	**300**
The Light Body	**301**
Consciousness Is All That Is, Was, Will Be	**309**
Important Conclusions About The Energy Body	**311**

30 WHAT ABOUT THE BRAIN? — **315**

The Brain Is Hardwired	**315**
Is The Brain A Computer?	**317**
The Brain As A Holographic Processor	**324**
The Brain Is The Holographic Processor Of Reality	**325**
Important Conclusions About The Brain?	**327**

31 THE QUANTUM SHOCK WAVE — **328**

Our Entangled Minds	**329**
Our Holographic Reality	**330**
Us Vibrating Humans	**331**
Science Is The Observer Of Its Self	**332**
The World Ain't Flat Anymore	**333**
Consciousness Changes Matter	**334**
The Ramifications Of This Are Simple	**337**
We Are Part Of A Universal Quantum Computer	**340**
Do We Live In An Intelligent Living Hologram?	**341**
All Energy Is Alive And Expanding	**342**
The Stages Of Evolution Of The Light Being	**344**
Important Conclusions About Quantum	**346**

32 MORPHIC FIELDS — **348**

The Morphic Field	**348**
Connections With Quantum Physics	**352**
Experiments On Morphic Fields	**353**
Important Conclusions About Morphic Fields	**354**

33 HOLOGRAPHIC REALITY — **355**

How Holograms Work	**355**
Holographic Awareness	**359**
The Holographic Projection Is Inside	**362**
Important Conclusions About Holograms	**366**

34 BASIC COMPUTER SYSTEMS — **368**

The Binary Digital Computer	**368**
The Binary Computer Chip Is The Workhorse	**370**

How Do You Program A Computer?	**373**
Analog Computers	**374**
Process Control Computers	**374**
Quantum Computers	**375**
Trinary Computers	**376**
Is The Trinary Computer Like The Human?	**377**
Important Conclusions About Computers	**378**

35 THE HUMAN COMPUTER SYSTEM **379**
Human Cells Are The workhorse	**379**
The Cell Protection Mechanism	**383**
The Human Versus Binary Systems	**384**
Important Conclusions About The Human Computers	**387**

36 WHAT HAVE WE LEARNED? **388**
Summary Of PART ONE	**388**
Summary Of PART TWO	**391**
Summary Of PART THREE	**394**
The New Supporting Evidence	**404**

37 THE DIVINE PROGRAMMER AND HEALTH MIRACLES **407**
The Programmer's Health Code	**407**
Setting The Healing Environment	**408**
Engaging In The Healing Process	**410**
The Suggested Program	**415**

38 THE DIVINE PROGRAMMER AND WEALTH MIRACLES **416**
The Programmer's Wealth Code	**416**
Setting The Wealth Environment	**417**
Engaging In The Wealth Creation Process	**418**
The Suggested Program	**421**

39 TO BE CONTINUED... **423**
Why Do These Processes Work?	**423**
How Does It All Work?	**424**

PREFACE

We feel it is important for you as a reader to meet us and to understand who we are, where we have come from in this lifetime, and why we have written this book. Having become centered in what you will come to know as the heart-brain, we wish to offer you what we have learned so it may help you in creating a better life.

Ed Rychkun   Aly McDonald

Ed's Story

Born as a Pisces in the rural backwoods of BC, Canada, I was always a curious kid, sensitive and independent, living close to nature in a simple but warm family life. Not fond of rules, schooling was a challenge for me but my parents encouraged me to go on so as to better my life they said; so I became what you would call a science junky at University. Here at the University of BC my curiosity and career took me 8 years as I delved into engineering, zoology, geology, physics, anthropology, computer science, economics, and mathematics. At the end of the day, when I graduated and headed into the world to make a living, it was a BSc. degree in mathematics and geology that won out. It led to a job in geological exploration with a major mining company.

And so it was that a traditional path of marriage and kids and a career in computer science and geology came forward as I moved into a position of an Operations Research programmer. In those days, computers were these giant punch card eating machines that used Fortran and Assembler. Here I delved in new research techniques for mining that could be programmed on a computer and this led to managerial positions with Placer Dome managing their computer department. My marriage brought a couple of wonderful boys but the spousal relationship seemed destined to end. It was a difficult time that eventually ended in divorce. Fortunately, it was not long after that I found my Soulmate and we headed off on a adventure that took us to Alberta where I became the Director of Information Services for a large coal mining company, and then to South Africa as a special computer consultant to IBM. Now married to my Soulmate, it was 1986 that we launched a new path of discovery. As the career churned, we came back to Canada where I became the CEO of a computer software firm engaged in subsurface geological modeling.

Well it all ended in 1997 and with health problems, as well as various financial challenges that terminated my career, it became the bumpy road of the corporate gopher wheel. As I engaged in the game of commerce I had become more and more detached from compassion and life. It was my Soulmate that kept me in a state of awareness that there was something missing. I had become more and more uncomfortable with that life of cold manipulation of others for the purpose of being a "successful executive". It should not have been a surprise that this stress would manifest itself in disease and disease. Having been diagnosed with an incurable disease of MS, and carrying some other issues like hypertension and neurological dysfunctions, it was still not apparent that these were a result of the stresses of the commerce boom and bust cycles. As a means of escape, I began to write books on recreation and humor. God knows I needed some! Having had my Mother and Brother die during that time of chaos, we became conscious of our health and became Reiki Masters. Here we could pursue healing techniques, engaging in ways in which I could overcome what I was told was going to be a serious problem with Multiple Sclerosis. At the turn of the century, I began to awaken to a niggling of a spiritual calling and a path that would hopefully create financial independence. Being discouraged with corporate life and working for others, we decided to follow a new path of independence.

I engaged in offshore business structuring, and this led to being a joint founder and CFO of a private bank and a mutual fund company in the Caribbean. It was a wonderful experience but it was all still subject to the boom bust cycles that appeared to follow me. With the eventual closure of these enterprises, and the financial calamities that it brought, my research and writing turned to the religious and commercial deception. It moved towards a more focused spiritual life and a quest for purpose and understanding of my life, and in particular, my life as to why it was the way it was. And so, as my evolution would have it, I began a more serious quest on the meaning of life and why these boom bust cycles prevailed. Of course, being disillusioned with the commerce and feeling that the functional years were limited because of the disease invading physical mobility; we decided to get financially liquidated and set out to enjoy the planet. It would involve continuing to engage in various business activities as a consultant, assisting others with writing business plans and helping them to attain financing for their projects.

With the years passing rapidly, I began the quest for healing myself. And as the traditional system showed no prospects, my spiritual inclinations led to the quest of energetic healing and creating one's own reality in a more proactive way, away from the norm of commerce, medicine and religion. It led to publishing many books on the topic, and attracting a new breed of people in our lives.

In this quest, I began to understand how we do create our own reality, and how we are not really victims; we are what we think. As a scientist at heart, it was difficult to understand how beliefs and the way we think and act impacts our health and wealth. So this led to a quest of better understanding the fringe sciences, with a subconscious urging to find the facts, and the need to be able to quantify a procedure from my management, financial, computer, and scientific background. The quest has not ended. The quest has been to level out and sustain a better life as it relates to proactive direct management of health and wealth. It has taken me into a new world of new science like quantum physics and the workings of subtle energies, higher divine forces, quantum computers, and the workings of our human architecture of DNA, subtle energetics, and biology. It led me to meet many wonderful people and many Healers. Aly McDonald is one of the precious ones.

This book is a result of this quest to heal body and mind. It is like a PhD thesis that brings things up to date on the research, findings, and results of many people. It will not answer all the questions because, I am not finished and there is much more to learn. However, my hope is that what you read here will assist you in opening up your mind to new beliefs and new opportunities to take a more proactive role in managing your wealth and health realities the way you want, without the traditional ups and downs of the gopher wheel of life.

I learned that my focus had to shift into a habitual pattern of thinking and creating perceptions about what I wanted, not what I did not want. I learned that these negative energies were silent thieves that stole reality and they had to be banished.

What is the highlight of this quest for meaning is my Soulmate and Guardian Angel who has stayed with my quest and supported me in everything I have engaged in, regardless of what it was or how it turned out. Her name is Hope, and that she has given me... the most wonderful lesson of all.

Ed Rychkun

Aly's Story

Many folks know by now we are in the Age of Aquarius. The symbol associated with my sign is the water carrier or water bearer; it is symbolic of the Gods nourishing the earth with life giving energies. One of the first to be called the water bearer was the Greek God Zeus in mythology. So it's no surprise that this is the sign in which I was born into. For the most part I fit into the biggest part of the description in describing the characteristics of an Aquarian.

Although an opportunity presented itself to gain education at an Art Institute at 19 years of age it was not supported by my parents. Life has always been very difficult having not been born with a silver spoon and coming from a broken family at a very young age. My own marriages have all been extremely difficult in that I have truly sought out the unconditional love that one seeks in a soul mate.

Higher Education came later in life at the ages of 34-38, then a loss of a child came into our lives and my attentions where drawn fully back into the family just before completing an Associate's Degree of Biological Science, Psychology & Art. It has been 10 years now since this event took place and I have since then taken a path onto other somewhat related areas of interest.

As a young child I loved to play outside, up trees and in the mud. My favorite thing to do that I always remembered was making mud pies and then taking the petals of the mimosa and sprinkling it on top for the décor always loving the sweet light scent of the blossom. Having lived in California at this time and being of young age I did not know growing up what kind of tree and flower that I loved so much as a child was, until one day as an adult in the deep south of the United States I saw the beautiful trees and I asked what it was. The blossoms look like little pink pom poms. I've always loved to create poems, sing, and draw pictures of the oceans and trees, still do. When I was young I could see spirits "good and bad" then one day I became so fearful of what I saw that I shut down that part of me. But I always knew and looked at the stars each night to make a prayer and a wish to my heavenly family, feeling homesick often, sending love and then drifting off to sleep.

In the spring of 1996. I had an experience where I accepted the Holy Spirit within my heart and the understanding of Yeshua "Jesus" and this is the earliest time of when I began to change spiritually. I was submerged into a full water baptism and when I came up out of the water I felt energy come over me as I have never felt in my entire life at that time. I knew I was loved, I was forgiven, and I was renewed and would never be the same again. I became very zealous for the church I was in at that time in that I was referred to as a Soul Winner for God. I shared my story with as many people that would listen. However, I craved the knowledge and understanding so much as I began to learn about the Bible, I also had multiple questions regarding all the understanding I was getting from the Pastor(s) and contents or missing contents of it. So, I began searching in other areas.

I continued and still continue in the path as some call Christianity; only it's not watered down understandings and many would probably think it's a new age way of thinking. So, I too have been on a quest or my purpose in bringing about more clarity of understandings for the importance of having a close relationship with our Creator(s). I view them as Masculine and Feminine, because we are also. This is the balance in which my daily life seeks and to assist this planet for higher consciousness in which it has been destined to achieve for some time now.

In 2009, I went through what I call my first spiritual clearing process. I did this mainly because I wanted to help my oldest child to overcome the death of the sibling which we had endured in 2004. The person I was working with spent much time and care with me and my many questions about his own beliefs, etc. After many scrutinizing hours of conversation, I said to him I want to be able to help her. He said his guides were telling him that I needed to heal myself first, because I had not had time to heal for taking so much care in my children and once I did I could heal many.

After my first clearing and healing process I became more open, similar to what I was like as a child. Many Angels of Light and Yeshua "Jesus" visited with me during this process. They gave me much understanding about my purpose and where I was headed. So, after many years of working outside of the home for various reasons I was advised by the Archangel Michael to go home. This did not come easy for me and I put it off until the spring of 2010 and then I resigned my position as Operations Manager for a local non-profit company. From this time till now life has been extremely interesting and it was imperative for my being to be in an environment that I felt protected and comfortable in while I began or continued the changes in my life and purpose.

I have always been very sensitive to the Earth and care of others and so after years of prayer to expand my boundaries and allowing myself to be utilized for the Creator's Purpose the time was upon me. So it began, I learned about the unseen things Good and Ugly, how to protect oneself and assist in others. How powerful one's intentions are especially when your battery is charged. I have learned a broader and continued understanding of our DNA, our energies, the Earths energies and higher divine forces.

One of the most important reasons I am participating in the writings of this book is to share my knowledge and how to become healed and healthy in your own mind, body, spirit and soul based on my own experiences and the facilitation of others. I am happy to be in service as a vessel of light in which the Creator's Love may flow through me to you and our planet for truly good health and happiness.

Much of the healing I have been involved in has been spiritual and physical and some even instant. As I become more of who I am energetically I am able to increase my bandwidth which allows more flow of Prime Creator/Creatrix's pure light/energy. I also utilize healers from Pleiades, Atlantis and Angelic and Native American spirits as well. Interestingly enough I have a team of light that assist. I am humbled by the amazing things that are allowed or done according to divine plan. I am always in service to the Divine Plan of the Creator most high.

I have facilitated healings around the globe, but never traveled outside the US. I find that unless one is connected and sensitive they generally do not feel much, but they do receive healing. Most folks I have helped have been spiritual and they either sense or see or both some of what the teams of light are doing to them... the biggest part of a successful and lasting healing are releasements. Some are very deep. Faith in the Creator and the heart are key. When we work in the physical I like to use crystals, Om tuning fork, Tibet bowls, essential oils, essences and the sacred healing tones as well as the teams of light.

I can feel discordant energies within the body as I run my hands over them. I also facilitate healing in places and animals. Everyone has free will though and if they truly don't want healing or they pick back up old baggage that was released they can manifest illness or disease in their life again. It is sad but I have also seen that happen to others.

When I do a healing, it can take a while depending on what all comes forward, that part does not need to be around others because sometimes very personal things bubble up or have to be addressed with the karmic Board.

I have discovered there are many beings on our planet who would be considered blueprinters or also considered programmers of and for the human beings on the planet for this cycle of what we know as the Age of Aquarius and also known as a time of the Return of the Divine Feminine. I wish to share this because I feel it is important to gain a little broader understanding of the importance of the Mother God essence not just Father God. There are a multitude of reasons why she has been forgotten in many areas of the world. Without going into all of these various reasons, I will talk about some I feel are important.

The Divine Mother God essence in which some also call Creatrix of this planet is not to be confused with the Prime Creator/Creatrix. She is not to be confused with Mother Earth or the one many call Gaia or Sophia. They are connected energetically however still different. As many know by now, there have been many non-benevolent beings (more than one race) from eons ago that came here to take over us and our planet and thus make us part of the food chain. How have they done this some may ask and I will just simply say this, every way possible "see and unseen."

I have seen that one of the biggest culprits is the unseen concerning the Matrix that placed us inside a box; one may view it like the binary system of the computer. You can only go so far within the perimeters of this system. Take that and place it around the world, now you've got your outer prison grid. Some of us have been incarnated to change this old animalistic system and assist in raising the consciousness back to where it should have been before this happened. Another big culprit was that Mother God has been forgotten or mixed in with watered down myths so that no one knows what to believe. Part of my journey is to bring her blueprint back to life one may say. Also, to show others that she does exist and is very much willing to help those she helped to create. One of the keys to manifesting healing, raising your vibrations and expansion of your consciousness comes from acceptance of her love. Not just the love of the Father but in Unity together.

Many feel that the non-benevolent beings that came to destroy the human race began this with the degrading of the feminine on this planet. Only a small handful of divine feminine are recognized even though it is through the feminine in which life is brought forth. Consider, the unconditional love of a mother, the nurturing, the guidance and so much more.

So we are in a cycle of a long awaited upgrade one may say. Viewing this as a binary system and thus creating into a trinary system, bringing back the trinity and unity.

The divine programmings of the new blueprint(s) are defined within my own experience and this is what I wish to share with the readers. So as I see it we have been allotted a timeframe to experience on a grand scale what the true depths of our emotions of darkness, deception and a feeling of disconnect have brought forth. Some of what we have experienced is cause and effect. However, much of the experiences encompassed with our purposes have been manipulated to a very high degree.

Aly McDonald

INTRODUCTION

"If you really believe that you cannot have a miracle in your life, then you won't. We are here to question your belief."
Ed Rychkun & Aly McDonald

The Divine Programmer

What is a Divine Program?

For the lack of any simple way to describe this, our definition of this from experience and observation is as follows. A Divine Program is that process that creates a miracle of healing. It is where a totally unexplainable process, that which we encapsulate as Divine Intervention changes the physical reality of the human body. The common procedures that trigger this unknown process are through placebos, hypnosis, regression, ritual, energy healing, prayer, or like process so instigated by one who believes typically to be a facilitator rather than a direct healer.

What is Divine Programming?

Divine Programming is to be an instigator for a Divine Intervention to take place. This is where someone or something typically a "Higher Force" corrects a physical dysfunction or re-writes the codes that trigger cells and biology to create new tissues in the body thus eliminating any dysfunction. The process that intervenes to trigger this reboot of the original program, to convince the human system of brain, consciousness, and cells to override the old dysfunctional program and instantly create a healing miracle would be called Divine Programming.

What is a Divine Computer?

The Divine Computer is the human mental and physical vessel. It, through its biological, biochemical, physical, electrical, and subtle energetic components, has the ability to store, retrieve, compile, boot, reboot, and run Divine Programs that change a human physical and mental behavior. It is important to understand that this Divine Computer is not just what we would see as the brain-mind and body of the human vessel; that which we refer to as our Lower Self. It is much more as it also encompasses our Light Bodies,

Souls, subtle energetic fields all that which many have come to call our Higher Self. Part of this Divine Computer is quantum in nature and behavior, as you will come to understand.

What is the primary working unit of A Divine Computer?

First let us look at a binary computer. At the basic level, in a computer, the primary work is a micro processor called a silicon chip, a semiconductor with transistors that are on or off so as to simulate two states of 0 and 1 as the binary bits. A computer chip is a semiconductor with gates and channels like a membrane. This simple unit is the fundamental building block of all that is around us as computer technology that stores, retrieves, processes, and displays this simple information. These are programmable from the outside.

At the basic level of the human computer, the primary work unit is a cell with a membrane which is a fluid silicon semiconductor as it conducts or filters through to the inside. It contains gates and channels as receptors and effectors to let nutrients in or waste out. Cells accept/reject food by membrane perception switches that are open or closed in a state of 0 off or 1 on by way of the their physical response configuration. A computer membrane is a semiconductor with gates and channels like a computer chip. Cells are the basic unit of any living organism, a living computer. A cell, all 50 trillion of them, is a single unit – the smallest in your body that is capable of carrying out life by itself and is the primary unit which conducts the work of storing, retrieving, processing, and displaying (running life support functions and learned behavior) from internal and external environmental information. These are also programmable from outside.

All our life processes go on inside these tiny units which are packed with even smaller organelles all busy carrying out chemical reactions. A cell also has a complete copy of the organism's genome, its DNA tissue is a group of cells that join together to do a specific job in your body. This processes are a result of creating, storing, and running of human computer programs to execute specific life tasks.

All the computer processes that we see everywhere today are created by the creating, storing, and running of computer programs designed to execute specific tasks.

It is our task here to determine how this process of Divine Intervening works and to attempt to quantify it in such a way that allows one to improve the odds of creating their own miracle.

The task here will be to play the role of a usual computer program that has to write a program to instruct the computer to do things. Basically, writing *software* (computer programs) is describing how to do something. In its simplest form, it is a task of writing down the steps as a *process*, or a *procedure*. One writes lists of instructions, as the *source code* representation of computer programs. A computer is very dumb but obedient. It does exactly what you tell it to do, which is not necessarily what you wanted, so it is important to define the steps and procedure with clarity of expression.

The big difference here, is that in our case, although we are looking to quantify the process and procedures as we would for a dumb binary computer, we are going to be cognizant of being a Divine Programmer interested in the process and procedure that result in instructing the human computer to give us a more predictable result of a healing miracle or a shift in external reality. To do this, we are going to look at many examples of Divine Programming and the many cases that a miracle or a transformation of physical or environmental reality has changed.

The millions of documented cases of instant healing, or instant shifts in the physical reality are the example of Divine Programming. Somehow, someone acting as a programmer has activated a computer program in the human that changes the physics. Whether it is a healer, a placebo, a near death experience, an out of body experience, or whatever, that triggers this applications software does not matter. It is undeniably a result of an applications program that is loaded into active memory and is executed.

In every successful case, a procedure was deployed in the form of a ritual, guided steps, environmental conditions, etc. that would be described as a systematic process. In computer terms, this process would be converted through programming languages to be a program (application code) that could be run over and over to produce the same results. This of course is how non-science (like fringe metascience) becomes science; when by observation, a procedure can be created which will produce a predictable result.

The 7 Steps of Manifesting Reality

Another aspect of this process quantification challenge we have here will relate to the way we actually manifest things as our physical or environmental reality. The Steps we follow are:

1. THOUGHT: We bring into consciousness an idea of a desired result.
2. VISION: We form a clear vision or what it is we want to manifest.

3. PLAN: We write or communicate a plan of how the result is to manifest.
4. PASSION: We become passionate and emotional about achieving the end result.
5. ACTION: We launch out intent to seek out and manifest the plan with a strong persistence to succeed.
6. RELATIONS: We seek out the resources, people and connections to others that assist in manifesting the plan.
7. MATERIAL: We succeed in manifesting the plan so as to engage in the joy and satisfaction of the end result.

It does not matter whether this is a simple project like making a chair, or a complex project like building a corporation with a special mission because we engage in these steps. And this is particularly true if you are a business man or woman. We will see that these steps will come up over and over in our detective work of finding out how to be a Divine Programmer.

The purpose of this book is to:

1. Attempt to rationalize the common steps, processes and procedures from what has been shown to work with miracles and the Law of Attraction type methods;

2. Look at the reasons <u>why these processes work</u> so as to find supporting evidence from science, metascience disciplines, and research that allows us to clearly believe in these as a possibility for proving our own health and wealth;

3. Create a Divine Programmer application program that can be run on the human computer system that will improve the odds of success.

Now, dear reader, if you really believe that you cannot have a miracle in your life, **then you won't**. And if you really believe you cannot have a more proactive control over your life's reality of heath and wealth, **then you won't.** This book will question this belief.

For those of you who believe that you can but it isn't happening, then what may be amiss is that belief at a subconscious level that you are not aware of - yet. This book will help you correct this misalignment.

Because humans like to delude themselves into believing these things like miracles and creating your own reality are not real, such cases are not recognized as even existing. But try to convince the many who have enjoyed the wonder and results of these "divine" interventions in physical reality. Of course, these results so witnessed and documented are not predicable, replicable, reliable or considered "science" so let us simply say that this process of changing reality is a Divine Intervention and someone, somehow has become a Divine Programmer.

At the base of this is individual belief that is resident in the subconscious memory. You put them all there either knowingly or unknowingly. It would seem that once these are recorded in this big subconscious disc drive, you cannot easily re-write these beliefs and behavior through the conscious mind; unless as miracle cases would suggest, you re-compile according to the rules of Divine Programming. But as part of this process, we have to deal with totally intangible words called belief, faith and trust that come up over and over.

The question is whether one can do this reprogramming consciously. We feel that you can. So our process of doing this has to first question those beliefs that are limiting by presenting many books, authors and healers that verify these processes do work. For example, our evidence will cover:

- Millions of Near Death Experiences report that their life force leaves the body with full awareness and memory.
- There exist millions of documented cases of healing miracles reporting instant emotional and physical healings that are unexplainable.
- Millions of documented cases exist where the placebo effect has healed the physical body—even eliminating surgery.
- Millions of Out Of Body Experiences are documented that created astounding differences in people's attitude and physics.
- There are millions of documented cases where hypnosis, through subconscious suggestion, has made dramatic physical and mental changes to people's lives.
- There are millions of documented cases reporting that prayer has created miracles unexplained by medicine and science.
- There are thousands of energy healers coming forward that can heal people instantly and document spectacular cases.
- It is estimated that 30% of drugs and surgeries are placebo effects that have created dramatic healings.
- There are millions of cases that use assertions and meditation to achieve incredible goals of changing wealth reality.

We do acknowledge that behind this awareness there is also a knowing that there exists a lack of consistency and a lack of attention on these incredible experiences. It is because people are not prepared to believe these are relevant to them. Their subconscious programs prevent any reprogramming no matter what they "say" consciously is the belief. The question is, would you also deem these "unbelievable" and of worthless consideration by science and medicine. Would you also deny yourself the true power we all have to make miracles "believable"? And would you continue to hold on to limiting beliefs driven by "science" and "religion" and "money" that may render your abilities dysfunctional to allow miracles in your life?

That is what this book is about. It is your shortcut to an end result of creating your own miracles of which the planet has an abundant supply. You may not have been tuned to the right frequency channels. At the end of this book, you will not have to spend the decade needed to figure these things out.

Miracles are real. But if you continue to believe otherwise because that is what you hear, read, or see then the change is unlikely to occur. In order for a change to occur, a new belief has to aligned with what is stuck in the subconscious mind.

The new reality that is coming to light is like a freight train ready to collide with the old reality of science. So many of the experts that have dictated what we program in our beliefs are just as confused as the non-experts. Many of us have set doctors and PhD's up as the almighty local gods of medical wisdom. So if they tell you that you are going to die of cancer or they tell you that miracles are nonsense because they are not proven, then that is what you believe. When a doctor tells you that you have 3 years to live, guess what? He programmed into your subconscious that belief and you believe it. The fact is that we have set experts up on pedestals but they have their own narrow belief systems and they are just as confused as anybody else. It is these people that we have placed in authoritative positions that program our subconscious minds. How do they do this? We are not even aware of it.

There are many ways miracles have occurred. The common original situations have been through evangelistic healers—they really used to get me riled up as a façade. But then there were Near Death Experiences, Out of Body Experiences, hypnotism, placebo experiments, Energy Healing, regression work, Psychoanalysis, Spiritual healers, and many other methods. More recently, Healers and Energy Workers have emerged by the thousands, along with many non-invasive biogenetic type clinics that do produce miracles. In the vast majority of these cases, there have been people who also have been perceived as an authoritative figure.

But these authoritative figures are typically facilitators, not healers. They have however, something else they align with; a greater power and authority which we refer to as Divine Intervention. In this way there have been millions of cases where something miraculous has happened instantly—totally unexplainable and mind boggling. Of course these millions of cases do not fit into the medical belief boxes that we have built so they in conclusion simply "do not exist". They are meaningless, strange, unexplainable and unscientific events that have no bearing in medicine. So the end result is that the fact these millions of cases are observable ways in which people have been fixed in a highly dramatic way is simply deemed by mainstream belief to be totally irrelevant! The truth is that a miracle process—whatever it is—does seem to be inconsistent. It is not predictable. It does not work all the time. But they happen. This is what the driving force for publishing this book was. Is there some consistency? Is there a bottom line that is eluding us? Can we be the authoritative figure that aligns with a higher power to reprogram the subconscious mind and create or attract a miracle?

These Authorities and Higher Powers instigate a change in biology. All you have to do is check out the work and results on Placebos that research says account for 30% of medical healing! Is it the doctor or the mind that does this? The doctors, as authorities, get the human machinery - the human computer - to make a spontaneous shortcut and change the program code, or execute the program code stuck in the nucleus of the DNA. And so that miracle of a mended bone, a vanished tumor, a healed disease or some dysfunction is gone!

How do they change the code? How do we change the code? Well, there are several ways that are open to you. Let us say you have a tumor or some fatal disease. Your desire to get rid of it according to the miracle workers and the gurus of creating your own reality, you have four ways:

Attraction: You think about the solution as it is paramount on your mind. You follow the systems and steps of those people in authority who say you can. They tell you that you attract the solution by following their medical procedures; perhaps several new options to heal this come upon you with surgery, treatment, medication, or whatever.

Manifestation: You visualize and see a clear solution of what you desire as your healing. You follow the systems and steps of those in the know who say you can. Your mind is filled with the prospect of a solution as you see yourself dancing with joy as it happens. And at some point you encounter situations, people, new things that you choose to manifest that result.

Co-Creation You know in your heart that a solution exists and it is only a question of finding it. You follow the systems and steps of those gurus who say you can. You hire them, take a placebo or you place your faith in a miracle healer, and suddenly the solution is upon you.

Creation You know you have the power to change the tumor into what was before it appeared. You follow the systems and steps of a Higher Power who says you can. You visualize that solution in your mind and change the hologram of the physical nature of the tumor instantly.

In a simple sense, if you desire an apple pie, these four options mean:

1. you can think about one until something happens where there is one before you like at a bakery,
2. you sit and mumble about wanting one until someone brings it to you or you make one with a recipe,
3. you can simply have faith that one will be brought before you,
4. you can materialize it before you.

As with miracles, there are examples all over the planet for you to understand that these are all possible. But it is a small minority. Why? Because those that can't create miracles are stuck in methods 1 and 2. That is where the beliefs of science and our subconscious say is the only way. It is metascience that says you can do it using options 3 and 4.

So let us now move on to a new reality of opening up our minds and dealing with options 3 and 4.

Our Goal Is Processes and Procedures

The process by which we plan to get your old beliefs out of the way is to use a bit of a clinical approach in that there are many professional people out there that have done a lot of research, are in the miracle business themselves, and have the credentials that so many look for to gain the status of "expert". Their methods, testimonials, and opinions are typically presented in many excellent books that they have written. The use of this information serves to save you a lot of testing and compilation time. It also provides you, the reader with a reference base to do your own research if you want to.

So here is a first focus in this book. It is to explain in simple terms how these miracles work from those that create them. We will look at the practice and common denominators from several cases that include different methods. We will then extract the essence of healing miracles. This will help to get through the science of belief limits you might have that may be blocking your way. There are two ways that we are going to place attention. Thus we have divided this into two parts. In PART ONE we will cover unexplainable shifts like healing miracles that occur <u>within the body as physical reality.</u> Let us call this **health processes and procedures**.

Next in PART TWO, we will cover miracles that <u>occur in our environment outside the body</u> like shifting our wealth reality through manifesting as in the Law of Attraction. Wealth in our terms may not refer to money, but to anything that you may desire in your life that would bring you a more comfortable and enjoyable reality. So let us call this **wealth processes and procedures**.

Our plan is to reduce the possibility of better health and wealth to practicality of personal application. Theoretically, once you understand the simple basis of these processes and procedure, you can follow the steps, you can have someone create a miracle for you, and then... yes, you can do it yourself—without rituals, props, devices, courses, procedures, certification, and all that jazz that is simply not necessary. Or you can take a more proactive programming of your wealth reality

We will bring in the new insights boiling forward that relate to quantum fields, subtle energies of the body, morphic fields and virtual reality. Many are now saying, and even science has established that we live in a holographic reality, an illusion so created by our sensory computer - the brain. We will explore this new information which, like miracles and other unexplainable phenomenon, has been relegated to a fringe science.

We will deduce what the authorities in the business of miracles do and say about their successes. Once we have extracted this, we will look for physical, scientific, biochemical, or collaborative information that will give us some reasons for why some of these work and speculate how they work.

We will bring in the model of a computer, how it works and provide the analogy to the human computer. The computer programmer requires a specific set of steps and procedures to create a program that executes a task in the computer. Our task is to see if we can determine these steps and procedures needed to execute a task of creating or attracting miracles through this human computer.

We are hoping to get you to understand that YOU are the higher Authority, and that you are free to align with, then bring you in contact with that Higher Power to reprogram your Divine Computer as a Divine Programmer.

As you delve into this mystery of miracles keep in your conscious mind the following:

"Your quantum self may be the Genie and your physical self the Lamp"

Ed Rychkun

PART ONE

CREATING MIRACLES

Aly McDonald
Ed Rychkun

CREATING MIRACLES
INTRODUCTION

"A divine programmer facilitates activation of divine intelligence operating system to bring back a state of perfection."
Ed Rychkun

When a computer program that runs a specific task becomes faulty or malfunctions from what its original design was made to be, a corrective rewriting or recoding is carried out to restore it to the original or correct functionality. In order to do this, a programmer has to re-compile the new instructions (program) into the disc storage so the central memory can rerun the new version via the operating system.

The result of Divine Programming is to recode the application program running within the human computer that has become dysfunctional or defective. What has effectively happened is that the old program that was defective (dis-ease) is like it had a virus attached (disease) and is recompiled into the subconscious disc drive with a new instruction program to run. These can be functions like the way cells build the tissues of organs. Or they can be activities like functions that we learn. So if you don't believe you can heal an organ subconsciously, you won't; just like if you don't believe you can walk again after an injury, you won't.

In our current reality, these events are beyond the knowledge of science as someone or some event or something has restored a physical or mental defect to its original functionality. For example, in the case of cancer or a tumor or a physical deformity/dysfunction is corrected to its original state before the issue occurred. The corrected program is rebooted and the correct functions become the reality. This correct program/blueprint had to come out of our cells where DNA sits; in the nucleus.

Such events have been typically classified as unexplainable fringe science and are a result of

- Energy Healing
- Placebos
- Near Death Experiences
- Miracle of Faith and God
- Out of Body Experiences

- Regression Therapy
- Religious Prayer
- Native Medicine Rituals

In most cases, there is a facilitator that triggers the result. A Divine Programmer has through some unexplainable divine intervention, rewritten and recompiled the defective program in the subconscious.

What we want to do in the next chapters is look at the people and cases where this has been documented. We are concerned only with successful transformations.

What is a pattern in so many cases is that the process or procedure simply did not work, or having worked, there is later return. It is like the delete function was temporary and the old program with the defect or virus rebooted itself.

The purpose is to extract a pattern, a system, a possible programming technique or language that can be used to improve the odds of creating a miracle.

But first, let us begin this section with a documented case that has perplexed the most brilliant medical minds. It clearly illustrates the power of the mind.

A very famous case was reported by Bruno Klopfer, a psychologist who was treating a man named Wright for advanced cancer. Bedridden in the hospital, Wright needed an oxygen mask to survive. Diagnosed with a few days left to live, this man was filled with tumors of the lymph nodes the size of oranges. All hope of *any* recovery was exhausted. But Wright did not want to die. He heard about Krebiozen, a new drug that was available for trial. Of course this was a waste of time to the doctor but with Wright's persistence, he finally gave in and the drug was administered to Wright on a Friday.

On Monday, when the Doc came in, he found Wright out of bed walking around. Inspections indicated his tumors had melted like snowballs on a hot stove. Ten days later, Wright left the hospital cancer free.

Wright was active for about two months until he read some articles stating that Kreibozen actually had no affect on cancer of the lymph nodes. Being very logical and scientific, Wright suffered a relapse and was readmitted to the hospital. The tumors were back, as were lung issues that required oxygen; it was all the same again.

Quite perplexed about this strange and dramatic shifting, the Doc decided to try something like a placebo. In this experiment he told Wright Kreibozen was actually effective and that the problem was some of the initial supplies had deteriorated during shipping. He said he had a new concentrated version and did Wright want to try it. The Doc had a plan to inject Wright with a plain water placebo but with the usual ceremony.

Again within days, the tumors melted, the chest fluid vanished and Wright was back on his feet feeling great. This went on for two months. Then Wright found out the American Medical Association announced that the nationwide study of Kreibozen had found the drug useless in treating cancer. Wright's cancer instantly blossomed and he died two days later.

What's happening here? Makes you think doesn't it? First, what does any pill really do? This Placebo Effect is not isolated as it is reported that 30% of medical treatments are due to placebo. And then there is the Placebo's evil brother called the Nocebo created in the mind by the power (or unfettered authority) of your doctor's statements that tell you negative news? What power does your mind actually have that you are not aware of? So is there any reason why anybody can't create an endless supply of placebo pills? Of course not, maybe they already have and it is the marketing hype and your Doc that convince you. Will they work? Not all the time. Why not? Well, do *you* believe they will? Yes, indeed, it is the magic question.

A Baylor school of medicine published in 2002, in the New England Journal of Medicine an article which evaluated surgery for a patient with severe deliberating knee pain. Dr Bruce Moseley knew that knee surgery helped his patients as he stated "*no good surgeons know there is no placebo effect in surgery*". To figure out what part of the surgery was responsible for most of the pain, he set up three groups.

He shaved the damaged cartilage in one group. He flushed out the knee joint removing inflammatory material in the second group and the third group got fake surgery. With the fake group the patient was sedated, got 3 incisions and he talked and acted like in a real surgery. He even splashed salt water to simulate the sound of knee washing. After 40 minutes he sewed up the incisions as if it was real surgery. All three groups got the same postoperative care.

The surprise came when the groups who received surgery improved but the placebo group improved equally. TV graphically illustrated the results. They all got better functionality even though the placebo group did not find out for 2 years.

Why do we present this special case? There are actually millions of these unexplained cases, some even more dramatic. We bring these forward into your awareness because sometimes it is the trigger that shifts belief. Did you believe any of it, or did you look immediately for reasons that it could be a fake? Most likely your conscious mind woke up to believe it, but your subconscious programming niggled you to look for reasons why it was a fake. And sometimes this subconscious training can be so well in place that you simply said: "what horseshit" and walked away. Well, dear Reader that is how the subconscious mind can sabotage what you "think" you believe.

These dramatic cases are documented, observed facts that give you a glimpse into what is a possibility that you may have never even considered. If you start looking and opening your awareness, the staggering truth of it is that these many cases are not isolated; there are thousands more. No one can be explained but they nevertheless exist. You have simply been conditioned to believe they are some sort of anomaly that is interesting and perhaps entertaining but of no relevance in your life. It was probably your Doctor that told you these were horseshit. Right? Did you believe him?

The first very important thing to understand here is that these physical anomalies like miracles and materialization do exist. Simply because they cannot be explained does not discredit them from existence. Secondly, how can you ever assume that you yourself cannot benefit from such an experience, or even do it yourself? Moreover, what makes you think that it can't happen again, and again, and to you? Yes, to you? Yes, let go of the beliefs that create the limits.

As you are about to understand the many writers and healers covered in the following chapters present wondrous examples of this peculiar shift in the body and mind. In most cases, this shift is facilitated by some event, person, or situation that is created as the experience. It could be a ceremony, a ritual, a process, a pill, an object, a morphic field or even the mind itself.

Our objective however is to extract a process as a common denominator to define what works and why. We really do not care about what did not work except to avoid the same mistakes. This process once defined can be used like a programmer uses; to create a new program compiled in the human computer system. As you read this, open your mind because whatever the program instructions are, it is the mind and its belief that is the common denominator to all of this. It has to be convinced or it has to be receptive before anything happens.

1

DIVINE PROGRAMMING
QUANTUM TOUCH

"Energy really does follow thought. Our love has more impact than anyone knows, and when you learn to direct the life-force energy, the possibilities are truly extraordinary"

Richard Gordon

We want to begin with the work of **Richard Gordon** of the USA. He started his miracle healing in 1978 and began to publish his findings thereafter. His extraordinary book **Quantum Touch: The Power to Heal** was published in 1999, 2002, and again in 2006. In his work he notes that his method of Quantum Touch (QT) teaches simple breathing and body awareness exercises that can be easily learned by everyone. This simple method of applying hands and breathing has created a dramatic list of healing miracles that baffle the best of medical doctors. Over the past eight years, he has taught QT to well over 4000 people. Without exception, professional practitioners of the various modalities have told him that this work can be seamlessly combined with what they know, and in most cases it has transformed their practice. This list includes chiropractors, osteopaths, physical therapists, acupuncturists, cranial sacral therapists, chi gung instructors, and Reiki masters, to name but a few. Lay people discover this as an elegant, simple, and profound hands-on healing method that they can use.

Richard's work has expanded to virtually every country. If you go to his website **www.quantumtouch.com** you will find hundreds of practitioners and lecturers in 70 countries. The site has an ongoing seminar series and workshops. So this man has been busy! He has healed defective bones, spines, physical issues, medical problems, you name it.

The method is a basic human skill learned immediately that we have simply lost or forgotten. It is as easy as eating! Cases happen where bones move into alignment, organs are balanced, pain is gone, emotional changes occur and scores of miracles simply happen—all through the use of hands and breath. He says it all works from a subatomic level into the physical level through resonance and entrainment activating healing—no symbols, no medicine, no rituals, no problem! Does the media or the medical profession talk about this? No!

Do the statistics give you any feeling for his credibility?

Are you wondering how this simple method works yet?

Richard's experience shows that disease or dis-ease is an out-of-tune energy behavior of an organ or something not working the way it was designed to work. He has discovered that when strong harmonizing rhythms are applied, the wrong interference waves of the organ start magically beating the right way again. This is because there is a tendency of two wave forms to vibrate sympathetically energizing and communicating with each other. The wave forms of energy entrain and influence each other. This is what happens in all creation. If you wonder what entrain means think about putting a large number of ticking clocks in one room. They will *entrain* their vibrations by eventually synchronizing vibrations and ticking together.

So when there are two wave forms of energy; one higher vibration, one lower that are brought together, resonance and entrainment happen. Either the higher will come down or the lower goes up. Or they will balance in the middle. It depends on the strength and frequency as to where they balance.

If you raise the vibration in your hands to a very high frequency and place them in the near proximity of a lower vibration pain or problem area in the body, it will be like a tuned circuit that will resonate and entrain to the hand's energy.

How do you get a high frequency? Guess. Through Yoga type breathing, meditation and filling your intent with love. Love is a very high vibration and it is a universal vibration that allows the transfer to take place—not very scientific is it? So the healer must hold the highest dominant frequency, and pushes that energy through the hands. The client's problem area of lower vibration will entrain to match it. All you are doing with the hand and mind is providing the resonant energy to allow healing to occur.

Sound simple? Yes? But there is an issue. Right, you knew it! How does one keep the dominant energy high so it does not get diluted? Well, Richard points out that the secret is in the breathing. It keeps the life force strong and keeps the frequency up, as does the love intent. The key is breathing to keep the higher vibration from dropping to the client's problem area vibration and draining yours.

Yes, life force. This is nothing new to many who clearly understand that life force animates life. We call it chi, Ki, manna, etc. In yoga for example, it is through proper (notice we used the word proper) breathing, that increases the life force (vibration). When the life force leaves we expire. When life force gets greater, we aspire, same as the terminology for breathing. Coincidence?

Here are Richard's basic principles surrounding this process he calls Quantum Touch. These are the things he has observed over the decade:

- Love is a universal vibration and the foundation for healing. It is the essence of the life;
- Ability to assist in healing is natural to all;
- Healing abilities grow stronger with practice;
- Energy follows thought;
- Love and intent are instinctual abilities we all have;
- Intention and meditation create a high energy field surrounding the healing area;
- Resonance and entrainment cause the area to change vibration as the area rises to a new vibration;
- No one heals, they only hold a resonance to allow healing to take place;
- Energy directed through a natural intelligence to do the healing in the right way;
- The healer also receives healing as well;
- The breathing amplifies the life force;
- Trusting that the healing will occur is essential;
- Combining breathing and meditation causes the energy to line up, to increase power like a laser beam;
- Creating a synergy between several healers is more powerful than individual;
- Healing can be done at a distance;
- Quantum Touch combines well with other healing techniques;
- Spiritual connection adds power to the healing;
- Body knows (divine intelligence) where healing is needed.

So how do you learn to do this "properly"? First, you learn to sense energy in your fingers, hands, and body by simply getting present to the body and its sensations. You "sweep" over the area and feel the sensations. You practice this by getting present and focusing your attention on the area. This is called running energy because when you can sense it and know it is there, you can direct the energy to a problem area. But running simply means you use your mind to imagine energy running through you to your hands and into the area of dysfunction. You may say: "Jeez, I can't do that!"

How do you know? Try it without your intellect interfering. It's called letting go of it and allowing your intuition to guide you. Just focus on breathing without expectations and accept the first thing that "pops" into your awareness.

Next you learn how to breathe "properly". This means taking full breaths through your nose drawing it down below the belly button to push it out then lifting it upwards. Richard explains how you learn to do this rhythmically in a certain way. The 4-4 breath is suck in for a 4 second count, then push out for a 4 second count. There are three main rhythms he uses, namely 4-4, 1-4 and 2-6. Note that deep pranic breathing in Yoga involves holding the breath for a few seconds after a deep breath so the life force is properly transferred into the body. Otherwise, shallow breathing does not make the transfer. Each rhythm has a different purpose but the objective is to learn these so they are natural, then you combine it with the first process of running energy.

So now we get to the healing part. You start with a love environment and relax. Begin the intent to move the high vibration energy into your hands. They may tingle, feel heat, or experience whatever you have learned to sense. Next engulf the pain area or dysfunction with your hands, and then intend healing for a better purpose. At the same time begin the breathing rhythm. Hold this for typically 5 minutes to an hour. Yes, some cases are more difficult!

Always keep in mind that the power is in love and intent. The breathing holds resonance high, replenishing the life force upon each breath. This means you don't keep your mind on your IRS issues! Keep the trust. If you connect with the Divine or Guides, or whatever, it serves to enforce your faith and trust that it will happen. Like a simple beam of light converted to a laser beam, you are intensifying the energy immensely and the body will know what to do with the defective energy.

Does this sound too simple? Well, Richard and thousands of people he has taught think it is. Some are realigning bones at sight, and fixing an unbelievable number of issues in people. Fibromyalgia, bone alignments, fractures, pains, energizing athletics, avoiding surgery, diabetes, burns, helping animals, pain relief, solving ADD, ADHD issues, and inflammation are but a few you can read about.

We quote Richard: "*Energy really does follow thought. Our love has more impact than anyone knows, and when you learn to direct the life-force energy, the possibilities are truly extraordinary. DNA, molecules, cells, tissue, organs and even the position of bones all respond to the powerful vibration of our love as expressed through the life-force energy that comes through our hands. Hands-on healing is real, natural, and an easily learned, basic human skill that clearly shows us that our love is far more wondrous and powerful than any of us know.*"

"*Quantum-Touch teaches simple breathing and body awareness exercises that can be easily learned by everyone. Over the past eight years, I have taught QT to well over 4000 people. Without exception, professional practitioners of the various modalities have told me that this work can be seamlessly combined with what they know, and in most cases it has transformed their practice. This list includes chiropractors, osteopaths, physical therapists, acupuncturists, cranial sacral therapists, chi gung instructors, and Reiki masters, to name but a few. Lay people discover an elegant and profound hands-on healing method that they can effectively use.*"

"*In principal the Quantum-Touch practitioner learns to focus and amplify life-force energy, which is most often referred to as Chi or Prana. This is accomplished by combining various breathing and body awareness exercises. When the practitioner holds a high vibrational field of life-force energy around an affected area, through a process of resonance and entrainment, the client naturally matches the vibration of the practitioner, allowing one's own biological intelligence to do whatever healing it deems necessary.*"

The Divine Programmer (Richard) triggers through his steps and environmental settings (Quantum Touch Program) to execute an application to correct an affected area back to its corrected state. Here is a summary of his process.

HEALTH PROCESSES & PROCEDURES QUANTUM TOUCH		
Setting	Have a belief and trust as it is essential	RG
Setting	Be in the higher vibration of love	RG
Setting	Become present to the body (lower brain waves)	RG
Process	Focus on and enfold issue area with hands	RG
Process	Breath in a rhythmic count to hold resonance high	RG

Process	Enter a space of higher vibration-love and intent	RG
Process	Intend healing for a better purpose as divine intervention	RG
Assist	Connect with Divine assistance	RG
Process	Imagine healing energy through you to your hands	RG
Process	See a beam of healing light connect	RG
Process	Allow biological Divine Intelligence to heal as it knows how	RG

2

DIVINE PROGRAMMING REGRESSION THERAPY

"If we were to remember where we came from ourselves, then we're coming from a place of unconditional love, because that source would be the one we call the Soul Energy that joins the human body when the baby is created."

Andy Tomlinson

Andy Tomlinson, author of **Healing the Eternal Soul**, founded the Past Life Regression Academy in the UK. It specializes in Regression Therapy, Past Life Regression, Life Between Lives Regression, and Hypnosis training. He has expanded his therapies throughout Europe, Asia and Australia. The Academy awards internationally accredited qualifications enabling its graduates to belong to independent professional associations, including the European Association of Regression Therapy and the General Hypnotherapy Register. The training program has been accredited by the International Board of Regression Therapy.

Andy is a psychotherapist, lecturer, author, and has been referred to as one of Britain's leading practitioners in hypnotic past life regression. This academy has scores of qualified graduates throughout Europe and they have, needless to say, dealt with thousands of cases, with many dramatic healings.

What is so interesting about this group is how they regress people back to previous lives where the trauma occurred, and they are asked to recreate the sequence of events the way they want—to release the trauma energies that created the problems in the current life. The events or situation regressed to can be simply visualized as changed and the memories, traumas are also changed—just like in a daydream where you imagine a situation changed. Somehow a quantum rearrangement occurs and a new possibility is created! Makes you think everything is simply in your memory, doesn't it? So with the mind alone, they are creating a completely new outcome. But there can be physical as well as physiological changes.

You may find this even more perplexing. They even regress people to the times between lives and follow the sequences of reported Near Death Experiences to identify information that can help them understand why the patients agreed to events that have resulted in trauma in the current, or any other life! Curious that people should already know the phases the consciousness (soul) goes through after death. And this is before they are consciously aware of them in the current lifetime! It all appears to be stored on the subconscious storage medium. The school has several therapy experts:

Regression Therapists have a holistic view that our body, mind, emotions and spirit have a fundamental inter-connectedness. All disharmony and disease has a root cause somewhere from the past. The healing process involves a reconnection with the root cause of the problem. This way they are allowing the client to deeply understand the issues associated with the problem before they are resolved at both a physical, emotional and spiritual level. It's like pulling out a thorn buried deep under the skin so that complete healing can take place. The problem may be from recent events such as the loss of a loved one or a relationship issue. Sometimes the root cause is a traumatic experience below the level of conscious awareness and has been affecting the client's well being. It could be from childhood abuse, rape or life threatening situations. Client experiences may go back beyond early childhood into prenatal experiences and into past life stories.

Past Life Therapists are trained to work with emerging stories that appear to be past lives. A migraine, chronic lower back pain or knee problem may be telling a story from an old accident or wound. A chronic sore throat may derive from strangling, hanging or choking. As the soul returns to life over and over, these traumatic past life memories are re-created in our current life often making little sense, and keeping us from living peaceful lives. Past life therapists work with past life residues and transform them in a way that is both safe and structured.

Past Life and Regression Therapists treat any client experience in an accepting and authentic way. Various psychotherapies may be used in the regression process such as hypnosis, gestalt, psychodrama, body therapy, together with various transpersonal and energy techniques. The symptoms dealt with by past life and regression therapists include low energy levels, emotional outbursts, anxiety, anger, guilt, depression, panic attacks, phobias, obsessions, nightmares, unexplainable physical pain, blocked feelings, loss of life focus and relationship difficulties. Often these are problems that keep being repeated. This therapy reaches further and heals deeper at the physical, emotional, and spiritual level than most other therapeutic approaches.

The Past Life and Regression Therapists are trained and certified by the Past Life Regression Academy to meet the content and quality standards agreed with other leading European training schools belonging to the European Academy of Regression Therapy.

Life Between Lives Therapists are sometimes referred to as LBL or Spiritual Regression Therapists. They use deep hypnosis to guide a client beyond a past life and into what appears to be soul memories between lives. From a therapeutic perspective the objective is to help a client to understand their soul progression and spiritual purpose for this life, and as a result to make major life choices and better cope with the pressures of modern life. It also provides the most accurate picture yet obtained of what happens after death.

Life Between Lives Regression has been progressively developed since the late 1960's by a number of professional Psychologists and Psychiatrists, the most prominent being Michael Newton. The regressions can last up to four hours and the main events that occur have now been confirmed by thousands of consistent reports from Near Death Experience research which we will cover in a later chapter.

However, following a past life death regression, clients often talk about being welcomed by deceased friends or family and receiving healings to shed the denser emotions and energies associated with the physical world. This allows them to re-enter the higher frequency vibrations of the spirit realm. Spirit Guides and Teachers review the past life. The only judgment in this review comes from the clients themselves, because all their actions and intentions are laid bare. At some point a client's soul group is encountered. These are souls working closely over many lives, although the relationships vary from lovers to family members to friends. Reuniting with them is described as a profoundly moving experience in which the client finally feels that they are really home.

At some point they meet 'Elders', who are spirits of light that have attained a level of experience and wisdom that does not require them to physically reincarnate. They review the progress of the soul before them and can replay any of its past lives and discuss aspects until the soul understands what will be expected in the next life. It is done with love, compassion and the participation of the soul until it leads to the next physical incarnation having a purpose.

Does this sound a bit far-fetched? Past lives, and in between lives being extracted from the patient's consciousness? The thousands of clients and the multitude of Therapists across Europe don't seem to think so.

The Academy has a formal training program that teaches people how to do this. The Regression Therapy Training Program is extensive. Past life regression training is included in the Regression Therapy training course. It's accredited by an independent certifying body called the International Board of Regression Therapy (IBRT) and meets the content requirements to be a professional member of the European Association of Regression Therapy (EARTH) which has professional members from the leading past life training schools across Europe. The training is normally done over a one year period.

Training includes lectures, demonstrations, experiential exercises, pair work, supervision and reading. The Regression Therapy and Past Life Regression course is led by Andy Tomlinson. Ideally students will be qualified in Psychotherapy, Counseling, Hypnotherapy, Psychiatry, Energy Healing, Body work or an approved complementary therapy. Also, qualification and experience using Hypnosis is required. For those without, a short intensive Hypnosis training workshop is offered which leads to a Foundation Certificate in Hypnosis. The Past Life Regression and Regression Therapy training program will be 16 days over 3 or 4 workshops.

This is an extensive program. On the successful completion of the Regression Therapy training program a Diploma in Regression Therapy is awarded. This enables the graduate to obtain insurance and work professionally with clients as a Regression Therapist. They will also be referred clients from the Academy website and can join the European Association of Regression Therapy as a professional Regression Therapist. In addition they can join the General Hypnosis Register as a practitioner.

So, we ask you, does this sound like a scam? It certainly tests one's belief system, does it not? One has to realize that healing and miracles are being created by identifying issues and blocks created in previous lives and in between lives.

In a nutshell, these are trained people that have learned to probe deep into the subconscious memories that obviously contains all of the memories of past and in between lives. Once they find the issue, you in your current life are then able to understand what it is, why it was caused, what it resulted in, and simply re-write the history of it into a new possibility—with the mind. And that not only affects behavior, it affects your physiology.

As a Divine Programmer, these people effectively delete and re-write the applications program from subconscious that controls the brains behavior. Here are the fundamental steps:

HEALTH PROCESSES & PROCEDURES REGRESSION THERAPY		
Setting	Have a trust and belief that healing will occur	AT
Process	Bring patient into a hypnotic state	AT
Process	Enter a holistic connectedness	AT
Process	Probe deep into subconscious memories	AT
Process	Regress patient to time and event of issue	AT
Process	Bring client into higher frequency vibration	AT
Assist	Allow higher realm Spirit Guides to assist	AT
Process	Hold the space of love and compassion at soul level	AT
Process	Understand the issue and why it occurred	AT
Process	Delete or rewrite the memory with the mind	AT

3

DIVINE PROGRAMMING
NATIVE MEDICINE

"Acceptance and surrender of the ailment meant that no one was obsessed with a cure. Instead, the strength of desire is the fuel for the birth of miracles."

Lewis Madrona

A wonderful example of healing is through the area of native miracles, Shaman, and ritualistic ceremonies. One timeless researcher and practitioner in this area will really capture one's interest. He is an MD and PhD named **Lewis Mehl Madrona**. He, a certified family physician, psychiatrist, geriatrician with 25 years of practice in emergency medicine, and a PhD in clinical psychology, wrote an eye-opening book called **COYOTE HEALING—Miracles in Native Medicine.**

This man has done many studies and has facilitated many miracles. He is more of a scientific type interested in figuring out what the common characteristics are. His studies of cultures reveal healing power is facilitated by spending time on individual attention, and having a relationship with intent of all involved. He says this process causes the mind to transform the inner body by awareness that healing requires profound life changes. Such awareness typically awakens through spirit and the spirit dimension as triggered by ritual and ceremony, or some such practice. As part of this process, he says family influences are important and the concept of taking ourselves apart is vital.

Focused on the study of Native medical miracles, he concluded that no one is healed alone—that it is the power of relationship that is vital. He said acceptance and surrender of the ailment meant that no one was obsessed with a cure. Instead, the strength of desire was the fuel for the birth of miracles. The focus was on the present—not on the past—as a narrow focus. He reinforces that prayer, meditation, and vision quest were their sacred processes of awakening, and the community nurtured a joint hope to healing. It is like energizing the joint consciousness influencing the spiritual dimension where spirit is the link.

He observed in cases of miracles, that a profound change is reborn where every thought is a prayer and every prayer is answered but you must have peacefulness. He noticed that there are no specific prayers more powerful than others but he certainly reinforces the *'God's will be done'* notion. He points out this really has nothing to do with religion as his opinion is that religious institutions are spiritually bankrupt. Hope, not despair is key. Denial and giving up are useless, only demanding success works. He says you are the healer. It is deep within yourself. He also says that doctors are now the third biggest cause of accidental death in the US so he doesn't like to relate to them. He reinforces that you must find the inner healer by using mind and spirit. Prayer creates the channels for spirit to enter but you must make a personal transformation first.

And to do this, one requires openness to making profound changes, have a willingness to embark on the inner world, involve the community to bear witness, and have an accurate appraisal of the health threat. Then, he observes, you have a foundation for a miracle. And the practice of retreat and ritual simply creates a concentrated focus—like a sweat lodge. These are just a means of focusing attention towards the Great Spirit and making the proper connections. What he is saying is that a certain kind of energy setting is created through these people and the means of joint ritual to Spirit. They are effectively creating an energy field of focused belief that supports a new outcome—one of healing administered by the Great Spirit or the Creator.

On a more philosophical side, he feels we carry healing wisdom in our DNA, but spirit needs the aids of hope, purpose, and meaning to trigger it. The ceremony connects the patient to their true being and concentrates attention there. He also reinforces that you get what you pray for; *'Thy will be done on Earth as it is in Heaven'*. So learn about compassion and love of the Creator. Also, indigenous healing uses touch to facilitate, and breath is the spirit to cleanse. He says imagine breath reaching everywhere and guide it with imagery. Get rid of fear, blame, and doubt. Everything is sacred to medicine people. Meditation is the connection to all living things. He reinforces that energy manifestation is through thoughts and emotions.

There is something he says that may interest those pragmatic left-brain readers. From his research, he says thoughts are mental electrophysiological events that affect the hypothalamus causing the adrenal glands to release calecholamines and activate the immune system. The electricity of thought and emotion is converted to chemicals in the brain's limbic area. Thought goes to the base of the brain where a neurohumoval transducer converts it to chemicals. A pleasant thought creates endorphins, a brain chemical 400 times more powerful than pure uncut heroin. A worried thought produces stress hormones. Science accepts the reality of electrical impulses being thought. He underscores that thought reflects core beliefs.

Now, on a more philosophical note, what he is saying is that every thought is a prayer and this means all thoughts are rising to the Creator. Every prayer is answered by our collective thoughts which shape the world. The Universe is our physical body, and we are all cells in the body of God. If all thoughts are prayers, we could say that thoughts are the electrical or energetic manifestation of each cell. Coherent thought means healthy organs and body. Incongruent and disharmonious thoughts mean dis-ease. Health occurs as disorganized thoughts become congruent. People are not disturbed by events, only the meaning they place on them. What we believe about cure affects the results.

The most fascinating aspect of his book is where he noted that there were common characteristics clearly evident before and after a healing miracle took place. Typically, these were miracles that occurred when there were no other alternatives. He documented these very carefully and we are going to summarize them here.

Before the miracle happened, the patients had a strong internal focus of control for healing. They had an accurate appraisal of the problem and its threat and they had a belief in self as agent for the healing. They believed a personal change was needed and that healing was very real. They had a belief in a personal capacity to heal through faith, all having a sense of self-empowerment.

It all has to do with the strength of belief. They knew it was serious but did not relinquish a faith that it could be healed. That is where we all seem to stumble.

He reported that with regards to life's meaning, the patients showed a common belief system as well. They believed their lives and suffering have purpose involving family, God, and love. They were so confident that they had a plan and projects for the future despite their fatal sickness. They all refused to give up and die and they believed a continued life would result in an increase in fulfillment. They thought life's purpose was to help and benefit others and a sense of joy would accompany fulfilling that purpose.

He noted that upon having a healing miracle occur, the patients underwent a personal transformation. They had changes in personality and they had an ability to identify feelings better. Not only that, they had an ability to express feelings better and had a new identification with a new self image. There was a sense of new values and valuation of life.

Upon completing the healing miracle, patients underwent a spiritual transformation. They had a change in sense of unity and connection with all things. They had a strong sense of presence of a higher power. There was an increase in importance of spirituality in guiding one's life, with an increase in feeling that life is directed by spiritual principles. They also had an increase in the sense of peacefulness—a sense of surrender of what cannot be changed. They all had an acceptance of all possibilities including death.

After the miracle, in looking at the patient's quality of life, the healing effectively impacted them in many ways. They had increased emotional well being, and had a new ability to tolerate and manage distressing emotions. They had increased comfort and enjoyment of the physical body, with enhanced feelings of self-worth and life satisfaction. They had a sense of being on the path of life's purpose, with increased pleasure, joy, and laughter in their lives.

After the miracle, the patients experienced a heightened sense of value in relationships. They had an increased experience of intimacy with much more pleasure and joy in relationships. They all developed a sense of being nonjudgmental with increased forgiveness as they released hurt and anger. They let go of the future instead of trying to control it. They expanded the degree of their relationships and had more ability to love. The family relationships were all improved as their values towards family changed.

Then, after the healing, the patients exhibited a new mindset desire to transform their lives to something new. They recognized the need to make a change and they knew they had the ability to take action on a change. They had a new willingness to initiate action on changes and set about applying themselves diligently to make the changes.

So what is happening here? A ritual of some sort creates a focus of energy. The process can involve chanting, prayer to the great spirit, sweat lodges, any number of things that "prepare" one for the miracle. Others are involved to reinforce the energy. It is a special morphic field that is being created by a group, one which can influence the individual's field of consciousness. The more people involved the more it reinforces the energy and the belief that this is all real and there is absolute trust in the faith of it happening. It has everything to do with focus of a belief. This process causes the mind to transform the inner body by awareness that healing requires profound life changes. Spirit and spirit dimension are accessed through ritual and ceremony. Faith and trust prevail as there is an acceptance of the facts that they must give their faith to some force and there is a faith that they will be fixed. The words belief, trust, and faith in something profound are crucial here. Well, if this is so, everyone's belief and faith are most certainly different on this topic so no wonder the results are unpredictable and hence "unscientific". No wonder, if this is the key, miracles do not work on everybody.

But there is something else. When they came out of this, their belief system—their boxes of belief they had before—changed. They then went on to accept life on different terms and made profound changes within that new life.

If the big variables were belief and faith in some force that could heal, total acceptance of the condition, this could definitely be a problem because how do you define or quantify it for programming? It was clear that you had to have this special mindset of belief. It was also clear that the process of eliminating this is to involve others and special ceremonies that create that morphic energy. It is sort of like walking into a pub where the morphic energy is usually social and with an air of fun. Some fields are stronger than others but we feel the energy of these fields all the time. The morphic energy of a church, or a party, or a special gathering is precisely this—an energy reflection of the individual energies. We assimilate into it by the process of harmonic entrainment which will be covered later. We sense it, feel it, and it creates changes in us depending on how these are received.

You may be wondering about this morphic field. Let us digress. It proposes that there is a field within and around a morphic unit which organizes its characteristic structure and pattern of activity. This field underlies the formation and behavior of units and can be set up by the repetition of similar acts or thoughts. So a particular form belonging to a certain group which has already established its (collective) morphic field, will *tune into* that morphic field. The particular form will *read* the collective information through the process of morphic resonance, using it to guide its own development. This development of the particular form will then provide, again through morphic resonance, a feedback to the morphic field of that group, thus strengthening it with its own experience resulting in new information being added (i.e. *stored* in the *database*). The morphic field is like a universal database for both organic (living) and abstract (mental) forms.

The easiest way to understand this is through a bunch of clocks on the wall that are ticking away independently. It does not take them long to entrain into each other's rhythmic ticking even though they are totally independent. The morphic field entrains into a specific rhythm. We have dedicated a chapter to this topic later. Here is Lewis's process simplified:

HEALTH PROCESSES & PROCEDURES NATIVE MEDICINE		
Setting	Have an acceptance of problem and surrender to the issue	LM
Setting	Have a strong belief and faith in healing	LM
Setting	Show strength and desire, willingness to embark	LM
Process	Focus on present, prayer, meditation	LM
Assist	Connect to the Great Spirit and Higher sacred processes	LM
Process	Engage in ritual & community to bear witness focus energy	LM
Process	Create a morphic field with the Great Spirit as the healer	LM
Process	Enter realm of inner healer through mind and spirit	LM
Process	Allow the inner Healer to do the work	LM

DIVINE PROGRAMMING DIVINE CONNECTION

"Natural healing is love, divine healing is supernatural love. It's about trusting the power of surrender."
Tiffany Snow

"Prayer talks to God, meditation listens."
Carolyn Miller

In delving more into the topic of the Divine, it is necessary to bring in a book by **Tiffany Snow**. She says she works with God, the Big Guy in the Sky she calls him. Tiffany is a Grand Ole Opry singer gone holistic who combines science and spirituality for the purpose of healing. She is a modern mystic, Reiki master, and spiritual healer. Her book **The Power of the Divine: A Healer's Guide -Tapping into the Miracle** shed an interesting light on this topic. In her practice she sees and facilitates miracles all the time. Once again, she is not some idle quack in the business of peddling supposed miracles. She has a long list of cases that support her success.

She points out that in her work she has found that the preconditions for healing miracles are *self healing and love*. She adds self forgiveness always resonates throughout, and self acceptance overcomes insecurities. When there is a balanced wholeness, it increases the greater good. The successful ones always choose love over fear, and forgiveness is always unconditional.

She also points out that prayer directs supernatural energy, as it is a two-way dialogue. It is not just positive thinking or wishful thinking. Prayer is pure love. She then concludes that you must visualize the outcome accomplished as it bridges the gap. Adding feeling is the key but knowing is better. She says that if you are a healer, you must get out of the way so healing comes *through* you. Pray for *his will to be done* as it is for the highest good. Do not allow ego to dictate what is good or bad. See the victim healed in your mind's eye. Begin with a loud prayer then be silent with hands on and invite the patient to make the connection to the source.

She notes that you can manifest extraordinary things through daily prayer. Feel deep love for every person. The heart is the seat of motivation. Whatever the heart is full of is what the mouth speaks. You must believe you are worthy, perfect, deserving, and forgiven to receive what is given. Love is the highest mission. It aligns with God's flow. She notes that balanced people take responsibility, do not cause harm, help others, and always know who they are. They do not blame others and show unconditional love to all. They clean out negative and false thought patterns.

She has now brought in a new perspective. It was going beyond a ceremony and making sure that the individual energy field was one of peace, unconditional love, without judgment and faith. Knowing that the miracle was done was obviously crucial. Praying was the communication channel that was activating the process.

Then she says faith does not heal—God does. She points out how to pray this way. First, talk to God like a trusted friend, be humble, and then show gratitude and thanks.

But here is the ultimate question. Does this model work all the time? No way. Why?

She says never show disbelief. Fear is a barrier, as is being unworthy, and peer pressure influence of what works. We are all born with the ability to heal. Natural healing is love, divine healing is supernatural love. It's about trusting the power of surrender. When you allow your natural spirit to be touched by the divine, it changes every aspect of your life and you see miracles happen. Trust and surrender to the Divine!

What are we hearing here? She says God and prayer heals, but what about all of the miracles others induce without God? And does prayer work all the time? No, not necessarily. What is true however is that there are common denominators. What are they?

The patient believes in a higher power that will heal. The patient in fact knows that this is true, regardless of what anyone says. The patient has accepted the nature of the ailment and is simply willing to place themselves in the hands of others' will or God's will. They do not judge, or become attached to the outcome. They let it all flow and it happens. Not always of course, but it can and does happen.

To further explore the notion of God's participation in miracles from the other side of the coin, one needs to include the book, **Creating Miracles**, by **Carolyn Miller** who clearly states that being "good" or being a sinner does not really matter, nor does faith or belief in God. All healing, she observes from many cases, depends on a patient's inner decision to release the problem to a solution. Now this lady is no academic piker. She holds a PhD in Experimental Psychology. She and her late husband Arnold Weiss are the founding directors of the Los Angeles-based **Foundation and Institute for the Study of A Course in Miracles**.

In *Creating Miracles,* Carolyn gets to the nitty gritty details of miracles in people's lives. In over 50 accounts of real experiences, she describes how ordinary people spontaneously entered altered states of consciousness and positively affected sometimes life-threatening events. Of note is that Miller is focused on a special breed of people that are in dire situations. This she calls the "Miracles of Deliverance" where these people for whatever reason are facing death.

Drawing on her scientific background as an experimental psychologist, she analyzes the common patterns in these situations as well as the scepticism with which these stories might be received. Part one of *Creating Miracles* spotlights "ordinary" miracles, where average people respond to extraordinary circumstances. She also explains how to create the personal conditions that are needed for a miracle to occur. Miller shows the importance of being able to tap into intuition (the inner divine guide) as well as disarming the ego in bringing a person into a state of miracle readiness. But note here that it is not God; it is the <u>Inner Divine</u> doing the intervention.

The author tackles the subject of miracles with regards to what they are, how they are created, and why some never seem to have them happen with the objectivity of both a psychologist and believer of 'faith' combined. She manages to analyze and explain just how the inner workings of miracles come about, how to recognize them, and how to work upon bringing more miracles into one's own life. She notes a commonality among those who have experienced miracles in their lives. What are these?

Miller noted that there was one thing all cases she related in her book had in common... they all came to a *point of surrender* just before the miracle happened. She noted that a *sense of peace* came over each individual, despite the sometimes horrific events that were taking place at that moment.

She observes that it is your free will that governs and means you are willing to change to solve self created problems. Explore your inner most thoughts about problems. It is a question your belief system has to answer honestly. Do you deserve the problem or the solution?

She points out as an observation that the successful patient's thoughts are *constantly for the highest and best outcome*. She also cautions from those cases where it does not work; striving for egos wants detracts from the solution, and worry only attracts the circumstances you worry about. You may have a right mind shared with God and a wrong mind shared with ego—it inhibits the process. When the right mind exists, miracles simply happen.

Now, the lady does not say that God is not the healer here, nor does she say that belief in God is necessary. In fact she points out that she is simply a facilitator. But what she is saying is this: if you do not have the right mindset, a belief that healing can happen, that you are worthy of it, it ain't gonna happen. Furthermore if you are not focused on the solution instead of the problem, it is most likely not going to happen. So God may or may not be part of the process in word, but there is certainly some higher power that she refers to an Inner Divine you facilitate, surrender to, have faith in and do higher good with at work here. And it is your attitude and belief about this that appears to be crucial to success.

She also points out something interesting in that she says: "**prayer talks to God while meditation listens**". If you don't want to hear, you won't. It is your belief and your mindset that dictates the degree of success.

She states: "*Miracles of deliverance, are what I call situations where someone is threatened with serious harm or even death, as the result of an accident, assault or illness, and things have reached a stage where most people would confidently expect a very negative outcome. Interestingly, those who survive situations like these, all seem to report that they found themselves slipping into a deeply peaceful, altered state of consciousness, variously characterized as totally fearless, unconditionally loving, intensely focused, and sometimes even humorous, or whimsical. Despite impending doom, they set aside fear and anger, and retreat into a detached and loving state of mind that sounds very much like a profound state of meditation. Often they say that time slowed down for them, allowing an opportunity for deep reflection in situations that were objectively occurring at lightning speed. Many report hearing an inner voice, or feeling a loving and authoritative inner presence prompting them to say or do something they would never have considered otherwise. And when they followed this impulse, their unusual response often turned out to be the very thing that defused the danger and led to the happy ending."*

So the key to miracles here lies in the peculiar shift in consciousness that always seems to precede their occurrence. By choosing peace and love over fear and anger, I believe we do our part to make divine guidance and intervention possible. We acknowledge our inability to solve the problem on our own, and truly turn the problem over to our higher power.

Miller describes how people have faced potentially lethal situations and avoided victimization by realizing in the midst of their ordeal that they could find and project a higher state of awareness on the situation. Their feelings changed their situations so much that would-be muggers and rapists walked away from potential victims, and a car plummeting off the side of the road landed safely in a lake... that had never been there before.

Miller tells numerous true stories that all share a common thread... in a time of need, people can and do create miracles. All that is needed is an attitude of love and "miracle mindedness". This attitude can overcome even the most horrific situations, bringing compassion to individuals who otherwise would show no mercy, and shifting reality in very profound ways.

What makes this book particularly fascinating and useful to me is that Carolyn Miller reviews dozens of stories to find some common threads... some ways that people have found to shift reality in these times of great stress:

Feel Love Move beyond the limited perspective of ego's worries and fears.

Expect a Positive Outcome Instead of assuming that the situation will continue to go in a negative direction, expect a positive (or neutral) outcome.

Turn Inward Feel a meditative sense of detached, non-judgmental peacefulness.

She states: *"It seems that by practicing achieving a meditative state on a regular basis, being optimistic, and being loving, we can predispose ourselves to experiencing wonderful miracles. I know this is true from my experiences with reality shifts!"*

Miller explains that it's not necessary to believe in divine intervention in order to create miracles. She explains that people who simply keep the miracle-minded attitude can bring miracles to even the most hostile situations.

Does God heal? If you believe so strongly enough, God can. Does an energy Healer heal? If you believe so, yes. Does prayer work? If you believe so, yes. Does hypnosis heal? If you believe so, yes. Can you heal? If you believe so, yes.

Do you need a ritual to heal? If it focuses your energy and belief, yes. Do you need religion to heal? If it focuses your energy and belief, yes. Do you need a Healer to heal you? If it focuses your energy and belief, yes. What do you need to heal? Focused energy and belief that the healer, or something, can heal. Do any of these work consistently? No. Why not? It is the personal degree of focus and belief.

So how do we deal with focus and belief? It seems to be a very nebulous, evasive thing that is virtually impossible to quantify.

When you truly believe, can any possibility happen? Yes. Why? Who cares? Just believe it. Your existing belief boxes are made of glass anyway. If these barriers do not come down, then nothing new can come in. So get used to this and keep your mind open. You do not need God or a Healer. You ARE the Healer—anybody else is just a Facilitator to make you believe it. Try believing that!

So what are these two experts in miracles telling us? The path (to the solution) is not the issue, the climb (belief box) is. What are these conflicting views of God's involvement telling us? The cases are biased to personal experience and point of view but the miracles are the same. They still happen. In either situation, the scene and the process are influencing or reinforcing the belief in their patients. And in all cases, the healer is simply a facilitator that helps set up an energy scene supporting the mindset that "it will be done" that's the end of it. But regardless of what you call the creator of the miracle, it is some higher power that you are yielding to and getting the assistance of. So let us extract the key processes.

HEALTH PROCESSES & PROCEDURES DIVINE CONNECTION		
Setting	Believe you are worthy	CM
Setting	Set the preconditions as self healing and love	CM
Process	Open a channel with prayer directed energy as pure love	CM
Process	Create a connection to Source	CM
Process	Visualize clearly the outcome in the mind's eye	CM
Assist	Surrender and trust in a Higher Power	CM

Process	Believe in a state of miracle minded readiness	TS
Process	Expect a positive outcome	TS
Process	Delete ego interference and feel love	TS
Process	Turn inward into a meditative altered state of consciousness	TS
Assist	Tap into the inner Divine Guide to look for higher good	TS
Process	Use free will to change or solve created problems	TS

5

DIVINE PROGRAMMING: ADAM DREAMHEALER

"Belief is a powerful form of intention but you have to create an edit button to take control and get out of old habits"
                                            Adam (Mcleod) Dreamhealer

Adam Dreamhealer claims at age 15, after hearing his mother suffering from extreme MS, he was moved by some invisible force, went up to her room, put his hands on her head, went into a trance, saw images of her head and a green pulsating light, removed it and healed her. He is a biologist and now a Healer. This man appears to have some controversy and has been accused of some scams on the Internet, but in the meantime, he is still giving conferences and workshops and has a long list of happy cases. In his book ***Intention Heals: A Guide and Workbook***, he describes his practice which we will summarize here.

Adam says that thoughts are energy and intention is focused thought which affects physical matter. Once you control the mind which regulates the body you are in control. Self healing knowledge resonates in your and other's energy field that you have been connected to in thought, word, and deed. In doing so, you help the planet.

He suggests that the use of precise visualizations of the issue such as pictures makes a connection to get the specific frequency unique to each. This is important to make the connection. Group healing merges the aura to a coherent group resonating together and has more power. He reports that he sees images of interacting frequencies. He focuses to reach specific frequencies to make them coherent by altering his own and does not know how it works. This ability to tune in resonance means more complete information is exchanged to get the past, present, future and determine the health issues. Using intention he transfers the information that is needed to manifest the health changes.

This, he states, is not attached to the physical self. It is a disassociated state of total awareness. His tune-in resonance allows him to know beliefs as to whether they are ready to receive the information and change. As the healer and healee resonate, they exchange quantum information in a "pinging" fashion. Clearly, the response depends on beliefs, attitude, relationships with self and others and the intention. When these are focused between the healer and healee it is strong providing the best results. When the intentions are a combination of fears, beliefs, doubts, low expectations and poor will to live, the results become less predictable.

Intention requires synchronizing conscious and subconscious thought patterns in order to invite change. Visualizations provide conscious focus and if they are fueled by emotional impact they are more powerful and can be more easily aligned with subconscious thought. It is the way to focus attention on healing.

In his experience, he says that life and healing are constantly changing; meaning there are infinite possibilities of possible outcomes which you can influence. Metabolism is based on enzymes (proteins) and these are directly influenced by intentions and thought. Think a thought and chemical reactions occur, and all reactions emit light. A thought is a light emitter. Even small amounts of light cause alterations in protein orientation and conformation of the entire enzyme.

This is why maintaining homeostasis maintains health. All your biochemical systems are constantly adjusting and reacting to new info down to the cellular level. He goes on to state that environment affects gene expression of DNA and a big part of your environment is your perception of it. Your genetic expression is affected by perception of which you control 100 percent. Harnessing self-empowerment through focused intention is the way to future medicine.

Healing needs physical, mental, emotional, and spiritual application in a proactive state. This means that belief influences like authority, media, family, education, thinking your limits are in your genes, thoughts that nothing can be done, or that it's in your head, in your family history are all limiting beliefs that will stop you cold. Healing needs synchronization of intention with beliefs which are mental constructs of all influences. Belief is a powerful form of intention but you have to create an edit button to take control and get out of old habits. When you do, there are no limits to imagination or how to interpret senses.

Adam has his ideas on emotions and what role they play. One constantly creates what they experience. Emotions are a choice and one can make a different choice about how you feel—your beliefs about emotions. A happy state associated with beliefs triggers the release of biochemicals and hormones such as serotonin and endorphins into cells. Stress on the other hand orders the release of cortisol and epinephrine biochemicals. Either is done by the choice of perception. Emotions fuel thought. An intention brought to memory stimulates response like electricity completes a circuit. Emotion triggers neurons of a particular frequency that triggers biochemical correlates for specific emotions. Intentions are goal based thinking sending signals to the neurons altering your being. The resonance created connects with all in the universe—the quantum sea of all possibilities.

So Adam believes that intention sets a cascade of biochemical reactions that get set into motion to influence events so they are aligned with your thoughts far beyond conscious awareness. We will get into the details of this in a subsequent chapter.

To give credibility to his thesis, he points out that the research Institute of HeartMath shows that DNA alters shape when intentionally focused emotion is directed at it. The research proves loving emotion unwinds DNA while anger contracts it. Each cell stores all and is interconnected so the energy of emotion is dynamically stored in all cells. Focused intent therefore changes memory in cells.

Beliefs are your filters. These are our perception of life so far. You must eliminate all limiting beliefs such as:

- I have no power to influence events
- I don't deserve health and happiness
- I fear death
- I always have bad luck
- Today will be worse than yesterday
- I fear failing so I won't get involved
- I have too much stress
- I cannot heal myself

Once you heal these beliefs, you must make an effort to maintain it as it is your responsibility to not fall back. Like after an operation, you must make an effort to behave a different way otherwise it does not heal. The power words are forgive, trust, love, sorry, thank you. These are words of high vibration that charge the energy. The words resonate with source and trigger quantum energy changes.

Once again, Adam's work points to the power of the mind and the belief system being intentionally aligned to positive vibrations. Once again, the energy field, referred to as the morphic energy that is created by you and the local influence is being harmonized and entrained to morph into a new visualized, emotionally charged outcome. This new outcome is magically merged into your field to become a reality.

Of large significance here is that his work reinforces this:

"Healing needs synchronization of intention with beliefs which are mental constructs of all influences. Belief is a powerful form of intention but you have to create an edit button to take control and get out of old habits. When you do, there are no limits to imagination or how to interpret senses. Emotions fuel thought. An intention brought to memory stimulates response like electricity completes a circuit."

What pops out here is that it always has to start with placing attention on something you want. Thoughts create morphic fields. Then there has to be some intention to change it. And then emotion fuels this process. Here are Adam's simplified steps:

HEALTH PROCESSES & PROCEDURES ADAM DREAMHEALER		
Setting	Eliminate limiting beliefs, belief is a powerful form of intention	AD
Process	Align to positive resonance vibrations to assist	AD
Process	Have precise visualizations of the issue with strong intent	AD
Process	Visualize, positive emotionally charged new outcome	AD
Process	Synchronize conscious and subconscious thought	AD
Assist	Tune resonance through to source and quantum energy	AD
Process	Invite change and launch intention to heal, merge into reality	AD
Process	Show faith, trust, love, forgiveness; all have higher power	AD

6

DIVINE PROGRAMMING
ANCIENT HO'OPONOPONO

"I Love You, I am sorry, please forgive me for whatever is going on in me that I perceive this in a certain way. Thank You."
Ihaleakala Len

You may have heard of a therapist named **Dr. Ihaleakala Hew Len.** He travels the world with **Joe Vitale** healing and teaching about an ancient Hawaiian healing process called **Ho'oponopono**. They are authors of ***Zero Limits: The Secret Hawaiian System for Wealth, Health, Peace and More.***

The mind boggling information that we will relate to you is that he is reported to have cured a complete ward of criminally insane patients without ever seeing any of them. Now that was just one of his miracles. There are many more. The process involved a study of an inmate's chart and then looking within himself to see how he created that person's illness. As he improved himself, the patient improved. Sounds crazy, right? How could anyone heal anyone else by healing himself? And how could even the best self-improvement master cure the criminally insane by remote control? And without the knowledge or consent of the criminal? Right, that's what many thought too!

As the story goes, Dr. Len worked at the Hawaii State Hospital for four years. The ward that he was associated with kept the criminally insane and was a pretty dangerous place. Psychologists quit on a monthly basis. The staff called in sick a lot or simply quit. People would walk through that ward with their backs against the wall, afraid of being attacked by the patients. It was not a pleasant place to live, work, or visit.

Dr. Len said that he never saw patients. He simply agreed to have an office and to review their files. While he looked at those files, he would work on himself using an old healing system he had learned. As he worked on himself, patients began to heal.

The reports are that as he quietly worked away things began to change. After a few months, patients that had to be shackled were being allowed to walk freely. Others who had to be heavily medicated were getting off their medications. And those who had no chance of ever being released were being freed. The staff began to enjoy coming to work. Absenteeism and turnover disappeared. Today, that ward is closed.

What was Dr. Len doing within himself that caused those people to change?

Dr. Len reported he was simply healing the part of himself that created these people the way they were. He explained that total responsibility for his life means that everything in his life—simply because it was in his life—was his responsibility. In a literal sense he believed the entire world was his own creation and it was all one. It was his creation of a hologram. So everything he saw, heard, tasted, touched or in any way experienced, was his responsibility because he created it. This means that anything he experienced and didn't like was up to him to heal. He said they didn't exist except as projections from inside himself. The problem wasn't with them, it was with him, and to change them, he had to change himself. What he was inferring here was that it was a big holographic movie. And everything in the movie was created by him. Far out? Not when you begin to understand modern quantum physics! But that is another chapter.

Doc Len was using the ancient art of **Ho'oponopono.** How do you suppose he did this **Ho'oponopono** thing which by the way means *'loving yourself'*? Dr. Len said that when he looked at those patients' files, he just kept saying, "*I Love You, I am sorry, please forgive me for whatever is going on in me that I perceive this in a certain way. Thank You.*" over and over again. He said he was talking to the Divinity in himself and Divinity knows what the memories are that need to be changed. But Divinity needed permission to purge the problem. He said loving himself was the greatest way to improve himself, and as he improved himself, he improved the world. He was re-writing the memories—sort of like regression therapy.

So? Do you believe this? Can it be this simple? Whenever you want to improve anything in your life, there's only one place to look: inside you? And when you look, do it with love? Wow!

Doc Len says that nothing can happen to us unless it is already in our data bank, namely our subconscious mind, because that is the Law of Cause and Effect. If you look within yourself and ask the Divinity part in you to erase the causes in you—whatever these memories are—that would cause you to see the world in a certain way, knowing that Divinity didn't create it that way, you can petition to have it deleted. Petition?

Doc Len explains when you say to The Divinity in yourself *"I love you; I am sorry; Please forgive me for whatever is going on in me that I am experiencing this; Thank You."* something gets attention and is erased. What gets erased by The Divinity is whatever requires your problems to stop. He explains: *"I have no idea what that is. That's Divinity's job, not mine! I am not doing Divinity's job. By saying the words, I am allowing The Divinity to transmute the errors (memories) in me."*

So what is this Ho'oponopono hocus pocus stuff all about? It teaches that the conscious mind is clueless and that it has NO idea of what is going on. So if you appeal to the Divinity who knows all to convert whatever memories are playing in subconscious mind to zero—nothing—and no-thing. Then you erase the problem from subconscious.

Ho'oponopono is a Hawaiian phrase that also infers *"to make right"*. In practice, the process is taking responsibility for all that you experience in your reality for the purpose of connecting to the Divine.

The philosophy of Ho'oponopono states that everything you *experience* is something that you have created. Whether you are pleased by the experience or harmed by it, whether it appears to be in your sphere of influence or not. Ho'oponopono requires that you take responsibility if you experience it even slightly.

By taking full responsibility for this creation, you also take responsibility for healing it. *You do not need to know how or why you are responsible, just that you are.* All experience comes from two sources. Your experiences and beliefs are either inspired from the Divine or they are the result of memories. These memories can either be ancestral group memories passed down from generation to generation, or they can be memories that you have created during your lifetimes. The goal of getting clear is to erase and eradicate memories so that you can more quickly access Divine inspiration.

In this case you do not need to know what beliefs, attitudes or memories are blocking your connection to Divine inspiration. Simply by taking responsibility, and identifying the issue, you can automatically begin healing the blocks between you and the Divine in you and everywhere else.

The bottom line is that if you want to solve a problem, no matter what kind of problem, take responsibility, realize you created it, and work on yourself first.

So Ho'oponopono is really very simple. For the ancient Hawaiians, all problems begin as thought. But having a thought is not the problem. So what's the problem? The problem is that all our thoughts are imbued with painful memories, memories of persons, places, or things. The intellect working alone can't solve these problems, because the intellect is the conscious part of the mind and only manages what it is aware of. Managing things is no way to solve problems. You want to let them go! When you do Ho'oponopono, what happens is that the Divinity takes the painful thought and neutralizes or purifies it. You don't purify the person, place, or thing. You neutralize the energy you associate with that person, place, or thing. So the first stage of Ho'oponopono is the purification of that energy. Then something wonderful happens. Not only does that energy get neutralized; it also gets released, so there's a brand new slate—a miracle! Buddhists call it the void. (It's the quantum zeropoint field but we will get to that in PART THREE). The final step is that you allow the Divinity to come in and fill the void with light; the way it was at point zero where everything was perfect with no issues.

To do Ho'oponopono, you don't have to know what the problem or error is. That is why Dr. Len studied the criminal charts. All you have to do is notice any problem you are experiencing physically, mentally, emotionally, or whatever. Once you notice something, your responsibility is to immediately begin to clean, to say those magic cleansing words. *"I love you, I am sorry, please forgive me for whatever is going on in me that I experience the world in me this way, thank you."*

When you are willing to take 100% responsibility for whatever you notice or experience in your life, you can then go onto the next step. When you state you are sorry and ask forgiveness, you are taking 100% responsibility for whatever is going on in your life and in essence saying to the Divine you are 100% responsible, the problem is within you, and you would like to convert whatever that memory, debt, block, error or problem is to nothing. And when the Divinity converts the block or memory to nothing, you return back to your original state, which is Zero or clarity. Hence the term Zero Limit. Only when you have clarity, can The Divinity provide you with insight, inspiration and whatever is perfect for you. So the secret is to stop looking outside of yourself for how you can solve the world's problems because that doesn't work. They are all inside.

In digging deeper into this notion, you encounter an interesting point of view in that Ho'oponopono suggests working on others is not our job. Dr. Len points out that he was trained as an educator from 1964 to 1982 to help the handicapped and developmentally disabled children, but then over twenty years later, he learned that that was not his job. Dr. Len then learned that his job was to help himself by letting go of how he perceived handicapped children. As he changed the way that he perceived handicapped children, they changed.

According to Dr Len, the person who had the most profound insight into the human condition was one that knew the woes that we experience now are the woes that we have experienced before. When we see the woe in a judgmental way, it means that it is already in us, but if we let go of it and do our Ho'oponopono cleaning by saying *"I'm sorry for whatever is going on in me that I perceive the woe a certain way"*, only then does it change. But the change has to take place in us first.

Doc Len says that cleaning memories from our subconscious mind takes incessant moment by moment Ho'oponopono cleaning. He points out that we never experience things correctly, but we always experience our reaction to them. Doc Len knows that when he meets people, he does not experience them the way The Divine created them, so he continuously cleans by saying to The Divine *"I am sorry for whatever is going on in me that I do not experience people the way You created them, please forgive me"*. By doing this, Len is asking the Divinity to cancel what is in him that causes him to react to people, and not see them as they truly are—Divine Beings. Once we let go of the dictate of memories by doing the Ho'oponopono cleaning, the memories stop playing, and not only the memories we hear playing, but many other memories simultaneously playing that we are unaware of.

He says that when we do Ho'oponopono, we are asking The Divine to remove the faults from our Soul and subconscious mind so that we can see people being perfect, the way the Divine created them, and when we respond to them, they will respond as being perfect. If we want to see people without problems, we need to get rid of our own problems first. Ho'oponopono is only about working on yourself and looking at the data and information in your personal subconscious mind that causes burdens and should be removed.

He goes on to state that when people are angry, it is not the person who is angry, but it is a memory replaying anger. He said that if we know this and keep it in mind, we can change the data. The Ho'oponopono we do is not changing the other person, because that person is perfect, but what is imperfect is the data, and we have to ask Divinity to convert that data to zero. He went on to say that the conscious mind does not take responsibly, and resorts to blame.

He continues by reflecting that as humans, we have stuff going on that we can't help because of the memories replaying in our subconscious mind, and these blocks prevent us from experiencing The Divine. Ho'oponopono is about erasing those memories that keep us from absolutely truly living and not being constrained by fear and how we feel. It is about working on whatever is going on in us that we are not able (generation after generation) to move through to a point where we can experience The Divine.

Ho'oponopono is about giving up those things in us that keep us stuck and constrained, and that we have no idea of what those things even are. We don't know what we don't know, so one does his Ho'oponopono cleaning on himself.

What have we here? First of all, what's Divinity? It refers to the operation of transcendent power in the universe and it is us—inside of us. What's the power? Who knows? Something we don't understand but anything that has the power and intelligence to clean up something and create a miracle is good enough for me.

Let us extract the basic ideas from Dr. Len's writings. First there is the **Divine** which is infinite and it creates self identity and inspirations. It transmutes memories to void. It is easily displaced by memories. It resides within us as part of the whole **Source.**

Then we have the **Super-conscious mind.** It oversees the conscious and subconscious mind. It reviews and takes appropriate changes in the Ho'oponopono petition to the Divine intelligence initiated in the conscious mind. It is unaffected by memories replaying in the conscious mind, always one with the divine.

Next we have the **Conscious mind**. It can make choices. It can allow incessant memories to dictate experiences for the subconscious mind or one can initiate the release of them through incessant Ho'oponopono. The conscious mind can petition for directions from Divine intelligence.

Next is the **Subconscious mind**. It is the storehouse for all the accumulated memories from the beginning of creation. Here is the place where experiences are experienced as memories replay or inspiration emanates. It is the place where the body and the world reside. It is the place where problems exist as memories replaying.

The Void is the foundation of self identity and the cosmos. It is where inspirations spring forth from divine intelligence—the infinite. Memories replaying in the subconscious mind displace the void (not destroy), precluding the flow of inspiration from divine intelligence.

A **Transmutation** is where a petition initiated by the conscious mind to Divine intelligence is made to void memories in order to re-establish self identity. It begins in the conscious mind.

Repentance is the beginning of the Ho'oponopono process initiated by the conscious mind as a petition to the Divine intelligence to transmute memories to void. Here you acknowledge 100% responsibility for the memories replaying problems in my subconscious mind.

Forgiveness is the petition from the conscious mind to the Divine Source to transform memories in your subconscious mind to void. Not only is your conscious mind sorrowful, it is also asking divine intelligence for forgiveness.

And so here is a very nice simple way of addressing problems. Is all this just quackery? Dr. Vitale, has partnered with Dr. Len. They have spoken publicly about Ho'oponopono and its practical uses in everyday life at venues around the globe. Dr. Len has been practicing the updated Ho'oponopono since November of 1982. He was taught the process by Kahuna Lapa'au Morrnah Nalamaku Simeona, who was designated a Living Treasure of Hawaii in 1983. He was staff psychologist in the forensic unit for the criminally mentally ill at Hawaii State Hospital for several years. He has taught the updated Ho'oponopono around the world and at the United Nations several times. Dr. Len has a doctorate from the University of Iowa. He has a Master of Science from the University of Utah and Bachelor of Arts from the University of Colorado. Check him out. He is now 70 years old and considered a recluse. Joe Vitale carries the torch.

Is this all a scam? You know the answer to this already. Yes it is a scam if you believe it to be! No, if you feel intuitively it will work for you. Is there a message here? Did you hear that you are simply part of a whole which is Divine. The question is whether you believe it or not. You can zero out the negative memories and energy blocks by focusing attention on them or some reflection of them. You don't even need regression? Wow! Not only that, you are able to do this to whatever you focus on. You are the whole and you can therefore take responsibility for the whole. This makes sense since DNA actually contains everything that exists—as does subconscious.

It gets even steamier. You are the Divine. Your gateway is through the mind and the subconscious via belief. Because you are the Divine, you are able to change things in that subconscious—zero out junk—through your own Divine intervention which operates on yourself. You are able to do this by a petition or request to your Divine counterpart by repeating "*I Love You; I am sorry; Please forgive me for whatever is going on in me that I perceive this in a certain way; Thank You.*" Do you need God to do this? No. Why? You are God! We all are! You just need to figure the way and environmental conditions where you can talk to yourself and do a divine intervention yourself!

So what are we being instructed to do here? It's pretty simple:

Start with the **conscious mind,** drop out a petition for **transmutation** to the **void** so **super consciousness mind** can instruct the **subconscious mind** to rewrite the defective program and reboot the computer. But if **repentance** and **forgiveness** are not stamped on the request then it simply ain't going to get mailed.

And this means that if these words are not enforced by deed, then "sorry, the request is on hold!" Here is Doc Len's simplistic process:

HEALTH PROCESSES & PROCEDURES HO'OPONOPONO		
Setting	Believe you are part of the whole which is divine	IL
Process	Zero out negative memories and energies by focus and reflection	IL
Process	Go inside and do it in a space of love	IL
Assist	Open the gateway through Divine and subconscious via belief	IL
Process	Bring into focus the issues that require attention	IL
Process	Send a petition to divine counterpart to erase memories of Cause	IL
Process	State I love you, I am sorry, please forgive me for this issue, thank you	IL
Process	Allow Divinity to erase errors in subconscious as the Effect	IL

7

DIVINE PROGRAMMING
JOHN OF GOD

*"Bring your scientists here, bring the doctors, bring them here.
There is no magic going on. Just the power of God."*

John of God

João Teixeira de Faria is referred to as John of God, the Miracle Man of Brazil. This man, called a psychic surgeon, has directly or indirectly healed millions of people over the years. For over 50 years he has been dedicated to using a unique gift. It is reported that some 500 people a day come for healing at a place called Casa de Dom Inác in Brazil. He charges no fee and for nearly 30 years, millions have visited the tiny village of Abadiania to see this man some call the most powerful spiritual healer since Jesus.

Every Wednesday, Thursday and Friday morning and afternoon, John of God, holds a free clinic for anyone who wants to attend. People come in the thousands from Brazil, elsewhere in South America, and around the world. They come to be healed not only of physical ailments but also of the fear, emptiness and left-brained materialism of our consumer society. Many come to test him and discredit him but he does not mind that. Soon after arriving, it becomes clear this is a very special place, a place of love, compassion, tolerance and healing. The experience at the clinic is truly extraordinary and transforming.

The clinic is set in a beautiful garden. Here you can rest and shelter from the hot sun, chat with clinic mediums and fellow pilgrims and have a quiet meditation. Also in the grounds are a shop, soup kitchen, and toilets. After the morning clinic, free soup is served to all.

Inside the clinic are a series of rooms where different healing procedures occur. The steps involve watching DVDs that familiarise people with the process before they go into a session. During clinic time, a long line of people wind their way from the outside hall through the rooms of the clinic to present themselves to John of God. It's often a slow process. But it's a time to relax, meditate, reflect on your reasons for being there and allow the powers of the various rooms to do their magic.

The first room of the clinic is the great hall. People gather here and in the garden before clinic starts. At one end is a stage where John of God talks and conducts visible operations. There is a series of pictures taken of people having visible operations on the stage in the hall. While all who attend the clinic are given the opportunity to participate in the healing sessions, it is the choice of the individual whether they have a visible or invisible treatment.

Next, the line goes through the Cleansing Room where you can sit and meditate while a clinic medium reads scripture and prays. Here you can be generally cleansed and prepared for your treatments with John of God.

Next is the Current Room. It gets its name from the palpable healing current that's generated by John of God himself, sometimes hundreds of meditators and the unseen throng of spirits that work in the room and its associated energetic hospital. This healing current augments the powers of John of God. The idea is that fear, the cause of the problems, is washed by Divine love and light.

Can you almost feel the morphic field of belief energy that is being set up here? People know others get cured here. The pictures, the priming, orientation, peace, love, divinity—all of it—reinforce a miracle happening to you, casting doubt out of your belief.

At one end of the room in a chair surrounded by flowers, John of God sits and treats each person as they present themselves in the queue. He will assess your state of health and then recommend one or more of a series of options; sit in the Current Room, come back when a more appropriate entity is present, take herbs, or have a series of crystal light bed treatments. John of God only speaks Portuguese. You can negotiate your own way to and around the clinic, or hire a Casa guide when at the clinic. You can even do a complete package for travel, accommodation, translation in the clinic, and then engage in tourist activities! There are pluses and minuses for each option. *But the bottom line is the shift in belief that you need to be familiar with before you go so you know what to expect and can immediately plug into the process. You need to be resolved that you want to be well and that a power beyond you and what you know will do it because you are worthy.* You are reminded that you ask and you shall receive.

John of God is reputed to be a very powerful trance medium for elevated spirit entities and powerful universal light healing source to work through. He performs his visible and non visible "operations" with the many different elevated spirits working through him. It is possible to observe and participate in some of these. Many serious cases are dealt with. All forms of cancer, (even the terminal or so called incurable ones), tumors, HIV and AIDS, motor neuron diseases, environmental diseases, lame people, addictions, (like drugs and alcohol) are a short list. People with psychological disturbances, obsessions and obsessive spirit attachments are also constantly being healed. There are many extraordinary healings that have even been measured by x-ray. There's also a room full of discarded crutches and wheel chairs.

There are cases of people being cured of HIV and AIDS, even when the symptoms had already taken over. Many people have had amazingly positive results in these areas most of whom have been cured completely, and are living healthy active lives. Although instant healings occur, often many people experience healing over time, like two to three months or more, sometimes after returning home. Some may have to return and sometimes there are many reported "visits" in sleep and dreams, as people being "worked on" set up a firm intention to visit the healing sanctuary.

Is this a scam? Is he creating miracles? Primetime TV followed the journeys of five people who sought out this man. They took a closer look at the amazing claims that surrounded him. The first traveler was Matthew Ireland, of Guilford, Vt. who was told he had a quick-growing inoperable brain tumor. He had undergone radiation and chemotherapy treatments. But almost two years after he was diagnosed, and after three visits with João, his tumor shrunk.

Annabel Sclippa of Boulder, Colorado was not able to walk since her spinal cord was nearly severed in a car crash in 1988. But after six visits with João, she said she could feel sensation in her legs and could nearly balance herself standing between handrails—something her physiotherapist said was unusual with her type of injury.

Mary Hendrickson of Seattle was diagnosed with chronic fatigue syndrome and powerfully debilitating allergies. She now feels much more energetic. *"There is no way I could feel this way if something hadn't changed inside me,"* she told Primetime Live. *"Something's made a difference."*

João is not a licensed doctor. Born in 1942, he is said to have been so rebellious he was thrown out of school after the second grade and could not keep a job. Then, at 16, as the story goes, the "entity" of King Solomon entered his body, and performed a miraculous healing. For years, João wandered Brazil offering healings. Twenty-seven years ago, he took residence in his casa in the plateaus and became known as "John of God."

Today, more than 30 doctors and notables can "enter" his body, João says. They're the ones that do the healing. Among those luminaries are Dom Inacio de Loyola, a 15th century Spanish nobleman; Dr. Oswaldo Cruz, who helped to eradicate yellow fever; and the late Dr. Augusto de Almeida, a meticulous and demanding surgeon. The "incorporating" happens in an instant, without warning. As João prepares to operate, his body suddenly jerks. He is said to take on the personality and even the eye color of the entity who inhabits him.

John of God's patients typically stay at Abadiania for two weeks, but they can stay for as long as they want. They can stay for an afternoon or morning and leave if they want to. Some people even arrive via bus on day trips. Everyone is told not to stop taking their medications or treatments such as chemotherapy. After seeing John of God, there are some strict rules. For 40 days, no sex, alcohol, pork or pepper, which are all said to weaken the body's aura, or energy field. John of God cautions that cures are not always instantaneous, but can take months or years and the entities cannot heal everyone. Some may be just too sick; others may not be ready spiritually. When patients come before him, he makes a diagnosis with just a glance—scribbles a prescription for herbs or even schedules an operation.

Some surgeries are "invisible". The entities are said to have such supernatural powers, they can heal without breaking the skin. Others are "visible" and only certain patients are considered eligible. They must volunteer, be 18 to 52 years old, and cannot be in wheelchairs, or have recently had radiation or chemotherapy. The "visible" surgeries can be graphic. Primetime witnessed one in which João took four-inch gauze-tipped steel forceps dipped them in a solution he called holy water, and shoved the forceps all the way up a patient's nostril and twisted them violently to heal him. It took 45 seconds, and the patient left bleeding. But João's assistants videotape such surgeries regularly and sell them at the gift shop.

It's against the law to practice medicine without a license in Brazil. John of God has been charged, fined and even jailed briefly. He keeps on performing surgeries, saying: *"It's the entities, not him, at work."* About the surgeries, he said: *"I don't do that. God and the spirits do that."* He admits even looking at the videotapes of the surgeries makes him queasy. He says he doesn't even remember the experience. *"I am unconscious,"* he told

Primetime. He likened his state to being asleep. Challenged over the propriety of these operations, João answered: *"Bring your scientists here, bring the doctors, bring them here. There is no magic going on. Just the power of God."*

Before we leave John of God it is of interest that he also performs distance healing. All you do is send him your full name, full address, date of birth, a recent average size full length photo, and a description of your condition that requires healing. You make an introduction by email with your formal request before sending payments for herbs via Paypal (around 60 bucks) on his website. Interesting that he uses Paypal since if you do a couple of scams with Paypal, you will hear about it fast and lose the account instantly as the client can demand money back! It certainly adds to his credibility of success.

Aha, it seems that John of God needs to bring you into his life with a photo, so you become his responsibility—just like Doc Hew Len of Ho'oponopono fame? Then new cleansing miraculously materializes as he puts attention onto the target, miraculously tuning into the right frame of mind with a new solution! Here is *João's* simplified process:

HEALTH PROCESSES & PROCEDURES JOHN OF GOD		
Setting	Enter a place of love and compassion	JG
Setting	Go through rooms to raise belief pictures, videos, demos	JG
Process	Cleansing room to meditate with a clinic medium	JG
Process	Engage in healing current to cleanse fear, cause of problems	JG
Process	Meet John to determine mode of treatment	JG
Process	Focus on the issue	JG
Process	Engage in a trance stage in preparation for healing	JG
Assist	Facilitate healing by allowing guidance through Spirits and God	JG

8

DIVINE PROGRAMMING
RELIGION & FAITH HEALING

God wants you well, God wants you to be prosperous; God wants you a whole person."
Oral Roberts

How could we write about miracles without mentioning religion? When we speak of religion, we mean the various followers of different gods, their chosen ones, and writings from which they derive their rules of behavior and belief. This may not be God. After all, that is where so many cases seem to have originated. The sense of religion is that most are founded on love, compassion, peace, and some divine force. And most seem to have some ultimate goal like a Heaven. But they all seem to have a different way up the mountain to where the ultimate place called Heaven exists. That's ok too. And each individual's belief about what to call their religion and how to get to the top is ok too.

What appears to be an issue, however, is that there appears to be so many at the bottom of the mountain fighting and hating others about which way to climb. It seems that there are different ways to love and show compassion— enough to fight over. It would seem more relevant to stick that love and compassion in one's pack sack, then start climbing—any path will do, don't you think? But religion is probably the originator of miracles.

Yet, these religions are a source of some new information on religion and miracles. For this one of the more controversial fellows in this business is **Oral Roberts** and his following is noteworthy. Roberts was a pioneer televangelist. He began broadcasting his revivals by television during 1955 and attracted a vast viewership.

Roberts became a traveling faith healer after ending his college studies without a degree. According to a TIME Magazine profile of 1972, Roberts originally made a name for himself with a large mobile tent that sat 3,000 on metal folding chairs where he shouted at petitioners who did not respond to his healing. During 1947, Roberts resigned his pastoral ministry with the Pentecostal Holiness Church to found Oral Roberts Evangelistic Association. He began conducting evangelistic and faith healing crusades, mainly in the U.S. and appeared as a guest speaker for hundreds of national and international meetings and conventions. Thousands of sick people would wait in line to stand before Oral Roberts so he could pray for them and lay his right hand on their afflicted body.

He founded Oral Roberts University in Tulsa, Oklahoma in 1963, stating he was obeying a command from God. The university was chartered during 1963 and received its first students in 1965. Students were required to sign an honor code pledging not to drink, smoke, or engage in premarital sexual activities. Another part of the Oral Roberts Evangelistic Association was the Abundant Life Prayer Group, which operated day and night. It should be noted, however, that the university is no longer part of the Oral Roberts Evangelistic Association due to the controversy stirred by the resignation of son Richard, as president of the university in November of 2007.

Somewhere along the line, Roberts fell from Grace. His fundraisings have been controversial among other things that questioned his integrity and intent. For whatever reason he fell from Grace, but the big question is: Did he or did he not facilitate healing miracles? One would not expect to hear that he always did. One would expect to hear that he sometimes did. And over the course of his career, he undoubtedly created a long list of people that would never be convinced they did not receive a miracle. That is significant. What is even more significant is how he gained the reputation of a healer and rose to fame.

Faith healing is a concept that Roberts was noted for. As a religious belief **faith** *is the confident belief or trust in the truth or trustworthiness of a person, idea, or thing.* The word faith can refer to a religion itself or to religion in general. As with "trust", faith involves a concept of future events or outcomes, and is used conversely for a belief *"not resting on logical proof or material evidence."* Informal usage of the word "faith" can be quite broad, and may be used in place of "trust" or "belief." Faith is often used in a religious context, as in theology, where it almost universally refers to a trusting belief in a transcendent reality, or else in a Supreme Being and/or this being's role in the order of transcendent, spiritual things.

Faith is in general the persuasion of the mind that a certain statement is true. It is the belief and the assent of the mind to the truth of what is declared by another, based on his or her authority and truthfulness.

As we see in placebos, faith can bring about healing—either through prayers or rituals. Prayer is the act of addressing a god or spirit for the purpose of worship or petition. Specific forms of this may include praise, requesting guidance or assistance, confessing sins, as an act of reparation or an expression of one's thoughts and emotions. The words used in prayer may take the form of intercession, a hymn, incantation, words of gratitude, or a spontaneous utterance in the person's praying words. Praying can be done in public, as a group, or in private.

Most major religions in the world involve prayer in one way or another in their rituals. Although in many cases the act of prayer is ritualized and must be followed through a sometimes strict sequence of actions (even going as far as restricting who may pray), other religions, mainly the Abrahamic religions, teach that prayer can be done spontaneously by anyone at any moment.

Scientific studies regarding the use of prayer have mostly concentrated on its effect on the healing of sick or injured people. The efficacy of petition in prayer for physical healing to a deity has been evaluated in numerous studies, with contradictory results. There has been some criticism of the way the studies were conducted.

Prayer is believed to evoke a divine presence. **Divine presence**, **presence of God**, or simply **presence** is a concept in religion, spirituality, and theology that deals with God's omnipotent abilities to be "present" with human beings. God is understood to be capable of interfacing with the natural world, and more importantly, with human beings, such that he can and does hold some influence with each and all human being(s).

According to the common theological view, God is omnipresent and telepathic. He can *read, see, interpret, evaluate, and understand* all human thought and concept, and can project his will in various ways. Such ways are commonly said to be quite subtle like through divine illumination. But religious texts typically deal with important occurrences wherein God deals directly with particular beings. There are three distinct but related concepts of divine presence:

- God's presence in nature
- God's presence among all human beings

- God's presence in each human being

In theological terms, God's presence in nature is irrelevant next to his presence among humanity. Such presence could be in the mind, but an unseen being that influences human perception would be perceived by human beings as an external, environmental, or natural entity.

This process of prayer which calls the divine presence can direct the power toward correcting disease and disability in particular indicated individuals. Belief in divine intervention in illness or healing is related to religious belief in general. In common usage, "faith healing" refers to notably overt and ritualistic practices of communal prayer and gestures such as laying on of hands. In its healing form, the **laying on of hands** is based on biblical precedent set by Jesus who would walk for days, offering his healing power to peasants and prostitutes, alike. Both Christian and non-Christian faith healers will lay hands on people when praying for healing, and often the name of Jesus is invoked as the spiritual agency through which the healing of physical ailments is believed to be obtained. This is common practice in many healing practices such as Shamanism, Sangoma, Nganga, Pseudoscience, Efficacy of prayer, Therapeutic touch, Energy Healer, and Reiki.

Claims that prayer, Divine Intervention, or the ministrations of an individual healer can cure illness has been popular throughout history. Miraculous recoveries have been attributed to myriad techniques commonly lumped together as "faith healing". It can involve prayer, a visit to a religious shrine, or simply a strong belief in a supreme being.

The term is best known in connection with Christianity. The Bible, especially the New Testament, teaches belief in, and practice of, faith healing. Advocates say that legitimate faith healings do occur today just as they did in the early Christian church—that faith healing has wide-ranging successes. There have been claims that faith can cure blindness, deafness, cancer, AIDS, developmental disorders, anemia, arthritis, corns, defective speech, multiple sclerosis, skin rashes, total body paralysis, and various injuries. Of course critics say it is "not effective" and have voiced concerns that those who pursue it may depend on it instead of (or delay seeking) conventional medical care.

The legacy of Faith Healing is carried by Oral Robert's son **Richard Roberts,** who has dedicated his life to ministering the saving, healing, delivering power of Jesus Christ around the globe. God has put a dream in Richard's heart of reaching the nations of the earth for Jesus. Since 1980, he has ministered God's healing power in 34 countries spanning 6 continents. In his miracle healing rallies, Richard has ministered to crowds of up to 100,000 folk in a single service. Regularly as much as 50% of the fans stand for prayer to receive Jesus Christ as their private Lord and Saviour. Hundreds and thousands more receive healings and miracles as Richard ministers God's Word and moves in the gifts of the Holy Spirit, especially the word of knowledge.

Richard is the Chairman and boss of Oral Roberts Evangelistic association and also co-chairman of World Charismatic Bible Ministries. He and his wife, Lindsay, host a nationally syndicated television program, the Spot for Miracles: Your Hour of Healing-a 1 hour, interactive daily broadcast that reaches out to millions. On this unique healing program, Richard ministers in the power of the Lord God, praying for people that are sick or hurting in some area of their lives, and often giving specific words of knowledge about how God is touching folk with His healing power. The place for Miracles has received more than 117,000 telephone calls to date from viewers who have reported miracles and answers to prayer.

Richard is a man aflame for God and consumed by the compassion of Jesus for sick and injured people. His meetings across the U.S. and around the globe are marked by an incredible move of the Spirit, resulting in all sorts of physical, psychological, emotional, financial, and religious healings. Richard announces: *"Jesus was born to step into an arena of difficulty and bring healing and deliverance, and that's the call of God on my very own life to reach out to folks in their troubles and heartaches, to pray and believe God, and to bring them His Word of hope and healing"*.

In addition to his responsibilities at OREA, Richard also served as President of Oral Roberts varsity for fifteen years and is now President Emeritus. Richard has authored a number of books, booklets, and other inspirational material, including **When it seems All Hope Is Gone, The Excellent News Is the Bad News Is incorrect, Claim Your Inheritance,** and his autobiography, he's the **God of a Second Chance**.

Here is what the Roberts boys tell you to do:

1. **Let the Word of God become real to you.** Sometimes, we hear the Word and know it's true in our heads, but it hasn't become real in our hearts yet. If that is your struggle, you can build faith in your heart by reading, listening to, and meditating on God's Word about healing. Faith comes by hearing and receiving the truth in God's Word. You may need to spend more time with God's Word than you usually do. You can also

be encouraged in your faith by reading and listening to stories of people who have been healed.
2. **Don't become discouraged when you don't see immediate results to your prayers.** It doesn't mean there is anything wrong with your faith if an answer doesn't come instantly. Continue to pray, continue to thank God, and ask others to pray and agree with you.
3. **Ask yourself if there is a spiritual or emotional issue that could be affecting your physical health.** It's important to open up every area of your life to God so He can heal your entire being. Ask God if there is something blocking your healing. If He reveals an issue to you, deal with it through repentance and whatever else you need to do to make it right.
4. **Continue to resist the devil.** He is the source of sickness, not God. And he will try to deceive you into doubting God's healing power. So put the devil in his place. Refuse to accept negative thoughts or doubts, and replace them with God's Word.
5. **Let God direct you about how to receive your healing.** Many times, when we are sick, we get it in our minds that God will heal us in a certain way, and we get disappointed when it does not happen as we thought it would. Often, we block God's healing power simply because we are not open to the many means God uses for healing. Your healing may come to you by prayer, by medicine, or by both. Be open to all of God's healing methods.
6. **You may need to see a physician.** It is not wrong for a Christian to seek medical care. Medicine is a gift God has given us. Doctors are a means through which God can bring you your healing, so be open to it and visit a doctor if you haven't already done so.
7. **You may need to simply receive.** Many Christians have not learned how to receive from God through simple faith. If you believe this is an area where you are struggling, ask God to help you learn how to receive from Him.

And what does Roberts say about when it fails?

> *"This is fear—a belief that God's power is not enough to beat sickness. If a person believes in the power of sickness more than the power of God, it will be hard for that person to receive God's healing."*

So what have we here? Does religion produce miracles? Yes, of course. And the process? Are we not hearing the same thing as with the other techniques? It is just a different form of application. The Evangelist certainly sets up the proper morphic field would you not agree? And the hands on healing, the trust in some Divine intervention coming to the rescue? Is this not the same process? But does it work all the time? No. Why? Belief.

Will the belief in a placebo pill create a miracle all the time? No. But when you really believe it will, it does!

What may be coming through here is a pattern. First, unexplainable miracles are certainly not new and they are most definitely not limited by scientific "rules" or type of people creating them. But we sure hear a lot about belief, faith, and Divinity and a procedure that sets the scene for consciousness to make a change to the programs. Here is the simple process used in Faith Healing of the Robert's legacy:

HEALTH PROCESSES & PROCEDURES RELIGION		
Setting	Have a belief and trust in the truth or trustworthiness of God	OR
Setting	Have a faith in future outcome and through a supreme being	OR
Process	Engage in a ritual audience to raise the awareness and energy field	OR
Process	Lay on of hands to simulate biblical precedent of Jesus	OR
Assist	Issue a prayer to address god or spirit for assistance	OR
Process	Create a conclusive slap, shout, situation to conclude the miracle	OR

9

DIVINE PROGRAMMING
ANCIENT PRAYER

"Research has shown that it is through a quantum field that connects us to the Universe that our beliefs and prayers within us are carried into the world around us".

Gregg Braden

This whole idea of prayer is highly intriguing because it is such a common part of the processes. In this area there is a writer and scientist that produces exceptional work. His books really take you out into the fringes of science. His name is **Gregg Braden** and you can find him at **www.greggbraden.com**.

As a crossover between science (he is actually a geologist) and spirituality, he has been on an incredible quest involving ancient wisdom and religions. What is really pertinent to this chapter is what he found out about what he called the lost mode of prayer.

Gregg says there are four modes of prayer that religions use but there is also a lost mode of prayer. The four types of prayer are *colloquial,* an informal prayer. There is *petitionary* which petitions for help, *ritualistic* where statements are made of the goodness of God, and *meditative,* where you create a deep sacred relationship. But the fifth is called *feeling*. Here the prayer has already been answered as the thing asked for was *'as done'* and surrounded with feeling.

This, he points out, was hidden from us. The conspirator was the church that deleted special wisdom from all books back in the 4th century—back in Alexandra and then they re-wrote the bibles and destroyed all of the writings that they believed were contrary to their beliefs. They took out empowering mystical information. Forty-five books were taken out and condensed.

Twelve hundred other translations to other languages further distorted the original truth. It was how this key powerful mode of prayer was lost.

It was, as he suggests, that this wisdom was too powerful because within it was the power of miracles. A prayer made in this faith could heal the sick. So the *"Ask and you shall receive"* prayer is not complete and does not work as is suggested in the new version! It was edited out. What is really fascinating is Braden's evidence in the King James modern condensed version of the Bible. He quotes: *"What so ever ye ask thy Father in my Name, he will give it to you. Hitherto have ye asked nothing in my name: Ask and ye shall receive, that your joy may be full".* But from the original version we have a whole different concept: *"All things that you shall ask straightly, directly… from inside My Name you shall be given… be enveloped by what you desire, that your gladness be full."*

Braden says that in the spring of 1998, he had the honor of facilitating a pilgrimage into the monasteries of central Tibet, searching for evidence of an ancient and forgotten form of prayer. There he found the language that speaks to the field that unites all things. The monks and the nuns who live there shared the instructions for a way to pray that was largely lost to the West in the fourth-century biblical edits of the early Christian Church. But it was preserved here in Tibet for centuries in the texts and traditions of those living there. He found this was the lost mode of prayer and it has no words or outward expressions. It was based solely in feeling.

Specifically, he says: *"this process of prayer invites us to feel as if our prayer has already been answered"*. It is different than feeling powerless and needing to ask for help from a higher source. In recent years, studies have shown that it is this very quality of feeling that does, in fact, *speak* to the field that connects us with the world. Through prayers of feeling, we are empowered to take part in the healing of our lives and our relationships, as well as our bodies, and our world! He says: *"Research has shown that it is through a quantum field that connects us to the universe that our beliefs and prayers within us are carried into the world around us"*.

If you are paying attention these days, you will see it has taken thousands of years to reveal the truth. But Braden reports another aspect of this as revealed in the Essene's Gospel which is 2500 years old. It says: *"When three become as one, you will say to the mountain move"*. This language is what speaks directly to the Force. The Essenes were the real ancient keepers of wisdom.

The three items Gregg is talking about are thought, feeling and emotion. It is the lost mode of feeling—already accomplished. It requires a faith that acknowledges our power in creation—it happened. You created it or the seed. Then you give thanks after you felt it. So you don't just pray for something, you have to feel it to really give it life. That is what creates the vibratory possibilities. Feeling is magnetic energy movement through us and around us. So if you can make thought, feeling, and emotion one, you can '*move mountains*' and create miracles.

But Gregg points out if you look at the old edited version it says: *"ask"* when the real version says: *"be enveloped by what you desire, that your gladness be full"*. That is a whole new picture. That is referring to visualization and feelings. Now there is more. He says the Essenes said: *"First, seek peace in his own body (emotion) then seek peace in the feelings, then seek peace in his own thoughts, such can shape the Heavens"*. Peace is the key. Demonstrate love and compassion. It is an anchor point. The Essenes said: *"go to Nature to nurture peace—reverence will help create peace"*. The Essenes said peace is the most powerful component. We can create it in our bodies through thought.

What is so interesting is that there is a universal template of prayer. It has input, function, output. The words are not key, the feeling is. Open the field, feel the feeling and give thanks. These are the three components. The template is the same in all world religions. The New Jerusalem version is: *"Our father in Heaven, may your name be held holy"*. King James Version is: *"Our father who art in Heaven, hallowed be thy name."* The original Aramaic Version is: *"Oh, Berther of the cosmos, may your name be holy..."* We seal the prayer in faith, truth and trust by *"Amen"* at the end. So we should use these components with our own words between. Create a feeling as if the prayers are already done. This is the way you communicate with the field and show faith.

Gregg points out that it is through subtle energy that science now acknowledges, the language of creation is words, thoughts, and emotions. The results are mirrored in the events we experience. Our visible world of what we see is a reflection of the invisible unseen world. What we become in our beliefs is what we experience in this world.

So what are we hearing here? Prayer is that petition like in Ho'Oponopono to the Divine Force asking for intervention. It seems to carry extra powerful resonance in the words and particularly with emotion. But does it work all the time? No. Can it create miracles? Yes, sometimes. Now we find that it is emotion that we need to be adding to the request memo. We also have to be in *now* time—it is done, thank you! And have faith that it is so. But is that all? No. What else? Perhaps strength of belief? And the proof stamps of love, forgiveness and repentance? Here is Gregg's suggestions quantified in our usual summary:

HEALTH PROCESSES & PROCEDURES ANCIENT PRAYER		
Setting	Believe that a higher source will answer your prayers	GB
Process	Believe the prayer has already been answered	GB
Process	Enter a state of peace, love, compassion without hidden motives	GB
Process	Bring forward the thoughts of your desire so your gladness be full	GB
Process	Create a clear visualization of that which is desired	GB
Process	Enfold vision with strong positive emotion to envelope the desire	GB
Assist	Ask the divine to fulfill the desire as in ask and it shall be given	GB
Process	Show gratitude that your joy is full	GB

10

DIVINE PROGRAMMING
MATRIX ENERGETICS

"At the level of the photon, consciously directed intent can alter the behavior of the fundamental constituents of matter."
Richard Bartlett

One of most amazing eye-opening practitioners of the application of quantum physics **and** energy healing is a man named **Richard Bartlett** who wrote the books: **Matrix Energetics** and **The Physics of Miracles**. Richard teaches seminars all over the globe and has a staggering amount of practitioners who themselves create miracles of healing daily. Now there are many more like Richard around the planet but he illustrates a whole storyline - the practical application of quantum physics. I (Ed) have also personally taken his Level 1 and Level 2 seminars. It also helps to sew together what we have been presenting.

There will be some repeat of earlier information but this will help to congeal things. Keep in mind that 30% of our practical science like lasers and MRIs are based on quantum physics, so there is no doubt about practical application and nothing here is really new. But what Richard does, is most definitely new. We are going to encapsulate Richard's words which come from a Level 1 and Level 2 three day seminar.

Richard explains that quantum physics teaches us we are one with the Universe and connected together via a mysterious energy called the Zero Point Energy Field—the sea of virtual particles that lies beneath every point in the Universe. We are made of high energy photons, the smallest known particle of matter, and we are just a pattern of light and information. When you understand this you unlock the powers to interact with the Zero Point. It provides a link to the indivisible One Spirit and us.

Richard adds that at the level of the photon, consciously directed intent can alter the behavior of the fundamental constituents of matter. As a matter of fact (and he is a Chiropractor as well) he points out that the issue of medicine is that focusing on symptoms, treatment, and conditions simply adds to the retention of the problem. It does so by adding energy for sustaining the unwanted state. You add validity to its reality and make the condition linear, predictable, and are self aware—exactly what you do not want. So anytime you perceive or observe from a framework of duality (a state of negative-positive or bad-good) it can reinforce the condition—a particle based reality or conscious reality.

By energy consciousness you can intercept a condition before inception and observe a different outcome—a new set of possible outcomes changing the manifestation of conditions and problems. By a process of morphic resonance, a certain amount of information is added and a new pattern of behavior simultaneously occurs. Our DNA acts as a tuner which receives instructions from energy in the morphic field like a TV that does not contain the pictures but picks up the correct frequency to create a picture.

Each organ, tissue, cell has its own field. You download into DNA biological traits from the collective fields of the human race—not your parents. Thoughts have morphic fields, as does the consciousness of you or a group. Once you believe and embody something, you link into a power grid of the morphic field. That is where healing occurs as you are in resonance with it and into an enormous database of universal energy.

An electron behaves like a particle when you are looking at it. It assumes a wave pattern when you look at it with different expectations or take attention off of it. This is called the Observer Effect. It means you can observe a different reality by attention to it.

Traditional atomic structure tells us an atom has a nucleus consisting of proton and neutron with electrons orbiting the nucleus. Quantum structure says the electron moves in probability or bits revolving into a predictable orbit only when observed. At the point where our consciousness enters into seeing it, the path materializes solidity into reality called forth by intention. Electrons choose from a realm of infinite possibilities the pattern that we limit it to by our observation. It goes from a seemingly unpredictable wave like behavior to a particle representation of reality when we see it that way. We don't know what the electron does when we are not looking at it. Consciousness collapses the wave function.

Yes, this is far out. But you have to check out the recent work in this area that confirms we live in a great hologram; a quantum universe. It is not compatible with our belief system that we observers create as we observe and that these electrons simply wait around for directives. If you are perplexed, think about scientists trying to explain this. It clearly does not compute within our "logic framework". There are millions of questions that pop out, aren't there?

We think we and our problems are solid physical material. The body is composed of organic structures (respiration, digestive, etc.) made from organs and specialized tissues and cells classified by their special morphology and function. Who says they are real? Our brains - the Observers! Don't fret; we will get into this topic in PART THREE! Cells are carbon based molecules composed of atoms but the observer can change the behavior. We are composed of light and information which is the same as consciousness. For, if a problem is just a pattern of high energy photons, then it can be reconfigured based on how we choose to observe them. We must imagine the problem not there.

You are the one who with help makes up the rules for your experience of this reality. When you get rid of measuring and observing boxes with your conscious limit of atoms, anything is possible. Science is a limiting box. Quantum energy principles, although not widely understood, have changed this and redefined reality.

So what if you let this archaic atomic belief of reality go and act as if everything depends on you the Observer. Atomic reality is lacking anyway! Set up the parameters of your manifestation before the crisis occurs. Remember that electrons or photons are observer dependent (perception & expectation). You are what you think. Everything you have believed, accepted, experienced or internalized is a matrix of your energetic signature; a perceptual lens used to subconsciously filter information in your world view. Your experience and senses make up what you think in your reality. To change this you must alter thoughts and feelings. You really don't want to "know anything" which opens you to the next moment. Ask open questions so the universe can answer.

What is he saying? Get out of the box and consider what normally would be impossible as very possible. You will see what you expect to see. Shift your awareness into a quantum state of consciousness. Get the mind to build confidence in a new quantum world. Mind over matter is the act of deciding what and how to observe at a quantum level causes the object of your attention to behave or move in a fixed or predetermined manner. Create a new belief system.

Quantum mechanics opens a virtual sea of possible solutions where you can use your imagination to pick out one you like. The concept you visualize can have significant power to drive an action to bring about a structural change in the physical body. It is because we are constructed of light and information and are malleable to focused intent. The reality is when intended changes are visualized clearly, belief is strong, emotional force behind intent is both focused and sustained, unbelievable things happen!

Human intention can strongly influence the physics of the unseen universe. Only our unconscious is aware of this quantum wave level of reality. Every one of us can influence all biological life forms via our biofield emissions and the information they carry. Whether we intend it or not we are already doing this in local and global reality.

In the normal material world (called 3D) we believe our power to influence the quantum is zero, thus the material world applies and human intention does not significantly influence reality. Yet we do it unaware all the time. We do influence and create events. We do create physical outcomes. We do create miracles and instant healing. What we have not realized is that we have the ability to cross between the two states of quantum physics. We, in fact were designed to do this. It is a cross between our "solid" reality and our imaginary quantum wave "dream" reality. With a significant field of consciousness present, there is the ability to straddle both realities.

So how does Richard use all this "wisdom" to heal?

We are going to describe something to you that will boggle your mind, particularly if you watch this. There is no doubt that Richard Bartlett reflects a new breed of healer—he calls healing a transformation. This transformation has been in many cases dramatic. And you can go to Richard's web site ***www.matrixenegetics.com*** and read for yourself the cases, the demonstrations, the testimonials.

Richard describes a process based on quantum physics which he calls Two Point. Here is how it works in a very simple case.

Let us assume that you have a client that would like to have a few things corrected. You are the one that is going to facilitate a transformation. This transformation is going to get you into the quantum zone of the heart so that a new outcome can be collapsed into the solid form from the quantum wave form. You are going to coax those electrons into a new possibility bypassing that subconscious Controller again.

Stand facing your client who is also standing facing you. The first step is to ask the client if they would like to see a change in them, what would it be? Let us say it is a pain in the knee or some dysfunction. You would ask the client to imagine placing that pain on an imaginary clip board say just about eye level. In other words, here is the list of things to do, dear subconscious. Ask the client to mentally or through some hand action place it there, then relax—like forget it is there. By this action, the issue does not exist anymore; it is on the clip board.

Now as the Transformer, you must get into the Zero Point zone of the quantum vortex of new possibilities. How? It is a process of "dropping to the heart." This is where the center of Grace—the Divine in you—resides. You do this with your own mind by taking a pebble (representing the physical quantum state) and throwing it lightly into an imaginary pond. The resultant ripples on the pond form (representing the quantum wave state) as the solid state is gone. This gets you into the Zero Point Field of the Heart. You can simply imagine dropping your intellect into the heart area. You do whatever you feel comfortable with that moves your mind (consciousness) into the heart area.

Next, without any hesitation, lag or thinking about it, move your left hand to a place on or close to the body which simply feels right and *attracts your attention*. There is no right or wrong here it is simply a spot that attracts your attention. It is without hesitation or intellect (higher brain waves) the very first thing that pops into your mind. You do not question it because you are being "guided". Keep your hand there. Let us say it is on the left shoulder.

Do the same with your other hand placing it wherever it is attracted. Remember this is the first impulse. Don't even think about it. You now have two points. This process now *places attention* on them and when you hold the hands in these two places and mentally link the two, *they are entangled*. Entangles is a term used to say you have now entered the realm of oneness with everything that exists in an un-materialized quantum state in the Zero Point vortex of the heart. There is no right or wrong point as long as you feel a pull and make the entangled quantum connection.

Now you are *waiting for a change* to occur in the client, and perhaps even yourself. You are looking for an energy pattern that will correct the condition you are entangled in. This process is called *collapsing the waves* into the new possibility. The result is that the client may waver, collapse, laugh, or show some visible sign that the change has occurred. Most of these demonstrations create a collapse on the floor indicating a shift has occurred. This can last from minutes to hours because the muscular system has been immobilized in the shift.

That's it. You are done. The affect is left to the Divine (Grace and the Heart are synonymous with the Divine). It can occur instantly or later—whenever the Divine decides, not you. You simply brought attention to the issues, got rid of your intellect and its normal Alpha interference, placed it into the heart or Divine jurisdiction, and looked for a change. On your part it was a mindless, faith leveraged activity left to do as it desired. On the client's part there was nothing done except when he or she collapsed on the floor.

You can now imagine you are linked or entangled with the other person or the area. When you connect the two points, you have consciously observed them as linked. This is a link with your imagination that already operates at this sub-atomic quantum level. You are observing at a subatomic level of high energy photons held in patterns of wave of interference. When you imagine at the level of a photon you have the power to change the pattern of light and information.

The act of focusing at this level where everything is made of light energy causes what you observe to behave differently. You collapse the particle based arrangement of your world into intricate patterns of wave fronts of light. You can normally sense and feel it happening.

But it is crucial to get into the heart. Imagine if you had no body nor did others. Feel the space as light waves of information and energy. Let go and allow the idea of a separate you and go away. This happens the instant you stop thinking about it if you give up trying to do anything and you just are. It is the real power of nothing. Feel what would happen as you merge with patterns of light. Practice this and get accustomed to the feeling. Don't think about it. Do it naturally like breathing. Train yourself by noticing the change at the two points. When you come back to a solid state particle awareness, they will be softer.

Richard says that when you get to the desired state, anything to do within the context of your intent will work. When you practice this art daily you begin to have glimpses of hidden reality behind the shroud of daily events. Things no longer happen to you and you begin to take responsibility for creative use of universal energy. You begin to grasp the scope and depth of infinite possibilities.

Finding the two points gives you something to measure. Second, the imagination interlocks with patterns of holographic representations of energy driven by consciousness. By focusing on the qualities of the two points, your imagination enters into a process and serves as the focus for intent. Here you embrace nothing and have access to ALL.

Sound nuts? This is the new quantum reality! Of course some will naturally do this faster and easier than others but this is a man, with practitioners all over the planet that are creating miracles and fixing some very dramatic dysfunctions.

One of the toughest things to do is to stop thinking. It is the intellect and the ego that will not be back-seated for long. That process is what is supposed to take you "inside", as a meditator would tell you. Inside is where you are **one with all that is.** It is the quantum state of un-materialized matter, ready to be chosen from an infinite realm of possibilities all of which can be in your mind. Here is a place where time does not exist. It is called NOW! Here is the place where you eliminated all the 30,000 or so thoughts per day the conscious mind is projecting, and establishing a direct connection to the computer system that manifests the material changes in the subconscious, that exists at that level of quantum state and the great intelligence that holds it together. The process actually takes you past the daydream state to cross into the physical, material reality.

Now, to continue, you are looking for ways to facilitate the process of how things are presented to the conscious mind. Shapes and objects (Reiki) can be used to trigger with the Mind's Eye. This builds a bridge between left and right brain to harmonize the two through greater coherence like the goal in meditation. The subconscious mind is the gate keeper to filter things not in step with the conscious reality expectations or belief. It can process 11 million bits/sec while the conscious does only 7 bits/sec. So flashes of intuition (from subconscious) are based on much more information than anything coming from the conscious.

We are not healing here. We are transforming. From a quantum model of altered awareness, you can change the manifestation of the physical outcome by coherently looking at it. The Two Point technique allows you to measure what you want to change. Having established the points, you then ask the Divine to do its work. By going to the heart with the pebble (or whatever way you prefer) you move into alpha state of relaxation taking your mind completely off the problem, when your consciousness intersects with the quantum state of matter, the very act of your measured, focused intent causes ripples and undulations of causative action to unfold the observer and observed together. You become one with the object of your intent momentarily fused together.

Thinking too much gets in the way because you are not in alpha. By practice, your subconscious mind begins to sift through the possibilities and you will slowly bring your creativity in.

It is useful to keep my example of the daydream in the back of your mind as you read this. Remember, we had no time here and we could time travel—teleport instantly. Richard calls this process Time Travel. He says using the quantum wave one can connect future events with past events by tracking back. These are simply memories recorded by you in your subconscious. The point of intersection creates the present moment. Past and present are just possibilities. You can travel back and reorganize things (like an injury) and access the pattern of wave format as well as the emotional state and the physical "change" on that event. Once entangled you choose a different possibility and resolve it just like hypnosis, regression and psychology do the same. And Ho'oponopono? Or you can imagine a new outcome in which case the event never occurred the way you previously remembered it. Here is the process:

1. Do the same as in the first simple Two Point to get your hands at the two points;
2. Ask the age which is your zero reference point;
3. Count back in increments of five years while holding the two points to arrive at the event in time you wish to interact with. As you approach you will notice the change as the client will waver, collapse or laugh;
4. Be prepared for an emotional release of energy. Let it be and encourage it;
5. When settled with conclusion, re-assess the Two Point. Repeat this as there may be multiple time frames that need to be accessed to resolve the issue or pattern more completely. For example with an injured knee, travel back to when the knee was injured and change the pattern of injury.

Time is a hologram and the past is configured by the way we remember events. Quantum theory says every moment has multiple possibilities (different perceptions of experience). When you begin to change the certainty about how past events are put together, you help re-establish a flexibility of consciousness. The pattern that holds that event together as a remembered construct can be loosened enough to allow for your mind (the best time travel machine-dream around) to re-encode, and enact the sequence of those events differently. This is precisely what we could do in our daydream!

Richard points out that the superstring theory says the universe is composed of vibrating loops of strings—12 dimensions in parallel (past lives). This can be used to travel back into previous dimensions (lives) to fix things there as well. You use the Two Point process and travel back the same way to feel the place where the issue originated. You feel the energy problem, fix it and leave.

Once the rational left brain realizes the concept of quantum physics, it lets go of its usual belief box to other possibilities and the box fades. That is where the pot of gold and infinite wealth/health possibilities are—in your mind.

Intent is the energetic foundation for manifesting the substance and structure of your beliefs into observable reality. To accomplish something you must first imagine it. Once you see it, then you conceptualize it, then see it happening. Then you take steps to do it. Quantum provides a real gateway into a realm of possibilities that allows instantaneous healing of physical manifestations and virtual transformation of every aspect of your life. Once you learn this in your body, there is no limit to your imagination and what you can do.

The ramifications of all this are very profound. Matter exists because we have thought it into existence and because so many hold that persistent delusion, it exists for all as our reality. We have taken the background cosmic energy and transformed it with one joint awareness and consciousness into our experience of what we call our reality—but it is really what we create and interact with in our minds. Once created, it is there for all to experience, but even though it is created, it can still be collapsed back into quantum waves and rearranged into a new possibility.

Richard, in his seminars, uses the audience to participate. His three day seminar is filled with laughter and wonder as he creates an incredible morphic field in the room, sort of like John of God and Oral Roberts. There is little doubt penetrating this kind of field! Now this is highly simplified as he illustrates how to use other tools such as the time travel, parallel universes, frequencies, and archetypes to assist in the transformation process.

Sound far-fetched? The hundreds of practitioners around the world do not think so. And their clients don't think so. At his last Practitioners four day seminar in Seattle, 700 people attended. Richard, who himself is a

Chiropractor also operates a clinic in Seattle. Here his miracles are indeed wondrous as he has aligned spines, broken bones, and facilitated miracles right on the spot.

To make this even more far out, the two point method is used as effectively in a remote, or distance transformation mode. In this situation, the Practitioner uses a figure representing the clients and goes through the same process. It is normally done on the phone so there are no collapsing surprises at the other end. I (Ed) can attest to this because I personally know six practitioners and their work.

The fact that the client is not present is not relevant because the Practitioner is simply tuning into a frequency representing the client or the wave form, then stepping aside so the center of Grace can do the healing.

But there is a final note here that is very important. Richard does not support the notion of procedure. There is no manual and he does not support discrete steps that you learn. What he supports is each taking the tools and developing their own style of transforming. He notes that he does not really know how it all works, and he does not care. It just does when you let go of analyzing, questioning and quantifying. The best practitioners are those that are essentially "mindless", have absolutely no reason to question it, know they are "heart centered", have no preconceived expectations, and are simply "guided" to see or feel subtle changes in energies reflected by a "change" in the patient.

How many of us can be purposely mindless? It means lacking the thinking capacity characteristic of a conscious being. Are you heart centered? Can you believe this? Try going to Richard's website. Or better still try one of his seminars. Let us summarize Richard's process:

HEALTH PROCESSES & PROCEDURES MATRIX ENERGETICS		
Setting	Get out of the old belief box	RB
Process	Get into a quiet still mode together	RB
Process	Ask if a change is required and what it is as in hypnotism	RB
Process	Ask to place the dysfunction on an imaginary clipboard	RB
Process	Drop into the heart as the divine in you (throw a pebble in water)	RB
Process	Enter into quantum state of waves on the pond and all possibilities	RB
Process	Place left hand onto a mindless point of attraction	RB
Assist	Place second hand on 2nd attracted area as being guided by Divine	RB
Process	Mentally link the two hands to enter entangled oneness	RB
Process	Wait for an energy shift in client to collapse new possibility	RB

11

DIVINE PROGRAMMING
CREATOR-CREATRIX

"I am humbled by the amazing things that are allowed or done according to divine plan."
Aly McDonald

Much of the healing I (Aly) have been involved in has been spiritual and physical and some even instant. As I become more of who I am energetically I am able to increase my bandwidth which allows more flow of Prime Creator/Creatrix's pure light/energy. Interestingly enough I have a team of light that assist. I am humbled by the amazing things that are allowed or done according to divine plan. I am always in service to the Divine Plan of the Creator most high.

I have facilitated healing around the globe and I find that unless one is connected and sensitive they generally do not feel much, but they do receive healing. Most folks I have helped have been spiritual and they either sense or see or both some of what the teams of light are doing to them... the biggest part of a successful and lasting healing are releasements. Some are very deep. Faith in the Creator and the heart are key. When we work in the physical I like to use crystals, Om tuning fork, Tibet bowls, essential oils, essences and the sacred healing tones as well as the teams of light.

I can feel discordant energies within the body as I run my hands over them. I also facilitate healing in places and animals. Everyone has free will though and if they truly don't want healing or they return to old thought patterns or addictions and pick back up old baggage that was released they can manifest illness or disease in their life again. It is sad but I have seen that happen.

When I participate in a healing, it can take a while depending on what all comes forward, I usually suggest it is helpful to be alone or with someone who knows you well or you do not mind them knowing your most hidden feelings or experiences if they are in the same area. In most cases it's better not to be around others because sometimes very personal things bubble up or have to be addressed with what I call the Karmic Board, High Council to the Creator.

In this work, I enter the space which I call the Creatrix of the Heart-mind. My humble understanding of the Creatrix (Mother God) is viewed as the Primary Mother of this Planet and to many beings. Prime Creatrix can be viewed as the next level up going into other Universes or even Omni-verses. I also refer to her as Universal Mother. Not to be confused with Mother Earth as she is a planetary being. Gaia to me is the essence of Mother Earth (a code carrier/aspect) made manifest.

My Creator-Creatrix Process

The first part is setting up for your healing process, talking to the individual and allowing them to feel comfortable in my own energy field. I like to ascertain whether or not they have a belief or acknowledgement in the Creator(s) at some point while we are discussing why they desire this healing session. I convey to them that I utilize the Creator's energies to assist in their healing and we call upon them and acknowledge them as we go through the process. This love energy connects right to the heart center and we move forward by saying a prayer of protection, what I call sacred space for myself and the ones we are working with. Sacred space is setting the desired energies in your area to be in the clean, clear and harmonizing environment without outside influence of random energies while you are facilitating a healing process.

It is my understanding that the Archangels that assist in the healing process each carry specific frequencies from the Creator/Creatrix. We can also view them as color ray frequencies, tones, and expressions. Some of the Archangels/Archeia are what I call intra-rays and possess certain multi-ray aspects that can be very powerful and have ranges like, Alpha, Theta, Beta, Delta and Gamma. This is likened to penetration into layers of the human vessel, and energy bodies. I also feel that each Ray of Angelic Light is associated with our chakra system. Solfegios are also similar and another example is the healing tones that John the Baptist used.

The Angelics help assist us to be rid of dark, negative, discordant energies. Encouraging us to see the beauty in oneself and life, harmonize between families as well as other relationships, and facilitate healing. They assist in guidance, balance and purification of thoughts, releasements and transformation, and so much more.

We are very much connected to and a part of them as we are a part of the Creation of the Creator/Creatrix only we reside in this physical experience. They have loved us for eons and have been around us to help us, even though we may not see them. When we shift our heart-mind consciousness enough to know that they can and will help us. This also assists in a broader belief and we begin to believe even stronger that the Creator/Creatrix truly does exist and has been there through all times of our existence. All we have to do is ask, because we have been given free will and intervention from them comes from asking and acknowledging them first.

Yes, I do believe we can do many things by ourselves with the Divine Heart-mind in a balanced environment. But who has a perfect, balanced environment, I certainly do not, at least not at this time. So, letting go of the ego mind which keeps one ensnared into believing *"I don't need any help"* is vitally important. I feel it is important to say that healers in this world, at this time should also allow others to come along side and give assistance from time to time for this is a very good thing.

They "our Angelic loving helpers" are there for us as many other galactic family members to assist in whatever type of healing is necessary as well as guidance in our life purpose.

Once I have had discussion and the client feels safe and secure I begin immediately with two prayers, one for releasement for the unseen entities and the other for a sacred space.

The second prayer is important because many etheric discordant energies and things can be attached to us, inside and out of our auric field. By stating these prayers you are empowering yourself to act and play a vital role in the success of your healing and awareness. Some have even measured these extra energies and one can see how much it can weigh a human down.

Feel free to change these prayers according to your own feelings and guidance; however, they are very effective as such for this venue.

Prayer 1: Clearing and releasement prayer for entities
"Father/Mother God, Infinite Spirit, I call upon your assistance to help these entities over into your realm of existence. I call upon the Christ Light, Archangel Michael and the Angelic realm for assistance."

"I call upon the Golden Christ Light to come in and anchor over this place and these beings. (You may visualize the shaft of light coming down to where you are.) I call upon Mother Earth to release the gravitational pull for the unseen."

Then speak these words and feel empowered:

"I command out all earth bound entities, demonic forces, negative thought forms, poltergeists, Incubus, succubus, negative space and negative earth beings. I command you out of my plain of existence now and forever. I command you to go to the Universal Light to be healed and awakened. I command you out now in the name of the "Father/Mother God, Infinite Spirit, and the I Am of myself. Through <u>Christ</u> Love, so be it."

Taking in a few deep breaths and releasing slowly helps in allowing this process.

Prayer 2: Sphere of Protection and Energetic space clearing

"I ask the Golden Christ Light to anchor down around me/us. I also ask Archangel Michael to bring forth his blue ray into a Sapphire sphere of protection around me/us. I also ask for the sacred Ruby/Rose Pink ray of protection and the Platinum White Diamond Rays of light of the Mother/Father God Creator/Creatrix to surround all the rays of light as a triple sphere of protective heavenly light. I also call forward lovingly the masses of Love Angels and Golden Angels to the outer perimeters of the spheres. Additionally, any other Teams of Light beings or Elementals that will be assisting for the session."

"We ask this in love, light, peace and harmony of the heavenly Mother/Father Creator, So be it."

If I am facilitating this session in person instead of remotely, I do like to utilize specific crystals, tuning forks, Tibetan singing bowls, incense or essential oil room sprays. These tools are very useful and one does not need to be clairvoyant to utilize this method. Actually you don't have to use them at all, but I like the vibrations they carry and it is a gift from Mother Earth so I use them when possible.

Crystals assist in removal of blockages in the meridians, chakras, as well as raising ones vibrations or battery which I feel is what assists in the powering up of a strong auric field. There are a multitude of crystals with healing properties of all types. So these are selected per session or individual then placed upon them in various locations of the body or around the body and under the body.

Once the Team of Light and client is ready, they begin using what I term as etheric light filters and energy swords/beams to cleanse clear and make adjustment to the individual. For myself or anyone that is assisting me I ask for a suit of light from the Creators and begin placing my hands over the individual, not touching them only above them approximately 5-6 inches or so. This process in the physical is for feeling the discordant energies. Many times I can point to it and ask what happened here and they then remember and say oh yeah, I had an injury there. Things such as this can hinder your energy flow as well as manifest negatively in different ways throughout your body. Then, I begin to also assist with removal "in the physical" as if I am shoveling off the stagnated energies.

After the teams have etherically cleansed the auric fields, energy bodies, chakras, intra-chakral spaces, etheric implants or devices, virals and bacteriums, we must remember what Yeshua/Isu "Jesus" said in Ephesians 6:10-18. This kind of stuff comes from the dark or negatives ones that seek out to control and destroy our very being in this dualistic experience we are participating in at this time.

I use a form of what some may view as Reiki and I place my hands above the top of the head and ask the Creator/Creatrix Pure Love energies to flow through me as a tube of light to the client in the top of the head and through the feet. My intentions of the "pure love" life force energy of the Creators are for physically cleansing and purging of the old energies and intentions to allow in the new higher vibrational DNA blueprint which is very important to the process of healing in today's times.

During the process, the Angels and guides assist the client in releasement of many things like; past experiences that are affecting them in this time, old thought forms and residues, spells, binding contracts, fears, hatred, discordant generational energies, releasement of reptilian/draconian DNA, even going into the akashic records for things that have been brought forward and need to be addressed. This is usually part of their individual purpose which can be quite the releasement and much healing will come from this type of understanding.

There have been times when the etheric body of a particular person is called forth to be addressed to the client in the example of allowing them to speak openly to that person(s) and say whatever they need to say. This allows the client to have closure and we believe the higher self of the individual who was brought forward will work with the physical body (if living) for the understandings that are needed. If they are open they will have some perception of what transpired between them. This experience can be very intense for the client, especially when they have had a long time of build up. It is very effective to be able to speak out and truly say whatever it is to release it once and for all in a protected sacred environment. Some clients are able to also use this experience for ones that have transitioned as well. This is very beneficial to ones who have a tragic loss of someone special to them and just needed to tell them in the comfort of the Creators' Love energy that they love and miss them.

When it comes to releasements and because of the ways of the world, our bodies generally speaking will continue this purging process as long as we are willing and desire change. Many view this process like the peeling of the onion, coming off in layers. The first cleansing/healing process is usually the thickest layer to go. Not necessarily the most intense because that is dependent upon situations or past experiences. In today's times it is important to LET GO OF THE OLD, FORGIVE YOURSELF, LOVE YOURSELF (not in a vain way but with a genuine loving heart way). Embrace the new higher vibrational energies.

Mother Earth can and will assist in this process also by asking, being in nature, sending her your love and thanks for all she has done to sustain each of us.

A closing prayer is simply giving thanks for all that assisted.

I have found that prior to this experience many do not know anything about what they have just experienced but are very pleased and feel lifted, healed and more awakened. Many go out and become zealous for more information and understanding - young and old, which I tend to get very excited about. It makes my heart so happy to be able to be in service to the Creators of this planet and beyond to truly help people lift up in a world that has been so oppressed.

When available I like to give the client crystals to take home to use for themselves and aid in continued meditation of their choice. If they ask I will give them ideas and assist. I also discuss the importance of continued maintenance for the physical body which also aids in the strength of the chakra system such as; eating healthy, toxic sludge cleanse, enzymes, good vitamins and minerals. Additionally keeping in mind their ph balanced at least 7.2 if possible and most of all praying to the Creator(s) for all things.

This process takes us way outside the box or framework of society in general, but not outside the understanding of the idea that we are likened unto individual computer systems and the Earth and the Creators are our protective mainframe computer support system, operating system, new DNA blueprints and anti-viral software and programs. We can accept it and move on or we may just simply fall away and become disabled with the old system. It is your choice.

This is a time for the New Earth, a time for the loving energies of the Divine Feminine to rise up and do what we do best. I ask all to please continually send strong intentions of the Unconditional Love of the Creators to the utmost and highest level that we may achieve to the planet and the beings on her. For I also believe in the transformational energies created from our positive loving intentions will catapult us into the higher dimensions collectively. Thank you for allowing me to share my love and experience.

Insights Into Return Of The Divine Feminine

I have discovered there are many beings on our planet that would be considered blueprinters or also considered programmers of and for the human beings on the planet for this cycle of what we know as the Age of Aquarius and also known as a time of the Return of the Divine Feminine. I wish to share this because I feel it is important to gain a little broader understanding of the importance of the Mother God essence not just Father God. There are a multitude of reasons why she has been forgotten in many areas of the world. Without going into all of these various reasons, I will talk about some I feel are important.

The Divine Mother God essence in which some also call Creatrix of this planet is not to be confused with the Prime Creator. These are male and female counterparts. She is also not to be confused with Mother Earth or the one many call Gaia. They are connected energetically however still different. As many know by now, there have been many non-benevolent beings (more than one race) from eons ago that came here to take over us and our planet and thus make us part of the food chain. How have they done this some may ask and I will just simply say this, every way possible "see and unseen".

I have seen that one of the biggest culprits is the unseen concerning the Matrix that placed us inside a box; one may view it like the binary system of the computer. You can only go so far within the perimeters of this system. Take that and place it around the world, now you've got your outer prison grid. Some of us have been incarnated to change this old cannibalistic system and assist in raising the consciousness back to where it should have been before this happened. Another big culprit was that Mother God has been forgotten or mixed in with watered down myths so that no one knows what to believe. Part of my journey is to bring her blueprint back to life one may say. Also, to show others that she does exist and is very much willing to help those she helped to create. One of the keys to manifesting healing, raising your vibrations and expansion of your consciousness comes from acceptance of her love. Not just the love of the Father but in Unity together.

Many feel that the non-benevolent beings that came to destroy the human race began this with the degrading of the feminine on this planet. Only a small handful of divine feminine are recognized even though it is through the feminine in which life is brought forth. Consider, the unconditional love of a mother, the nurturing, the guidance and so much more.

So we are in a cycle of a long awaited upgrade one may say. Viewing this as a binary system and thus creating into a trinary system, bringing back the trinity and unity.

The divine programming of the new blueprint(s) are defined within my own experience and this is what I wish to share with the readers. So as I see it we have been allotted a time frame to experience on a grand scale what the true depths of our emotions of darkness, deception and a feeling of disconnect have brought forth. Some of what we have experienced is cause and effect. However, much of the experiences encompassed with our purposes have been manipulated to a very high degree.

Having said this it is my understanding at this time the beings that came to ultimately destroy the human race went as far as rewriting some of our soul contracts. When I say soul contracts I wish to describe this as our purpose for being here on the planet at this time. Really? Some may say. However when you view the complexity of the deception and manipulation of our planet along with us, you begin to see with clearer vision. If you are a reader and have never heard this before, I would like to add, I was once in your shoes also. I went through a long period of time searching and finding things out for myself and there was a time it brought forth much anger and sadness, thinking there was no way out for us as a race. But there is and this is why I wish to share with you my understanding. It may not be perfect, but something is better than nothing in this case.

Now, each of us before we incarnate we lay out for ourselves a life plan. It can be short or long with windy curves or the straight and narrow. This is determined in various ways with the assistance of the Creator/Creatrix and your higher self. Some may say Really? Look at my life, it's a mess or I have been through horrendous times. Why would I do this to myself? Well, this part can get complex, but we do come into this world sometimes with Karmic Debt to balance. So this has played a role to some degree, until you realize you can actually either remove or lessen this by acknowledgment to the Karmic Board, High Council and oneself. Also, remembering many have come to work specifically on areas to bring forth the Divine Plan of the Creator. In this we have needed to go into certain threads of energy or experiences for reasons of connectedness, to attempt to reach the darkest of the dark for some of us.

Let's expand the consciousness even further, unfortunately certain races have been acting as guardians and very cleverly manipulated let's just say with fine print areas in our life plan or contract for their benefit. So some of the hardships we have endured or not endured (possibly still struggling) are because of obstacles placed in our way to keep us from becoming the true beings that we are or an attempt to stop us from the work on the Divine Plan. Does this sound extremely paranoid to you? Perhaps, I simply ask you to step outside of your comfort zone and really look around. When I was a younger woman I used to ask myself how God could allow all the bad things in this world, the fighting, beatings, starvation and disease. It wasn't until I accepted the Holy Spirit "The Creatrix Love" into my heart that I then was able to step outside my comfort zone.

My answers came from self discovery and reading or acknowledging others self discovery of course. The bottom line is many of us have had our life purposes interfered with. When you accept this, then you can change it. Because we do have loving Creators and they want us to grow and learn and overcome. They are there for us and we are coming out of this veil together with the Mother's nurturing love and care. The Father is protecting while we are reaching the higher vibrations and dimensions.

In closing, I feel when people say go within, it is a step to knowing yourself at a much deeper level and understanding the Heart-mind. Understanding what is the true source or underlying issues and feeling you can have. This healing is relief in a way that we should have had a long time ago. Because of the ways of this world, many have been entrained to simply go to a doctor. Doctors are useful for some things yes. Many doctors are not healing all, in my observations and experiences instead it's a lot like a masking of the true issue, and then you end up with another issue.

We have also been heavily distracted with simply going to work just to pay the bills and have some food on the table. Then we have been entrained with all the electronic devices to entertain our minds, *"hey, you can stay at home, save gas, order apps online, you don't even have to get out of bed."* But this is good— right, because you're tired and stressed out. It's all a part of the plan to sedate the human race and I haven't even touched on all the other things...but I feel you will get the drift.

Everything is energy, it is a proven fact. These energies come in various forms and can be positive or negative. In order to have positive intentions for oneself and/or others that are affected by your thoughts you must relinquish the negative. This can be easy attained or difficult, however, please know you are never alone. By allowing yourself to become humble and more loving in an unconditional love, this not only assists you but also assists the masses for we are all connected energetically.

Here is a summary of my healing process:

HEALTH PROCESSES & PROCEDURES CREATOR-CREATRIX		
Setting	Ascertain in belief in the Creator, understand desire for healing	AM
Setting	Inform of assistance of Creators' energies	AM
Process	Empower action with 2 prayers for releasement and sacred space	AM
Process	Command negative energies to heal in the name of Christ Love	AM
Process	Enter a sacred space and harmonizing energies/rays to facilitate	AM
Process	Ask Team of Light to cleanse and clear with hands over individual	AM
Process	Assist in the removal shoveling off stagnated energies	AM
Assist	Ask Creator/Creatrix pure love energies to flow from head to feet	AM
Process	Show pure love intention to bring new DNA energies, purging old	AM
Process	Allow purging of old thoughts, residues, spells, contracts, fears, hatred, discordant energies	AM
Process	Allow closure and release by speaking about what has occurred	AM
Assist	Allow Mother Earth to assist by asking and sending her love	AM
Process	Offer a closing prayer giving thanks for the assistance	AM

12

DIVINE PROGRAMMING ENERGY UNBLOCKING

"At the root of every bodily dysfunction is a living energy form that was created in the past and has manifested itself as dis-ease in the current life."
Ed Rychkun

After studying the many ways that energy healers apply their craft to facilitate the Divine Programming, what comes up over and over is that a prime objective is to locate these energy blocks and dysfunctions as to source and then alter, integrate or remove them. This is done through a guided meditation where the person in a totally conscious way, becomes present, getting to the core and gateway to the world and other dimensions/lives—through the heart. The heart has intelligence to tell us what we need to know. It is the very core of our bodies on all dimensions. It is our heart mind which is connected to all that is. It is connected to all consciousness, including Prime Source Creator. Others would call this God! This is the Quantum aspect as there is no difference between what is past, present or future. It is all happening NOW!

To illustrate this, I (Ed) am now going to take you through another detailed healing process that I am very familiar with. Although I do not go out and actively do work as a healer, I do use some methods and study many. I prefer to engage in healing of external environment as many of my books suggest; through Managing Subtle Energies. This method I learned from a Healer friend and have used it to clear out "boogey men several times. I have, however, seen my friend create a list of impressive results. For a lack of a better name, I call it Energy Unblocking.

It is well known that when the person becomes relaxed through a guided meditation, an inspection is possible to identify and quantify the energies that are creating the issues. All energies are like little children and have communication abilities. This allows a communication channel to be created and the energy identified. Needless to say, we are putting attention and focus on the energy. By locating the energy with the mind, identifying and objectifying it we click in to its location and totally unique vibratory signature. Because it is all in the mind, we find these energies and change them with the mind, it becomes part of the psychological world. Whereby working together we can either, alter, integrate or remove the energies through conscious intent of the mind.

Once identified and communication begins through the sub-conscious mind, the energy can be asked to co-operate and to change, integrate or agree to be removed. Part of the process is to send it away for recycling to the sun with love and light from where all that is, comes from in our Solar System.

One can refer to the sun and earth as Father Sun and Mother Earth with the healing procedures. Sometimes there is resistance with different energies in the body and this is where experience in how to coax the energy—and sometimes even force them—into removal.

Part of the process is to enter into a process of cleansing every cell and DNA strand of the memory and programming of the energy and releasing anything that has been created by its presence with the assistance of the Almighty I AM presence inside the person. The people will feel the results immediately, typically resulting in a new freshness of life almost like a NDE and with a new perspective. These energies reside in layers and once they are altered, integrated or removed, they do not change back or return to what they once were. In many cases, this opens to a new layer which can also be worked on. This is the healing aspect of this procedure. Although energies are simple, and the concept of communication with these energies is also, the game that must be played to identify and seek them out can become complex.

The game is one of hide-and-seek with a bunch of children who have different motivations for hiding. Even more difficult is that they can hide in any previous lifetime. Here one must work with the heart or some other organ to find and identify energy using different but set processes you will develop to be effective. In order to better understand this whole process, the following steps can be used as guidance. Typically, a session can last around an hour and it follows the following steps:

Paramount to the success is the belief that this is a way that healing can be effected. Although the conscious belief by way of the conscious mind and the intellect is energetically placed on the side, this is not a guarantee that the subconscious is willing to cooperate. The process undertakes to seek out and eliminate the issue but if it is entrenched in the subconscious it can easily be recalled through habits of intellectual activation even after a healing occurs.

Let me take you through the steps:

Step 1: Becoming Present This is the initial step which gets the person into a relaxed state called being present. It is similar to meditation where the purpose is to drop into the Alpha brain state so as to bypass the conscious intellect and access the subconscious. It is here that the client can be asked to imagine taking their intellect and placing it on the shelf.

Step 2: Connecting to the Heart Mind This is a very important step. It is taking the attention of the mind from a focal point on the person's forehead on a journey down into the person's heart. It is here where the mind then checks out the heart for the first time from a sub-conscious perspective. It is here where the person can actually see, sense or feel their own heart. Here ask the heart to communicate and through the person's own voice and their sub-conscious mind it is possible. It is here where we connect to the heart mind, the quantum world of all time. Here we get the heart mind to agree to assist us. This is our connection to the Divine Consciousness, through our hearts. It is through our hearts where we can connect to all that is, our connection to Prime Source Creator where we all are a part of God. After all we all have God within us.

Step 3: Energy Identification This step focuses on the person becoming familiar with identifying, sensing, feeling, and communicating with the various energy forms in the body. In particular, the heart mind, the organs, the pineal gland, pain and other energies then become the attention for communication.

Step 4: Energy Block Detection In conjunction with the heart or some other energy ally, this step puts focus on the area of dysfunction targeted. The process is one of locating the energy or energy block in terms of what the person can see, sense or feel through their internal sensory abilities and the mind. Then they are asked to identify the shape, color or size of the subtle energy or energy block in order to identify, objectify and qualify it for focus, attention, intention and communication.

Step 5: Quantum Scanning This is a process of locating in the past or in a past lifetime, the age and time frame when the energy or energy block entered the patient's body. This process is an exploratory search to locate the energy, whether it be by interrogating the Heart, the Pineal or any other part of the person, including the energy or energy block to determine the details as described in step 6.

Step 6: Energy Communication This develops a rapport between the energy or energy block, myself and the patient (as reported through the patient). The communication process is one of determining the energy or energy block origin; why it was placed there, what purpose it has, what beliefs and what behaviors have been placed in the body and mind as a result. The tone of voice should be low and slow so it has a tendency to vibrate at a lower, clearer frequency which allows one to tap into the subconscious mind easier. It is crucial to understand that it is here where the energies will communicate with us through the person's voice as we do with the heart mind.

Step 7: Heart Mind Healing This process is one which deploys a healing of the energy block. This can be a cooperative process or the energy can be resistant. The process of healing is to alter, integrate or remove the block and the layer within which it resides. This is facilitated with the patient and healer—and possibly other assisting entities—to extract, alter, integrate or contain the energy block.

Step 8: Release Process This is where you work with the patient and the energy to either integrate or to assist or to leave the body. This becomes the final step where the pineal (that knows and is also connected to all that exists) and the Almighty I AM essence inside each of us is called upon to release and remove all decisions and expectations, beliefs and rules of behavior, judgments, values and ideals that resulted from the presence of the negative energies. If this turns out to be an energy from a past lifetime one can call upon the person's Third Eye to open. This is located on the bridge of their nose between their eyes. Call upon the third eye to release all past life energies from their body during the remove all process as well.

Step 9: Cleansing Process This is where Archangel Michael, the Almighty I AM presence and the pineal are asked to clean away all negative energy from every cell in the body through the toes starting from the top of the head, like sand in an hour glass, with grace and ease. Also call upon the third eye as mentioned in step 8. Then ask to send all the negative energy to the sun with love and light. Using the Ho'oponopono words; I'm sorry, please forgive me, thank you, I love you!

Step 10: Rescanning Ask the patient to look around with their mind to see if there is anything else that draws their attention. If yes, then you go back to step 3.

Step 11: Pineal Review Ask that the patient go back to focus on the pineal and ask if there is anything else that needs to be looked at or attended to. If yes, then go to step 3. If no, then the session is closed.

Step 12: Session Close Ask the patient to come back out slowly when they are ready.

In line with our usual process summaries, here it is:

HEALTH PROCESSES & PROCEDURES ENERGY UNBLOCKING		
Setting	Validate that the belief in healing is strong and not an issue	ER
Process	Become present by becoming aware of self as in a meditative state	ER
Process	Ask to place the intellect on the shelf to open to subconscious	ER
Assist	Connect to the heart mind of quantum space and Source Creator	ER
Process	Ask to identify energies that are not feeling right in the area of issue	ER
Process	Scan back in time to when the energy block was created	ER
Process	Open communication with energy block to solicit cooperation to leave	ER
Process	Extract the energy block and release all that created it	ER
Assist	Request Higher Powers to cleanse cells of memories and conditions	ER
Process	Go back and rescan area to see results (issues) as done	ER

13

SUBCONSCIOUS MIND POWER

"At the level of quantum energy, our subconscious is the link to all that exists."

Ed Rychkun

Let Us Summarize Health Processes

We have covered a lot of wisdom on how to improve your health in an unconventional way. We have covered Divine Programming through:

1. RG: Richard Gordon: Quantum Touch
2. AT: Andy Tomlinson: Hypnosis & Past Life Regression Therapy
3. LM: Lewis Madrona: Coyote Healing & Native Medicine
4. TS: Tiffany Snow: God & Power of the Divine
5. CM: Carolyn Miller: Power of You and Creating Miracles
6. AD: Adam Dreamhealer: Power of Intention
7. IL: Ihaleakala Len: Ancient Practice of Ho'Oponopono
8. JG: Joao Teixeira Faria: John of God
9. OR: Oral Roberts: Religious Faith Healing
10. GB: Gregg Braden: Ancient Prayer
11. RB: Richard Bartlett: Matrix Energetics
12. AM: Aly McDonald: Creator-Creatrix
13. ER: Ed Rychkun: Energy Unblocking

Let us now attempt to summarize all these methods. Any Programmer would attempt to extract specific steps to identify the processes and procedures to be able to quantify them. If there is any possibility of creating a step by step procedure, that is what we need to be a Divine Programmer. If you look at the following tables of processes, you will see a pattern that can subdivide each technique into Setting, Process and Assistance:

	HEALTH PROCESSES & PROCEDURES QUANTUM TOUCH	
Setting	Have a belief and trust as it is essential	RG
Setting	Be in the higher vibration of love	RG
Setting	Become present to the body (lower brain waves)	RG
Process	Focus on and enfold issue area with hands	RG
Process	Breath in a rhythmic count to hold resonance high	RG
Process	Enter a space of higher vibration-love and intent	RG
Process	Intend healing for a better purpose as divine intervention	RG
Assist	Connect with Divine assistance	RG
Process	Imagine healing energy through you to your hands	RG
Process	See a beam of healing light connect	RG
Process	Allow biological divine intelligence to heal as it knows	RG
	HEALTH PROCESSES & PROCEDURES: REGRESSION THERAPY	
Setting	Have a trust and belief that healing will occur	AT
Process	Bring patient into a hypnotic state	AT
Process	Enter a holistic connectedness	AT
Process	Probe deep into subconscious memories	AT
Process	Regress patient to time and event of issue	AT
Process	Bring client into higher frequency vibration	AT
Assist	Allow higher realm spirit guides to assist	AT
Process	Hold the space of love and compassion at soul level	AT
Process	Understand the issue and why it occurred, results	AT
Process	Delete or rewrite the memory with the mind	AT
	HEALTH PROCESSES & PROCEDURES: NATIVE MEDICINE	
Setting	Hold the acceptance of problem and surrender to the issue	LM
Setting	Have a strong belief and faith in healing	LM
Setting	Have a strength and desire, willingness to embark	LM
Process	Focus on present, prayer, meditation	LM
Assist	Connect to spirit and higher sacred processes	LM
Process	Engage in ritual & community to bear witness focus energy	LM
Process	Create a morphic field with the Great Spirit as healer	LM
Process	Enter realm of inner healer through mind and spirit	LM
Process	Allow the inner Healer to do the work	LM
	HEALTH PROCESSES & PROCEDURES: POWER OF YOU & DIVINE	
Setting	Believe you are worthy	CM
Setting	Set the preconditions of self healing and love	CM
Process	Launch prayer to direct energy as pure love communication channel	CM
Process	Create a connection to Source	CM
Process	Visualize clearly the outcome in the mind eye	CM
Assist	Surrender and trust in a higher power	CM
Setting	Believe in a state of miracle minded readiness	TS
Setting	Expect a positive outcome	TS

Process	Delete ego interference and feel love	TS
Process	Turn inward into a meditative state altered state of consciousness	TS
Assist	Tap into the inner divine guide look for higher good	TS
Process	Use free will to change or solve created problems	TS
	HEALTH PROCESSES & PROCEDURES: POWER OF INTENTION	
Setting	Eliminate limiting beliefs as belief is a powerful form of intention	AD
Process	Align to positive resonance vibrations to assist	AD
Process	Have precise visualizations of the issue with strong intent	AD
Process	Visualize, positive emotionally charged new outcome	AD
Process	Synchronize conscious and subconscious thought	AD
Assist	Tune resonance through to source and quantum energy	AD
Process	Invite change and launch intention to heal, merge into reality	AD
Process	Faith trust love forgive have higher power	AD
	HEALTH PROCESSES & PROCEDURES: HO OPONOPONO	
Setting	Believe you are part of the whole which is divine	IL
Process	Zero out negative memories and energies by focus and reflection	IL
Process	Go inside and do it in a space of love	IL
Assist	Gateway is through divine and subconscious via belief	IL
Process	Bring into focus the issues that require attention	IL
Process	Send a petition to divine counterpart to erase memories of Cause	IL
Process	State I love you, I am sorry, please forgive me for this issue, thank you	IL
Assist	Allow Divinity to erase errors in subconscious as the Effect	IL
	HEALTH PROCESSES & PROCEDURES: JOHN OF GOD	
Setting	Enter a place of love and compassion	JG
Setting	Go through rooms to raise belief pictures, videos, demos	JG
Process	Cleansing room to meditate with a clinic medium	JG
Process	Engage in healing current to cleanse fear, cause of problems	JG
Process	Meet John to determine mode of treatment	JG
Process	Focus on the issue	JG
Process	Engage in a trance stage to request Higher Assistance of God	JG
Assist	Allow healing to be done by guidance through Spirits	JG
	HEALTH PROCESSES & PROCEDURES: FAITH HEALING	
Setting	Have a belief and trust in the truth or trustworthiness of God	OR
Setting	Have a faith in future outcome and through a supreme being	OR
Process	Engage in a ritual audience to raise the awareness and energy field	OR
Process	Lay on of hands to simulate biblical precedent of Jesus	OR
Assist	Issue a prayer to address god or spirit for assistance	OR
Process	Create a conclusive slap, shout, situation to conclude the miracle	OR
	HEALTH PROCESSES & PROCEDURES: ANCIENT PRAYER	
Setting	Believe that a higher source will answer your prayers	GB
Process	Believe the prayer has already been answered	GB
Process	Enter a state of peace, love, compassion without hidden motives	GB

Process	Bring forward the thoughts of your desire so your gladness be full	GB
Process	Create a clear visualization of that which desired	GB
Process	Enfold vision with strong positive emotion to envelope the desire	GB
Assist	Ask the divine to fulfill the desire as in ask and it shall be given	GB
Process	Show gratitude that your joy is full	GB
	HEALTH PROCESSES & PROCEDURES: MATRIX ENERGETICS	
Setting	Get out of the old belief box	RB
Process	Get into a quiet still mode together	RB
Process	Ask if a change is required and what it is as in hypnotism	RB
Process	Ask to place the dysfunction on an imaginary clipboard	RB
Process	Drop into the heart as the divine in you (throw a pebble in water)	RB
Process	Enter into quantum state of waves on the pond and all possibilities	RB
Process	Place left hand onto a mindless point of attraction	RB
Assist	Place second hand on 2nd attracted area as being guided by Divine	RB
Process	Mentally link the two to enter entangled oneness	RB
Process	Wait for an energy shift in client to collapse new possibility	RB
	HEALTH PROCESSES & PROCEDURES CREATOR-CREATRIX	
Setting	Ascertain in belief in the Creator, understand desire for healing	AM
Setting	Inform of assistance of Creators energies	AM
Process	Empower action with 2 prayers for releasement and sacred space	AM
Process	Command negative energies to heal in the name of Christ Love	AM
Process	Enter a sacred space and harmonizing energies/rays to facilitate	AM
Assist	Ask Team of Light to cleanse and clear with hands over individual	AM
Process	Assist in the removal shoveling off stagnated energies	AM
Assist	Ask Creator/Creatrix pure love energies to flow from head to feet	AM
Process	Show pure love intention to bring new DNA energies, purging old	AM
Process	Allow purging of old thoughts, residues, spells, contracts, fears, hatred, discordant energies	AM
Process	Allow closure and release by speaking about what has occurred	AM
Assist	Allow Mother Earth to assist by asking and sending her love	AM
Process	Offer a closing prayer giving thanks for the assistance	AM
	HEALTH PROCESSES & PROCEDURES: ENERGY UNBLOCKING	
Setting	Validate that the belief in healing is strong and not an issue	ER
Process	Become present by becoming aware of self as in a meditative state	ER
Process	Ask to place the intellect on the shelf to open to subconscious	ER
Assist	Connect to the heart mind of quantum space and Source Creator	ER
Process	Ask to identify energies that are not feeling right in the area of issue	ER
Process	Scan back in time to when the energy block was created	ER
Process	Open communication with energy block to solicit cooperation to leave	ER
Process	Extract the energy block and release all that created it	ER
Assist	Request Higher Powers to cleanse cells of memories and conditions	ER
Process	Go back and rescan area to see results (issues) as done	ER

It is a pretty long table but it reflects a lot of different techniques, wisdom and cases. It is noteworthy that this table is based on the opinion of others that tell us what is the common setting, process, and assistance **_when these miracles do work_**.

If you go through this table, a common pattern begins to emerge and it is like this:

The Common Denominators Of Healing Miracles

By this time, you will have detected a common pattern in the Processes. Quite important is that there are obviously a lot of different ways that these miracles can occur. So it is not so much a set system of procedure as much as a set of processes that make up different systems. The enlightening part of this is that once you get these common processes down, you can create your own system that suits you, and even take from these experts parts that vibrate with your heart essence as being "right" for you. What are these common elements?

A belief that one is worthy, that they can be healed, is important to all these cases. It is a belief that is created by way of inner convictions, experience, enforced by an authoritative expert such as a doctor, a healer who has a reputation, of some authority on the topic that is believed to know what they are doing. Regardless, the patient surrenders mind control to an authority who they believe can heal the issue. This belief incorporated a trust and faith that the process to be engaged in will work.

An altered state is required to open into subconscious. It is through hypnosis, ritual, regression, becoming present, meditation, or a situation where the higher brain waves of the conscious mind are out of the way so as to not interfere with the subconscious. It is a morphic field that is created to gain access to the subconscious.

A state of well being is required as so reflected in a morphic field of love and peace as it opens to the gateways for a change to occur. This is induced by creating a setting of higher vibration by creating a space without conflict or anger, or fear, only of positive energies.

An identification of the issue is required so as to be clear on what it is that needs to be corrected. It is done by visualizing, by hands on, by focus of thought and intention, by hypnosis or regression.

A Higher Power is engaged so as to make the change and correction. It is a surrendering process where God, Spirit, Divine Self, Source, or some Guides, Higher Self, or higher power is called upon to assist in the healing thus creating a Divine Intervention.

A removal of the issue is simulated through various ways such as erasing memories, using intent, visualization, imagination or some induced process like simulation that removes it. Visualization of the desired result, enfolded with the emotion of completion adds to the power of its removal.

If you look closely at these processes and procedures, there is another thing emerging here as a step by step process we originally identified as **The 7 Steps of Manifesting Reality**. After the Healer sets a scene of peace, love, surrender and faith, there are seven steps engaged in. The Healer, becoming unified with the Healee into a morphic field of peace, then creating a setting where the patient is in an altered state:

1. Brings into thought the belief of being healed
2. Brings into vision the image of the issue which is to be corrected
3. Communicates to find the source of the issue or solicits help
4. Brings in the power of emotion to surround the corrected desire
5. Launches the intention to correct the issue
6. Surrenders control of the correction to a higher power
7. Allows the Higher Power to materialize the correction

These **7 Steps of Manifesting Reality** are well known to any businessman or anyone engaged in a project where an idea is taken to be created in our material reality. These are recalled below.

1. THOUGHT: We bring into consciousness an idea of a desired result.
2. VISION: We form a vision or what it is we want to manifest.
3. PLAN: We write or communicate a plan of how the result is to manifest.
4. PASSION: We become passionate and emotional about the achieving the end result.
5. ACTION: We launch out intent to seek out and manifest the plan with a strong persistence e to succeed.
6. RELATIONS: We seek out the resources, people and connections to others that assist in manifesting the plan.
7. MATERIAL: We succeed in manifesting the plan so as to engage in the end result.

These steps will be discussed again in a later chapter but let us get back to the common denominators.

Belief is not a variable that can be quantified easily. The big silent belief parameter is that these miracles had a setting with someone that was an expert, had a reputation, or provided a setting which made the person feel comfortable that what the healer was going to do was credible. In the case of the placebo, it was a doctor that simulated the surgery or gave a pill. It was his credentials, and reputation that impacted the belief system where there was no question that it would work. In the case of religion, it was a faith healer that had a reputation for getting results and the person had a trust and faith in a higher power. In the case of an energy healer, there was a history, a presence, a confidence of authoritative knowledge that convinced the belief system to surrender to the process and take over control.

This may well be a reason why so many healers cannot heal themselves. They can heal others acting as a conduit but they have difficulty in healing their own ailments.

It is the common denominators, however, that are of interest here and one begins to question why these are so important. Why do these prevail in these procedures? The systems are quite variable but these denominators, once you clear off the marketing hype and fluff to create unique marketable branding, the basic processes are the same. Why is this important? Is there anything that can substantiate why these somewhat intangible processes are important?

The answer is yes indeed. In order to investigate this let us delve into this from a more scientific inspection of these key processes. Let us look at what some of the emerging science of new biology has to say.

The Subconscious Is The Missing Link

The recurrent steps here seem to be focused on bypassing the conscious mind to convince the subconscious mind to awaken some Divine Intelligence to direct the brain and the cells to reconstruct tissues, as in a healing of bones, organs, or deleting a tumor. In the end, it was the cells that were told what to do; and they listened! These processes seem to do this by putting the conscious mind on the shelf so it shuts up and gets the hell out of the way. Why? Obviously it is not quite as easy as telling the conscious mind to give the directives to the subconscious and then to the big dummy brain who gets the cells to tow the line. Did we have to talk to God or Spirit?

Apparently this does not matter, yet some Divine Intervention or some higher unknown power to reprogram is clearly at work here. Obviously it just wasn't a simple order or petition because most certainly could not do it. But we get the conscious mind to get things done all the time. They don't happen to be dramatic shifts like miracle healing but nevertheless we do trigger the 7 Steps all the time. What is the difference?

What becomes very relevant here is the information and books related to Hypnosis, Placebos and psychiatric work. The placebo effect as we have presented in the beginning is perhaps the most dramatic. Here someone with a problem is given a fake pill that the doctor knows does nothing. At the same time others are given a pill that is supposed to do something—like get rid of some physical issue. What mystifies the medical profession is that many times the placebo cures the problem. Why? Because the patient simply believes they took the pill that will cure the problem. That belief that it will work is so strong it bends physical reality.

Does it happen every time? No, of course not. That's why it is not a medical practice. What's the thing that makes the difference? There is really only one variable here and it does not take a nuclear scientist brain to figure it out. The individual belief is the variable. The patient was simply led to believe that the right pill was being taken and it miraculously cured the problem. Something created a physical transformation in the body because of a belief—no prayer, no God, no ritual, zip. On the other hand, there may have been some private parts of the belief, and the environmental setting that, like in the case of miracles happening some of the time, set the conditions needed to happen?

It turns out that the one who is holding the cards is the subconscious. Somehow, just like in the processes of the hypnotist or the regression therapist, the tactics were to get by that conscious brain and they were able to issue behavior change and healing directives to change biology. To get a better handle on what is happening here, we have to bring in some technical information about these brainwaves.

The Importance Of Brainwaves

Let us take a quick diversion into the science of brain waves.

Your brain is made up of billions of brain cells called neurons, which use electricity to communicate with each other. The combination of millions of neurons sending signals at once produces an enormous amount of electrical activity in the brain, which can be detected using sensitive medical equipment such as an EEG or ElectroEncephaloGram, measuring electricity levels over areas of the scalp. The combination of electrical activity of the brain is commonly called a *brainwave* pattern, because of its cyclic, "wave-like" nature. Below is one of the first recordings of brain activity.

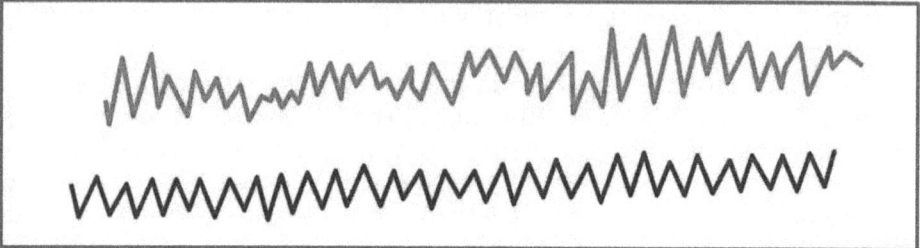

With the discovery of brainwaves came the discovery that electrical activity in the brain will change depending on what the person is doing. For instance, the brainwaves of a sleeping person are vastly different than the brainwaves of someone wide awake. Over the years, more sensitive equipment has brought us closer to figuring out exactly what brainwaves represent and with that, what they mean about a person's health and state of mind. Here is a table showing the known brainwave types and their associated mental states:

Wave	Frequency	Associated Mental State
Gamma	27 Hz and up	Gamma is associated with the formation of ideas, language and memory processing, and various types of learning. Gamma waves have been shown to disappear during deep sleep induced by anesthesia, but return with the transition back to a wakeful state.
Beta	12hz - 27hz	Wide awake. This is generally the mental state most people are in during the day and most of their waking lives. Usually, this state in itself is uneventful, but don't underestimate its importance.
Alpha	8hz - 12hz	Awake but relaxed and not processing much information. When you get up in the morning and just before sleep, you are naturally in this state. When you close your eyes your brain automatically starts producing more alpha waves.
Theta	3hz - 8hz	Light sleep or extreme relaxation. Theta is also a very receptive mental state that has proven useful for hypnotherapy, as well as self-hypnosis using recorded affirmations and suggestions.

Delta	0.2hz - 3hz	Deep, dreamless sleep. Delta is the slowest band of brainwaves. When your dominant brainwave is delta, your body is healing itself and "resetting" its internal clocks. You do not dream in this state and are completely unconscious.

From this table, you can see that Beta and Gamma are brain states that are rife with mind chatter that is all about intellect and mundane affairs. It is not a surprise that to get to subconscious mind you have to stop this incessant noise. You can tell a lot about a person simply by observing their brainwave patterns. For example, anxious people tend to produce an overabundance of high beta waves while people with ADD/ADHD tend to produce an overabundance of slower alpha/theta brainwaves. At least that is what the medical "gurus" tell you.

Researchers have found that not only are brainwaves representative of mental state, but they can be stimulated to *change* a person's mental state, and this in turn can help with a variety of mental issues.

The Neuro-Programmer uses sound and light to directly affect the brain through a complex neural process called *Brainwave Entrainment*.

Brainwave Entrainment refers to the brain's electrical response to rhythmic sensory stimulation, such as pulses of sound or light. When the brain is given a stimulus, through the ears, eyes or other senses, it emits an electrical charge in response, called a *Cortical Evoked Response*. These electrical responses travel throughout the brain to become what you "see and hear". This activity can be measured using sensitive electrodes attached to the scalp. The example below shows how the sound pulse has evoked a cortical response.

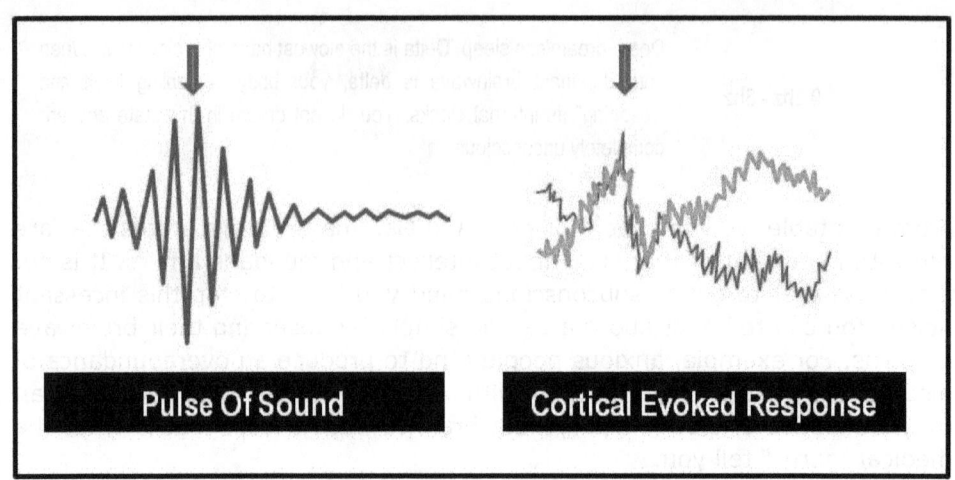

When the brain is presented with a rhythmic stimulus, such as a drum beat for example, the rhythm is reproduced in the brain in the form of these electrical impulses. If the rhythm becomes fast and consistent enough, it can start to resemble the natural internal rhythms of the brain, called brainwaves. When this happens, the brain responds by synchronizing its own electric cycles to the same rhythm. This is commonly called the Frequency Following Response (or FFR).

FFR can be useful because brainwaves are very much related to mental state. For example, a 4 Hz brainwave is associated with sleep, so a 4 Hz sound pattern would help reproduce the sleep state in your brain. The same concept can be applied to many other mental states, including concentration, relaxation and meditation. If you listen closely during an NP3 session, you will hear small, rapid pulses of sound. As the session progresses, the frequency rate of these pulses is changed slowly, thereby changing your brainwave patterns and guiding your mind to various useful mental states.

For those that are not familiar with NP3, it is Neuro-Programmer 3 which offers mind technology as techniques to affect the mind much like an engineer would program a computer. NP3 implements the methods of psychologists, EEG researchers, neuroscientists, hypnotherapists and meditators. One aspect of the Neuro-Programmer that makes it unique is that it targets specific brainwave patterns which have been shown to make the mind more receptive to psychological change.

Entrainment is a principle of physics. It is defined as the synchronization of two or more rhythmic cycles. The principles of entrainment appear in chemistry, neurology, biology, pharmacology, medicine, astronomy and more.

As an example, while working on the design of the pendulum clock in 1656, Dutch scientist Christian Huygens found that if he placed two unsynchronized clocks side by side on a wall, they would slowly synchronize to each other. In fact, the synchronization was so precise not even mechanical intervention could calibrate them more accurately.

Is It Important To Be In an Altered State?

When a hypnotherapist relaxes the patient he attempts to get the mind buzz out. The process is to get by the conscious mind interference and have the body and brain relaxed into the level of the mind called Alpha. Normally our minds are buzzing away generating millions of thoughts, getting input from the external world in a frequency range of 14 to 40 cycles per second. It's called the Beta range and this is the place for the conscious mind. The Alpha range occurs when we are able to ignore all that noise and become more calm and relaxed—like when you do meditation and Yoga. It is called going inside. We will talk about this later. Alpha means getting to a point where you are at the same frequency buzz as the subconscious—like being able to change the frequency on your radio. All sorts of things can happen here when you can talk the same lingo. Here it is susceptible to these entrainment and NP3 techniques. It is where the subliminal programming process likes to target

Regardless, hypnosis uses the "power of suggestion" where a suggestion by the hypnotist is registered as a program in the subconscious. It becomes temporarily "hardwired and recompiled", unbeknown to the person hypnotized, to load and run at some other time, trigged by some environmental signal. It is also where the regression therapists go to locate an issue, acknowledge it, and release it, then change or delete it from subconscious memory. In our miracle lingo, this would be to place attention on it, understand the issue as to why it is there, let go of it by forgiving it, then replace it (new vision) or delete it (divine assistance).

In this light, you begin to shed some light on techniques like Ho'Oponopono that are a simple process to do the same thing.

In order to shed more light on why this state of the brain, and the various processes used to bypass the conscious mind of Alpha, Beta and Gamma are important, all one has to do is look at a lot of biological research. On this topic, we are going to focus on the book **The Biology of Belief** by **Bruce Lipton, PhD**.

As Bruce explains the brain and nervous system must interpret environment stimuli and send signals to cells which then integrates and regulates life sustaining functions of body organ system to support survival. Notice it says regulate and integrates, not analyze and decide! For this purpose, as we have said before, the brain dedicates vast cell numbers to catalogue complex perception and remember millions of experienced perceptions and integrate them into a database to give them "consciousness" or more like **self-consciousness** which is the prefrontal cortex – the neurological platform to realize personal identity and experience the quality of thinking. So the brain has a direct connection to consciousness and self consciousness. In general, "consciousness" can be divided into three categories:

Consciousness can process 40 nerve impulses/second that enable assessment and response to environmental stimuli at that moment so one can participate in life.

Self-consciousness allows one to factor in the consequences of past and future as self reflection through free will.

Subconscious can process 40 million nerve impulses/second and monitors and controls automated stimulus-response (also unconscious) programs. It is like an automated record-playback system of recorded habits. It has no creativity, once learned is automatic (note Yogis can drop to delta and control body through conscious mind function which is under subconscious control). Subconscious controls body behavior not attended to by self-conscious mind in the present time.

Ok, with this in the back of your mind, let us look into the research that has been conducted on kids and their brain wave states as they evolve their automated stimulus-response programs so they can engage in life. It has been found that during the lower brain waves of 4-8 Hz, kids are in a highly suggestible state almost like hypnosis. To better quantify this process, have a look at the following interesting graph.

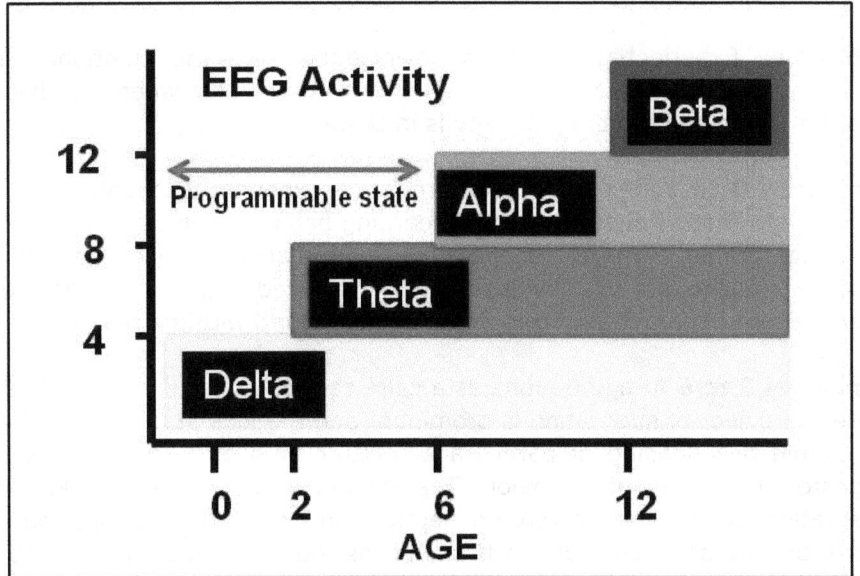

- DELTA During pregnancy and Age 2 years the human brain is in operation in the delta range of .5-4 Hz. This is the sleeping or unconscious region
- THETA Between 2 and 6 years, the human brain is operating in the theta range of 4-8 Hz. Imagination enters
- ALPHA Between 6-12 years the brain goes to more alpha of 8-12 Hz. Here calm consciousness like in meditation is added.
- BETA At 12, the brain goes to beta 12-35 Hz. This adds focused consciousness.
- GAMMA After 12, the brain can go to 35Hz during times of peak performance.

The most powerful programs are recorded in the first 6 years of life by observing and listening to people, parents, teachers, and environment. The role of the brain is to create coherence between its programs and real life as quickly as possible; these being inventoried in the subconscious. It unconsciously generates appropriate (or inappropriate depending on perception) responses that assume as truths of its programmed perceptions. With reference to the EEG Chart showing the state of awareness, there are three primary sources:

1 **Nature** First programmed perception is through inheritance such as instincts (nature). These allow the basic survival as encoded in DNA to be brought into the subconscious database.

2. **Nurture** Experiential memories downloaded from the emotional and mental/physical patterns of the mother. This is the time when the child is in the womb and the brain activity is in Delta.

From ages 0 to 2, the brain is recording all experiences, motor, speech, running, information about the world, learning behavior patterns, acceptable or unacceptable. These shape life automatically because Alpha consciousness has not yet developed. What is added in awareness at age 2 is Theta. Here Theta which mixes the imaginary world with the real world.

From ages 2 to 6 At age 6 Alpha as a calm consciousness is added. Here is where the power of suggestion is prominent and the kids in Delta and Theta have rapid downloading of parent and cultural "wisdom" to be stored as suggested programs of behavior. The infants quickly pick up skills by observation to become hardwired synaptic pathways in the subconscious to control biology and behavior. To the subconscious, because the purpose of the life form is to learn to adapt and react as quickly as possible so as to survive, these "truths" so suggested become facts, beliefs, truths, and programs ready for survival.

From ages 6 to 12 Alpha brings about the brain activity that opens conscious processing but before it can the brain must acquire a working awareness of the world into the subconscious. That's its duty up to age 6. As we get older we move more in Alpha and become less susceptible to outside programming as it is where the usual five sense observation systems interacts with consciousness. This phases into the mode of discernment where the conscious mind's ability to make a decision by observation before the belief is stored in the subconscious becomes more prominent. It is where the prominent development of self-consciousness begins.

At 12 there is focused consciousness where more academic activity is prominent and the Beta kick in to the consciousness pot to take on life.

3. **Actions** of Self Conscious Creative platform of perception by imagination that generates unlimited beliefs and behavior patterns through free will. That's when you have a full brain wave card deck to work with so you can build your personal identity and survive with this free will that you are given.

Of significance here is that Delta and Theta are below consciousness and called hypnagogic trance which is the same state hypnotherapists use to download new behaviors. So kids up until the age of 6 are in a hypnotic trance where perceptions are downloaded without discrimination or filtering of analytic self-conscious mind which does not yet fully exist.

Also an important note is that these five stages of brain wave activates with special purpose are not given to you all at once. They are additive by age, exactly the same way your body develops by age.

Thus the hard core perception-response programs as well as beliefs are set in the first 6 years. This has relevance later when using the Conscious Mind to rewrite programs of behavior; it is like talking to a tape recorder. This can sabotage the conscious by limiting programs!

Research shows that as adults, 5% of cognitive action is through self-conscious while 95% is through subconscious. This means that decisions, actions, emotion behavior, for example are directed from unconscious serial processing of the subconscious. So part of the mind imagines who we are as 5% while 95% is controlled by subconscious to be who we are. Hence positive thinking may not work if the subconscious does not agree. Fate is based on recorded programs many of which you don't even have an awareness of!

Becoming conscious of subconscious beliefs is the gateway. We will see that we must activate a process (like forgiveness) to replace beliefs. Jesus said: *"if it were not for limiting beliefs, we could all perform miracles."* Forgiveness is the reality that gets us unstuck from the past.

Hypnotherapists bring the patient down to Theta to do their work. What the hypnotist is doing is starting to shut out the conscious world of noise and bypass the process where the conscious mind gives directives for loading bio-programs at the subconscious level. Again this is in the lower Alpha to Theta range. Now the hypnotist starts suggesting things like you are very relaxed, you are going to have heavy eyelids and not hear anything but me, etcetera, etcetera. It is called getting present to you and now. It eliminates the outside noise. They are effectively taking you down into those more programmable levels of Theta.

When the hypnotist knows he has you in that state, he checks to see if you—now the subconscious—agree to listen. You are now under his spell as he is able to suggest things to the subconscious mind. He makes some suggestions for later when you are in the conscious buzz state. He may suggest that when someone claps, you will bark like a dog. Now be aware that the subconscious mind simply takes orders and responds—if it has been given the orders properly and it does not have something encoded that is in conflict—like your true belief that this hypnosis is crap. If you believe hypnosis is a joke, your subconscious will protect you and not let the suggestion through.

And in many cases the process works because that suggestion has now been programmed and loaded into the bio-computer to be run at a specific time by the operating software. So suddenly 10 minutes later, when someone claps, you start barking like a dog in your seat. Of course everyone laughs and applauds the hypnotist. Your subconscious is doing this all the time—filtering what comes in on the basis of your belief system.

Sound crazy? Research it for yourself. The Hypnotist bypassed the consciousness to input into the bio-computer what he wanted to. There was nothing there in the belief system to negate it. In self-hypnosis one does it by themselves. It works—not all the time of course.

Now be aware that this process is done all the time by some medical doctors, psychologists, psychiatrists and energy therapists. Some serious and spectacular issues have been solved this way. Some cases have even bypassed surgery. Does it work every time? No. Why not? Because, what is already programmed, and in agreement with the belief system, does not agree with the new information.

In the profession of psychiatry, the process goes a step further. In regression therapy, a patient is brought into a hypnotic state and is slowly regressed (taken backward in time) to a point where a problem (which can be a trauma or a physical injury) occurred. In the case of a trauma, once the patient gets to that point and it is revealed, it is released simply by saying it (and believing it to be so). It gets erased! There are millions of documented facts of incredible trauma healings. Likewise, there are millions of documented cases that have eliminated serious illnesses like cancer, AID's, and other problems.

In the physical case, a patient is regressed to the point of injury or before. The patient imagines, and is aided by reinforcement from the therapist to see the issue gone. That is it, and in many cases, poof, it is gone. The belief it is so gets the subconscious to make it so and it is. A miraculous unexplained anomaly happens instantly

What was clear is that all these processes worked. They all created wonderful results and they all created miracles. However, not all the time. So what was missing here that could control success?

The bottom line was this. Whatever was impressed on subconscious is expressed as a condition to experience an event. The subconscious is the objective responsive process while the conscious is subjective. The subconscious works at the quantum level, the conscious does not. (We will get to this quantum stuff in PART THREE). In fact, as we have stated, in comparison to a computer the subconscious mind can process 20 million environmental stimuli per second. The conscious mind can process 40 environmental stimuli per second. The conscious mind can look back and forward, but while the conscious mind is out dreaming and playing, the subconscious mind is always on duty dealing with the moment now. It effectively is the manager, the overriding authority and manages things the way it was trained. In simple terms, if the subconscious does not agree with the conscious, guess who wins?

One follows energy instructions; the other makes them up and uses imagination. When thoughts are conveyed to subconscious as energy, impressions are made on brain cells and as soon as subconscious accepts the idea, it proceeds to put it into effect.

The subconscious does not reason and compare and decide. Yet it can act by suggestion. And it can revise programs that control biology like in miracles. So how does one get through to this big processor; obviously one had to get it to accept something as its "truth" and bypass conditions or anything that limits and prevents reprogramming.

So back to our common denominators. It is important in these processes and procedures to bypass the conscious intellect so it cannot interfere and we can go directly to the source where the programs that create behavior are written. This, like with the kids in early years, is done by inducing techniques like meditation to get into that altered state of awareness.

Is an altered state important? What do you think?

Is There A Biological Process To Belief?

We have already mentioned the work by **PhD Bruce Lipton**, who released his mind-bending study results in **The Biology of Belief.** Here Bruce expounds on the fact that everything in us is expressed in one cell. A cell is intelligent and can survive on its own. It is capable of learning through environmental experiences and creates cellular memories which they pass on to their offspring. Each of the 50 trillion cells is a miniature copy of us.

Cells are highly organized communities that subdivide workloads. He underscores that the Earth and all species are living organisms and that we are not subservient to genes. Scientists, he says, have never found genes cause a disease.

His research points out the cell membrane is the brain controlling cellular life. Here is the secret in how your body translates environmental signals to behavior. All living cells have membranes with the same three layer structure. The membrane is very aware and sets in motion a response by the group of cells called the nervous system. These molecules of the membrane behave like a fluid liquid crystal. The membrane is a semiconductor as it conducts or filters through to the inside. It contains gates and channels as receptors and effectors to let nutrients in or waste out.

A computer chip is a semiconductor with gates and channels like a membrane. These are programmable from outside. The nucleus is a memory disk containing the DNA programs that encode the production of proteins.

Genes containing nucleus do not program the cell, data is entered through the membrane receptors into the cell/computer like a keyboard. Receptors trigger effector programs which act like a CPU and convert environmental information into the behavioral language of biology! So Lipton states that we are the drivers of our own biology like a WORD program. We can be masters of our own fate not victims of genes.

But what was clear also is that you need more than positive thinking to harness the control. The conscious and subconscious are independent. Conscious can create positive thought but the subconscious is the repository of data it acts on. It is habitual, millions of times more powerful. If desires of conscious are in conflict, the subconscious will win. You can affirm over and over your cancer will go but if deep down you have learned you are sickly and worthless it will undermine your best efforts.

So one can understand more clearly from Lipton's research that our conscious mind relies on a unique mechanism that converts chemical communication signals into sensations that could be experienced by all cells—emotions. The conscious mind reads signals and generates emotions which are manifested through the controlled release of regulating signals by the nervous system.

Through self consciousness the mind can use the brain to generate molecules of motion and override the system. Subconscious is a stimulus response playback device. It does not ponder and works in the "now" and there is no disagreement with the instructions once they are accepted.

Subconscious is rapid about downloading and emphasizing perceptions about threatening situations. Our perceptions control our biology, namely our beliefs.

So back to our common denominators, the cells respond to outside environmental stimuli that trigger the response action to activate tissue changes. The perceptions and beliefs create the stimuli that have a direct bearing on what the brain and the subconscious need to retrieve as a response.

Why Do We Need To Be In A State Of Well-Being?

In order to answer this question, we can again look to the work *Bruce Lipton as* reported in his books *Biology of Belief* and *Spontaneous Evolution*.

Cells are unconsciously driven to the fight or flight reactions to service a hostile environment. These cells have moving parts as proteins, as building blocks to generate the cells behavior. Each has 150,000 parts as pathways as assemblies of proteins for breathing, digestion, etc. These behave as switches in the cell's membrane and get proteins in motion. Biological gauges convert information via sensation from by-product chemicals. For example when threatened, immune cells release messengers such Interleukin 1 into the blood. When these are recognized by membrane receptors on blood vessel cells in the brain they forward a byproduct molecule Prostaglin E2 into the brain which activates fever pathways to produce shivering and high temperature. Signals are both energetic and physical (air, food, news) and all activate protein movement to generate behavior. Coupling of protein molecules with complementary environment signals causes a shape change expressed by movement in the cell membrane which animates the cell, bringing it to life.

The brain of this operation is in cell membrane where these switches respond to environment signals thus relaying information into internal protein pathways. Some respond to estrogen, adrenalin, and calcium for example. There can be 100,000 switches in a cell. Each membrane switch is a unit of perception with receptor and effector proteins. Receptor receives signals (through senses) and moves to bind the effector. A second signal is sent by effector into cytoplasm that controls specific protein functions and pathways. So once again, perception controls behaviors. These switches also activate genes in nucleus to draw out a blueprint from DNA if it is required.

Dis-ease and dysfunction is because of defective proteins or distorted signals from three situations:

1. Trauma – twist or misalign spine, impede nerve signal transmissions
2. Toxicity – distorts signals
3. Thought – action of the mind to misinterpret environment

Cells, tissues, and organs do not question information from the nervous system. Once triggered, the brain and supporting nervous system are the regulating mechanism that coordinates all these pathways. These pathways will include using genes as blueprints to make protein parts. But it had to get through the cell brain first!

Let us work through an example. Cells accept/reject food by membrane perception switches (histamines for example). A body wide system emergency response like this is adrenalin—alpha (protection) and beta (growth response present) switches. When both histamines and adrenalin are released by the nervous system, adrenalin overrides histamines signals that are local.

Consider the power of thought as the system does not distinguish between real and non-real. The placebo effect studies prove mind over matter which is positive thinking. Similarly the placebo effect of negative thinking is possible (i.e. nocebo, you have cancer, you have 3 months to live, it won't work). Negative thoughts can truly manifest disease. It is reported that one third of medical healings are placebo. But what percentage is nocebo when 70% are negative thoughts brought on by fear or doctors?

But let's get back to our example. Protection mode inhibits the creation of energy, growth, and vitality. This is controlled by the nervous system in response to stress. This happens through external HPA (Hypothalamus-pituitary-adrenal) like the fight or flight reaction where stress hormones are triggered in the body suppressing or inhibiting normal function everywhere. Where? The key ones are the immune system to fight disease, the visceral digestive area, and the ability to think. This is why if you are frightened you are dumber. Obviously the built in firmware doesn't think you need to waste any resources on eating, thinking or internal immunity when the shit hits the fan! Trouble is, this system doesn't know if the shit is in the imaginary or real perception fan!

We live in a world of fear and threat activating HPA and releasing stress hormones continuously. It is estimated that 70% of our thoughts are negative. . Almost every illness has now been linked to stress. Subconscious is an emotionless database of stored programs that creates hardwire behavior response with no judgment; a programmable hard drive into which our experiences are downloaded. The subconscious does not decide whether an order is bad or good, positive or negative. It simply checks its disk drives to see what is ok (belief sub-drive) and does it.

The two mind components are like a dynamic duo operating together. Subconscious takes over the moment conscious is not paying attention. To alter the program one for sure had to change the belief because it is the program that creates patterns in realty. The universe of thought and emotion changes belief because they are already working at a quantum level; ready to put input into those micro chip cells. When you really know, and really believe you deserve something, then you can have it. You simply know it to be true so it will happen.

The state of stress and negativity either physical or emotional suppresses many biological processes that inhibit normal functions. This why a state of well being of peace and love are enhancers of these biological functions.

Consider the opposite power of thought to heal. Elisabeth Fischer Targ, M.D. (1961 - 2002) was a psychiatrist with many interests including psychic phenomena and the role of spirituality in health and healing. She earned her undergraduate degree and her medical degree at Stanford University. In one of her studies, she found that group therapy was as useful as Prozac for fighting depression. She is probably best known for her study on the effects of prayer on patient outcomes in a group of people with AIDS. This randomized, double-blind study which was published in the Western Journal of Medicine found that the subjects who were prayed for had significantly better health and lower morbidity than the subjects who were not prayed for. She experimented with positive and negative thoughts to see if they influenced events. Could prayer influence AIDS? She got 40 religious and spiritual healers with known credibility to participate.

In this double blind study 20 patients in 2 groups all received the same medical treatment. The healers all got the name, photo, and T-Cell counts of one group. Each had to hold the intention to heal as well being one hour per day for 6 days a week for 10 weeks. This meant 40 healers were praying for 10 patients so each patient got prayers from 4 healers. After 6 months the control group had 4 of 10 die and the Healer group had 10 alive all improved. Many other experiments confirmed the same

So, is it important to have a state of well being? Well guess who is the emotional conscious dude operating in the higher brain wave area to not let go of meddling when you are trying to get it out of the way. And how can a stress environment be conducive to those entrainment and harmonious brain wave patters? We will get to this later.

What Is The Programmable System?

If you begin to rationalize the different ways in which these miracles occur and look at some other common denominators, it becomes clearer as to what the common steps and requirements are. For now, let us summarize what the Healers do and say is important to success:

1. **BELIEF**: The recipients' belief system must be one that believes in the healing process and is aligned with the subconscious belief;

2. **STATE**: The recipient must be in a programmable state where the brain does not interfere and the subconscious mind says it is ready to accept a new program. This is through guided meditation, regression, becoming present to lower the brain wave interference of the conscious mind;

3. **ENVIRONMENT**: The process of setting the environment whether a ritual, a gathering, a process by the healer is important in creating the focus and attention for the intention of healing and reprogramming to take place. This creates a morphic field of energy that enforces the belief so as to allow the reprogramming;

4. **WELL BEING**: The internal environment of the recipient and the healer is one of love, forgiveness, compassion, peace and harmony as the morphic field of energy around and in the body. The elimination of stress is needed here to better entrain the body and mind into a higher state of vibration;

5. **FOCUS & INTENT**: By triggering the intention, the issue is identified or located so as to direct the process of healing to that location. At this point, the clear vision of the correct state becomes the focus as surrounded by the joy of its completion. This through words, prayer, emotions, or guidance, creates the directive to correct the issue.

6. **HIGHER POWER**: Engagement in a Higher Power or Guides is the necessary process as some form of Divine engagement to assist in the process of correcting the issue and instigating the subconscious reprogramming.

7. **MANIFESTATION**: The healer, as higher authority and the conduit for some form of Divine Intervention that is triggered to actually replace the program in the subconscious mind. The process of reprogramming convinces the brain and the cellular community to respond by instituting a new or old program from DNA held within the nucleus of the cells.

So to follow the Ho'Oponopono line, once the environment is set, one begins with the **conscious mind,** drops out a petition for **transmutation** to the **void** so **super consciousness mind** can instruct the **subconscious mind** to rewrite the defective program and reboot the computer. But if **repentance** and **forgiveness** are not stamped on the request then it simply ain't going to get mailed.

In these cases, a common denominator is that a Healer who is accepted (Belief) as an Authority on the process acts as a conduit leading the recipient. The issues here are that some of these variables are not clear cut, like the strength of belief, the right state, and the proper environment; but nevertheless, we can begin to rationalize all these into some simple steps. In looking at a process where you wanted to get healed, you could summarize these following steps. First, you must come from a place of belief that you are worthy and believe in miracles. Then the Healer:

0. Creates a setting where the patient is in an altered state
1. Brings into thought the belief of being healed
2. Brings into vision the image of the issue which is to be corrected
3. Communicates to find the source of the issue
4. Brings in the power of emotion to surround the corrected desire
5. Launches the intention to correct the issue
6. Surrenders control of the correction to a higher power
7. Allows the Higher Power to materialize the correction

These steps were under the control of an Authority such as a Healer, not yourself. The other difference is that you are not going to regress yourself to find the issue, you are going to use your power of intent, love, and emotion to shift an issue which you already know exists without a hunt for what caused it. It is best to follow the more simple methods of Quantum Touch, Power of Intention, Ho'Oponopono, Ancient Prayer, and Matrix Energetics to be your guide. Here you will trust that the Divine Intervention will know what to do. Let us use an example of a dysfunctional knee.

0. ALTERED STATE: Bring yourself into an altered state by imagining a peaceful place, breathing softly, and becoming present to yourself in the heart.
1. THOUGHT: In your thoughts assert your beliefs that you believe in miracle healing, you believe you can heal yourself, you believe you are worthy and you believe in a higher power that will assist you.
2. VISION Visualize clearly in your mind a picture of the healed knee or a situation where it is healed.
3. SPEAK out stating that you are asking for Higher Divine Intelligence assistance to manifest your vision.
4. HEART EMOTION In your imagination feel the result of the knee being completely healed and surround this vision with the joy and bliss of it being so.
5. INTENT With your intention to correct the issue, you state to the area of problem, I love you, I am sorry for creating this issue and the reason for its being, please forgive me, thank you.
6. HIGHER POWER In your mind, connect to a higher power to feel the energy flow into your total being and into your cellular structure to the knee. You can use hands or imagine the flow of healing energy.
7. MANIFEST Feel the gratitude of completion and thank the higher power or those you have called to assist you.

Essentially, you can try any one of the techniques to begin telling your subconscious that it is time to believe. Pick a technique that "resonates" with you and go through the steps. They all work, and they all have produced some spectacular results. Yes, some of the time, but how do you know that you are not one of the ones that it will work for? Choose an area of attention that is a small issue, like the bad knee. The difference here is that you are going to be the Authority, not a doctor, healer, or third person facilitator. And how do you know you are doing it the right way? When it works! So engage your belief, intent, and accept that there is a Higher Power, drop your intellectual expectations and get on with the programming.

These simple steps would be where we stand so far. You may have doubts and questions about whether your belief is strong, are you in the right state and so on but why not try it and see. If you are still in doubt, then that is fine; let us move on to the process and procedures when you want to change your reality without a Healer or conduit. And understanding what has been programmed into the subconscious. So in order to further quantify the processes and procedures, let us move on to another area of "miracles". This is the one that changes the **reality around you**, not within you. These we are going to label **wealth** miracles so **created by You as the Facilitator.**

PART TWO

ATTRACTING MIRACLES

Aly McDonald
Ed Rychkun

ATTRACTING MIRACLES INTRODUCTION

"The world is nothing but an objectified dream and whatever your powerful mind believes very intensely instantly comes to pass."
                                              Paramahansa Yogananda

There is another kind of miracle that we are going to address in this part. It is about creating your own reality around you, not within you. Although it may encompass the healing miracles as a process of Divine Programming, it deals with creating a different miracle which may not be instant. The well known Law of Attraction is most adequate to describe this. These are miracles that are proactively planned for so it isn't the body that is being reprogrammed; it is the physical and mental reality in and around you. There are two types of reality, namely mental and physical. It is easy to understand that you can control your mental reality because it is in your mind and you can choose the perception of any situation as positive, neutral or negative. But to think you can also change your physical reality, that is a different matter, isn't it?

At the "heart of this matter" is the notion that we live in a holographic world where we as a Light Being or Soul take up temporary residency in a physical body to experience a virtual reality like hologram created by our old buddy in the attic - our brain. As such, if were able, like on the Starship enterprise go over and program the holodeck computer to give us a new hologram to engage in, we could choose any reality we wanted. It would be just like engaging "physically" in our mind's imagination. Well, besides the new breed of quantum physicists that are out there screaming that is exactly true, there are not too many guys around that can do it.

What is being suggested in this part of the book is that you do and can. When we get to the next part of the book, we will investigate what these new breed of scientists are saying.

Ester and Jerry Hicks have brought forward The Law of Attraction to thousands of people. The Law of Attraction says, *"The essence of that which is like unto itself, is drawn."* These teachings come from Abraham who is suggested as *"infinite intelligence"* so says Ester Hicks.

What they are inferring is that you create energy through your thoughts and actions that attract like energies. So if you want to walk around being a jerk, you are going to attract more jerks. If you walk around thinking you lack things then it is more lack you will attract. It is the same as we discovered in Part 1 where it is the subconscious that stores these behavioral attitudes and beliefs so it overrides and in many cases, if you think through the conscious mind to the contrary, and think you are being positive, it is really irrelevant because the subconscious rules. But here is a different twist; the inference is that maybe this subconscious mind has some kind of influence on the reality we attract in our lives? Yes, big question.

This may seem a bit contrary to the way we usually behave in the wake of issues but it seems to be a common denominator to the suggestions that allow you to take a more proactive control of what comes into your reality. As you carry this forward, into bigger and better schemes, the suggestion is that there is a process that they report can be used to change your wealth and health reality for the better.

In fact there are many around the planet that have grown to be the "gurus" of this idea, branding their own systems and steps as the answer to your health and wealth problems. And in the traditional marketing material, they quote many cases where these procedures have resulted in spectacular success.

With the miracle gurus, the problem is that they don't work all the time. In fact, they are like the miracles only working part of the time on some people. This does not discount that they do not work, it simply means that like miracles, there are other variables included that are not so quantifiable - sort of like belief or state of consciousness- that you really can't put into a formula, measure, or define. You know those intangibles; faith, trust, love, belief.

Whatever the case may be, in this section we are going to look closely at these top "guru attractors" and see what they say about their secret systems and processes. The purpose is to try to extract the common denominators to give our Divine Programmer instructions so as to change our realities.

Once again, we will start with a dramatic case to open your mind. This involves a special case of creating your own reality as documented and observed by many. The importance of this is to open your mind to the possibility that there really is a holodeck you can program. So let us begin this Part with an incredible example that distorts the physical beliefs of science. It has to do with materialization—creating an object instantly out of thin air. The most famous modern day materializer and miracle maker is **Sathya Sai Baba** an Indian Holy man who lived in Southern India.

It is said that a pilgrim to Puttaparthi suddenly developed acute appendicitis. At the time, there was no hospital there nor was there a surgeon, so Sai Baba was asked to come to the room where the patient lay groaning. He waved his hand in the air and produced a surgical knife out of nowhere. A second wave materialized vibhuti which he used as an anesthetic. With these aids he performed the operation to remove the inflamed appendix. Then the surgical knife vanished into thin air. He applied the vibhuti on the wound which healed immediately, leaving only a small scar

Now, given our description of John of God in the previous section this should not be too hard to believe even though no one can really explain it. Relevant to this Part however, is that this fellow was reported to materialize lockets, rings, jewelry, delicacies, sacred ash, and specific objects that were requested by others. He created these out of thin air then passed them out as gifts. Thousands have witnessed this. Scientists who studied this were befuddled by it of course, so they simply discounted it claiming it is a hoax.

In his book ***Modern Miracles: An Investigative Report on Psychic Phenomonena Associated with Sathya Sai Baba***, author and researcher **Erlendur Haraldsson** presents his work on this man who truly boggles the mind. He, a Professor of Psychology at the University of Iceland, set out to research this strange phenomenon and report his findings.

When interviewed, Sai Baba insisted: *"Daily and spiritual life must grow together."* He reported that Baba is deemed a saint, and he is visited by many daily to materialize vast quantities of food; even sizzling hot delicacies fall from his hands and feet. He can produce exotic and rare objects, fruits, and even anomalous ones like half apple, half orange on two sides. He walks about producing sacred ash with the wave of his hands. Haraldsson reports these have been observed and filmed endlessly. He states it is not mass hypnosis and Sai Baba has been doing this since the age of 14. He produces things from nothing using the attention of his mind. No one has ever been able to discredit him.

Sai Baba was also a biolocation example. Numerous witnesses report watching him snap his fingers and vanish instantly reappearing several hundred feet away.

This is not an isolated case. There are many Holy men in India with this ability. In the book, ***Autobiography of a Yogi, Paramahansa***

Yogananda, the first eminent holy man of India is reported to materialize out-of-season fruits, gold plates and other objects. He said: *"The world is nothing but an objectified dream and whatever your powerful mind believes very intensely instantly comes to pass."*

What is his secret? Well let us see if there are any clues in his the **Eleven assurances Sai Baba made to his devotees:**

1. No harm shall befall him, who steps on the soil of Shirdi (town of India).
2. He who comes to my Samadhi, his sorrow and suffering shall cease. (Samadhi is the spiritual height of divine consciousness)
3. Though I be no more in flesh and blood, I shall ever protect my devotees.
4. Trust in me and your prayer shall be answered.
5. Know that my spirit is immortal, know this for yourself.
6. Show unto me him who has sought refuge and has been turned away.
7. In whatever faith men worship me, even so do I render to them.
8. Not in vain is my promise that I shall ever lighten your burden.
9. Knock, and the door shall open, ask and it shall be granted.
10. To him who surrenders unto me totally I shall be ever indebted.
11. Blessed is he who has become one with me.

Like the acts of the Divine Programmer in our previous sections that reprograms organs and issues in the body, this fellow is somehow reprogramming physical reality to create something out of nothing.

Throughout history, psychokinesis has been a radical topic and in the modern day, there are stories of people who performed superhuman abilities... abilities that defy the norms of what we humans are able to do. In certain cultures however, abilities involving energy manipulation with the power of the mind (or soul/lifeforce) is believed to be real. A good example of this is in some Chinese martial arts, which claim to harness the body's natural lifeforce. The Chinese call this energy "chi", and with training they strive to master its manipulation.

This is the ability of affecting objects with the mind is suggested by a school that gives courses in developing this ability. They state that the secrets are:

1. The Power of Materializing is possessed by everyone (belief)
2. The power resides in a Higher source and connection to it
3. Slow Down and Relax to be in the present, get into the subconscious
3. Begin Meditation (get into theta brainwaves)

4. Create an Image of What You Desire
5. Trust It Is Yours
6. Focus Without Attachment
7. Believe It Is On Its Way
8. Feel It Is Yours
9. Say Thank You

Sound familiar? That computer language as an interface between the Programmer and the Computer allows the specific functions and processes to be understood by the computer so that it can consistently run to produce the same results. Once again this computer appears to the human one.

In our day to day affairs, we train our body to attain/mind new functionality which is coded into programs stored in the subconscious to be run as required. In our day to day reality we train our minds to interpret and perceive situations using these programs. In our daily lives we train ourselves to create, seek out experience, relationships, so as to control our physical reality as much as we believe possible. It seems to be the same process regardless of where we look.

Under the Law of Attraction and Cause and Effect, that which one creates as a Cause becomes program instructions that have been known to create an Effect in the physical reality. Or does it give instructions to find the solution desired? In this case the Divine Programmer simply knows the results desired, not the steps of the program to stick in the subconscious. The petition becomes the result and the Divine Intervention becomes one of manifesting the result either instantly in the case of psychokinesis, or over a period of time by attracting the experience, event, or situation that satisfies the energetic blueprint created by the mind and body.

Let us first look at the way we create things in our physical and nonphysical worlds. Then we will look at the Gurus who say they know how to do this the "easy way" through various techniques and see if we can extract some new "truths" for Divine Programming guidelines.

14

PROCESS OF CREATION IN THE "REAL WORLD"

"What you believe is what you see. Seeing is believing is a limiting scientific box. Drop it and you can change your life."
Ed Rychkun

We commonly refer to the "real world" as 3D or "reality". It is not the mathematical length, width, depth reflection of science. The second term applicable here is "Creation". We create things in 3D all the time, either mentally or physically.

What is creation?

It is defined as the action or process of bringing something into existence. This is actually quite different than the word "manifesting" which means that something is *"clearly apparent to the sight or understanding; obvious; to show or demonstrate plainly; reveal; to be evidence of; prove; readily perceived by the eye or the understanding; evident: to make clear or evident to the eye or the understanding."*

There is a subtle difference here. If you read this carefully, it can mean that you alone can see this in reality through the senses; and it need not be a physical creation. We have grown used to using sight as our reality check; to see is to believe. Creation actually creates the material version while manifesting is a bit looser in that it is the eye of the beholder and what one believes is seen does not necessarily represent the existence of the material version. This may not seem an important difference but what if the process of manifesting something is not the same as the process of creation?

Now, what about the word "reality"?

It is defined as the state of things as they are or appear to be, rather than as one might wish them to be; something that is real; the state of being real; that which exists, independent of human awareness; the totality of facts as they are independent of human awareness of them.

In our world of 3D we create things all the time. We brought these forward before as the 7 Steps to Manifesting Reality.

In the simplest cases, let us use a simple example of creating a chair. Usually we follow certain steps:

1. We form a thought that we would like to make a chair
2. We form a vision of what that chair will look like
3. We make a design or description of the chair
4. We get emotionally excited about creating the chair
5. We launch the intention to act on its construction
6. We engage with wood, saws, nails, etc to make it
7. We create a chair which physically enters our reality

These seven steps are typical of anything we create in our reality. This is our physical world. This is the way we do things. Even in the more complex situations, like making a million dollars or building a corporation, it is the same process

1. We form the thought of making a million dollars
2. We form a vision of a company that sells chairs
3. We make a business plan of the company and product
4. We get emotionally excited about the plan/company
5. We launch the intent to execute the business plan
6. We engage others, money, etc. to make it happen
7. We create the chairs/company that enters our reality

Now here is the big question.

Was it the thought process that actually first manifested, and then created the end result? Or was it simply the idea and then the dedicated physical effort that created the end result by some unknown way of attraction? Or was it just hard work and perseverance? Regardless, the examples serve to show how we create first mentally through the thoughts; visions, words, and then we create physically from the intent, relationships, and materialization. What we did was first manifest it in our minds, and then create the physical counterpart.

The reason for this question is that either way, the 7 steps reflect what is alchemically known as "As Above, So Below". Although this term has been bantered around for thousands of years and interpreted many ways, it reflects a well known process of creation.

In the seven steps, the first "above" would be in the thoughts, images, words that are not yet reality. But you can see these clearly and even write them down but you have only manifested them, you have not brought these into reality as a creation. It is still all mental manifestation but it is the clarity and belief in doing it that become the driving force to success. In the last three steps of "below" would be the intent to act, engagement, materialization that bring it into reality. That is the creation part. In the middle is the emotion that is the catalyst that actually creates the conversion from above to below; the strength of the passion and emotion drives this.

Now, you have to ask, in the more complex business cases, why do some succeed and others not? Well, we have developed many aids and tools and techniques to assist in this process. For example the level of emotion, of focus, clarity, passion, attention, of action, of intent, dedication, all go towards the success of the end result. The attraction of the right people, money, resources, events, all need to be in alignment with the plan; all attracted and acted on to create the infrastructure of the 3D process. Some use assertions to drive them. Some us prayer. Some are so passionate they are driven to completion by fierce dedication and perseverance. Whatever we use, the truth is that the clarity, passion, dedication all affects the time and the exactness of the end result. And of course, depending on the complexity, size, and time to do it, the result and the probability of success varies considerably. The vast majority simply fail. So whatever process we use, we cannot guarantee the final creation.

If we go back to the questions, one could say it was just idea clarity, passion and hard work that brought the result into reality. The other way was that when the idea and clarity was created, it attracted the rest of the below elements that came forward to choose the relationships with others that would create the end result. This process is suggested in the proliferation of stuff around the Law of Attraction.

But either way, sometimes the end result does not get created into reality. Our business plans fail and the Law of Attraction does not work all the time.

And if something does not work "most of the time" or cannot be explained, then it is not a law and it is discounted as no sense or nonsense. It is not part of our reality. As we have learned, the most obvious is the millions of healing miracles that occur around the world. Because they cannot be replicated or explained, they simply become discounted and cannot be "statistically significant" to enter the reality of the medical world. So although they exist, they do not exist. For those who have had or engaged in the creation of miracles, they certainly exist; even though they can't be explained - try to convince them otherwise.

What is also very significant is that in our 7 Steps, the last steps are being done by Divine Intervention in the case of miracle healing. There was no need to see a doctor in Step 6 and have the operation in Step 7. It just happened spontaneously by taking the proper steps of changing the program of mind and biology.

It is so with the idea behind the Law of Attraction and many other processes sold by the reality changing gurus. They bypass the last steps so it is we in some joint partnership with a higher force that changes our reality by assisting over time to make the desire come true.

What if we all exist in a programmable holodeck of reality and the computer that is programmed is just another level in our Divine Computer?

15

PROCESS OF CREATION IN THE "UNREAL WORLD"

"When you enter the state of quantum oneness which exists in the now, you have the realm for infinite possibilities."

Ed Rychkun

So let us go into our Holodecks.

To summarize the last Chapter, in the "real world we manifest mentally and create physically all the time in that above to below process. To most, the conventional process is simply that we create things by <u>making them with work</u>. And we <u>select the options</u> to create that end result. This is contrary to the notion that we <u>create</u> our reality by <u>attracting</u> the options to get to the end result.

To go into a Holodeck, let us delve into how the mind also works with your imagination. In this process of creation, there is no physical reality to do the "below" steps of intent, relationships and materialization because it is all imagined.

Your mind can bring into its reality any possibility you can think of. From the soup of no-thing, some-thing as an image, idea can be brought forward into your imaginary reality simply by shutting out your senses like closing your eyes and creating the picture in your mind. An event, experience, object, people; can all be brought into reality. If you are tuned into the new science of quantum physics, you will understand that the conscious mind is a perfect example. It begins with quantum nothing and like in the Observer Effect of quantum physics nothing becomes something simply by way of your mind placing attention to it. There need not be space or time. You can flip from one scene to another, you can play a movie like a dream, you can bilocate, materialize, be invisible, meld into other things, even deploy your physical senses given practice. You are engaging in the Creative process within you as a creator and here there are limitless possibilities to be "formed" by the conscious awareness of your mind. Everything can be everywhere, anywhere, nowhere at once. It is nonlocal. You entangle by way of conscious intent to manifest whatever you desire to create.

But what if manifesting in the imaginary world is the same as is creating in the real world. Quantum physics and holograms tell us there is really no difference.

Perhaps this reality IS a holograph of your imaginative world and you can even feel the engagements with emotion of bliss, fear, or whatever you choose to perceive as the result of an experience in the "non reality". There is a link to your physical reality as one can affect the other.

A New Look At Creating Reality

At this point, there is a bit of a diversion that I (Ed) want to bring forward. It occurred when I was researching this topic in March of 2010 and occurred when I was in deep Theta. I was then actively involved in "channeling" asking about this process of materialization. Here is what I got:

"On your practice, we speak of materialization which will evolve as your vibrations rise and body lightens. This is indeed a higher vibration ability that lies dormant in all. Again, it is attention and intention and love as the substance of power that allows an image to congeal into a material representation of an object in a hologram."

"This means that the Divine Mind must be the total agent of the image of some object that is simply created in your mind's eye. It will be a clear image so you need much practice here. At the point at which your Higher Mind and the Heart—the congealer—create that image, it is projected onto a place of choice by intent and at the same time the image of the mind is projected to the God Source of the one to be reflected back like a mirror as a beam of divine light to the same place of choice—yes it is like converging laser beams of light that create the 3 dimensional holographic image."

"As these two actions converge upon the place of choice from you and the Divine beam from the Source, they form a holographic duplicate representation of the object that is to be replicated or materialized. Yes, from a wave form to an atomic form as the electrons arrange themselves into the image which is your higher consciousness choosing a new possibility from the no-thing."

"No, you do not concern yourself as to how the chemistry, atomic structure and so one occurs as it is all under natural cosmic law that such an arrangement is created. These laws understand how this is done and your divine consciousness abides by these so they all understand what this is made up of to congeal this into the expression of the holographic image to be interpreted as such by your and other sensory systems of your brains—your sensory receiving stations."

"What we want you to get used to is this concept as you will begin with simple things all in your mind. As you sit quietly one with your heart and Source, knowing your higher mind is totally you; you form the image and project it. Then from your image, project it to the source to reflect back onto the same spot to see it materialize."

"You still need to enhance your image and vibrations which are doing so rapidly now. So do this in your mind and then there will be a surprise one day when you open your eyes and it will be there as you imagined."

"You will develop and expand over time as you begin to understand the laws of nature—and the Divine laws of Cosmic creation. At first you will not see material results of your efforts as your belief system adjusts and you surrender command to the Higher Mind. Here you are adjusting to the belief that the infinite possibilities of your mind are awakening. We only want you to begin this process to instil it as an eventual automatic process of a Creator."

When I researched holograms and how they are created, there was a striking similarity to the process. Now I have not been able to perfect this process but it does bring out a need for perhaps a better belief system to create physical reality? We will revisit this later.

So I was told that you first create a clear image in your mind's eye with the assistance of the heart, and then project it to a place of materialization. Then you project this to the One to project back to the same place. A holographic image is created. This is similar to the way a holographic image is created with beams of light that are split, reflected and converged again. What is it? A hologram. What form is it? It is whatever you see clearly that your brain understands and has meaning for or memory of.

In the next Part Three, we will see that it is your brain that does the final work as a material representation by retrieving what it knows and what cosmic rules apply in the material representation. It retrieves information and the cosmic rule simply "knows" what it is.

So let us say an apple is chosen. Is it big, small, red, or yellow? What kind is it? The brain is designed to hold its own local knowledge—like a copy of its own experience that is held current. It uses this to fill the gaps of creating this from what it knows about the apple. The brain, and of course your consciousness or mind has information and the cosmic rules of its composition, formation, are drawn to complete the picture.

So a word, an object, and image, all have meaning to the brain by its experience and it with the assistance of cosmic law reverse engineers the process to create the result from memory and let us call it technical information as to its composition or material makeup. Although an image of the apple is only a representation in your lower mind and brain, it already has the appropriate material characteristics from higher sources as to how it would be materialized. So anything can indeed happen in materialization therefore it requires a high degree of responsibility.

You see, the brain which interprets senses also fills in the gaps to complete it. Many times, you will not actually see things exactly as the brain only picks up half of what is there, filling in the rest by itself—unless you place strict attention on it and see the difference. The brain fills the gaps, holes, missing information and uses a process you call extrapolate and interpolate from its memory what is needed to complete the picture. If you see and read the words "I luv yu" or "wht a wndrful da" you know what this is meaning, do you not? Your brain is interpolating the true meaning even though parts are missing. But by closer inspection and attention, you see the difference. So it is with an image of an apple.

As we will see later, the brain is the holographic processor because like consciousness, it behaves quantumly. It creates the meaning, composition, representation through its memory and the interpretation of the senses of your lower body. You see, feel, taste an apple and it seems so real. So if you take the senses of see, feel, taste and the memories of this, then reverse engineer the process back through the brain—with divine assistance—it will create the apple appearing solid in the hologram.

The message went on to get into the Law of Attraction:

"What you have not done is to do this outside of your imagination in an eyes open conscious state of awareness. Yet as you know, some can indeed do this—like holy men—by a reverse process which is easy in your mind but not in your hologram of 3D. But you are learning. It is what you are learning as your vibration reaches a certain level. Yes, this is so because of a certain

level of responsibility, and partnership with the Higher Divine Self is required as reflected by the alignment of heart, purpose and Divinity—the One."

"You are creating energy that will either seek out and energy mate or it will materialize into something that the energy represents into a new form from the essence of particles of what consciousness is made up of—electrons you call them—common to all things whether material or non material. This is what you call a reality, the attention of your awareness within the total consciousness—the mind of God. Each energy lives and has purpose and once created, lives to expand itself according to its purpose and its design which will behave according to cosmic laws of creation. Once live, it remains so and evolves as it was perceived at the time of creation, then it grows, changes and evolves."

"Think also of how we have informed you of materialization and how you form the holographic image of some thing that can materialize—but with the alignment of the divine partner—approval to actually create—knowing the divine cosmic laws and being are explicitly in the heart so you are indeed the creator."

"Each particle is of the whole and all is one therefore all that exists, existed or will exist resides here in the hologram which is the mind—the total consciousness of the One—the Creator. In your lower form of mind and body, this becomes like an individual compartment of the whole which is your local individual consciousness."

"Once thoughts or actions of the lower form create, these energies remain to attain their purpose. They may be transmuted if you have attained the level of vibration that is of the Higher Body and Divine Mind. However, this responsibility is not of the lower form. If the energies are created from the Lower Selves, they will simply congeal into a transitional etheric state, attract, evolve and interact as they are designed by intent and attention to do—fulfilling either a cosmic or a purpose assigned by the creator you."

"Through your senses of the Lower Self, the experiences are interpreted and perceived with the brain being the interpreter. The mind is what creates, sets, interprets the instructions and is the actual link and control center of all this interacting energy and the body which itself is energy. A body is thus a hologram formed the same way and once created; a genetic code is set creating a signature of its makeup like in DNA. It is like this in all things as an initial blueprint that can replicate and evolve once given life."

The Creation Of Perception

One thing about the mind's creation is that you create your own world of perception and belief. The way you receive input is through your senses but the way you interpret and perceive things as a result is of your own choice. Your world of reality is built upon that choice. Is it real? No. It is the result of the choices you make as a result of experiencing through your sensory systems. And here is the kicker; real or not these perceptions and reactions all go into your subconscious as well as being recorded as stimuli-response or perception-reaction right down to your cells.

Not many will argue that this world of perception is real even though it is part of the 3D life. Yet these invisible perceptions have an effect on our 3D lives-physically.

Each of us has this unique world gathered from experiences. The result is a storehouse of things we can conjure up as memory, thoughts, images, words typically carrying some emotion; love, fear, hate, bliss, all contributing to that invisible world we call belief. They are all stored!

Does this perception have anything to do with creating physical reality? If you consider the physical body, yes! Does stress and a lowered immune system plus eating dysfunction have any affect?

Do they assist in creating your physical reality outside the body? You may say no but it is your perception and belief (above) that influences your acts and deeds (below). So at first you may say that these do assist in the creation process indirectly. Let your mind open a bit and consider that these thoughts, images, words, emotions that can manifest anything above in the imaginary world can attract the things that you create in your physical reality. This is what we are going to delve into now.

Many Gurus, much like the Healers, say that it is possible to bypass all the work effort in the below part (all the work) as in the 7 Steps of Manifesting Reality and create directly. In the last Part, at the extreme end was the instant healing miracle, and now at the extreme end here is the Sai Baba instant material miracle. Is this possible for us? In this second part of this book we will see the answer to this may be a resounding YES!

Let us start by learning how the experts tell us we can attract miracles.

16

NAPOLEON HILL: THINK AND GROW RICH

"Whatever the mind can conceive and believe, it can achieve."
Napoleon Hill

Napoleon Hill in 1928 published a book that has been reported to be one of the best-selling books of all time. His famous quotes were:

"The starting point of all achievement is DESIRE. Keep this constantly in mind. Weak desire brings weak results, just as a small fire makes a small amount of heat."

"Whatever the mind can conceive and believe, it can achieve."

"You are the master of your destiny. You can influence, direct and control your own environment. You can make your life what you want it to be."

For many years when you went into business, particularly if you took an MBA course at Harvard, there was a book that became your business bible. It was a book by Napoleon Hill. It was originally called The Law of Success in 16 Lessons and was his first book set, published initially in 1928 as a multi-volume correspondence course and later in more compact formats in recent years. The work was originally commissioned at the request of Andrew Carnegie at the conclusion of a multi-day interview with Hill, and was based upon interviews of over 100 American millionaires across nearly 20 years, including such self-made industrial giants as Henry Ford, J. P. Morgan, John D. Rockefeller, Alexander Graham Bell, and Thomas Edison. Napoleon Hill, as a Great Depression era author and former advisor to President Franklin D. Roosevelt, interviewed the most successful men this country has ever known to figure out the key to their good fortune. He wrapped all of his insights in a 200-page package and published **"Think and Grow Rich,"** which went on to become one of the best-selling books of all time.

The Law Of Success

The Law of Success was first used as a lecture, and was delivered by Hill in practically every city and in many smaller localities, throughout the United States over a period of more than seven years. What did this "best selling book of all time" say? Let us look at a summary of the Lessons:

In Lesson 1: INTRODUCTION Here Hill introduces the concept of The Master Mind, which Dr. Hill defines *"as a mind that is developed through the harmonious cooperation of two or more people who ally themselves for the purpose of accomplishing any given task."* Hill used ideas from physics to illustrate the synergy that occurs between like-minded individuals. He also warns of the danger to the master mind group of any single member who thinks negatively. Another key insight from Hill is that knowledge is not power; it is only potential power. He defines power as *"...organized knowledge, expressed through intelligent efforts."* The master mind group makes this happen.

He explained the 15 Laws of Success as follows:

I. DEFINITIVENESS OF PURPOSE will teach you how to save the wasted effort which the majority of people expend in trying to find their life-work. This lesson will show you how to do away forever with aimlessness and fix your heart and hand upon some definite, well-conceived purpose as a life-work.

II. SELF-CONFIDENCE will help you master the six basic fears with which every person is cursed: the fear of Poverty, the fear of Ill Health, the fear of Old Age, the fear of Criticism, the fear of Loss of Love of Someone, and the fear of Death. It will teach you the difference between egotism and real self-confidence which is based upon definite, usable knowledge.

III. HABIT OF SAVING will teach you how to distribute your income systematically so that a definite percentage of it will steadily accumulate, thus forming one of the greatest known sources of personal power. No one may succeed in life without saving money. There is no exception to this rule, and no one may escape it.

IV. INITIATIVE AND LEADERSHIP will show you how to become a leader instead of a follower in your chosen field of endeavor. It will develop in you the instinct for leadership which will cause you gradually to gravitate to the top in all undertakings in which you participate.

V. IMAGINATION will stimulate your mind so that you will conceive new ideas and develop new plans which will help you in attaining the object of your Definite Chief Aim. This lesson will teach you how to "*build new homes out of old stones*", so to speak. It will show you how to create new ideas out of old, well known concepts, and how to put old ideas to new uses. This one lesson, alone, is the equivalent of a very practical course in salesmanship, and it is sure to prove a veritable gold mine of knowledge to the person who is in earnest.

VI. ENTHUSIASM will enable you to "saturate" all with whom you come in contact with interest in you and in your ideas. Enthusiasm is the foundation of a Pleasing Personality, and you must have such a personality in order to influence others to co-operate with you.

VII. SELF-CONTROL is the "balance wheel" with which you control your enthusiasm and direct it where you wish it to carry you. This lesson will teach you, in a most practical manner, to become *"the master of your fate, the Captain of your Soul."*

VIII. THE HABIT OF DOING MORE THAN PAID FOR is one of the most important lessons of the Law of Success course. It will teach you how to take advantage of the Law of Increasing Returns, which will eventually insure you a return in money far out of proportion to the service you render. No one may become a real leader in any walk of life without practicing the habit of doing more work and better work than that for which he is paid.

IX. PLEASING PERSONALITY is the "fulcrum" on which you must place the "crow-bar" of your efforts, and when so placed, with intelligence, it will enable you to remove mountains of obstacles. This one lesson, alone, has made scores of Master Salesmen. It has developed leaders over night. It will teach you how to transform your personality so that you may adapt yourself to any environment, or to any other personality, in such a manner that you may easily dominate.

X. ACCURATE THINKING is one of the important foundation stones of all enduring success. This lesson teaches you how to separate "facts" from mere "information." It teaches you how to organize known facts into two classes: the "important" and the "unimportant." It teaches you how to determine what is an "important" fact. It teaches you how to build definite working plans, in the pursuit of any calling, out of FACTS.

XI. CONCENTRATION teaches you how to focus your attention upon one subject at a time until you have found a way to master that subject and have put that knowledge into operation. He gives you techniques on how to insure that your goal is concentrated on until you have completed that goal.

XII. CO-OPERATION will teach you the value of team-work in all you do. In this lesson you will be taught how to apply the law of the "Master Mind". This lesson will show you how to co-ordinate your own efforts with those of others, in such a manner that friction, jealousy, strife, envy and cupidity will be eliminated. You will learn how to make use of all that other people have learned about the work in which you are engaged.

XIII. PROFITING BY FAILURE will teach you how to make stepping stones out of all of your past and future mistakes and failures. It will teach you the difference between "failures" and "temporary defeat," a difference which is very great and important. It will teach you how to profit by your own failures and by the failures of other people.

XIV. TOLERANCE will teach you how to avoid the disastrous effects of racial and religious prejudices which mean defeat for millions of people who permit themselves to become entangled into foolish argument over these subjects, thereby poisoning their own minds and closing the door to reason and investigation. This lesson is the twin sister of the one on ACCURATE THOUGHT, for the reason that no one may become an Accurate Thinker without practicing tolerance. Intolerance closes the book of knowledge and writes on the cover, "Finished, I have learned it all!" Intolerance makes enemies of those who should be friends. It destroys opportunity and fills the mind with doubt, mistrust and prejudice.

XV. PRACTICING THE GOLDEN RULE will teach you how to make use of the great universal law of human conduct in such a manner that you may easily get harmonious co-operation from any individual or group of individuals. Lack of understanding of the law upon which the Golden Rule philosophy is based, is one of the major causes of failure of millions of people who remain in misery, poverty and want all their lives. This lesson has nothing whatsoever to do with religion in any form, nor with sectarianism, nor have any of the other lessons of this course on the Law of Success.

Napoleon Hill Summarizes

"Wishing will not bring riches, but desiring riches with a state of mind that becomes an obsession, then planning definite ways and means to acquire riches, and backing those plans with persistence which does not recognize failure, will bring riches."

In one passage, he sums up six steps to turning a desire for wealth into "its financial equivalent":

First. Fix in your mind the exact amount of money you desire. It is not sufficient merely to say *"I want plenty of money."* Be definite as to the amount.

Second. Determine exactly what you intend to give in return for the money you desire. There is no such reality as "something for nothing".

Third. Establish a definite date when you intend to possess the money you desire.

Fourth. Create a definite plan for carrying out your desire, and begin at once, whether you are ready or not, to put this plan into action.

Fifth. Write out a clear, concise statement of the amount of money you intend to acquire, name the time limit for its acquisition, state what you intend to give in return for the money, and describe clearly the plan through which you intend to accumulate it.

Sixth. Read your written statement aloud, twice daily, once just before retiring at night, and once after arising in the morning. <u>AS YOU READ, SEE AND FEEL AND BELIEVE YOURSELF ALREADY IN POSSESSION OF THE MONEY.</u>

It seems basic, but if you actually compare this to just about any personal finance guide out there, you'll find exactly the same simple steps. They just come with a lot more bells and whistles. But also note here a very critical thing; it is already **manifested reality** in the mind and you just put it to paper as a plan. But in terms of a physical reality it s still not created.

What is Hill saying as the bottom line? Begin with **thought** and make it very clear in your mind as to what you want. Know what you are going to **share** with others as a result, create a clear plan, then **see, feel and believe yourself** already in possession. Firmly entrench this into your mind by reading this daily. Who does this translation of unreal to real? Some of the wealthiest people on the planet.

And so thousands of people have used this wisdom to achieve their dreams. And one would say that many more have not. It did not work for all. But as you go through his wisdom, you pick out the seven steps of above to below. Thoughts, visions, words (plans), and passion are manifestation. Intent, relationships, and materialization are creation. Intensity, clarity, emotion, perseverance, relationships all go into the belief you can create your visions. What else? Give, share, feel good about yourself, believe, and have a pleasing personality... NO negative stuff here!

Do you see a similarity between the 7 Steps and what we determined as the common processes in creating miracles? The big question here is that by programming your wealth desires into your subconscious by repetitive conscious thoughts, images, words, passion (emotion) and intent are you:

> Directing the course of your reality towards creating the end results by attraction?
>
> or
>
> Directing your focus and attention to the course of your reality to create the results?

It is noteworthy to understand that in these procedures there are two key suggestions to assist in the self suggestion process, namely *"get out of the emotion of failure and misery"* and *"see, feel and believe yourself already in possession."*

But here is the bottom line. This process is most definitely working at changing your belief about yourself and reprogramming in your subconscious a new set of procedures. Let us now quantify Hill's process.

	WEALTH PROCESSES & PROCEDURES: THINK AND GROW RICH	
Setting	Have self confidence, definitiveness, habits of saving, initiative	NH
Setting	Have imagination, passion, and enthusiasm	NH
Setting	Show self control, pleasing personality, accurate thinking, concentration	NH
Setting	Know cooperation, profiting by failure, tolerance, harmonize	NH
Process	Fix your mind on the exact amount of money or the final desire	NH
Process	Determine what you intend to give in return	NH
Process	Establish a definite date for completion	NH
Process	Create a definite plan for carrying out the desire	NH
Process	Write a clear concise statement, time, return, and the plan	NH
Process	Read the written statement daily before bed and upon awakening	NH
Process	Have great passion and emotion to succeed	
Process	See, feel and believe yourself in possession of the desire	NH

17

WAYNE DYER
THE POWER OF INTENTION

"Change the way you look at things and the things you look at change."
Wayne Dyer

Dr. Wayne W. Dyer, affectionately called the "father of motivation" by his fans, is one of the most widely known and respected people in the field of self-empowerment. He has published more than 20 self-help books and audio lectures, many of which have become best sellers.

He teaches there are 8 ways to tap into the **Power of Intention** and feel great every day. He is very much tuned into feeling good about himself, getting out of the failure and misery mode:

1. Make meditation a regular practice in your life. You need to take time to get quiet, to go within, and from this silence make conscious contact with the source of intention. You're already connected to everything that you perceive as missing from your life; go with a realign.
2. Become conscious of the foods you eat. Foods high in alkalinity such as fruits, vegetables, nuts, soy, non-yeast breads and virgin olive oil are high-energy foods and will strengthen you, while highly acidic foods such as flour-based cereals, meats, dairy and sugars lower energy and will weaken you.
3. Retreat from low-energy substance. Alcohol, cigarettes, caffeine, sugar and virtually all artificial drugs, legal or otherwise, lower your body's energy level and weaken you.
4. Become aware of the energy level of the music you listen to. Some rap music—filled with profanity and messages about killing, for example—is an energy drain, while music that has a more soothing impact on the soul has been proven to be beneficial.

5. Become aware of the energy levels of your home environment. Make your home a nurturing, cheerful and peaceful environment.
6. Reduce your exposure to low-energy commercial television. Children see 12,000 simulated murders on TV before their 14th birthday! Television news puts a heavy emphasis on the bad and the ugly, leaving out the good.
7. Enhance your energy field with photographs. Every photograph contains energy. Carry and display photos taken in moments of happiness, love and receptivity.
8. Become conscious of the energy levels of your acquaintances, friends and extended family. Choose to be in close proximity to those who are empowering, who see the greatness in you, who feel connected to spirit.

In his talk on **OVERDOSING ON SEROTONIN** he explains about the effects of kindness on your brain. It goes something like this:

"Serotonin is the drug that makes you feel good. It's what all the pharmaceutical companies pump into those wonderful little anti-depressants. It's also a little drug God decided to pump through our brains when we do things he/she/it likes. It's kinda like a little reward for good behavior, ya know?"

"Anyway, get this: When you do something kind for someone else, the person you're helping has serotonin released in her brain—she feels happier. And so do you. Good news! Two more serotonin-induced happier people in the world! Woo hoo! But the most incredible thing is this: not only do you and the person you helped feel better, so does some random person who happened to watch your act of kindness."

So what does Wayne, as a world known motivational speaker, and follower of Napoleon Hill, say about the steps to create your reality? Here they are in his words:

1. ACT AS IF Act as if everything you desire is already here... treat yourself as if you already are what you'd like to become.

2. COME INTO YOUR SELF Connect to The Power of Intention with Four Steps of <u>Discipline</u>, <u>Wisdom</u>, <u>Love</u> and <u>Surrender</u>.
    1) Exercise your <u>Discipline</u> by building strong habits. DO the things you know you should do. Live with integrity to your ideal!
    2) Develop your <u>Wisdom</u> as you learn in this classroom that is our lives.
    3) Open your heart as you learn to <u>Love</u> more and more—loving who you are, what you do, and those around you. And,

4) <u>Surrender</u> to the force that's bigger than you, the force that beats your heart, the force that Wayne calls, "The Power of Intention"!

3. BOW TO THE DIVINE WITHIN YOU When you meet anyone, treat the event as a holy encounter. Make every encounter we have today an opportunity to see the Divine within ourselves and others.

4. SAY "YES!" One of the most effective means for transcending ordinary and moving into the realm of extraordinary is saying yes more frequently and eliminating no almost completely. I call it saying yes to life. Say yes to yourself, to your family, your children, your coworkers, and your business... He states: *"I rarely let the word No escape From my mouth Because it is so plain to my soul That God has shouted, Yes! Yes! Yes! To every luminous movement in Existence."*

5. CONNECT TO SERVICE If you want to feel connected to your own purpose, know this for certain: Your purpose will only be found in service to others and in being connected to the something far greater than your mind/body/ego. You'll feel most on purpose when you're giving your life away by serving others. When you're giving to others, to your planet, and to your Source, you're being purposeful. Whatever it is that you do, if you're motivated to be of service to others while being authentically detached from the outcome, you'll feel on purpose, regardless of how much abundance flows back to you.

6. WHAT ARE YOU SEEKING? You must be what it is that you're seeking. This is a universe of attraction and energy. You can't have a desire to attract a mate who's confident, generous, non-judgmental, and gentle, and expect that desire to be manifested if you're thinking and acting in non-confident, selfish, judgmental, or arrogant ways... What are you seeking? Who are you being? Are they matched? Let's make it so.

7. FACES OF INTENTION Describing the field of intent: Say: "It grows my fingernails, it beats my heart, it digests my food, it writes my books, and it does this for everyone and everything in the universe." There are Seven Faces of Intention: Creativity, Kindness, Love, Beauty, Expansion, Unlimited Abundance, and Receptivity. Say and believe *"I am Creativity, Kindness, Love, Beauty, Expansion, Unlimited Abundance & Receptivity"* Soak into your mind (read out loud):
    How can you be more creative today?
    How can you be more kind today?
    How can you appreciate beauty more today?

How can you embrace the expansion of our universe and grow today?
How can you flow with the unlimited abundance of the world today?
How can you open up to the world more today?

8. IN-SPIRITED If you've ever felt inspired by a purpose or calling, you know the feeling of Spirit working through you. Inspired is our word for in-spirited. What inspires you? When do you feel the Spirit working through you? Let's feel it more. And more... And more...

9. EMPOWERING PEOPLE Choose to be in close proximity to people who are empowering, who appeal to your sense of connection to intention, who see the greatness in you, who feel connected to God, who live a life that gives evidence that Spirit has found celebration through them. This sentiment is echoed throughout the wisdom of all the great teachers.

10. TRUE NOBILITY True nobility isn't about being better than someone else. It's about being better than you used to be. Don't compete. Come from your soul and CREATE. Be you. The best you imaginable.

11. DELETE! Hit the delete button every time fear appears. And ask yourself the question: *"What would I do if I wasn't afraid?!?"* By banishing doubt and trusting your intuitive feelings, you clear a space for the power of intention to flow through.

12. FLOAT The Wright brothers didn't contemplate the staying on the ground of things. Alexander Graham Bell didn't contemplate the non-communication of things. Thomas Edison didn't contemplate the darkness of things. In order to float an idea into your reality, you must be willing to do a somersault into the unconceivable and land on your feet, contemplating what you want instead of what you don't have.

13: GOOD MORNING, THIS IS GOD Good morning, This is God. I will be handling All of your Problems today. I will not need Your help, so have A miraculous day.

Dyer, a prolific author whose first book, *Your Erroneous Zones*, hit the bestseller list in 1976, has made a career of mining topics that include the law of attraction, the power of imagination, losing the ego and living in gratitude. His 37th book: *Wishes Fulfilled: Mastering the Art of Manifestation* is based on an idea from William Blake, "that everything that now exists was once imagined," Dyer said. *"So, if you want something to exist, you must first be able to imagine it."*

Dyer has helped thousand achieve their dreams.

What is he saying:

Believe you already have it, connect with the power of intention directly, be clear about what you want, find like synergies, share, feel wonderful about yourself and believe you can. Open your heart. Reprogram your beliefs and habits that are subconsciously limiting your potential. Ask the Divine to assist and surrender to it. Wayne does however add a new variable to the considerations, namely the type and quality of foods.

Let us summarize his process.

	WEALTH PROCESSES & PROCEDURES: POWER OF INTENTION	
Setting	Engage in meditation, proper foods, avoid low energies, awareness to empowering relations	WD
Setting	Create strong habits, open your heart, develop wisdom, surrender to a bigger force	WD
Setting	Banish doubt, allow God to handle your problems, say yes to life	WD
Process	Come into your self	WD
Assist	Bow to the Divine within you	WD
Process	Connect to service	WD
Process	Define what you are seeking	WD
Process	Act as if the desire is already here	WD
Process	Launch intention: kindness, love, beauty, expansion, unlimited abundance, receptivity	WD
Process	Feel Spirit working through you	WD
Process	Choose to be close to empowering people	WD

18

JOE VITALE
THE ATTRACTOR FACTOR

"Our own doubts and fears are the only things that prevent us from attracting greater wealth or achieving any expansive goal. The vast majority of the work it takes to succeed is internal — dealing with our doubts and fears."

Joe Vitale

In PART One we learned about Dr. Len and Ho'Oponopono. Joe Vitale is his buddy so while Dr Len was travelling teaching and creating health miracles, Joe was, and still is, flogging the world of wealth miracles. He has built a pretty big reputation as the world's only "spiritual" marketer. He is reported to have successfully coached thousands of people, through his seminars, books, DVDs, webinars, and TV/radio appearances, on the Law of Attraction. Thousands of testimonials from all over the world prove Joe's 5-step method for attracting wealth, health, love, and happiness work. It is stated that his system has helped countless people become millionaires and find happiness.

Joe Vitale developed his 5-step system when he went from literally being homeless, living on the streets of Houston, to becoming one the most prolific writers and entrepreneurs. Granted, he has a pretty strong marketing background but it is the published testimonials that say he is credible. Now he is financially independent living the life most only dream about. His life's mission is to help others to do the same.

In his book **The Attractor Factor: 5 Easy Steps for Creating Wealth (2005)** he reveals the keys to what he calls his Attractor Factor:

1. Know what you don't want;
2. Select what you do want;
3. Clear all negative or limiting beliefs;
4. Feel what it would be like to have, do, or be what you want;

5. **Let go as you act on your intuitive impulses, & allow the results to manifest.**

Joe explains:

1. Know What You DON'T Want This may seem counter to what some say. Some say always focus on the positive. Always look on the bright side of things. Be grateful and always look for things to appreciate. This is good advice. Being appreciative and grateful will definitely open you up to have more things to appreciate and be grateful for. It's a simple (though, at times maybe not easy) way to put a 'positive spin' on the Law of Attraction and create more good in your life.

But when your life is less than ideal, when you don't have things that you want, or when you're struggling in any area of your life, you can USE these conditions beneficially. You can use them to gain clarity. That's why you want to ACKNOWLEDGE them: You can use them like a springboard to take you to the Next Step. So, while being grateful and appreciative for things, also recognize what you DON'T want, and even list them out. What are the things in your life that are less than ideal? What are the things in your life you DON'T want?

- I don't want to be short of money.
- I don't want to struggle.
- I don't want all the stress I'm feeling.
- I don't want to be arguing, especially with the people I'm closest to.
- I don't want to be unhealthy and out of shape.
- I don't want to have to beat myself up to get healthy or into shape.
- I don't want to be unhappy with myself.

2. Know What You Want Now that you have your list of Don't Wants, use the list to create your Wants. All you need to do is turn them around and state the opposite positive condition you want. For example:

- I want plenty of money.
- I want to be enjoying life and feeling good with what I do.
- I want to be feeling relaxed, at ease and in the flow.
- I want my relationships to be harmonious, mutually beneficial, loving and kind. I want to be at peace and enjoying my relationships.
- I want to be healthy and fit and feel good in my body.
- I want to enjoy the process of getting fit and healthy and feeling good, and maintaining this condition.
- I want to be happy with myself.

3. Get Clear This step is all about 'getting out of your own way. It's all about recognizing the 'counter beliefs' you have, the 'limiting beliefs' that prevent you from having what you want. (Note: If you didn't have any limiting beliefs, you'd probably already have what you want.) Here are some examples:

- I don't deserve it.
- I'll have to work too hard to get it.
- It's not possible for me to have it.
- I'm better off without it.

To me, there's a very EASY way you can tell if you have a 'limiting belief' about something you want, and this will tie in with the next step. To see if you have limiting beliefs about something you want, just notice how you FEEL when you think about what you want. If you don't EASILY feel some very good feelings, if instead you feel unwanted feelings – doubt, fear, guilt, shame, anger, etc., you probably have some unlimited belief(s) you need to clear.

One of Joe's famous quotes:

"Our own doubts and fears are the only things that prevent us from attracting greater wealth or achieving any expansive goal. The vast majority of the work it takes to succeed is internal — dealing with our doubts and fears."

I can't go into all the details of HOW to get clear of your limiting beliefs in this short article. There are many books, programs, methods, exercises, CDs, DVDs and extensive seminars that have been produced on how to get clear of your limiting beliefs. But however you do it, this is a crucial step, one that needn't be completed perfectly, but the MORE you get clear, the EASIER your manifestation experiences will be.

4. Feel What It's Like To Already Have What You Want. If you have taken care of most of your limiting beliefs it will make this step much easier and mostly, if not completely enjoyable. This is just like it says, but it's something for you to DO. It's a kind of inner practice or routine, -- an Innercise, as opposed to Exercise -- that helps keep your inner mind, your subconscious, attuned to and focused on bringing you what you want, in the easiest, most effortless, happy, loving and peaceful ways. Simply, you need to practice feeling what it's like to already have what you want.

Using the examples above, you need to:

- Practice feeling what it's like to have plenty of money.
- Practice feeling worthy and deserving.
- Practice feeling what it would be like to be in the flow, happily, peacefully and easily creating and attracting and having and maintaining what you want.
- Practice feeling what it feels like to know that what you want is very possible, or something even BETTER.
- Practice feeling how you'll feel even BETTER having what you want.
- Practice feeling happy with yourself, now.
- Practice feeling loving, approving, appreciative and grateful for yourself, being the person you really want to be.

And, if you find you have trouble with this step then realize that you probably need to work more on Step 4 of Getting Clear. Ideally, you want to get to where this step of feeling how you want to feel will be easy and effortless. Ideally, you'll be able to think of what you want and easily and effortlessly FEEL the wonderful feelings of having what you want, even if it's nowhere to be seen in your current physical reality.

5. Let Go This step is about detachment, or not being attached to the outcomes you want. And, again, if you've done the previous steps this one will be effortless. This is because, if you've done the previous steps you will realize that life, just as it is, no matter how it appears on the outside, is already wonderful and complete and worth living and enjoying.

Letting go means not being concerned about 'how' what you want is going to show up in your life. To me, it also entails being open to 'something even better.' In other words, not only are you unattached to the outcome, you are also completely open to 'something even better' or better ways to have what you want showing up in your life. I have a quote of someone who seems to me to exemplify the attitude of someone who is living freely, unattached to outcomes, open and ready to receive and act when the time comes.

"I am the happiest man alive. I have that in me that can convert poverty to riches, adversity to prosperity and I am more invulnerable than Achilles, [mis]fortune hath not one place to hit me." Sir Thomas Browne (1642)

What is it that Sir Thomas had in him that could convert poverty to riches, adversity to prosperity, etc.? Of course, he had somehow learned or taught himself to think, believe and act constructively, no matter what.

So, that's the basics of Joe's 5 Steps, the steps that took him from broke (and worse) to rich, free and happy.

One more thing maybe worth mentioning: You've ALREADY taken these 5 steps, probably many times, though you may not have been aware of them. And, probably, mostly without knowing it, you've unwittingly used these 5 Steps to create exactly what you DIDN'T WANT. You have to begin considering that The Law of Attraction was actually working but your energy and focus was on the wrong things; namely what <u>you didn't want</u> in your life.

And also, with anything good or bad you've already created, you might be able to go back now and notice something: With the ones that came easily you probably unknowingly completed all the steps. And the ones that involved struggle were the ones you probably missed a step or two. Now you know there is a lesson in keeping toxic crap of what you don't want in your mind! Now you can lessen the struggle and increase the flow, peace and joy.

Joe says: *"I've enjoyed writing this, and learned something just as I wrote it. I've learned that the steps intertwine and build on each other. I hope it benefits those who read it. Making your life more like you want it to be is not so mysterious. It's really about realizing what you're already capable of being and doing, and being it, and doing it more effectively."*

"When you vigorously reject the concept of personal limitations and become enthusiastic about your own self it is astonishing what new qualities will suddenly appear within you. You can then do and be what formerly would have seemed quite impossible." Norman Vincent Peale

Remember to breathe.

Joe's 7 Ways to Attract Money

That book was in 2005. In 2008, Joe brought an update on ways to attract money. Like the other gurus of Hill, Dyer, Joe has other "lessons" on bringing the energy of money to you as he is a firm believer in the Law of Attraction.

1. Give money away.
It sounds counter-intuitive but the more you give, the more you will receive (unless you block the receiving, which ties into the next step). Give openly and freely to wherever you received spiritual nourishment. Give on a regular basis, too. The rule of thumb is to give 10% of whatever you receive, but it's

also smart to give more when you feel inspired to do so. Remember, you don't have to give to a church; give to the person, place, or group that has kept your spirit alive. Just ask *"Where was I most inspired today?"* and give to *that* source. And ask the question daily or weekly as the source will often change.

2. Get clear.
Most people push money away with their hidden limiting beliefs, such as "money is bad" or "rich people are evil." Those are beliefs, not facts. Get clear of them and money will come to you (as long as you also do the next step).

3. Take action.
Too many people sit and wait for money to materialize in front of them. I believe in magic and miracles, but I also believe that your role in the process of attracting money is to actually *do something* to bring it your way. Act on your ideas. Now. "Money likes speed" is my favorite mantra. If you don't act now, you'll see your idea manifested in a store some day and somebody else will be attracting money from it.

4. Support a cause.
Most people push money away because they don't feel they deserve it. One way around this (while you still work on getting clear inside yourself) is to want money for a larger purpose. I created Operation YES to end homelessness. Raising hundreds of thousands of dollars (or more) for that cause will remove any remaining prosperity limitations within me. While I won't receive a dime from Operation YES, my working on its behalf will attract money to me in other ways, such as the contacts and goodwill I'll create. In short, want money for a larger reason than your own ego.

5. Get support.
One of the wisest things you can do to achieve any goal is create or join a master mind group devoted to it. I co-authored *Meet and Grow Rich* with Bill Hibbler for this reason. Attending a seminar can give you the same result.

6. Be grateful.
This is huge. Be thankful for the money you have — which is probably considered true wealth by people starving in third world countries — and you'll begin to attract more money. Gratitude sends off a signal of appreciation, which brings to you more to be thankful for. Begin with whatever is in this moment that you can be sincerely grateful for.

7. Do what you love.
There's no sense in working at something you hate. If you are currently at a job you don't like, find a way to enjoy it for the time you are there while working towards doing your passion. Following your passion is the greatest secret of all when it comes to attracting wealth. Everyone from Donny Deutsch to Donald Trump to Bill Gates to little ole me agree that passion (combined with the other steps above) is your ticket to financial freedom. Finally, expect success.

The mindset of *expectation,* expecting that you are now attracting money and playfully looking around, asking *"I wonder where and how big money will come from to me today?"* — will keep your brain turned on to seek and find opportunities. You of course then have to take fearless action when you see them.

What is Joe saying here? Know what you want, get clear, feel you have it, allow the universe to create it for you. Thank the Universe for giving it. And he has some more advice for those who are not creating their dreams:

1. Forgive yourself for not attracting
2 Wake up from the victim scarcity notions
3. Give from the heart
4. Use appreciation and gratitude to feel better
5. Don't learn from the past, learn and let go
6. Remove counter beliefs
7. Let the Universe create it for you

	WEALTH PROCESSES & PROCEDURES: ATTRACTOR FACTOR	
Setting	Clear out all limiting beliefs	JV
Setting	Believe you are deserving and worthy, take action to do something	JV
Setting	Give money away so you can receive, support a cause of good will, give from the heart	JV
Setting	Know what you do not want, do what you love, join a group with similar minds	JV
Process	Get clear on what you want	JV
Process	Become highly passionate as it is the greatest secret	JV
Process	Forgive yourself for not attracting your desires	JV
Process	Feel what it would be like to have, do, or be what you want	JV
Process	Let go and detach from the outcome	JV
Process	Feel what it is like to already have what you want	JV
Process	Let go as you act on your intuitive impulses, and allow the results to manifest	JV
Process	Be grateful that the desire is already in your possession	JV
Assist	Let the Universe create for you	JV

19

ESTHER AND JERRY HICKS
THE LAW OF ATTRACTION

"The essence of that which is like unto itself, is drawn."
Esther Hicks

The next Gurus in this game of creating wealth and health in 3D is a pair which say they get their wisdom on this topic from Abraham. Their teachings suggest that it is the thoughts that are the creators of things in 3D reality. They add a spiritual dimension and highlight the importance of creating that energy that attracts the end result.

They have brought to thousands of people The Law of Attraction which says, *"The essence of that which is like unto itself, is drawn."* These teachings according to Esther Hicks come from Abraham who is suggested as *"infinite intelligence"*. We will now cover this belief system that they teach. Their programs given around the world are very focused on shifting that old subconscious belief system by way of repetitive conscious statements such as:

1. You Are a Physical Extension of That Which is Non-physical.
All-That-Is, or that which you call God, is not finished and waiting for you to catch up. You are the leading edge of thought, here seeking more: more of all that feels good to you, more of that which is fresh and gloriously uplifting. You are, in essence, bringing heaven to earth.

2. You Are Here in This Body Because You Chose to Be Here.
You chose the opportunity to experience this delicious contrast in time and space, and with great anticipation you came to co-create with other joy-

seeking Beings, to fine-tune the process of deliberate thought. What, where, when and with whom you create are your choices, too.

3. The Basis of Your Life is Freedom; the Purpose of Your Life is Joy.
You are free to choose to discover new avenues for your joy. In your joy you will grow; and in your growth you add to the expansion of All-That-Is. However, you are also free to choose bondage or pain... but everything anyone chooses is only because they believe it will help them feel better.

4. You Are a Creator; You Create With Your Every Thought.
By the Universal Law of Attraction, you are attracting the essence of whatever you are choosing to give your attention to — whether wanted or unwanted. And so, you often create by default. But you can know by how your emotion feels if what you are attracting (creating) is what you are wanting or if it is not what you are wanting. Where is your attention focused?

5. Anything That You Can Imagine is Yours to Be or Do or Have.
As you ask yourself why you want it, the essence of your desire is activated, and the Universe begins to bring it to you. The more intense your positive feelings, the faster it is coming to you. It is as easy to create a castle as a button.

6. As You Are Choosing Your Thoughts, Your Emotions Are Guiding You.
Your loving Inner Being offers guidance in the form of emotion. Entertain a wanted or unwanted thought, and you feel a wanted or unwanted emotion. Choose to change the thought and you have changed the emotion — and you have changed the creation. Make more choices in every day.

7. The Universe Adores You for it Knows Your Broadest Intentions.
You have chosen to come to earth with great intentions, and the Universe constantly guides you on your chosen path. When you are feeling good, you are, in that moment, allowing more of that which you have intended from your broader perspective. You are Spirit Incarnate.

8. Relax into Your Natural Well-Being. All is Well (Really It Is!).
The essence of all that you appreciate is constantly flowing into your reality. As you find more things to appreciate, your state of appreciation opens more avenues, to more for which you feel appreciation. (As you think, you vibrate. As you vibrate, you attract).

9. You Are a Creator of Thoughtways on Your Unique Path of Joy.
No one can limit where you can direct your thought. There are no limits to your joyous journeys to experience. On the path to your happiness you will discover all that you want to be or do, or have. (Allowing others their experiences allows you yours).

10. Actions to Be Taken and Possessions to Be Exchanged
Are By-products of Your Focus on Joy. On your deliberately joyous journey your actions will be inspired, your resources will be abundant, and you will know by the way you feel that you are fulfilling your reason for life. (Most have this one backwards, therefore most feel little joy in their actions or their possessions).

11. You May Appropriately Depart Your Body Without Illness or Pain.
You need not attract illness or pain as an excuse to leave your body. Your natural state — coming, remaining or leaving — is that of health and Well-Being. (You are free to choose otherwise).

These form the foundation for Jerry and Esther's teachings. But the key to their thesis is the Law of Attraction.

There are many, many versions of this Law but best publicized by Esther and Jerry Hicks who state the *Law of Attraction as* **that which is like unto itself, is drawn.**

The Law of Attraction simply says that you attract into your life whatever you think about. The Law of Attraction states that every positive or negative event that happened with you was attracted by you. Say that a special friend loaned you money when you didn't have any. You attracted that, even without your awareness of using the law. Say that teacher, classmate, client, or co-worker gave you a hard time during the day. You attracted that, too. Again, we are using the law every second of every day. You've even attracted reading this article! There are really only three basic steps: ask, believe, and receive. However, the point of this article is to break those three steps down into actions that you can do. Here they are:

1. Relax your mind. Meditate for 5 to 10 minutes. Doing this will increase brain power and have your mind at that relaxed state. This step is optional but recommended.

2. Be sure about what you want and when you do decide don't doubt yourself. Remember that you're sending a request to the Universe which is created by thoughts and therefore responds to thoughts. Know exactly what it is that you want. If you're not clear/sure, the Universe will get an unclear frequency and will send you unwanted results. So be sure it is something you have strong enthusiasm for.

3. Ask the Universe for it. Make your request. Send a picture of what you want to the Universe. The Universe will answer. See this thing as already yours. See How to Visualize. The more detailed your vision, the better. If you're wanting that Nintendo Wii, see yourself sitting down playing a game on it. See yourself feeling the controller, playing your favorite game(s), touching the console. If there's that person you have a crush on, see yourself walking with her/him, touching or caressing the person, or even kissing the person. You get the idea.

4. Write your wish down. Start with "*I am so happy and grateful now that...*" and finish the sentence (or paragraph) telling the Universe what it is that you want. Write it in the present tense as if you have it right now. Avoid negation terms (see Warnings for more on this). Every day until your wish comes true, close your eyes and imagine your desire as if it's happening right now.

5. Feel it. Feel the way you will now after receiving your wish. You must act, speak, and think as if you are receiving it now. This is actually the most important, powerful step in using the Law of Attraction because this is where it starts working, and sometimes if you do this you don't feel like you need it anymore because you FEEL like you already have it! And then the universe will manifest this thought and feeling and you will receive it.

6. Show gratitude. Write down all the things the Universe has given you. Be thankful for what you already have and be thankful for all the things the Universe has given you. The Universe has done a lot of things for us. Paying the Universe back with some gratitude will motivate the Universe to do even more things and will draw more things into your life. If you were once bullied and that person stopped, that's one thing to be thankful for. If the person you're crushing on likes you back, or doesn't but she/he didn't send their lover out to hurt you, that's another thing to thank the Universe for. You should also thank the Universe for this process too. Showing gratitude will turbo boost the Universe to manifest your request faster.

7. Trust the Universe. Imagine an alternate dimension that is almost exactly like the real world but whatever you truly desire comes true in an instant. See yourself in that dimension, where whatever you ask the Universe for comes to you in an instant. Don't *look for* what you asked for; this is where people tend to mess up. If you have to keep an eye out for an event that manifests your wish, it's only telling the Universe you don't have it and you will attract... not having it. Be patient. Don't get upset if these things don't happen immediately. Don't stress the "how" of things. Let the Universe do it for you. When you take the Universe's job of worrying about the "how", this says you're lacking faith and that you're telling the Universe what to do when the Universe has far greater knowledge and power than human mankind.

And here is some more advice on making this work:

If your current reality is bad, try not to think too much about it. Most of the people pay attention to their current reality and attract the same. Focus on what you wish to experience instead. It works.

Try this... if you experience an event that makes you so happy and overjoyed that you want to attract more into your life then try and remember your inner emotion that you had (your heart beating faster/ stomach jumping) whatever it was try and replicate that by remembering the event and then if your vibrational energy is the same as you felt in that joyous moment then it will manifest and you will attract it into your life.

Have a vision board or a picture from a magazine to help you see and feel what you want, look at that picture everyday (better to do this in the morning since this will help you to feel better throughout the day), and focus on emitting happy feelings to the Universe.

Focus as often as you can on what you DO want rather than on what you don't want. For example, if you are angry or upset about a war/conflict that has been going on, do your best to be 'pro-peace' rather than 'anti-war' - focus on the peace, and the kinds of solutions that you would like to see, instead of whatever it is that you do not like about the situation.

Good feelings = good reality. Feel GOOD. Put on your favorite song, paint a picture, have fun with your pet, or think of someone or something that you love something that makes you happy, and just shut your eyes and dwell on this. These can be called Frequency Shifters, so have a few up your sleeve. Different thoughts work for different situations, so think of a few now you can use later.

But there are also some warnings: If you want something to happen, such as you want a bike, don't just say I want that bike; believe you are going to get that bike. Instead of telling yourself you want the bike, envision yourself riding that bike. It doesn't matter whether or not you know when you're going to receive it, just believe you're going to get it and have no doubts about it. If you have any doubts, quickly change your thought pattern to the positive and focus on receiving or having what you want.

You can't have any resistance in your mind, for example: if you have just tried using the law of attraction and you say "*this stuff isn't working*" then the Universe will give you more of "*this isn't working*".

Be careful what you wish for because you just may get it, is not a statement to joke around with. This law is so powerful your request could manifest instantly and powerfully without warning. Remember, this Law could be used to create or destroy.

If you are constantly worried about bad things happening, or negative outcomes, then you are using the law of attraction AGAINST yourself. To worry is really to apply most of the above steps, towards a NEGATIVE outcome. You are visualizing the negative outcome and asking the universe for it with pictures of the negative outcome, you are feeling the feelings of the negative outcome ... Stop Worrying and follow step seven above.

Avoid using those negation terms. For example, if you want to get out of debt and you say "I want to get out of debt," the Universe only sees the word 'debt' and will send more along your way. It pays no attention to negation terms like, 'no', 'not', 'none', 'out' and so forth. Instead say "I am rich/wealthy and have lots of money."

You can't use the Law of Attraction to control people. However, if you have a friend who you haven't seen in a long time and you want her to come to you, nstead of saying "I want my friend to show up at my door," just say, "I want to walk down the street and see her pass by," or something like that.

Ok, that is what Eshter and Jerry say. You are once again seeing the same elements as before, just different marketing attached to the same process. But... and here is the BIG but; they have been doing this for years and even though Jerry has since departed from Leukemia, Esther still carries the same torch and is obviously helping people. Here is our simplified process table.

	WEALTH PROCESSES & PROCEDURES: LAW OF ATTRACTION	
Setting	Believe you are a creator, anything is possible, your purpose joy, relax into well being	JH
Setting	Good feelings are good reality, eliminate any limits or negativity	JH
Process	Relax your mind into a relaxed state	JH
Process	Be sure about what you want	JH
Process	Write your wish down	JH

Process	Visualize your desire	JH
Process	See yourself feeling the result of the desires	JH
Assist	Send your request to ask the Universe	JH
Process	Show gratitude and be thankful for receiving the desire	JH
Process	Have faith and trust the Universe to manifest your desires	JH

20

JOHN KEHOE
MIND POWER

"Everything we can see, hear, touch, taste and smell is made of different wavelengths vibrating at different frequencies."
John Kehoe

For over three decades, **John Kehoe** has earned worldwide recognition for his pioneering work in the field of Mind Power. He is reported to be a warm and energetic teacher, author, socially conscious individual, and proponent of the amazing human potential to transform the world and our lives with our thoughts. John has lectured on every continent and his seminal book, **Mind Power Into the 21st Century**, has topped bestseller lists in over a dozen countries. His teachings relate directly to the powers held within every person to conclusively shape his or her destiny.

In 1975, John Kehoe withdrew to the wooded seclusion of the British Columbia wilderness to spend three years in intensive study and contemplation of the inner workings of the human mind. During this time, Kehoe forged the first straightforward and successful program for developing Mind Power. In 1978, he began traveling and teaching people the principals he had formulated, and the phenomenal success of his speaking tours soon grew to literally encompass the world. Mind Power Into the 21st Century has sold millions of copies, and has become an international bestseller, translated and published in a multitude of languages including, French, German, Japanese, Korean, Russian, Bulgarian, Lithuanian, Italian, and Serbian. John has also written other books, **Money Success & You, A Vision of Power and Glory, The Practice of Happiness and Mind Power for Children** to name a few. -

Let us look into John's wisdom. These are John's words.

Visualization What you focus on, you attract. The reason this is true is simple. Even though we are not consciously aware of it, we live in an immense quantum sea of vibrating energy that is ever responsive **to how**

and **what we think**. Our thoughts are forever trying to express themselves in our lives. Our thoughts are creative forces, and the sooner we realize this, the sooner we can begin designing our lives with clarity and purpose.

How can we use this reality in our lives? Again the answer is simple. Focus daily on what you want. And here is where Mind Power techniques can come to your assistance. The Mind Power system consists of easily learned techniques that help you focus and direct your thoughts. The first technique I want to teach you is visualization.

Visualization is simply mental rehearsal. You create images in your mind of your having or doing whatever it is you want. You repeat these images over and over again. I suggest to my students that they practice this technique for five minutes each day. In your five-minute practice, you use your imagination to see yourself being successful, closing the deal, having the relationship, healing the illness—whatever the goal is that you wish to manifest. The key to remember when visualizing is to always visualize that you already have the thing you want. This is a mental trick. You don't hope you'll achieve it, or build confidence that some day it will happen. No, with the visualization technique you "live and feel it" as if it is happening to you now. Now on one level you know this is just a mental trick, but here is an important truth to understand. The subconscious mind cannot distinguish between what is real and what is imagined. Your subconscious will act upon the images you create within, regardless of whether those images reflect your current reality or not.

Does it work? Ask Arnold Schwarzenegger. *"It's all in the mind,"* says Arnold, who is five-time winner of the Mr. Universe title, a successful real estate tycoon, movie star, and past governor of California. Arnold has it made, but it wasn't always so. Arnold can remember when he had nothing except a belief that his mind was the key to getting where he wanted to go.

Arnold goes on: *"The mind is really so incredible. Before I won my first Mr. Universe title, I walked around the tournament like I owned it. I had won it so many times in my mind, the title was already mine. Then when I moved on to the movies I used the same technique. I visualized daily being a successful actor and earning big money."*

What worked for Arnold will work for you. I know this because I have taught this system to millions of people worldwide and have seen the results. It's not magic and it doesn't happen overnight, but if you persist in your vision, you will achieve it. What you focus on, you attract

Affirmations Another technique of Mind Power is that of affirmations. Affirmations are statements that you say either out loud or quietly to yourself. You affirm to yourself whatever it is you want to happen. For example, if you have an important interview coming up, you could affirm to yourself, "*A great interview,*" and you would repeat this statement over and over again for several minutes. Or, let's say you're recovering from a leg injury, you could repeatedly say to yourself, "*I have strong and healthy legs.*"

Why do affirmations work? They work because whatever you verbally repeat to yourself will influence your thoughts. Say to yourself, "*A great interview,*" and you will automatically begin thinking about your upcoming interview as "*a great interview.*" Repeat to yourself, "*I have strong and healthy legs,*" and your mind will begin imagining strong and healthy legs. And what you focus your mind on, you attract, so begin focusing on whatever it is you want.

Now let me give you three simple rules to remember when using affirmations:

1. Always affirm in the positive. Make your affirmation a positive statement. Avoid asking yourself, "*What happens if it's a terrible interview?*" or saying to yourself, "*I'm so nervous.*" These statements focus on what you don't want to occur. If you want to be confident, use that word in your affirmation. If you want to be dynamic, use that word. Use the words that reflect what you want to happen. Be specific.

2. Make your affirmation short and simple. Use a phrase or at maximum one sentence. Your affirmation should be like a mantra that you can repeat over and over again without even thinking about it. Don't ramble on.

3. Don't force yourself to believe it, just say it. All you have to do is repeat it over and over again and the affirmation will quite naturally have an affect. After all, you don't force yourself to believe that the medication your doctor has given you will work. You just take the prescribed dosage and assume it will. So too with affirmations; just repeating the statement many times will cause it to work for you.

Affirmations are simple, easy to use and very powerful. Many professional athletes use them to perform well on the field. Successful business people use them to close deals and run their businesses. Artists use them to be creative and come up with innovative ideas. You can use them too, in any area of your life. Now repeat after me, *"I am successful, confident and achieve my goals. I am successful, confident and achieve my goals. I am successful, confident and achieve my goals"*.

Acknowledging There is an old maxim that says, *"Nothing succeeds like success."* And it's true: a success vibration acts like a magnet that attracts success and opportunities to you. When you *"think and feel success,"* you vibrate with success energy and act accordingly.

Those of you who are already successful, you have momentum on your side; the law of attraction is already working for you. You are attracting to yourself even greater success because of the nature of your predominant thoughts. Your success vibration is a great asset to you. Those of you who are struggling and not yet successful, don't despair; you too can create the same success vibration using the technique of "acknowledging."

The acknowledging technique begins with searching for areas of your life where you are already successful. Unfortunately most of us are quicker to see our own failures and shortcomings than we are to acknowledge our achievements and successes. To create a success vibration you must change this self-defeating habit and become success-focused. Examine your personal qualities and present situation and find things to feel successful about. Can't find anything? Look again. Are you a loving parent? Are you a good friend to someone? Do you have certain skills? Are you positive? Do people enjoy your company? Are you generous? Do you dress well? Are you a safe driver? You are not limited to the narrow definition of success as someone who is rich, famous and good-looking. There are literally hundreds of other aspects of your life that are equally important. The key is to find aspects that help us feel successful in our life. Doing this creates a success vibration.

You can also look to your past and acknowledge yourself for past achievements. *"But that's the past,"* you might argue. It doesn't matter; you can use anything, past or present, to make yourself feel successful. I suggest that you reflect upon your life and make yourself an acknowledging list—ten or fifteen attributes that make you feel successful. Spend five minutes every day reading this list over and acknowledging your positive traits, feeling successful. Let these elements seep into your consciousness.

An acknowledging list can be either general or specific. For example, let's say you're going to a job interview for a sales position. You might make a specific acknowledging list that highlights the particular qualities you possess which will help you succeed in such a position, such as: I'm a good communicator, I have great people skills, and I'm organized, and so on. By focusing on this list you are building a specific success vibration. But the same principle works whether you're closing a million-dollar deal or getting an entry-level job or finding that perfect partner. Create a success vibration and you will attract success. What are you waiting for? Get started today.

Everything is energy. Everything we can see, hear, touch, taste and smell is made of different wavelengths vibrating at different frequencies. Our brain is like a translator that has the ability to interpret these frequencies into what we perceive to be our physical reality. So we interpret an energy cluster as a chair, or a tree, or another person. We perceive them as physical or solid, but break them down to their smallest particles and they're all just energy. There are non-physical energies as well, of course. Our thoughts, for example, are just different vibrations.

Every time you think a thought, you send out that thought's specific vibration. If a thought makes you feel good, if it's a "positive" thought, it is vibrating at a higher frequency. If a thought makes you feel bad, if it's a "negative" thought, it's vibrating at a lower frequency. So, "I hate you" has a much lower frequency than "I love you", for example.

The more focus you give to a thought, the more thoughts of the same vibration will join it. This is the Law of Attraction in action - like attracts like. As the vibration grows, it becomes stronger, more stable, and more able to attract other, equal frequencies. The more attention you pay to a subject, the easier it becomes to think about it, and the more evidence you see in your world supporting your thoughts about it. If you think the world is a terrible place and spend a lot of time watching negative news, looking for horrible and sad stories in the paper and spending hours talking to others about how the world is going downhill, more stories supporting this world view will literally find you. Whenever you meet someone who thinks the world is a wonderful place, they're probably going to annoy you - the energy of their thoughts is completely foreign to you.

The thoughts you think form a collective vibration. Some of your thoughts are more negative and some are more positive, but the majority of your thoughts are going to be in pretty much the same range. If you think predominantly positive thoughts, your overall vibration is going to be higher than if you think predominantly negative thoughts. And this collective vibration will affect what thoughts or vibrations you have access to. If you are a predominantly negative person, you'll have a very hard time thinking a cheery, sunshiny, happy puppy thought. It's not *impossible*, but it's very difficult.

So, are we then merely a collection of our thoughts? No, not really. Who we are is pure, positive energy. Our natural state is one of high vibration. So, if you have no thoughts, as in the state of meditation, you will naturally return to that high frequency. Any thought which deviates from this high vibration, however, will have the effect of bringing your overall vibration down.

The thing to remember, though, is that we have the ability to deliberately choose which thoughts to think. We do not have to be at the mercy of our thoughts, letting them determine our collective vibrations. We can change our energies at any time.

There are many ways to raise your vibration:

- **Meditate**. When you meditate, you stop thinking, including limiting and negative thoughts. This allows your vibration to rise. While your vibration will not be permanently reset to the new higher vibration achieved in the meditative state, it will also not return completely to where it was when you started. Just twenty minutes a day will gradually change your vibrational set point to a higher and higher frequency.

- **Do something that makes you really happy**. Happiness and joy vibrate at a much higher frequency than almost any other emotion. When you're in a state of happiness, you cannot also be in a state of depression, anger or frustration. Find something that makes you happy, even for just a few minutes a day, and do that. Play with a child, take a bath, dance to your favorite song, kiss your significant other like you did when you first started dating, play a video game, for example.

- **Breathe**. Breathing deeply and slowly will raise your vibration. You can do this anywhere and anytime you need a bit of relief.

- **Take a nap.** When you sleep, you naturally return to a high vibrational state. Your body and mind get some relief from all the heavy vibrations you're carrying around. Taking even a short nap, will help you to reset your vibration. You'll generally wake up feeling better than you did when you lay down.

Try to incorporate several of these methods into your day. Start slowly and take it easy with this. If you miss a day of meditation, for example, don't beat up on yourself (this would lower your vibration). Do the best you can, and choose whichever methods make you feel best. How do you know if you're doing it right? You'll feel better. You'll be more relaxed. Things won't bother you as much. And the world will just seem to become a little prettier every day.

And you can work your way up the emotional scale one "issue" at a time, such as in the one used by Abraham Hicks below showing the emotional scale.

Level of Control	Responsibility	Emotions	Thoughts	Appearance*
Full Control	It's MY doing that things are good.	Joy/ Knowledge/ Empowerment/ Freedom/ Love/ Appreciation/ Passion/ Enthusiasm/ Eagerness/ Happiness	I can do it! I WILL do it! I can't wait to get out there and do it!!! I love myself! I love my life!	😊
	It's Fate's doing that things are good.	Positive Expectation/ Belief/ Optimism/ Hopefulness/ Contentment	Things can get better. Good things do happen in the world. If other people can do it, maybe so can I.	🙂
	Neutral.	Boredom	Neutral.	😐
	It's Fate's fault that things are bad.	Pessimism/ Frustration/ Irritation/ Impatience/ Overwhelment/ Disappointment/ Doubt/ Worry	Bad things just happen. That's just the way it is. The world is a bad place. Might as well accept it.	🙁
	It's THEIR fault that things are bad.	Blame/ Discouragement/ Anger/ Revenge/ Hatred/ Rage/ Jealousy	It's all their fault. If other people weren't so selfish, I could have more. Why does nobody care about me??	😠
No Control	It's my fault that things are bad.	Insecurity/ Guilt/ Unworthiness/ Fear/ Grief/ Depression/ Despair/ Powerlessness	It's all my fault. Nobody loves me because I'm unlovable. There's nothing I can do. I hate myself.	😢

*for those who'd rather look at pictures. :o)   www.deliberatereceiving.com

But the most important thing to remember is that you have the power to choose your thoughts and therefore you have the power to change your vibration and how you feel. Make a commitment to yourself today that you will no longer put up with not feeling good, not being who you really are. Reclaim your power and deliberately choose to feel the way you were always meant to; because, you are supposed to feel good. It's your natural state. All you have to do is allow yourself to return to it.

What is John telling us?

If you read this in terms of what we have already discussed, John is revealing a process of reprogramming the subconscious. By repetition of words, through assertions, by imagining the bliss of the results, by pumping your conscious mind full of these desires, you are in effect writing or rewriting the programs stuck in your subconscious. You are by repetition, changing your beliefs that something IS possible and that you ARE worthy, and you are bombarding the subconscious in an environment of well being positive morphic energy until it literally gets its shit together and changes the program. You are actually being a Divine Programmer but you are not working on your body physics, you are working on your environmental reality.

Here is a summary of steps:

	WEALTH PROCESSES & PROCEDURES: MIND POWER	
Setting	Believe you attract reality, your are energy, what you focus on you attract	JK
Setting	Raise vibrations: meditate, be joyful, breathe, nap, choose positive thoughts	JK
Process	Create images in your mind over and over	JK
Process	Affirm to yourself out loud what you want, in a short simple way over and over	JK
Process	Always affirm the positive	JK
Process	Visualize your desire	JK
Process	See yourself feeling the emotional result of the desires	JK
Assist	Send your request to ask the Universe	JK
Process	Show gratitude and be thankful for receiving the desire	JK
Process	Have faith and trust the Universe	JK

21

THE LAW OF CAUSE AND EFFECT

"Good deeds bring good results. Bad deeds bring bad results. Your own deeds bring your own results."

Buddha

Do these Processes all work? Have people achieved results? Yes! All the time? No.

Why?

The gurus haven't figured it out.

Figured what out?

How to create a true law where it works all the time.

Of course the degree of clarity, emotion, belief, determination, and complexity all make a difference. But that is the same in business. Some fail, others don't.

And can we really expect the Universe to pay the bills and take care of our health and wealth? Obviously not yet... even the gurus like Jerry Hicks and it seems Wayne Dyer suffer from things like Leukemia. However, one has to understand that their life path, their contracts, their residual karma, and many other factors besides a stubborn subconscious can have an effect on the results.

But like the existence of miracle healings, we cannot take away the fact that these gurus all have a pretty long list of testimonials. What is pretty consistent here is that all these gurus admit that we **already create our own reality**. And there is no distinction to "the Universe" as to whether this is bad or good, positive or negative resultant reality. The estimates on the number of thoughts per day is 50,000-70,000 thoughts! Over a year that's around 18 million and over 50 years we are near a billion thoughts. If thoughts create reality wow, that's a lot of things to happen!

The truth of this matter so far is that there is really nothing new here at all from when Napoleon Hill published his Think and Grow Rich process. He does not solicit assistance from a Higher Power because he is saying that YOU already have the power. It is easy to understand that we all certainly choose our own perception of reality but is this true of our physical reality? It has always been the clarity of vision (thoughts, visions, and words), the passion of the mission (emotion), the drive of the individual (intent), the building of relationships (engagement) that determines the success or failure of the end reality. And no matter what marketing hype, secret proprietary technique one may attach to this process, there appears to be no law that guarantees it will work.

So many have **an answer** but nobody has **the answer**

Soo…. here is the big question.

Do we create our own reality by choosing the thoughts, visions, plans that become a passionate drive to achieve the resultant reality by **hard effort**?

Or do the thoughts, visions and plans, once energized **attract** the resultant reality?

And the big question; Can we really get God or the Universe to pay our bills?

Before we leave this topic let us see what the experts say about why these processes don't work all the time; so we can learn and modify our processes.

On a life path, there may be many excuses as to why something you desire never comes true:

It may be that your destiny is different,
It may be because your karmic path is different,
It may be that you have a contract to fulfill from before you incarnated,
It may because you have created a backlog of different energies that need to be cleared off first,
It may be that you may not understand the process,
It may be that the time to complete the desire is not yet,
It may be that you are not clear on what you are asking for,
It may be you may not understand the process by which energy and the Law of Attraction really works,

It may be that you do not believe.

Well, that is a lot of ifs. In this process is a law that we are engaging in called the Law of Cause & Effect. It states that absolutely everything happens for a reason. All actions have consequences and produce specific results, as do all inactions. The choices we make are causes, whether they are conscious or unconscious, and will produce corresponding outcomes or effects.

The Law works the same for everyone at all times. Distilled down to the simplest possible terms, this Law states that for every outcome or effect in one's life, there is a specific cause; poor diet and exercise habits result in poor health, constant and uncontrolled spending results in debt and money worries, not putting effort into your key relationships results in poor relationships and all of the associated issues.

Remember that this law is not the same as the Law of Attraction. This is about what you put out (cause) will have a result (effect). *The trick is to know which one you are using at any one point in time, and when you do to use it properly.*

The law can also be applied in the physical sense through examination of Sir Isaac Newton's third Law of Motion, which states that *"for every action, there is an equal and opposite reaction."* If, for example, you were to hold your hand over a candle's flame (the cause) the effect would be that your hand would burn and it would hurt! While this is an extreme example, it serves to illustrate the point very well.

At the point of making this idea of putting your hand over the flame, you made a decision to act on it (cause). You made a choice and then got the result or (effect). The decision you make becomes the cause and the effect is the result of the decision. The same holds true with your personal relationships. If you treat the important people in your life with respect, love, compassion, dignity and honesty (cause), you will most of the time experience loving, solid relationships – which lead to happiness, fulfillment and peace of mind (effect). Most of the time!

The law of Cause and Effect is the foundation of Buddhism and is made up of three essential guidelines:

Good deeds bring good results.
Bad deeds bring bad results.
Your own deeds bring your own results.

Every effect has a cause and a condition. A cause and a condition combine to make an effect. All effects have a cause. All effects have a condition. There are no exceptions.

So if we create our reality this way, it has nothing to do with a Law of Attraction that suggests that a concentrated focus on what we really desire attracts a likeness. It infers that everything will just happen because the Universe will take care of it. That's ok to manifest. But Cause & Effect says you have to do more than sit on your butt to create; you have to do something like taking action when the opportunity arises. That may be a good strategy for trying to get what you want, especially the taking action step, but will that "create your reality"? In other words, what you want will apparently not "just get created" no matter how intensely you focus or how much action you take. But people like Sai Baba can! What are we missing?

The business of taking action does not mean the Universe will simply pay the bills if you sit there forever visualizing the bill paid. The physical reality of the bill does not go away except in the unreal world. And by action, we are back to doing something in the physical like Napoleon Hill said. So you can sit and visualize winning the lotto, but if you don't get off your butt to buy the ticket, how can the possibility even come to you, even if that possibility does exist in the Universe?

Moreover, it won't even occur to you to take action in a reality where what you want is impossible because you have already constructed the "reality". Change your reality by eliminating your limiting beliefs and virtually anything becomes possible.

So what does this suggest? Under The Law of Cause & Effect you instigate a Cause that returns you an Effect. The Law of Attraction is suggesting that you create the effect which is attracted into your reality. What makes more sense is that the Law of Attraction is how you can influence how the reality will occur or what that reality may be, if you get off your butt and choose some alternatives that come before you.

The truly wonderful thing about this law is that by definition then, we should be able to manifest that which we truly want (the effect) simply by exerting the same causes that others before us have exerted and been successful. If you have a desire to be a successful and highly paid businessperson in your chosen field, then you should be able to look back and study what made others, before you, successful. What books did they read, courses did they study, beliefs did they hold, actions did they take?

If you were to emulate the things they did to be successful, you would achieve the same results over a period of time. If, over time, this does not occur, it is likely because there is something different in what you were doing – some vital piece of information that is missing.

There are three action exercises, which you can put in place immediately, to help you get more of what you want:

1. Determine the Cause & Effect relationships in the areas in which you want improvement or success. Identify the specific things you will need to do in order to get the results that you desire. In this aspect having a thorough, proper understanding of yourself and how you work as a person and a good knowledge of your belief systems will go a long way in assisting you to properly understand and use cause and effect.

2. Take action! Make the decision to focus on, and do, the things that other successful people have done in those areas. Half the battle is taking action. It is your ability to actually begin that will set you apart from the majority of the population. In some way fake it until you make it. It will follow through. That is the law, the iron law of human destiny that is!!!!

3. Persevere. If you take action and do the things that others have done, you will eventually get the desired results. Rome was not built in a day and it has taken you a lifetime to get into the position in which you now find yourself. Success takes time, so if it doesn't seem to be working immediately, don't give up! Stay focused, analyse your causes to ensure you are doing the right things; tweak your approach if necessary – you will get the desired results!

When The Law Does Not Work

The Law of Attraction says that we can manifest into reality anything that we can imagine with our minds, and that our vibrational energy must correspond with the thing to be manifested. Until we are a match, it will remain in escrow.

So we should pick the end result and give thanks and rejoice, because the Universe works backwards and will create the reality leading to that end. You might be having the same lack of connection to that statement, or you might relate to it. But, wherever you are, especially in business ventures you have to hang on to that truth, see it, meditate on it, and incorporate it in your life because whatever law is at work here, that is how you will make that million.

Joe Vitale said after Jerry Hicks died of leukemia: *"I drifted away from Jerry and Esther when I realized Abraham's feel good formula was missing a step.* **That's when I began writing about "getting clear" as an essential ingredient to attracting what you wanted.** *I wrote about this in my book,* **The Attractor Factor***, and spoke about it in my audio program,* The Missing Secret. *It's the core of my Miracles Coaching program."*

Steve Pavlina says: Failure experiences with the Law of Attraction can result because:

1. You fail to hold the intention.
Think of intentions like electromagnetic waves that flow out into the universe, as if you're transmitting a radio signal. The universe receives your thoughts and reflects them back to you via the physical universe. **The more thought and emotion you put into your intention, the stronger the wave you're sending out, and the stronger will be the bounce-back reflection**. Failing to hold an intention means you don't put enough energy behind it. The reflection (i.e. the manifestation) may be so weak you can't even detect it. Perhaps the #1 reason people **fail to hold an intention is a lack of persistence**. Physical matter is really just energy, but it's a very dense form of energy. It takes time for our thoughts to manifest here in the physical realm. On other planes of existence, such as in your dreams, matter is much less dense, so your thoughts can manifest far more quickly. In the astral realms your thoughts can manifest instantly. But in the physical universe, reality is more solid, yet it's still powered by intention-manifestation. It just takes more energy to get things moving, so initially it may seem like they aren't moving at all. It isn't unusual to hold an intention religiously for a week or longer and see no apparent results. Then suddenly the floodgates open, and the manifestation comes pouring through.

2. You put no energy behind the intention.
When it comes to intentions, emotion equals energy. If you aren't really passionate about an intention, it's like turning on a flashlight with no batteries. The most powerful intentions are those that will help you manifest joy.

3. You hold a fuzzy intention.
The best intentions are clear and focused. Be specific. General intentions have very little power. Make your intentions like lasers instead of candle flames, and you'll see them manifest much more quickly.

4. You inadvertently cancel the intention.
Every thought is an intention. One of the greatest challenges with intention-manifestation is that you must drop all thoughts that conflict with your desired intention. You cannot hold thoughts like, *"I hate being depressed,"* while intending to be happy. I hate being depressed is an intention to remain depressed. If you want to use intention-manifestation successfully, you must stop acknowledging what you don't want.

5. Your intention conflicts with your beliefs.
If you try to hold an intention that conflicts with your dominant beliefs, that intention will simply fizzle and die. With practice you'll build mental discipline, and you'll find it easier to stay focused on your desires without so much internal resistance.

6. Intentions are polar.
The energy you apply to your intentions also has polarity, much like a battery. It can flow one way or the other way. You'll know you have a strong intentional current when you experience strong emotions. No emotions means you have no current.

When it does not work:

1. Law of Cause & Effect requires intent to act and choose
2. You are not getting clear
3. We fail to hold intention long enough 30 days
4. You need to surcharge with high joyful emotion energy
5. Need more time to manifest in physical realm
6. Intentions are fuzzy and unfocussed
7. You cancel the intention by thought conflicts
8. Intention conflicts with beliefs
9. No strong emotion to create current flow of intention
10. Thought alone is not creative, belief is

So once again, we have the same pattern in the processes. And here we have some added things to learn from and not do.

Now, let us get on with extracting a simple set of steps from these experts' processes.

22

SUBCONSCIOUS MIND POWER AGAIN

"What you believe is what you see. Seeing is believing is a limiting scientific box. Drop it and you can change your life."

Ed Rychkun

Ok, that is a lot of wisdom taken from the secrets to success of some very successful people. So if you seek health and wealth, all the clues are here for you. We have looked at:

Napoleon Hill: Laws of Success
Wayne Dwyer: Power of Intention
Joe Vitale: Attractor Factor
Jerry & Esther Hicks: Law of Attraction
John Kehoe: Mind Power

Here is a summary table of all of them.

	WEALTH PROCESSES & PROCEDURES: THINK AND GROW RICH	
Setting	Have self confidence, definitiveness, habits of saving, initiative	NH
Setting	Have imagination, passion, and enthusiasm	NH
Setting	Show self control, pleasing personality, accurate thinking, concentration	NH
Setting	Know cooperation, profiting by failure, tolerance, harmonize	NH
Process	Fix your mind on the exact amount of money or the final desire	NH
Process	Determine what you intend to give in return	NH
Process	Establish a definite data for completion	NH
Process	Create a definite plan for carrying out the desire	NH
Process	Write a clear concise statement, time, return, and the plan	NH
Process	Read the written statement daily before bed and upon awakening	NH
Process	Have great passion and emotion to succeed	NH
Process	See, feel and believe yourself in possession of the desire	NH
	WEALTH PROCESSES & PROCEDURES: POWER OF INTENTION	

Setting	Engage in meditation, proper foods, avoid low energies, awareness empowering relations	WD
Setting	Create strong habits, open your heart, develop wisdom, surrender to a bigger force	WD
Setting	Banish doubt, allow God to handle you problems, say yes to life	WD
Process	Come into your self	WD
Assist	Bow to the Divine within you	WD
Process	Connect to service	WD
Process	Define what you are seeking	WD
Process	Act as if the desire is already here	WD
Process	Launch intention: kindness, love, beauty, expansion, unlimited abundance, receptivity	WD
Process	Feel Spirit working through you	WD
Process	Choose to be close to empowering people	WD
	WEALTH PROCESSES & PROCEDURES: ATTRACTOR FACTOR	
Setting	Clear out all limiting beliefs	JV
Setting	Believe you are deserving and worthy, take action to do something	JV
Setting	Give money away so you can receive, support a cause of good will, give from the heart	JV
Setting	Know what you do not want, do what you love, join a group with similar minds	JV
Process	Get clear on what you want	JV
Process	Become highly passionate as it is the greatest secret	JV
Process	Forgive yourself for not attracting your desires	JV
Process	Feel what it would be like to have, do, or be what you want	JV
Process	Let go and detach from the outcome	JV
Process	Feel what it is like to already have what you want	JV
Process	Let go as you act on your intuitive impulses, and allow the results to manifest	JV
Process	Be grateful that the desire is already in your possession	JV
Assist	Let the Universe create for you	JV
	WEALTH PROCESSES & PROCEDURES: LAW OF ATTRACTION	
Setting	Believe you are a creator, anything is possible, your purpose joy, relax into well being	JH
Setting	Good feelings are good reality, eliminate any limits or negativity	JH
Process	Relax your mind into a relaxed state	JH
Process	Be sure about what you want	JH
Process	Write your wish down	JH
Process	Visualize your desire	JH
Process	See yourself feeling the result of the desires	JH
Assist	Send your request to ask the Universe	JH
Process	Show gratitude and be thankful for receiving the desire	JH
Process	Have faith and trust the Universe to manifest your desires	JH
	WEALTH PROCESSES & PROCEDURES: MIND POWER	
Setting	Believe you attract reality, you are energy, what you focus on you attract	JK
Setting	Raise vibrations: meditate, be joyful, breathe, nap, choose positive thoughts	JK
Process	Create images in your mind over and over	JK
Process	Affirm to yourself out loud what you want, in a short simple way over and over	JK
Process	Always affirm the positive	JK

Process	Visualize your desire	JK
Process	See yourself feeling the emotional result of the desires	JK
Assist	Send your request to ask the Universe	JK
Process	Show gratitude and be thankful for receiving the desire	JK
Process	Have faith and trust the Universe	JK

What do these world famous "motivators" of wealth tell us over and over?

Be clear, positive, know what you want, see it already achieved and be passionate about it. Each one of these gurus has put a new marketing twist to the same process that we talked about in the first chapters, namely our 7 steps:

1. We form the thought of making a million dollars
2. We form a vision of a company that sells chairs
3. We make a business plan of the company and product
4. We get emotionally excited about the plan/company
5. We launch the intent to execute the business plan
6. We engage others, money, etc. to make it happen
7. We create the chairs/company that enters our reality

Notice however, these top sellers have injected a more and more spiritual aspect to the process. Once again with the exception of Napoleon Hill who does not bring in a higher power (it is YOU) we see that it is important to **believe**, and get some help with the **divine intervention (Universe)** again and again.

Notice that we have moved also from "doing the hard physical work" to "letting the universe" bring the result to you. But the Setting, Process, and Assistance are similar except that one must be repetitive and engage in choices that are now going to be attracted to you. The important difference from PART ONE is that the Universe is not going to create a miracle of a healing desire by Divine Intention; the Universe is going to focus on attracting either the desired result or steps to the desired result over time. But again, we have the same basic steps:

1. change the **belief** of limiting factors
2. create an **environment** of well being of physical and mental health
3. change the **belief** self, your worthiness, your truths
4. be very **clear** on the desire
5. supercharge the desire with **emotion**
6. drop into **lower state** to **reprogram** the subconscious
7. to get into a mode of **feeling good**
8. be **repetitive** and persistent
9. **engage** in the choices that come forward

When we bring our deductions from Part One on miracles forward, we had seven key steps.

0. ALTERED STATE Bring yourself into an altered state by imagining a peaceful place, breathing softly, and becoming present to yourself in the heart.
1. THOUGHT In your thoughts assert your beliefs that you believe in miracle healing, you believe you can heal yourself, you believe you are worthy and you believe in a higher power that will assist you.
2. VISION Visualize clearly in your mind a picture of the healed knee or a situation where it is healed.
3. SPEAK out stating that you are asking for Higher Divine Intelligence assistance to manifest your vision.
4. HEART EMOTION In your imagination feel the result of the knee being completely healed and surround this vision with the joy and bliss of it being so.
5. INTENT With your intention to correct the issue, you state to the area of problem, I love you, I am sorry for creating this issue and the reason for its being, please forgive me, thank you.
6. HIGHER POWER In your mind, connect to a higher power to feel the energy flow into your total being and into your cellular structure to the knee. You can use hands or imagine the flow of healing energy.
7. MANIFEST Feel the gratitude of completion and thank the higher power or those you have called to assist you.

There are several differences here. First, we are creating new realities outside of us, not healing. Second we are doing this by ourselves. Third, we are being told to create habits to create well being, Fourth, we see it may not be instant, repetition and persistence are required. But the basic steps are the same. We still have to trust a higher power to do it. We still require the belief it will be done, we still need to create a clear vision of the desire, surround it with passionate emotion and launch the intention to a higher power to materialize the plan. Only in the case of Napoleon Hill is it critical to modify this process a bit. The big difference here is that Napoleon Hill says you have to get off your butt and engage in the relationships and make choices which come before. In a simple sense, you can go through steps 1 to 4 all you like about winning the Lotto but if you don't engage in the choice of buying a ticket, it ain't going to happen! So learning from the Law of Cause & Effect, when the Law of Attraction brings a choice to you, you must act on it.

So this is NOT the same as a spontaneous healing. It is a drawn out process that relies on depth of belief, perseverance, clarity, strength of passion, and faith in a higher force.

What would our steps, processes and procedures look like for this?

In an environment of well being, believe you are worthy, and positive energy:

0. Bring yourself into an altered state by imagining a peaceful place, breathing softly, and becoming present to yourself in the heart.
1. Assert your beliefs that you are worthy of your desire, you believe you can change your reality, and that the Divine Intelligence will assist you.
2. Visualize clearly in your mind a picture of the desired result.
3. Speak out stating that you are a believer in your ability to manifest your desires and ask for assistance.
4. In your imagination feel the result of the desire being completed and surround this vision with the joy and bliss of it being so.
5. With your intention send the request for the desire/visualization to be completed.
6. In your mind, connect to a higher power or the Universes to assist in the completion.
7. Feel the gratitude of completion and thank the higher power or those you have called to assist you.

Then in an environment of continued well being, faith and trust, repeat the process until you begin to see people, events, and situations come before you and act on these options.

Too simple?

Try it for 30 days on some simple desires and see...

Let us leave you with some final simple answers assuming you are still a skeptic:

You: *"How do you know something is right?"*
Me: *"I say it to be so."*
You: *"How do you create the right attention?"*
Me: *"By bringing something into your mind."*
You: *"How do you go inside to the Heart?"*
Me: *"Anyway you like or just say it to be so."*
You: *"How do you detach from the conscious mind?"*

Me: *"Stop thinking."*
You: *"How do you vibrate with desire?"*
Me: *"Feel the bliss of being perfect."*
You: *"How do you fulfill a desire?"*
Me: *"Form a clear vision of it in your mind."*
You: *"How do you believe without doubt?"*
Me: *"You act in accordance with it."*
You: *"Is there a specific procedure?"*
Me: *"No, it is what works for you."*
You: *"How do you know?"*
Me: *"By launching intent."*
You: *"So how do you know you are doing it properly?"*
Me: *"When it works."*
You: *"How long will that take?"*
Me: *"As long as you take to make it work."*

23

MEASURING BELIEF

"You can do whatever you set your mind to do, assuming you can set your mind."

Ed Rychkun

You may have come to the conclusion that the biggest variable in whether something works or not is the degree of belief. But belief was just some nebulous thing—or was it? How does one know what that belief is stuck in subconscious? Especially when the majority of these were programmed into you in the first 12 years. In managing external energy to better control the things in one's life, one has to create procedures and practices to do this. When you begin to determine the secrets to dealing proactively with the outside (wealth) world, you have to conclude that you have to effectively recode and retrain the belief system until belief—and subconscious—know it as truth and there is no conflict with the conscious mind.

As an example, perhaps when you were a kid, your Dad made a point of telling you that you were not worthy of something you wanted. Your reaction of unworthiness caused certain behaviors to come forward in you. Pity, remorse, anger, sadness, a barrage of physical reactions. So the brain and its buddy the subconscious that got a good shot of negative emotion from your reaction, doing its job of creating perception-response programs, tucked all this away for your future survival. Then one day when you were older and excited about a great job opportunity and an upcoming interview, your conscious mind seemed to be excited, frothing with this great prospect. But during the interview and even with the times before with preparation, behavior, suddenly the worthiness issue surfaced and erratic behavior is created so the whole thing flops. The subconscious sabotaged you and you did not even know it. It said to its little buddy the conscious mind; hey hold on a minute, Pal, this is what I have in my disc drive, so get your little intention out of the way.

Needless to say, quantifying the level of belief is almost impossible. If there was a belief scale of 0 to 100, you could say, at 100 I could levitate but at 0 I have to use a car like the others. Conversely, if I can't levitate then I am surely not at 100. If I am at 100, then I can levitate. Sound silly? It is. But how do you measure belief? There is a book on levitation where it studied 350 cases of well documented levitation so obviously it can be done. It sounds crazy but levitation is one of those higher functions that we expand to as we raise vibrations. It is real despite what science says. Have you ever seen a fourth degree martial artist put his hands through bricks because he sees his fingers go through the bricks and simply knows he can? Is that not the strength of the belief system?

To strengthen belief is like convincing yourself to quit a bad habit. It needed attention, focus, and discipline to create a new routine that got rid of the old habits and began to reinforce new beliefs. Now, if you can do this quickly, great, but most folks cannot. You first have to put the flaps of your current belief boxes down and open the mind to new possibilities, just as you have to train the mind to entangle in the quantum level and manifest new possibilities.

This is an answer to re-conditioning the belief side and slowly converting all the energy around to behave and manifest a different way. But it did not solve a really big issue of health. .

As we have seen in the first part of this book, there were common elements to healing miracles but none of the methods were consistently successful. The common variable was the strength of the belief system.

But we will explore in PART THREE subtle energies to understand how they exist naturally in the quantum world of invisible wave forms at different frequencies of vibration. Matter does not exist the way we thought. We are made of ever changing fields of energy which intersect with one another to create our world of possibilities not certainties. Quantum energy exists either as visible particles or invisible waves. The particles can be in one place, two places or several at once but still act as connected.

Quantum particles can communicate with themselves at different points in time not limited by past, present or future—only now and here, just like subconsciousness. Now is all they know about. Obviously some intelligent force is holding the particles of you and me together just right. It is like the force of magnetism that works a specific way.

The universe of thought, images, words, emotion and belief are simply quantum energy waves waiting to change form into visible particles. What can do that? Belief and intent can do that. Changes in belief, means programming the subconscious. Miracles are a result of the belief programs that bypass the limitations of science.

The Wiezmann Institute of Science has been studying what is known as the Observer Effect. They conclude we change the reality by watching it. We are connected with everything from cells in the body to atoms of our world. Our experience of consciousness expressed as a feeling and belief is doing the connecting—we are participants. We are connected at this quantum wave level where everything exists because we have not yet chosen the infinite possibilities that make things look real. Do the placebo effect that bypasses surgery and millions of miracle healings not illustrate this clearly? This is very hard to comprehend; that we are living in a world so real and diverse that is effectively imagined by collective and individual consciousness! But this is what science is so befuddled about.

But let us look at this problem of belief. We must believe in belief for it to have the power in our lives. Faith and belief are used interchangeably but faith is to trust as a firm belief in something for which there is no proof. Belief is a conviction of the truth of some statement of reality or some phenomenon with evidence.

This sets the two apart as much as science and spirit. Belief is the certainty that comes from accepting what we think is true in our minds, coupled with what we feel is true in our hearts. Belief is the very stuff that makes our universe. It is the language that touches the quantum stuff of our bodies and our world and appears to create it. It is through the deepest beliefs that limits of physical time are a thing of the past. Beliefs are not right or wrong, do or don't. It is the acceptance of what we have witnessed, experienced or have known for ourselves.

Belief holds the key to the single most powerful energy in the universe; ability to change our lives, bodies and our world by choice. Beliefs must travel through a medium beyond our bodies to the quantum level that connects all. Beliefs must rearrange the atoms to pick a possibility in order to make something physical that we observe. We do it all the time and we witness what it can do. But we have not learned to understand it and manage it.

And because there is no time in that world—it all simply exists—we must also believe as if that which we need already exists as well. And the most charge given to that belief is when you add the emotion of the heart in line with the other quantum energy generators in the body. That is what changes things at the core level. It is what changes the state of the atom from invisible wave to visible atom.

We will take you into the subtle world of the heart in PART THREE. We know that when placed in an external field, (magnetic) the energy of the atom changes. The heart field radiates out and connects the world to create belief waves; belief of matter translation converting perceptions of experience and imagination into coded language of waves that communicate beyond the body.

But if you have a consciousness that is projecting 12,000 to 50,000 thoughts per day, how can any order come of what all those thoughts are representing? What will come out are those that are strong, aligned and focused in line with your beliefs. So if you spend a lot of time worrying about your health or the IRS getting you, guess what you are reinforcing at the quantum level?

Belief is a form of feeling. Your emotions can reflect a belief without knowing it. And you have no idea how strong it can be. Like resonance, it is an exchange of energy. Pick a string on a guitar and the same string will vibrate on a guitar across the room. It is like the resonance of the words, or eye contact, or the merger of hearts reflecting "I love you". If you experience resonance, you believe it is true. Goose bumps, ringing, and flushing are similar body truths from the chakra centers. The opposite signals are cold sweat, pasty face, and weakness where the body knows of danger.

Well, the whole idea of belief and measuring the strength of it is hardly a cold hard science but one could easily conclude that if you do not have the degree of belief you need for a miracle then the miracle won't happen. And the converse is just as ridiculous. It is that if the miracle didn't happen, then your belief wasn't strong enough. Although ironically this may be true, it does not help a hell of a lot. How could one figure out what their beliefs really were? Well, as it turns out, there actually are always things happening in the body and mind that tell you what is true and what is not. Some people simply "know" like a gut feel or intuition that subconsciously they do not believe. For sure you have had encounters with many stubborn people who simply state *"miracles are pure horseshit"* or *"how could anyone be so stupid as to consider miracles as real?"* Needless to say this type would not be reading this book. But there are many who simply cannot verify what that disc drive holds.

How Do You Test Belief?

In studying this, a rather incredible simple process called Muscle Testing—Kinesiology is relevant. It is a means of measuring communications to the subconscious to see if it believes what you are saying, feeling or thinking. It gets to that set of programs that are resident in the subconscious—the ones we have spent our lives putting in place.

Muscle testing works like a lie detector does. Here is the background. The subconscious controls the autonomic nervous system. It is responsible for physical functions and sends signals for a task from the brain. It is like having a set of bio-computer programs for running, walking, and other motor functions. When the subconscious decides to do something as a result of conscious, unconscious or automatic signals, it loads the appropriate program that you have learned, and it signals the brain to get the appropriate muscle/chemical actions going.

The strength of the signals from the brain determines the strength in the muscle response. When the mind holds a stressful thought, a conflict is created in the brain and the signal strength is reduced. The same happens when you make a statement that the subconscious disagrees with. It is not that it sits there like a judge and jury. It does not judge and it only knows what it has been programmed to know as your personal "truth". So the subconscious does a quick hard drive check to see what it has recorded and to see if a known or unknown (true or false) condition exists. If false, it causes a weakened response in the muscles as they are "confused" just like in a lie detector test. The process is simply true or false. Well, the great news is we can test this truth.

The body is not as much of a liar as the conscious mind is. If the body does not like something, you get a reaction. It is the judge in the system as your body will react a negative or positive way. The conscious mind is the one that is ego driven and biased through its own intellect. The subconscious is the one that cannot lie about what it is programmed to believe. The body-subconscious connection will give answers to things that are submerged and unknown to the conscious processes. And it will give answers without being biased by wishful thinking or social maneuvering.

You see, the subconscious is simply an objective bio-computer that knows nothing about right or wrong. It just does what it is told to do, unlike the conscious mind that can imagine things and make judgments determined through the domain of the ego. But it has a protective system you need to get through—like in hypnosis.

So how do you find out what the subconscious holds as its beliefs—those you have spent a lifetime programming? There are several simple ways that you can use.

Muscle testing technique
Have someone help you on this. You stand and hold one arm out horizontal with the floor at shoulder level, palm down. Then you make a statement like "my name is Ed." If your name is Ed when your partner presses down on the arm say at your wrist, you will resist this. If this is the truth, you will have a strong resistance because this is truth resident in the belief system of the subconscious and the muscle electronics is in harmony.

If it is not true, the muscle will have little resistance. It is because the statement does not correlate with the truth in the subconscious and the muscle—in this case the deltoid—is in temporary electrical dysfunction. Now say "my name is Zorro," or some such lie. Have the partner push the arm down again. You will not be able to hold the arm up with the same force. The muscle response system is weakened by your untruth. Try it and see for yourself.

Now, you may want to be private about this and do this on your own so there are several ways to do this. But first, you need to set the scene properly. For the most accurate results, here are some pointers—this is what the experts say. First you need to be well hydrated so your electromagnetic circuitry is functioning at its best. So drink plenty of water well before you do it. Secondly, you need to get the ego out of the way so you are less attached to the outcome. This means, get quiet and get all the noise out of your mind. Sit quietly, breath in deeply and focus on the breath—just get present to yourself and now. Remember you need to apply the same pressure to the muscles when doing it. Then, you should make sure when you make a statement, you do it in such a way as to receive a yes (strong) or no (weak) answer. Do not state something and think something else because it can give a false response. Then when you are doing it, look down.

Here is an easy way. If you want to follow on the horizontal arm test, you can use a 5 Kg dumbbell on a shoulder height shelf which you can lift with ease for a strong response but which feels welded to the shelf for a weak response.

Now here is an addition to the muscle testing that is relevant and rather extraordinary as it fits with the chakra energy system. If during the process of testing, your eyes move upwards they are processing thoughts visually (making pictures via the third eye chakra). Straight ahead is auditory (throat chakra) and down is kinesthetically—feeling (heart chakra). By looking up in a muscle test it is nullifying a physical response from the subconscious (which it depends on) through the physical body. The individual needs to be experiencing necessary feelings for a proper muscle test. People with trauma look up—a strategy to disassociate from unpleasant memories disconnecting feelings necessary to create a conflicted (weak) response. Normalize them by looking down.

The thumb-finger technique
But the easiest, most portable way is to form a ring with your thumb and little finger of the non-dominant hand. Make another ring with thumb and index fingers of the other hand, and then interlock the two rings. Make the statement and then try to pull the dominant second ring through the non-dominant ring at its weakest point where the thumb and finger meet. Keep the tension constant. If you break the ring, the muscles are weakened (no). If it holds the muscles are strong (yes).

Alternatively, pinch the thumb and a finger of the dominant hand together as if forming a beak, and try to spread the thumb and finger of the first hand apart with them. Or use your forefinger and thumb of the dominant hand to break the loop.

Now, bear in mind that you can "think" the statement as well. You can also use this to test whether a food or pill is good for your body or not. You would take the food in your hand and place it up against your solar plexus. You can do the test then. See if a bottle of wine is good for you! If you want to free one hand while you do this, do the dumbbell method. Some people use hand grip exercisers. There are spring loaded devices specially designed to be squeezed between thumb and middle finger.

The Sticky-smooth Technique
From the field of radionics comes the sticky-smooth technique. Using any convenient smooth surface, let one finger rub gently across the smooth surface. You can ask your body to show you what a strong response feels like (my preference), or you can program it so that strong is smooth and for weak, the finger will just stick (or the other way around if you prefer). You can Google "self muscle testing" for more ideas.

So here is a way to test your beliefs. If you make a list of these, like you believe you can heal yourself, and some real doozers that are critical to your subconscious not screwing up your desires, you will begin to see where you are fooling yourself and your beliefs are not in alignment with your desired intent. So make a list and see. Try these:

- *I am able to heal myself*
- *I am deserving of wealth and prosperity*
- *I am part of God*
- *I can create prosperity and abundance*
- *I am an infinite being*

Pick out some of the questions you are curious about, especially as they relate to the heath and wealth processes and see how you come out. You can make this a habit and get good at it. Then you can work at making a belief change, measuring the result.

The Dousing Technique
Just as radios pick up information from unseen radio waves, the pendulum is a powerful antenna that receives information from the vibrations and energy waves emitted by people, places, thoughts and things.

Noted physicist, Albert Einstein, was known to perform impressive feats with such dowsing tools. He believed that it had to do with electromagnetism: just as birds migrate following the earth's magnetic field, dowsers react to energies that are unseen and still not fully understood.

Some people say that the pendulum creates a bridge between the logical and intuitive parts of the mind. Some say that the pendulum connects them with a higher power and call it **divining** as the information is believed to come from a divine source. Research by many scientists indicates that the pendulum responds to electromagnetic energy that radiates from everything on Earth.

No one knows for sure how the pendulum works, but the important thing is that it does work! As Thomas Edison is said to have replied when asked about electricity: *"I don't know what it is, but its there, let's use it."*

Other famous dowsing advocates in history include Leonardo De Vinci (inventor), Robert Boyle (father of modern chemistry), Charles Richet (Nobel prize winner), and General Patton (U.S. Army).

Another way of looking at it is realizing that a TV antenna can pick up invisible rays and translate them into pictures, so perhaps the inherent electrical current of the brain can also act as a receiver for which the pendulum serves as a transmitter.

But regardless, even if you do not understand how the pendulum works, just as most people don't know the inner workings of a television or telephone, you can still benefit from its use. You do not have to be psychic to use a pendulum; there is nothing magical or mystical despite the fact that friends and family are always amazed at its uncanny accuracy.

How you believe it works may be secondary to the fact that it actually does work - and you can experience it for yourself.

Dousing instigates a way of asking questions of the Divine—which is resident in all of us. It uses a pendulum, or some metallic object hanging from a string or chain. The easiest is a needle on a string. Some form of handle may also be attached to the upper end of the thread to decrease the chance that the direction of movement would be caused by your hand.

The key here is that when you begin by connecting your pendulum to your Higher Self, what happens is that the answers go from your Higher Self, to your subconscious (which makes tiny movements in your wrist and hand to make the pendulum swing) and then to your conscious mind, when it sees which way the pendulum is swinging. So, when you use a pendulum, you are moving it unconsciously. Spirits do not move the pendulum for you. It is a spiritual thing (in that it comes from the spirit in you).

Once you have assembled your pendulum, sit down in a comfortable position. Hold the pendulum by the string a few inches away from your body. You can use one hand to stabilize the other to make sure the weighted portion is still. The pendulum handle or chain should be held loosely between the thumb and first finger. Place your second hand under the pendulum holding it flat. Next, keeping the hand holding the string perfectly still, say to the pendulum, *"show me yes"*. If it works, you will see the weight move, either in a circular motion or back and forth. Now ask the pendulum, *"show me no"*. Once you have seen what "yes" and "no" look like to you (it can vary from person to person), you can start asking questions like *"Is today the 15th?"* or *"Is my middle name Superman?"*

It's important to relax and clear your mind so as to focus only on the question being asked when using a pendulum. It can be quite easy to project the answer you want into your reading, but with time and practice, you will start to get a sense of whether or not the reading is a "good" one. The pendulum can be used to answer "yes" or "no" questions. If you ask a question and the pendulum doesn't respond, rephrase the question or ask again at another time. Basically, this is a tool to tap into your intuition, or alternatively, your spirit guide, to get information. For this reason, it works best if you are asking questions about things that are in your power to control. If they are things you do control in your personal realm, that you can control, then the answer will not be dependable. And make it a simple yes or no question.

It is best to first begin with a benchmark. As a programmer, a benchmark is always used to set the constraints for how a program is supposed to work. It is a benchmark against which the programmer can compare. So start with a few things you know are right or wrong to see if is responding.

- Is my name Ed?
- Do I have two legs?
- Is my name Zorro?
- Am I married?

Then try "*Do I believe in miracles*?" If the response is no or it does nothing, rest assured that your subconscious does not agree with your belief.

Remember a belief is just thoughts that are repeated over and over. So sit down quietly later and drop into a lower state - like in meditation to get into the subconscious morphic field and repeat *"I believe in miracles."* over and over for at least 30 seconds to start reprogramming. If it is just a single thought, it may not have much energy, so like an affirmation, repeating it gives it life. When you do this try to feel how great a miracle would be. Then try the test again.

There is a list of key questions that if not yes, are potential sabotagers of your miracle work:

- *Do I believe in miracles?*
- *Do I believe I can create miracles?*
- *Do I believe I can heal myself instantly?*
- *Do I believe I am worthy of healing miracles?*
- *Do I believe a Higher Power will assist me?*
- *Do I believe I can heal others?*
- *Do I believe I can create my own destiny?*
- *Do I believe I can change my physical reality?*
- *Do I believe I am worthy of well being?*

- *Do I believe I am worthy of money?*

You can add to the list but may be surprised at how psychic you are!

When you get no answers and the conscious and subconscious are both screwed up and there is no clarity on the issue, this may be a great signal to get into a lower brain state and clarify it by repeating the belief over and over until it is clear. Remember it becomes difficult to instigate any instructions from the conscious mind because the subconscious is the emotionless database of stored programs that create hardwire behavior responses with no judgment – a programmable hard drive into which our experiences are downloaded. Once we accept perception as truth it becomes hardwired into our brain as well to become our truth. Conscious and subconscious are independent but in terms of neurological processing are millions of times more powerful. If the subconscious is not aligned with the conscious, positive affirmations/thinking, it wins. So repeating an affirmation that a tumor be gone and being loveable may be futile because the subconscious can override or undermine if it does not agree.

The two minds are a dynamic duo operating together. Sub takes over the moment conscious is not paying attention.

The bottom line was this. Whatever was impressed on subconscious is expressed as a condition to experience an event. The subconscious is the objective responsive process while the conscious is subjective. The subconscious works at the quantum level, the conscious does not. In fact, as comparison to a computer the subconscious mind can process 40 million environmental stimuli per second. The conscious mind can process 40 environmental stimuli per second. The conscious mind can look back and forward, but while the conscious mind is out dreaming and playing, the subconscious mind is always on duty dealing with the moment now. It effectively is the manager, the overriding authority and manages things the way it was trained. In simple terms, of the subconscious does not agree with the conscious, guess who wins?

Energy Focusing

We will leave this chapter with one more simple process which shows you the power of the subtle energy of your mind when you place attention on something. It enforces the whole idea of the power of intention as we say with Adam Dreamhealer.

This requires a piece of brass wire like the thickness of a coat hanger. Bend it into a 90 degree shape so you can hold the part vertical in your hand and the other end points horizontally. It should be allowed to swing freely.

Now, bring attention to the wire and take a few deep breaths. It requires another person or persons to be in the room. Then ask it to show you that person, say the name is Hope. Say, *"point to Hope"* and focus attention on the wire. The wire will rotate along the line between you and Hope. Say, *"point to Bill"* and see how it then rotates to point to Bill. That is the power of focused intention.

24

CHANGING BELIEFS

"What you believe so shall you receive."
Ed Rychkun

Unlike the creating of miracles internally, creating reality externally seems to be talking to a different computer and requires belief, focus, and persistence.

So clearly, if something does not work, as we have learned, there may be many reasons that are intangible variables not easy to define in a program. Measuring belief is part of the process to see if you are aligned with the subconscious and if you have to do something about aligning it.

We have seen that certain "environmental factors" are conducive such as a positive attitude, a healthy cellular environment, a better feeling of self worthiness and a dissolving of limitations. Also important is this overall field of love and compassion that are the conductors of movement of intent and prayer within this field. Clearly, this field is also conducive to cell life and the well being of the body.

The surest way to change a belief is to launch a repetitive act. Like if you want to quit smoking, a repetitive act of intent and action of not smoking will convince the biology and subconscious that it is not needed. This can be around 30-60 days to write a new behavior program.

If you want to program a new physical ability into your subconscious, you take intent to repeat the enhancement physically over and over until you get it perfected and the program is placed in subconscious to execute at any time.

If you want to change a belief you use affirmations and repeat images, words repeated over and over until it is programmed into your subconscious.

If you want to feel good, you need to feel good about yourself by denying the intrusion of stress and negativity and engaging in a healthy diet of body and mind behaviors.

If your desires are not becoming real, then something is cancelling them out; your trust and faith in yourself that they will happen may be clouded by conflicting thoughts and emotions of stress, so be persistent and repetitive.

We will see in PART THREE that the center of energetic force is critical in this process through the emotion and the intent. We have heard this over and over. Once a thought is brought to life (7th energy center in the body) it is clarified as a vision (6th energy center) defined and enforced by words (5th energy center) surcharged with emotion at the 4th energy center and launched by way of choice and intent through the third energy center when the choices begin to come forward. The law of cause and effect takes over.

When you take the initiative to determine what is out of alignment between your subconscious and conscious minds, then it is habits and subconscious programming that are your allies.

We have earned that the subconscious mind as in children is most open to programming behavior at early ages because that is when the conscious mind is not yet interfering. The brain is operating at the lower levels of brain waves. So what is the big lesson here? Get out of the influence of higher brain vibrational interference. It is commonly known as meditation. Here is where you instigate a repetitive program to shift beliefs and it is through the intent and free will that this can occur. This is where affirmations come in.

Practice Will Change Your Beliefs

So if you want to create miracles, believe you already can. It is your confidence and belief that is still in doubt. Your beliefs limit you so we suggest you set up a special mantra that you can activate instantly when you are ready to do your healing. Let us do that now. Think of a special word that you will use as a mantra. Silence your mind and body then place yourself into a deeper state of lower brain vibrations. Move your attention to your etheric heart chakra. This is called "getting present" as in the technique of healing. The present is **now**; that is the domain of the subconscious.

Now go through your items where you have found disbelief. And will your self through the power of will and intent to believe those things your subconscious needs to be convinced of.

I will myself to always be in my heart
I will myself to believe in miracles

I will myself to heal myself
I will myself to always react from the heart
I will my emotional body to always be bright and strong

The 30 Day Mind Plan - Daily Routine

If you paid attention to your thoughts and were like most, you would find that 65% of them are negative or redundant. Many need a simple Mind, Body, and Spirit plan to get rid of a lot of old habits that insidiously get imbedded in just about everything you do. If you are a business man, it would be the time to become the real CEO of the new 30 Day Mind Plan.

Such a plan would work away at modifying the belief system to set a course of action. Essentially, daily routines designed to get one kick-started on four crucial areas of Life, Spirit, Body, and Mind would be a logical purpose of a Mind Plan. This new program would be to reprogram the subconscious.

As we have learned from the experts, there are some key items here that can be mindful assertions to help keep strong mind focus on these important beliefs so they are drummed into the belief system:

1. My Spirit (linked with my heart) is there to help me live well and prosper; to help me expand my consciousness towards a quality life;
2. My Heart-Mind is the true manager and it must always be conducting the orchestra of subtle energies from a higher perspective;
3. The orchestra of subtle energies works best when the instrument sections of body, mind, and spirit are playing the same tune in positive harmony;
4. My being conscious of the laws of Subtle Energy always gives me an advantage in managing them to my benefit;
5. I have a life plan to fulfill and no one other than me can accomplish it;
6. My body, mind and spirit are the vehicles to complete my mission;
7. I am a wonderful, confident machine of subtle energies that deserves anything I want that will make my life better;
8. My belief system is what allows my empowerment to blossom;
9. My management of my subtle energies will get better and better and stronger and stronger over time to shorten the time lag between thought and manifestation;
10. I am the Genie and the Lamp and I have awakened the powers.

To further this implementation it is important to create a simple list of activities that one needs to pay close attention to because like trying to get rid of any bad habit, one has to consciously work at it and drum activities into a routine. Here are the key guidelines:

1. I must always take my times of peace in the morning and evening before bed so as to find solutions and imagine my desired life movie;
2. I must always be on the lookout for immediate reactions and negative thoughts, stop the process and convert them through the heart;
3. I must always engage in deliberate creation of positive thoughts, images, words and emotion;
4. I must always look for ways to determine something positive that arises from any event or situation;
5. I must always look to ways to make things better and focus attention on those things;
6. I must always look to support my desires with constant surges of positive thoughts and emotions;
7. I must always look to ways of balancing the energies of ego with those of the heart;
8. I must always fuel the expansion process by raising the emotional thermometer towards the high positive end, seeing the positive side to all that exists;
9. I must always let others be, without judgment as they also are the creators of their own destinies;
10. I must always be aware the past and future do not exist except in my memory and my mind. What is past is gone and what is before me is to be determined;
11. I must always look to the past as a valuable experience and change my perception of any negative energies by forgiveness and thankfulness of the opportunity to advance;
12. I must always think in solutions that are done, not dwell on problems, I must enjoy that the solution is so, then be thankful for it being that way;
13. I must always be aware of what I am, who I am, and that my beliefs are what my life will be.

The Energy Investment Portfolio

If you are of the pragmatic type who likes to have rules and reasons, this section is for those business types who like to engage in having a balanced investment portfolio that provides short term and long term returns.

Everyone has 24 hours in a day to create energies, like 30-50,000 a day, 60% of which are negative or redundant. It is simply our culture. The underlying belief here is that these critters called thought, visions, words, and emotions are lethal when they are given life and charged with negativity. So here is a great tactic; one of setting up a human subtle energy fund where you take full responsibility for managing four portfolios. Take the management of the fund away from the usual broker—namely ego and take responsibility for managing it with your new Consulting Advisor; the Heart. It would guide you on a great growth scheme. The Heart is going to help manage energies of thoughts, images, words and emotions so bad critters that would come back to bite you in the ass never get a life.

The fund is made of four different portfolios with energy you create as assets. These are related to the way you give life to different energies. The more positive the energy the higher the value of the investment. The more negative the energy, the lower it would fall.

The initial investments in the four portfolios would reflect four types of energy generating activities. The first two portfolios are **reactive** energies. One is a result of thoughts created from the news, the media, television, papers, what others said, things that were outside. This group is *media*. Here one listens, hears, sees, reads and reacts, creating energy. Perhaps 60% of your total time in the 24 hours is of this nature. These are the ones that cause the cells and the brain to go into the negative reaction mode that inhibits growth.

The purpose is to not react in a negative way. No negative thoughts, no adding of negative emotion, never getting angry or saying things shooting from the ego's lip, or doing things that would not be in alignment with the heart. Yes, it is not an easy task in such a negative world.

So here you stop a thought before you give it life and remember it is there to teach you what you do not want or focus on it, not the reverse. If you react instantly in rage, it is ego. You simply stop the thought for three deep breaths, let ego subdue and let the heart take over. Then you create a new reaction that saw a good reason for the issue, or do not react at all; keeping it neutral. One has to remember the objective to invest in a future life of goodness, so the more goodness you can energize; the more you can build up the value of the portfolio and the return on investment. At some point it will return through the Law of Attraction. Positive grows the asset, negative diminishes the value.

The second portfolio to set up also comes from outside as part of the reactive process. It has to do with events that happen seemingly not under one's control. This is the **events** portfolio like if you had a dreadful accident, or you got involved in a terrible situation. This may be about 10% of the energy fund. The immediate ego instinct to clash, react, or do something that one could be sorry for later is the issue. The focus is NOT to do that; not to create a huge energy action that is negative. Try to see some reason why this occurred and read something good out of it. Take a higher perception and see it as a lesson of what you did not want or find what is good about it. If this is some terrible thing that would create anger and vengeance you still have a choice. It is a choice to go ballistic but if the portfolio is to build rapidly, this is the place you can make huge strides. Even though many of these could be a result of old karma or negative energy in escrow from the past, the tactic is to create a perception that if it was a terrible problem that brought fear or hatred, ok but then leave it alone for three days to get the ego out of it then you have time to look at it with the heart in mind more calm and collected.

The next two portfolios are **proactive**—those energies that you create in your own time, purposely and with positive purpose from *inside*. The first is easiest described as *free thinking*. It is the time you would spend letting the mind simply generate thoughts about whatever is on the mind. This could be about 20% of the time, or 20% of the energy fund.

This is like when you created a thought about personal affairs, like about a feeling of inadequacy, doubt, fear of the future, crisis from the past, not enough money, or feeling sick. Perhaps it was about how great the world was, what you had to appreciate, what is good. The focus here is to add to the positive investment energy in the fund and with purpose and intent add positive thoughts. Any negative thoughts like "*it pisses me off*", or "*I hate this*", or "*I feel crappy*", are not to be allowed to enter the portfolio. You learn to stop this and convert it; not give it any negative life.

The last portfolio has to do with plans. It is the **plans** portfolio, also from *inside.* This could constitute 10% of the fund allocated toward it. These energies are for investing in major desires, solutions, and passions to create in the longer term. Here, rather than being focused on the problems, like not enough money, having to work hard, do this do that to get more money, you change the focus to the solution to feel the energy of completion, add the emotion of enjoyment, be grateful for it being done, and put the positive energy of completion out to the Zero Point Quantum Field to attract the solution. You would place this energy in the fund. This could be a very small part of the fund but it could have an immense effect on the positive energy of joy that could come back into the fund and its future value.

When this is instituted, you will begin to see a dramatic change in life as the fund grows from positive energies. The objective is learning to generate new positive energy or converting more and more negative energy until there is no room for negative events and experience to enter each day. It is like a business where you take old energy companies that are failing, and then put new energy into them to be successful.

Those residual energies in escrow that were looking to materialize—things one had already given life to also have to be dealt with. Some may be there as lessons or karma that would manifest an experience that needed to be converted. These would be celebrated as a great opportunity to create a big impact in the fund. They would be great opportunities to point a different way.

The Paradigm Shift In Energy

Now, this is a process that I (Ed) instituted years ago and I have to report on it. When I incorporated the new Life Plan into my life, it changed things within 30 days. The subconscious was responding. A dramatic shift unfolded. The balance of energies and events, and experiences began to shift to the positive. As I paid attention to managing the subtle energy, got my body and mind into the same mode, I began to build a resilience that quickly converted negative energy to positive energy. This naturally led towards a more positive based existence that put excitement into everything I did, thought, wanted and reacted to.

I began to view things differently. I began to look for challenges from experiences that I was previously afraid of. Life started to become a patchwork of fantastic adventures, experiences, and good emotions, regardless of what I encountered. I have tested others with it and the results are the same. I found that there are five critical changes that resulted from the practice of managing my subtle energies the way I have outlined here. I wish to share those with you before we move on.

First, by trying to see the good in experiences arising from some uncontrollable events, I avoided falling victim to negative energy, activating the intent to create more negative energy that further attracts other situations.

Second, by monitoring the ego that always wants me to have more things and strive for power and money, I became aware of the rebellious, protective, angry, conflictive thoughts it projected almost instantly—the ones that would infect my health and my attitude. My conscious awareness allowed me to stop these thoughts from being projected out to find more buddies of the same mind. I found that I was able to attract more positive energy in the form of people, events, and opportunities. They simply began to appear from nowhere.

Third, there is a proactive component where I would purposely engage in positive situations, positive people and work towards creating positive manifestations as I moved forward. When I started to dissolve old energies by forgiveness and a new look at negative situations, I began to clean out residual energies that were still looking to manifest.

Fourth, I deliberately transmitted more positive energies and engaged in training my energy systems to generate positive energies while on autopilot. I effectively learned to train the ego to take orders from the heart. This eventually began to snowball as the dark side got more and more light into it.

Fifth, I launched a plan of coherence between all my subtle energy centers. This was my plan to bring me wealth and health through my passions the way I wanted. I would focus on the solution not the business problems. This I knew would grow to improve my health and longevity as my reasons to live expanded and the anger, fear, anxiety, and tension—the most consistent dis-ease, and disease manifestors—fall away. The physical, physiological, and psychological aspects of my life would harmonize and respond as they were designed to do in the first place.

I now know many people that have been miraculously attracted into my life. They have a wonderful resilience that others notice and the body, mind and spirit come into a wonderful balance of harmony.

By changing the balance through managing the human subtle energies, I believe that you can also make that paradigm shift. The change in belief and a daily change in habit will unfold a new life—the one you design, not the one you default to. That means you can start creating a better life now and it can only get better and better. It will get better beyond your comprehension. You will simply take control and begin to create the life you want—not have a life that reacts to everything. Proactive management of Human Subtle Energy will insure that your current limited comprehension, and limited physical state, does not inhibit what you can really do.

25

SHIFTING THE ENVIRONMENT

"The worst thieves of your dreams reside with what you eat, what you believe and what you perceive."
Ed Rychkun

Well-Being At The Cellular Level

We have seen that the setting required for miracles includes Well Being, to be in a positive space of emotion and love, compassion, forgiveness, and giving, over and over. But there is a whole new variable that has come to light, and that is the cellular environment. We have learned how the outside and inside environment governs the behaviour of cells. We have seen how research shows how the thought, image, word, and emotion energies, regardless of whether they are real or perceived, create the hormones that the brain uses to run certain firmware to trigger the HPA Axis or the **hypothalamic–pituitary–adrenal axis.** This axis causes a sequence that results in a response that depletes growth in the digestive and immune systems as well as numbs the mind to be "dumber" The stress, induced in any way creates a stimuli response mechanism that automatically triggers programs to be executed from the subconscious disc.

We also see that through the Genome Project that the progression of stimuli is ENVIRONMENT - DNA - RNA - CELLS, and that DNA is not the top of the heap as once believed. Research is coming forward that also shows that diseases are not inherited as there has not been any link of diseases to any genes. What is key here is the Environment that sets the mood and functional abilities of the cell.

In research conducted by **Bruce Lipton**, a cells biologist (**Biology of Belief**) he confirms that the cell can be made sick and dysfunctional with toxic environments but that it recovers when the proper environment is re-established. As stated, this proper environment has to do with the foods we eat and the stress we create. The stress limits the immune system and its ability to live or function. The food we eat limits the environment the cells live in. Research has shown that certain foods like pork for example, create a lining or a barrier on or within cell walls to render the cell wall, the biological micro chip, dysfunctional. It would be like a chip on a microprocessor overheating. The issue here is that a toxic environment, particularly when compromised by toxic stress (either real or perceived) is just as bad in compromising cells as is the toxic environment produced by the foods eaten.

In this respect, it would be logical as part of a health maintenance plan to reduce the toxicity in the food and water, but more relevant to this chapter to enhance the cellular environment to effectively make the cells happier in their work. The way to do this is to assist them with enzymes.

What Are Enzymes?

Enzymes are biologically active proteins found in all living cells. Metabolic enzymes catalyze and regulate every biochemical reaction that occurs within the human body, making them essential for cellular function and overall health. Digestive enzymes turn the food we eat into energy which may be utilized by the body for various biological processes. Our bodies are designed to naturally produce both digestive and metabolic enzymes as they are needed but this can change dramatically.

Enzymes are protein chemicals, which carry a vital energy factor needed for every chemical action and reaction that occurs in our body. There are approximately 1300 different enzymes found in the human cell. These enzymes can combine with coenzymes to form nearly 100,000 various chemicals that enable us to see, hear, feel, move, digest food, and think. Every organ, every tissue, and all the 50 trillion cells in our body depend upon the reactions of metabolic enzymes and their energy factor. Nutrition cannot be explained without describing the part that enzymes play.

Enzymes are catalysts, which means that they make chemical reactions go faster, but are not changed by the reaction. For example, digestive enzymes cause food that you eat to be broken down much faster than would occur without them. Research has shown that people who have a chronic disease or have low energy levels also have lower enzyme content in their blood, urine, and tissues. While there is clearly a direct relationship between disease states and a person's enzyme levels, only recently has the nature of that relationship been better understood. Researchers began to question if a person's enzyme levels were low because they were sick or they were they sick because their enzyme levels were low. The researchers found something surprising.

A person may not have a low enzyme content because he is sick or old, but instead, the reason a person may be sick or old is because of low enzyme content.

As a result, the old concept of *"I am sick, therefore my enzyme levels are low"* has recently been replaced by a new concept which is *"my enzyme levels are low, therefore I am sick."*

Why Are Enzymes So Important?

So research confirms that enzymes are one of the most essential elements in our body. Enzymes are more important than the air you breathe, the water you drink, and the food you eat. Why is this? Enzymes are required for your body to function properly because without enzymes you wouldn't be able to breathe, swallow, drink, eat, or digest your food. To do all of these things, your body needs some help. You must have enzymes to help perform these tasks. Enzymes are an absolute necessity to live. But there is a big problem here because as we have noted, this can change dramatically.

Enzymes are your body's workers. They are responsible for constructing, synthesizing, carrying, dispensing, delivering, and eliminating the many ingredients and chemicals our body uses in its daily business of living. When you were young, you had an abundant supply of enzymes. You felt great. Your energy level seemed never ending. You had "enzymes to burn" which kept you running at tip top efficiency.

As time goes by, you slowly begin to lose this efficiency. For years you don't even notice the changes. But then you are less able to eat the spicy foods you love or less able to recover as quickly from the aches and pains of weekend sports. This reduced vitality and stamina can signal a weakened and compromised body. The issue us you are running low on the enzymes you need to fuel your life. The process of depleting your enzymes is a slow one, and most likely you didn't notice your energy and vitality disappearing until one day something you once loved to do was suddenly too much work. You aren't getting too old to enjoy life; you are running out of enzymes that would ensure you the energy you need to enjoy life. You simply need to restore your enzyme potential.

The reason we are running out of enzymes is a **lifestyle problem**. Our poor dietary habits, fast food obsessions, and excessive intake of fat and sugars, all require excessive amounts of enzymes to digest our foods. Also, stress kills and damages cells, resulting in our enzyme-making machinery having to work overtime to help rebuild and replace them. Environmental pollution causes cellular damage requiring ongoing assistance from enzymes just to maintain a healthy immune system. And time is a big factor. Time and the process of living uses up enzymes that must be replaced if we expect to retain the healthy active lifestyle we have grown accustomed to. Every one of these factors diminishes our body's capacity to act, to do, to feel the way we want to feel; and, as many reputable scientists will tell you, these factors may even shorten your life.

The difficulty is that enzymes are essential but your enzyme potential is dropping. Many researchers now view the aging process and death itself as nothing more than an enzyme potential which has decreased to a level where the living organism can no longer be repaired and maintained in its existing environment. You may slow down this trend by fortifying your body with supplemental digestive enzymes. You can help minimize this inevitable downward spiral in your body's efficiency, a spiral created by a growing shortage of available enzymes. There is much you can do to combat your waning enzyme potential. The sooner you start, the quicker you begin to restore and extend the vitality you once had.

In current times we need to consider this seriously because of the depletion in our soils of naturally occurring enzymes and minerals. We are not getting the amounts we would have been getting say 50 years ago in many parts of the world. Some of this is because of an undesirable environment; from chemicals in the air to biochemically engineered pesticides to improper care of soils where mass crops are grown. Add to this the stress factor and with the chemicals placed into meat products and soft drinks, this creates a toxic hostile environment for a body to be unsustainable at length.

What we also see is more children being born with what are termed diseases. Naturally occurring enzymes are also what Mothers should naturally transfer to the unborn child as this is vital. However, some children are being born without these enzymes and one has to ask why is this so.

As a side note, from a perspective of the higher vibration (Rainbow or Crystal and even Indigo) children being born, they come with extreme sensitivities to chemicals in unnatural forms of food products. These are burning enzymes at a faster rate than others and many are not getting enzymes at all! These issues results in what some of the medical society are calling ADD, ADHD, Autism, Food Allergens or Sensitivities, and many other invented diseases. Even if a mother breastfeeds a baby, it may not be enough because in society today with what we have readily available to us at the grocery store and the enormous stresses of everyday life the mother may already have a deficiency and not pass on the appropriate enzymes. Even if a baby is bottle fed it is still questionable what they truly are getting. Being aware is the first step in being able to do something about it.

To better understand digestive enzymes, we must first understand the role of nutrition in our health. Nutrition is the body's ability to use and metabolize food. There are 45 known essential nutrients that are required in specific amounts for the body to function properly. The term "essential," as used here, means the body cannot synthesize them internally. Therefore all "essential" nutrients must come from exogenous, or outside, sources. In addition to carbohydrates, fats (lipids), complete proteins, and water, there are at least 13 kinds of vitamins, and at least 20 kinds of minerals required for proper metabolic function. Once consumed, the food containing these nutrients must be digested, meaning they must be broken apart and reduced to a state that the nutrients can be absorbed into and transported by the blood stream to all parts of the body.

Our body's cells are programmed to direct each nutrient to combine and interact with other nutrients and chemicals to create still other chemicals and compounds which, in turn, are used to build and repair the body's cells, bones, tissue, and organs. The process is called metabolism. Each metabolic reaction is started, controlled, and terminated by enzymes. Without enzymes, no metabolic activity will occur. A body that does not consistently and efficiently metabolize the essential food nutrients necessary cannot maintain optimum health.

Enzymes are classified into three categories.

- METABOLIC ENZYMES
- DIGESTIVE ENZYMES
- FOOD ENZYMES

Metabolic enzymes run the body. They exist throughout the body in the organs, the bones, the blood, and inside the cells themselves. These enzymes are instrumental in the growth of new cells and the maintenance of all tissue. Every organ and tissue has its own group of specialized enzymes. They are trained to run and maintain their host. When these enzymes are healthy, robust, and present in adequate numbers, they do an excellent job carrying out their mission.

The two kinds of enzymes we are concentrating on here are DIGESTIVE ENZYMES and FOOD ENZYMES. These two are active only within our digestive system. These enzymes have only one job — to digest our food. Digestive Enzymes are made by our body's organs. Digestive enzymes are secreted by the salivary glands, stomach, pancreas, and the small intestine. Food Enzymes are already present within the food we eat. Food enzymes exist naturally in raw food. If the food is cooked, however, the high temperature involved in the cooking process will destroy the enzymes.

Digestive enzymes and food enzymes basically serve the same function, which is to digest our food so it can be absorbed through the walls of the small intestine into the blood stream. From this viewpoint the only real difference between food enzymes and digestive enzymes is whether they come from inside our body or from the food we eat.

Most food, when it is uncooked, contains enough natural food enzymes to digest that food. When you cook the food the enzymes are inactivated (denatured) and can no longer assist in the digestive (breaking down) process. Eating raw food is totally acceptable in some cases and quite unacceptable in others. We eat raw fruit and many raw vegetables, but less often do we eat raw meat, raw fish or raw pork. Here's where the problem occurs. Cooked food contains no enzymes because they have been destroyed. If you eat a meal consisting of a salad, a steak and a baked potato, there are likely enough food enzymes contained in the salad to digest it (break it down so your body can use its nutrients). But, there are no extra enzymes available to help digest the steak or the baked potato. Because the steak and potato are cooked, there are no food enzymes available to digest them, so our body must take over and internally create the needed amount of digestive enzymes to handle the digestive task.

The more we depend on our internally generated digestive enzymes, the more stress we put on our body's systems and organs and the less time these systems and organs have for rebuilding and replacing worn out and damaged cells and tissue and keeping our immune system strong. Your body's top priority is making sure it has enough nutrients to run its systems. This means digesting food and converting it into nutrients. There is no activity more important to the body than this. This takes a lot of energy and enzymes, particularly if the body must make most or all of these enzymes. Remember that no food can be digested without digestive enzymes.

Dr. DicQie Fuller-Looney, in her book *The Healing Power of Enzymes*, emphasizes the importance of enzymes for digestion:

"Eighty percent of our body's energy is expended by the digestive process. If you are run down, under stress, living in a very hot or very cold climate, pregnant, or are a frequent air traveler, then enormous quantities of extra enzymes are required by your body. Because our entire system functions through enzymatic action, we must supplement our enzymes. Aging deprives us of our ability to produce necessary enzymes. The medical profession tells us that all disease is due to a lack or imbalance of enzymes. Our very lives are dependent upon them!"

You know that proteins, carbohydrates, and fats are the three main food groups that make up the bulk of our daily diet. A "balanced" diet means we consume the proper proportions of these three basic food groups on a daily basis. This balance, when combined with the assurance that we also get the essential nutrients, can help provide a healthy life; iF we properly process and metabolize these nutrients. To do this we also need an adequate source of the major types of digestive enzymes: Proteases, Amylases, and Lipases.

FOOD GROUP	% OF DAILY DIET	ENZYME CLASS	ENZYME'S FUNCTION
Proteins	20-25 %	Protease	Digests Protein
Carbohydrates	50-60 %	Amylase	Digests Carbohydrates
Fats	20-30 %	Lipase	Digests Fat (lipids)

How Are Enzymes Utilized In The Body?

Let us summarize this as it is important.

Metabolic Enzymes are an essential component for optimal cellular function and health. These descriptions are not without merit. They speed up the chemical reactions within the cells for detoxification and energy production. They enable us to see, hear, feel, move and think. Every organ, every tissue and all 50 trillion cells in our body depend upon the reaction of metabolic enzymes and their energy factor. Without these metabolic enzymes, cellular life would cease to exist.

Digestive Enzymes are secreted along the digestive tract to break food down into nutrients and waste. Most of the digestive enzymes are produced by the pancreas. The liver, gallbladder, small intestine, stomach and colon also play pivotal roles in the production of these enzymes. Digestive enzymes allow the nutrients found in the foods we consume to be absorbed into the blood stream and the waste to be discarded. Some human digestive enzymes include lipase, protease, amylase, ptyalin, pepsin and trypsin.

Food Enzymes are introduced to the body through the raw foods we eat and through consumption of supplemental enzyme products. Raw foods naturally contain enzymes, providing a source of digestive enzymes when ingested. However, raw food manifests only enough enzymes to digest that particular food. The cooking and processing of food destroys all of its enzymes. Since most of the foods we eat are cooked or processed in some way and because the raw foods we do eat contain only enough enzymes to process that particular food, our bodies must produce the majority of the digestive enzymes we require, unless we use supplemental enzymes to aid in the digestive process. A variety of supplemental enzymes are available through different sources. It is important to understand the differences between the enzyme types and make sure you are using an enzyme product most beneficial for your particular needs.

Why Take Digestive Enzyme Supplements?

We have seen that when stress occurs, the reactions are to activate the flight or fight syndrome to **lower the immune system, take energies from the digestive system and become dumber**. Nearly one in three people in the U.S. experience some kind of digestive problem. We breathe and consume toxins continuously through the food, water and air; it all goes to compromising the cellular environment. The typical benefits of enzyme supplementation include reduced digestive distress, increased energy and improved regularity. This makes it a pretty tough environment for those 50 trillion cells to function!

For example within the cell biology/environment, enzymes play the following roles:

Soothe Digestive Distress: When undigested foods travel through the intestines they can irritate and potentially damage the sensitive intestinal wall. Over time, this irritation may reduce our digestive capacity and negatively influence the vital absorption process.

Increase Energy: According to *Yuri Elkaim* author of *Eating for Energy*, in most cases, up to 80% of our body's vital energy is spent on digestion. By aiding the breakdown and absorption of foods, you can free up enormous amounts of energy, increasing physical vitality and enhancing energy levels.

Promote Regularity: Promoting proper digestion may encourage a healthy intestinal environment, and help relieve occasional constipation and irregularity.

Typically Available Enzymes

Plant-Based Enzymes are the most popular choice of supplemental enzymes. They are grown in a laboratory setting and extracted from certain types of fungus and probiotics. The enzymes harvested from aspergillus are called plant-based, or fungal. Of all the choices, plant-based enzymes are the most potent. This means they can break down more fat, protein and carbohydrates than any other source.

Plant Enzymes consist of bromelain and papain. Bromelain is a proteolytic (breaks down protein) and milk-clotting enzyme derived from the pineapple stem. A concentrate of this enzyme has been known to promote a healthy inflammatory response, is used as a meat tenderizer and is used in the chill-proofing of beer. Like pepsin and papain, bromelain has an optimal temperature higher than normal body temperature. There is always greater heat at the sight of inflammation than any other part of the body. Bromelain is used in Repair, Repair Gold and Natto-K. Papain is an enzyme derived from the latex of papaya. This enzyme becomes active in an environment of 6.0 - 8.0 pH and requires temperatures above normal human body temperature. Like bromelain, it too supports the body's natural recovery from overexertion.

It is important to know that vitamins and minerals work together. For the Papain enzyme to activate your body's pH must be between 6.0-8.0 ph. It is likened unto your body being able to heal itself with the right environment when it is in the alkaline level of ph 7.0 or higher. A healthy baby is born with a ph of 7.4. Babies born with a lower level of acidic ph generally have problems.

Glandular/Animal: Chymotrypsin, pancreatin, pepsin and trypsin are enzymes from the pancreas, stomach and small intestine derived from animal glands and organs. These enzymes require an alkaline pH level of 8.0 to become active. For example proteolytic products are 100% vegetarian, thus enzymes derived from animals are not used in the formulations.

The bottom line is this: Give those hard working cells some help! They are dealing with a toxic environment that they have to react to. And aging does not help them! Research this for yourself and when you get to the end of the chapter on the 30 Day Body Plan, make this a top priority.

The Importance of Minerals

Another important factor in the cell and body well-being is minerals. Minerals are elements that originate in the Earth and cannot be made by living organisms. Plants obtain minerals from the soil, and most of the minerals in our diets come directly from plants or indirectly from animal sources. Minerals may also be present in the water we drink, but this varies with geographic locale. Minerals from plant sources may also vary from place to place, because soil mineral content varies geographically.

Major minerals are considered a major issue when they are not available to the body. They are required by the body in doses of 100 mg/day or greater; i.e. greater than 0.01% of body weight. Calcium and phosphorous are the greatest in amounts in the body. Minor minerals are required by the body in amounts of less than 100 mg/day; i.e. less than 0.01% of body weight and are also called trace minerals or trace elements. Minerals, made of metals and other inorganic compounds, are as essential to bodily functions as vitamins. They form the structure of our bodies and help our systems work. Major minerals are: calcium, phosphorus, potassium, sodium, chloride, magnesium, and sulfur. Minor minerals are: chromium, cobalt, flouride, zinc, selenium, silicon, boron, iron, copper, iodine, manganese, molybdenum, nickel, arsenic and vanadium.

The table below is a small hint of what the deficiencies are when minerals are deficient. This table is on the site *www.thetotalman.com* which is dedicated to keeping the soul, spirit and body whole. In humans the most important dietary minerals can be seen below:

Mineral	What the Mineral does	Effects of mineral deficiency	Good food sources
Calcium	Strengthens the bones and teeth. Also needed to help regulate the heartbeat and help muscle and nerve functions.	Its minor deficit can affect bone and teeth formation.	Milk, dairy Products, green leafy vegetables, salmon, sardines, turnips, tofu, almonds, broccoli
Chromium	Required for the proper metabolism of sugar in the blood.	Can affect the potency of insulin in regulating sugar balance.	Beans, cheese, whole grain food , peas, meat
Copper	Important for nerve functioning, red blood cell formation and maintaining energy levels through iron absorption. Also good for healthy bones and the	Anemia, hair problems, dry skin, vitamin C deficiency	Beans, raisins, chocolate, nuts, meat, shellfish

		immune system.		
	Iodine	Helps keep your thyroid glands working. Your thyroid gland helps regulate the rate at which your body carries out its necessary physiological functions.	Enlargement of the thyroid gland.	Seafood, seaweed, dairy products, iodized salt
	Iron	Helps the blood and muscles carry oxygen to the body.	Tiredness and lethargy, feelings of weakness, iInsomnia, palpitations.	Liver, red meat, egg yolk, legumes, whole / enriched grains, dark green vegetables
	Magnesium	Helps muscles work, aids metabolism and aids bone growth.	Fatigue, numbness, poor memory, muscle twitching and ilrritability, tingling, rapid heart beat.	whole grains, nuts ,legumes, apricots, bananas , soy beans , green leafy vegetables , spinach
	Manganese	Helps bone growth and cell production.	Rarely documented but one case showed in a patient a decrease in serum cholesterol, depressed growth of hair and nails, scaly dermatitis, weight loss, reddening of his black hair and beard and impaired blood clotting.	whole grains, fruit, vegetables, tea egg yolk
	Molybdenum	Helps cells and nerves to function.	Very rare but one observation has shown a patient to have developed rapid heart and respiratory rates, headache, night blindness, and ultimately became comatose.	dark green vegetables, peas, milk, beans, grains
	Potassium	Essential for nerve function, muscle contraction and maintenance of fluid and blood pressure in the body.	Depression, fatigue, hypertension, decreased Heart Rate	Oranges, bananas, peanuts, beans, potatoes, spinach
	Selenium	Helps to prevent damage to cells and aids in the functioning of the thyroid gland. An antioxidant for the body.	Poor heart function, osteoarthropathy, mental retardation	brazil nuts, tuna , eggs , grains, chicken, shellfish , fish
	Sodium	Helps to regulate water in the body's blood and tissue	Fatigue, apathy, and nausea as well as cramps in the muscles of the extremities.	table salt, dairy products
	Zinc	Helps wounds to heal and aids taste and smell sensory.	Growth retardation, hair loss, diarrhea, delayed sexual maturation and impotence, eye and skin lesions, and loss of appetite.	whole wheat, peanut, poultry, eggs, legumes , beef, shellfish

The above discussion is not meant as a dietary program, nor a pitch to sell products. It is meant to convey that in order to assist the cells to do a better job, it is important to attend to a cellular well-being plan that gives them the enzymes and minerals they need in addition to a less toxic "mind" environment. Just consider how much of the minimum requirement you are actually providing. As you continue into the 30 Day Body Plan, it may be advisable to keep this in mind.

The 30 Day Body Plan

In conjunction with the earlier 30 Day Mind Plan and the Energy Investment Portfolio addressing the mental environment, it would be logical to conclude that one also should engage in a regiment of physical habits that reprogram the subconscious behavior to create a better environment for the body and the cells. As these cells are as vital to life as the microchip is to a computer, it would be logical to keep them in the best of health.

As we have brought forward, the body is used to sense the experiences and the mind records it as a perception and a belief, which if toxic develops dysfunction, dis-ease and disease. Here are some ways you program by repetitive action to respond and reprogram, as well as create a better environment for the 50 trillion cells. We call it the 30 day Body Plan to train yourself into a new behavior.

Love your body It is your sacred temple and it is unique. Remember, it is an extension of purity and responds best to positive energies such as love, compassion and peace. It has capabilities and abilities that you are not aware of so treat it as a very precious thing. Remember also that you have to love yourself and your body first before anybody else loves it. Understand that the way you feel about it is directly affecting or infecting its incredible capabilities. It is your choice. The best tactic is to talk to your cells and body in an altered state and say: *"I love you, I am sorry for causing any dysfunction or disease in you, please forgive me, thank you."*

Decontaminate your body You have spent most of your life contaminating it with bad fuel and stress. You may want to go to a Naturopath or Dietician and find out what your food sensitivities are. If you are overweight or unhealthy, you will probably find that the stuff you like best is the worst for you. That is your ego running the show. Get your body to tell you how it feels, not your ego. What's the difference? The body may thank you for a new eating plan and it all goes to giving the body a chance to get into a better state so it can perform what it was designed to perform. It was designed to heal itself but if your machinery is not functioning well because of a lack of proper physical and spiritual food, it becomes dysfunctional, lowers its vibration and becomes susceptible to dis-ease.

Exercise your body The body is designed to give you mobility. It is your mind that decides what type of mobility to engage in to maintain best performance. If the ego has much to say about this in later years, your mobility and muscle performance may be compromised. The muscles and particularly the main pump—the heart—simply need exercise to function well. If that engine is not attended to then you know the result. Even if it is a walk in the park 2-3 times a week, the body will thank you for it. Your body is designed to perform as an incredible machine, but it needs to be worked to work well. It will quickly atrophy its functionality if you don't.

Water your body Seventy percent of you is water. Your brain is even higher in water content. Part of effective subtle energy management must include providing the body with the proper amount of uncontaminated water it was designed to use. A regular amount of water helps to flush the junk out of the body and the organs have less of a tendency to get overloaded and let toxins accumulate. A high majority of people do not take in anywhere near enough to help flush, so of course, many little bad guys like heavy metals and toxins like to build up a strong team to inhibit function.

Ventilate your body The blood needs oxygen to work well and feed the rest of the system. If it does not receive sufficient oxygen, it cannot transfer air and food into the rest of the system and itself becomes dysfunctional. Deep pranic breathing and aerobic activity helps get more of this fuel into the blood so it can do what it was designed to do, namely make the body work. From best to good is skipping, running, bikes, aerobics, or walking. Take your choice of cure but DO IT. Your blood will thank you for it. You will digest food better and get more oxygen. Even when you are stressed, deep breathing will calm you.

Nourish your body with proper food This is where you need to start thinking seriously about that hard fuel that the body needs. The ego likes to conduct the orchestra here but you know it would set up a diet of chocolate bars, ice cream and fries for you if you let it. Most don't let it get away with this kind of tune but it always likes to try another craving on you. Don't listen. Your body may have been vibrating to the ego's tune too long and it cannot even tell you what it needs. The statement "you are what you eat" is highly appropriate. Eat junk food and you will rapidly prepare your body for the junk pile. Look to high vibration foods on your plan. And this means supplements, like ENZYMES and MINERALS!

Calm your body The most important activities to engage in to calm it are Meditation and Mother Nature. Take your time to create clarity and peace. Get out and be one with Mother Nature. Don't get old, get outdoors! The key word here is REVERENCE. Use your senses to see, feel, smell, hear, and wonder at Nature. Nature is one of the greatest dividend payers on the planet. Go out and learn to hug a tree. Make it a habit to get into Nature and merge with it — and leave your cell phone behind! Make a ritual of this little sanctuary with Nature. Really feel it and understand the grand beauty of it all.

Finally, get a dog! Dogs are trained stress reducers and nature lovers.

PART THREE

THE DIVINE PROGRAMMER

Aly McDonald
Ed Rychkun

THE DIVINE COMPUTER INTRODUCTION

"A mirror of all that is energy is in your mind; harness it and you have the genie at your command."

Ed Rychkun

There are still many questions about our "science" of creating and attracting miracles. We have seen that there are many supporting reasons; scientific reasons, why these systems and steps have been chosen by the healers and the attractor gurus. But there are many more scientific and fringe scientific reasons as well. These have to do with what is known as the Light Body and its components which are essentially subtle energy fields that have been relegated to the esoteric sciences, particularly in western cultures where the pharmaceutical and surgical approaches to medical issues reign supreme. Yet this esoteric knowledge and its ability to address many of the causes of medical issues refuse to go away; and are emerging into the consciousness of humanity more and more.

What has also emerged, however, out of the scientific closets some 80 years old is the theory of quantum physics. Even today, with quantum physics being used in many of our daily practices, like MRI's for example, it is still relegated to a fringe area because it explains so many things, like consciousness, that the old scientists who have been subconsciously programmed under the Newtonian physics, refuse to acknowledge. In this new tsunami of new thought, it has been accepted that Newtonian physics is dreadfully wrong and lacking. The big issue is that quantum physics explains how all the fringe and esoteric sciences actually work! No one can use the classical science to explain consciousness, or PSI, or many of the subtle energy fields because it can't. But quantum physics can, as well as many other unanswered phenomenons.

So, in this part of the book, we are going to further investigate the business of creating and attracting miracles in view of the many subtle "light body" energies integrated into the human body. These are like the heart field, the chakras, meridians, auras, morphic fields, vortexes, torroids and look towards additional supporting evidence that assist in shifting belief. We will also look into holograms and how quantum theory explains that we because of the brain and consciousness operating according to quantum physics actually create a hologram which we see as reality. And, of course, it is only appropriate that we delve into some basics about Quantum Physics.

From all this, there is another purpose to this part of the book. It is dedicated to understanding the major components of what we are calling the human computer and how it relates to a regular computer. In doing this, we will first look at some of the more subtle energetic systems of the body because these form a part of the Divine Computer. We will also look at how these fields are quantum and morphic in that they act as transmitting and receiving systems that are "intuitively" detected. This will also help us refine our findings on what defines our System and Processes for internal and external miracles with the purpose of understanding why these steps that are common to the practitioners and Gurus are important considerations for success. We will also look at our traditional computer and attempt to develop an analogy to the Divine Computer so that we can develop our own process.

Now What?

So at this point, we are going to introduce both esoteric and non-esoteric "truths" about the human body to develop a different model of its function, and energetic systems under a title of morphic energetics. We are going to look more closely at subtle energies and how the body works.

We shall attempt to determine whether there is any information that further substantiates these findings up to now. Then we shall attempt to modify our ideas about the human computer and how it compares to the traditional systems. We will then attempt to summarize our findings into a set of steps, systems and processes that we would use as a Divine Programmer that proactively reprograms the Divine Computer.

If for some reason, you are not so keen on technology, especially the fringe type, you can skip to Chapter 36 which summarizes all three parts of this book. It is called "What Have We Learned" and is provided as a repeat of the conclusions we came to in all three parts of this book. You can always come back to read the details.

26

WHAT IS CONSCIOUSNESS?

"It is not death we need to change our beliefs on, it is our view of life."

Ed Rychkun

We have seen that consciousness simply can't be explained or defined by conventional scientific wisdom. And this mystical nothing of the subconscious is even more perplexing because how the hell does it store all these programs and information? Where is it? Traditional scientific wisdom simply says it is part of the brain. Well there is a whole new science and thought emerging that says it is quite independent of the brain.

Most people, when asked what Consciousness is, will reply that it is the state of being awake. That is most certainly true, for that it is. But when people reply with this answer, they are almost always talking about the state of being physically awake. This is not the kind of consciousness we're talking about here. For one could be physically awake and still be largely or totally unconscious in their overall awareness. Here is an interesting definition.

Consciousness is the ability of a being to recognize patterns and meaning with respect to events taking place, both within oneself and in the realm in which the self exist and operates

If we consult a standard dictionary or encyclopaedia, we find that Consciousness is commonly defined as *"the characteristics of a being generally regarded to comprise qualities such as subjectivity, self-awareness, sentience, sapience, and the ability to perceive the relationship between oneself and one's environment."* That's a mouthful too!

Subjectivity means one's own perceptions of one's existence. Self-awareness means that one is able to ponder and comprehend the fact that one is actually aware of one's own characteristics and perception - being aware that you are aware, so to speak. Sentience is the capability of having perceptions and feelings. Sapience is discernment or wisdom - the ability to know that some things are more desirable than others if a particular condition or outcome is preferred.

This definition of Consciousness does an overall good job of accurately describing the condition. But we could express the basic definition of what Consciousness actually is in a more concise and simplistic way. Keeping in mind and building upon the popular dictionary definition, one could say that at its essence, Consciousness is the ability of a being to recognize patterns and meaning with respect to events taking place, both within oneself and in the external realm in which the self exists and operates.

This ability is the fundamental driving force of all Creation. It could be said that all of Creation itself IS Consciousness in various forms and states of awareness. Consciousness is required for matter to exist. Consciousness creates the observable effects we perceive in our world. Everything that exists in the seemingly "external" domain first exists as a construct in Consciousness before becoming manifested through form.

But ask a scientist to define it and out comes a vague conundrum. The more recent developments in quantum physics suggests that consciousness is a quantum field as it can be nowhere, everywhere, create things, be no thing, have no element of time and behave according to the rules of nonlocality and collapsing; all depending on The Observer Effect of creating that imaginary reality by simply focusing on it. We will discuss this in a subsequent chapter but let us first look at understanding consciousness when one experiences a Near Death Experience.

Consciousness And Near Death Experiences

NDE's are short for Near Death Experiences. There are millions of people dying all the time—then coming back to tell about it. What is of particular interest is that there were so many of these cases coming back with miraculous changes—like big, big changes in their lives and even in their bodies. Yes, miracles—totally unexplainable miracles. Among many other books and websites, one of the best is **The Big Book of Near Death Experiences** written by a timeless researcher on this subject, **P.M. H. Atwater**. She has herself experienced and survived 3 NDE's. And this is a *big* book. Being a new breed of clinical professional that has dropped the flaps of their own belief boxes, she has studied thousands of cases. She has compiled her observations about people pronounced clinically dead. These have returned to tell about their little vacation.

Now, you must understand that NDE's mean the person is dead! Gone! "clinically" dead for some period of time like 15-60 minutes! Heart stopped and the body weighs one half to one ounce less! Yes, something left the body. This means that the cells are dying in the brain from lack of oxygen, and it is coffin time. At least that is what the medical belief box tells us. After all, if you stop feeding oxygen to the brain, cells die rapidly, right? Wrong!

Atwater reports there are 13 million cases of NDE's that have been recorded. Of the thousands that she has herself studied, she reports that an energy force of approximately one ounce simply leaves the body (nice to know a ghost weighs an ounce!) and floats up and away to take a little vacation. Is this consciousness that has left—the force that gives life? Yes, we say so; the Light Body encompassing the Soul! But whatever it is separates at the point of death and the NDE people are completely aware of this separation as they see their bodies lie lifeless below.

Consciousness--Separate Intelligent Energy Form

Now here is the mind-bender that should flatten the side of any belief box. This consciousness that separates can see, hear, think, move, communicate, tell jokes, and retain senses regardless of distance from the body. In fact the senses are even better—heightened. How can this be without the brain or body? It even keeps a memory of everything that was ever learned, experienced, and felt along with all of the senses (perhaps taste may be questionable unless you can get some ghost food!). It actually hauls out consciousness! And this includes sub consciousness which has stuff in it from previous lives according to past life therapists. These are left completely intact. But did we not learn that the brain was responsible for all that? And when you croak, that memory is no more? Not so.

Consciousness, which clearly includes the life giving force, leaves the body, goes on a little trip, then comes back and ta dah, the body has life again. All the dead cells are happy again. Rigamortis has no say here—the white face gets pink again, and it is wakey, wakey time! All is better than before—sometimes with a few miracles kicked in.

But what about the little vacation that this consciousness takes when it leaves the body? It is like a little visit to an amusement park. Where does it go? What happens?

Well, here is what is very astounding. Atwater clinically confirms with thousands of cases what one of the foremost early researchers found when he checked out this little vacation away from the body. We will get back to Atwater, but his name was **Raymond Moody** who did this as far back as 1975 when he published the highly controversial book **Life After Life**. In this book, he described the little vacation in detail. Now Moody built his study on some 150 cases of near death experience, not a lot according to a statistician, but nevertheless relevant because he clearly pioneered the definition of the NDE stages and this is what Atwater confirms in her studies with thousands.

He defined his cases as people who were either resuscitated after pronounced dead, had severe injuries and were close to dead, or those who were present and being told what was happening as the patient "died". He noted that these cases were all disconnected and knew nothing about each other's experience. This was important because then the stories would be personal and not influenced.

This little trip that the life force—consciousness takes exhibits striking similarities between cases. Moody broke these down to specific stages and observations not particularly in any set order. What were they?

Well to begin with the people had what he called ineffability—a difficulty in describing the trip with any literal justice. It was unexplainable and beyond their comprehension. Then he outlined the stages.

The first stage was **Hearing the news**. They heard the news of dying from the Doc or others around the croaked body. They saw people and events around them.

Another stage was that they had the **Feeling of peace and quiet**. They experienced wonderful feelings of comfort, peace, quiet, relief, and no pain. No hell and brimstone, just peace.

Now the next stage was the **Noise**. They had unusual auditory sensations of buzzing, ringing, and clicks. I guess this was like getting tickets at Disneyland.

Then there was the **Dark Tunnel**. They were pulled rapidly through a dark space, tunnel, valley, pipe, or some such thing in a wonderful worry free ride. Sort of like getting into the amusement park.

But get this one. They had an **Out of body** experience. After they *died* they would find themselves looking at their body, watching and hearing things as a spectator. They felt like pure consciousness that was indescribable—most called it a spiritual body—but they could not touch other bodies or material things. No one could hear or see them. They were separate, weightless, floating, going through things like a cloud. They had projections like rounded limbs but all their senses were intact. Consciousness existed outside the body! What we would commonly call a ghost! So the other part of us—the ghost—was the one invited to the amusement park.

The next stage was what he called **Meeting others**. They encountered other spiritual beings, people they had known before, like friends and relatives that came to greet them. They were recognizable ghosts. Everything was filled with white light and was beautiful—like a feeling of coming home. These beings had a clear body outline but no physical body. Moody says the type of people encountered depended on a person's background. But there was no speaking. Thoughts were communicated as a direct transfer—no language. They were totally telepathic with no need for any language.

At this stage he says there are typical questions that come forward telepathically like: Are you ready to die? What have you done in your life that is sufficient? There was a point of stressing preparation yet there was no condemnation or judgment, only total love and acceptance coming from the light.

It gets even more bizarre at this amusement park visit. The next stage is the **Review appearance**. This is where a bright light Being presents a high speed video panorama review of life. Here the intent is only to provoke reflections. Get this; rapid temporal memories in chronological order occur almost instantaneous. The images generate emotions as they flip by. The being asks what they have done with their life, stressing love, and pointing out things. No one could gage time. It is like the stories you hear about when people drown. They have their whole life flash by in a moment—instant replay of consciousness. It is the same as the notion that your life flashes by in one instant at the point of drowning.

After the review stage, the reports reflect **Border or Limit approach**. There seems to be some limit like a fence or border where over the line there is peace, tranquility, golden light, and joy. But the ones that come back don't go over this limit and go through the last stage. Obviously if you do not come back, that is a whole different story! This must be the world of life between lives.

At the **Coming back** stage some would come back spurred by some Being which many said was God. They would be sent back for obligations, or pulled by relatives. Some actually felt a re-entry into the physical body.

Now, this is really interesting. With those that came back, they inevitably had a totally changed life, just like in many of the miracles cases. Moody goes on to say that most times this experience created a totally new attitude in life. Some reported enhanced senses, some picked up on other's feelings better, expressed a need to cultivate love of others, seek knowledge, became morally purified, and created new clear goals mostly in service of others. The bottom line is that their belief systems and behavior had changed dramatically—an unexplainable miracle.

Moody makes a parallel to the works of Plato, the Bible, and the Tibetan Book of the Dead. He says they contain a description of the steps of the Soul after physical death. They are exactly the same. First, the Soul departs the body and enters a swoon and a void where consciousness still exists. The Soul may hear alarming noises and it enters an envelope of gray misty illumination. There is a surprise of the Soul to see itself outside of the body, but then hears relatives and friends morning over the body. There is a feeling of regret and it wonders where it should go. It is a shining body of no material substance with intensified senses. The Soul may then meet other beings and sees clear white light. There are feelings of immense peace and contentment as a mirror of the entire life of all deeds good and bad are reflected.

And we can certainly attest to the *Tibetan Book of the Dead.* Although it is pretty hard to understand it certainly scopes out what Moody concludes.

When people go through this they inevitably become conscious of a Life Force (whatever you want to call it matters not—Universal consciousness or the mind of God). Once you know this and really believe it, and it is very hard not to when you yourself have experienced it, it is impossible to worry about fear and death.

This is something that has been known all along, from the Ancient Tibetan Book of the Dead to studies in the 70's and now. But back to Atwater. She confirms it all again in a professional, objective, clinical way. This book is indeed a revelation about what happens. And if you care to check this topic out yourself, there are hundreds of books and thousands of websites on this topic.

What Does Near Dying Tell Us?

What is Atwater saying in her studies? Besides confirming all the other NDE works, she gives us some relevant insights from her work. She tells us that life is immortal consciousness that grows in an unlimited way. Most of her cases see a book of life—a full history of everyone. Their faculties are heightened and they retain that expansion upon return. During the little NDE vacation, the consciousness always has the power to make choices. She observes the intuitive mind is a sacred gift, and the rational mind is a faithful servant. We have forgotten this and honor the servant.

What are we being told here? This consciousness of ours—or life force—is alive and does not croak like the body. In fact it IS LIFE as it gives such to the body upon entry and exit. It can take a vacation, come back and remember the vacation even if the brain and body are dead! It is the field of transpersonal experience that is the source of all knowledge and memory—not the brain. It is independent of the person's physical and mental system. Whole consciousness is stored somewhere in space not in the brain. The brain serves as a relay station for connecting to our bodies when we are in a conscious state of being awake. Interesting how regression therapy is able to tap into this vast information bank, is it not?

The rest of the lesson was that death is a passing, a simple shift in vibration from one state of energy to another. The body is a temporary vehicle to have fun in while we are on the Earth—so why don't we?

What else? Here is the big one. There is something most people called God—some—angelic or Divine type ghost—that they met and had a telepathic experience with. Is it some figment of the mind? Is it really the Force or God? What is relevant is that *there is something* and it is consistently part of our consciousness. Period! It does not really matter what it is, does it? What matters is when this ghost of God appears—in the mind or in person—life changes big time!

Now, some scientist could tell you that this is just pure crap and it was people's imagination that made up this story but we would ask why is it that so many unrelated cases came up with the same story? Do all these documented cases just copy each other to piss off the scientists? Is that just a coincidence with no statistical significance?

There is one more thing before we leave Atwater and her incredible information as she is no stranger to documenting miracle healing cases. She notes prayer and meditation top the ways to set up for miracles to occur.

What is pretty obvious is that we have some invisible and separate energy field that gives us life. And when it decides to leave the old body, the life ceases. That is not exactly a mystery. But having this energy measured and keeping all of our consciousness and sensory abilities intact; wow! That's a bit different from the old belief box. Actually there may be many people who are not so surprised at this notion but they are not willing to readily admit it in public—peer pressure from "science".

What is indeed difficult to overcome was that when people came back to life—into the dead body that is—the body was still ok—not death smelly and dead brain cells clogging life, but fine. And then there was a life transformation. This little episode that consciousness took altered something in the mind and body resulting in life changing habits. Their belief and faith had been completely altered to produce new habits. These sometimes involved healing miracles but the greatest miracle was that within seconds to a minute, that person's life was totally transformed. And this transformation became centered in the "heart" not the ego or the brain.

Now, if you came back after you croaked for an hour, floated around in a tunnel, got your ticket to this wonderful, peace filled amusement park, talked to some friendly ghosts, met the big boss in the sky, then had an instant replay of your life's movie, remembered everything out of your body, what would it do to you?

Would you believe anyone—scientific or otherwise—that told you when you croak that's it? Not likely! What if they said it was nonsense what you saw? What if they told you miracles like the one you had was nonsense? You would not care much to associate with them and simply keep your new knowledge to yourself. They would become the idiots, wouldn't they? Simply knowing it would be your truth. And no one on the planet would convince you otherwise. Your belief system would have taken a paradigm shift because you knew your own truth. Period.

Would this change your approach to life? Would you then be afraid of dying? Would you not realize you needed to do something meaningful and had been given a new chance? Would you be grateful? What would you be like after? Would you be completely freaked out and shrivel away? The possibility of that would be remote because you would have gained a new will and purpose to live. And where would that notion be? In a thing called consciousness—your mind.

Perhaps if you listened to the people living inside their limited belief boxes on this you may think you had gone mad, but maybe you would change your consciousness—your awareness—to accept beliefs outside of your usual belief box. You realize you don't need to croak to go through this. But you do have to change your beliefs and be totally faithful to facilitate some changes—especially miracles. That is what miracles do. They provoke a paradigm shift in the mind—in your consciousness and your beliefs.

In addition to the conclusion that consciousness - all of it subconscious and conscious - is a field separate from the body, is another conclusion. It is that this floating consciousness had a meeting with that illusive Higher Being, Divine self, The Force, that other energetic system that allegedly had the power to issue the instructions to change belief, reprogram the subconscious, create a miracle, and then send you back to a body that was stiff.

So perhaps the enormous lesson here is that in our steps, sending this petition, or asking a Higher Power for assistance is not such a silly idea?

Now let us go back to another energetic component of our bodies, the chakra system which science gives little credence to. But before we do that let us sum up the important conclusions.

Important Conclusions About Near Dying

With relevance to our quest as to why miracles exist, there are several important conclusions:

The first conclusion is that subconscious and conscious is an intelligent field separate from the body. This consciousness that separates can see, hear, think, move, communicate, tell jokes, and retain senses regardless of distance from the body. In fact the senses are even better—heightened. It even keeps a memory of everything that was ever learned, experienced, and felt along with all of the senses.

The second is another conclusion separate from the brain and that the brain does give orders to the subconscious. The brain serves as a relay station for connecting to our bodies when we are in a conscious state of being awake.

The third conclusion is that there is something most people called God—some—angelic or Divine type entity that they met and had a telepathic experience with.

The fourth is that through this experience of total detachment from reality, many came back healed mentally or physically. Some process of Divine Intervention was encountered which changed them - some for the rest of their lives.

27

THE CHAKRA ENERGETIC SYSTEM

"As you create in the mind above the heart so you manifest into the material below the heart."

Ed Rychkun

The Chakra Energetic System

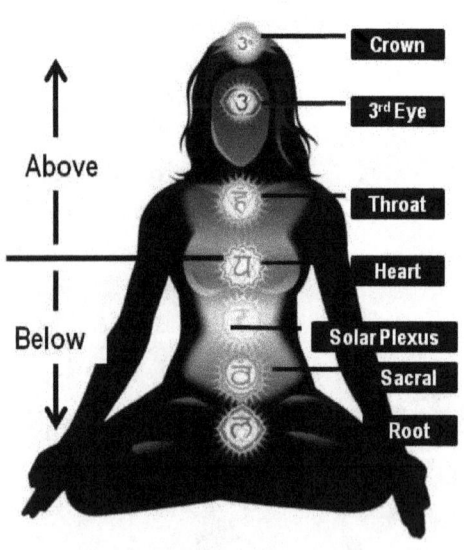

Chakra is a Sanskrit word meaning wheel, or vortex, and it refers to each of the seven main energy centers of which our consciousness, our energy system, is composed.

These chakras, or energy centers, function as pumps or valves, regulating the flow of energy through our system by rotating the flow of energy in a clockwise direction. The functioning of the chakras reflects decisions we make concerning how we choose to respond to conditions in our life. We open and close these valves when we decide what to think, and what to feel, and how we choose to perceive and experience the world around us. The main chakras are described below.

1. Root Chakra - Represents our foundation and feeling of being grounded. It is located at the base of the spine in the tailbone area. Emotional issues are survival issues such as financial independence, money, and food.

2. Sacral Chakra - Our connection and ability to accept others and new experiences. It is located in the lower abdomen, about 2 inches below the navel and 2 inches in. Emotional issues are a sense of abundance, well-being, pleasure, sexuality.

3. Solar Plexus Chakra - Our ability to be confident and in-control of our lives. It is located in the upper abdomen in the stomach area. Emotional issues are Self-worth, self-confidence, self-esteem.

4. Heart Chakra - Our ability to love. It is located in the center of chest just above heart. Emotional issues: Love, joy, inner peace.

5. Throat Chakra - Our ability to communicate. It is located in the throat. Emotional issues are communication, self-expression of feelings, and the truth.

6. Third Eye Chakra - Our ability to focus on and see the big picture. Its location is in the forehead between the eyes. (Also called the Brow Chakra). Emotional issues are intuition, imagination, wisdom, ability to think and make decisions.

7. Crown Chakra - The highest Chakra represents our ability to be fully connected spiritually. It is located at the very top of the head. Emotional issues are inner and outer beauty, our connection to spirituality, pure bliss.

The chakras are not physical. They are overlay aspects of our consciousness like our auras are aspects of our consciousness. The chakras are more dense than the auras, because of the amount of energy which flows through them, but not as dense as the physical body. Chakras interact with the physical body through two major vehicles, the endocrine system and the nervous system. Each of the seven chakras is associated with one of the seven endocrine glands, and also with a group of nerves called a plexus. Thus, each chakra is associated with particular parts of the body and particular functions within the body controlled by that plexus or that endocrine gland to which it is associated.

All of your senses, all of your perceptions, all of your possible states of awareness, everything it is possible for you to experience, can be divided into seven categories. Each category is associated with a particular chakra. Thus, the chakras represent not only particular parts of your physical body, but also particular parts of your consciousness.

Understanding the chakras allows you to understand the relationship between your consciousness and your body, and to thus see your body as a map of your consciousness. It gives you a better understanding of yourself and those around you.

Maintaining balance within your chakras is important, because when your chakras are not functioning correctly this can cause the glands associated to it and surrounding it to also function incorrectly. When your chakras are not balanced you can usually feel this on both an emotional and physical level.

As Above So Below

Unlike the physical nervous system in the body which is like a hardwired sensing and response system, the chakra energetic system of subtle energy is more like a wireless network that provides sensing abilities from the outside environment on a more subtle level. This is not a well understood phenomenon but as said, it links with specific biological, biochemical and chemical functions in the body. Much like the communities of cells, there are major functions that have been known for hundreds of years.

You may have heard the expression As Above, So Below. It's a pretty common expression brought forward by Hermes and Thoth. What does it mean? Does it mean that everything above in the cosmos is the same as on earth? Does it mean all that we think above in consciousness is the same as below? What is above and what is below?

With reference to the picture at the beginning of this chapter, let us give you a new perspective on this. Essentially above relates to conscious reality which is not real; we could say it is manifested. Below is the created physical reality. In simple terms, what is in consciousness can be created below in physical reality. The central chakra is the balance point from one to the other. As you manifest in the mind *above* the heart so you create into the material reality *below* the heart. You are deploying energy centers that phase from invisible energy (thoughts, images, words) through the heart (emotion) to the visible (intent, relationship, material). As you create intent above in the higher dimensions, through the heart, so you create in the lower dimensions.

Each of these seven main chakras has a responsibility within the human body. The energy process changes from non-physical to physical as it proceeds from the three above to the three below. These subtle energy centers are known to have a direct affect on seven major groups of physical organs. These organs control the physiological and psychological functions related to the *verb* actions (see table) on the left. In other words starting in a non-physical world, proceeding down the axis. With reference to the picture below, to quantify this process from the top down:

1. In the Crown Chakra, we form or know a *thought*,
2. In the 3rd Eye chakra, we *see* an *image*,
3. In the Throat Chakra we *speak words*,
4. In the Heart Chakra *we feel* an *emotion*,
5. In the Solar Plexus Chakra *we will the intention to act*,
6. In the Sacral Chakra, *we relate to other things needed to assist*,
7. In the Root Chakra *we have and indulge in the material reality.*

Although each of these have biochemical functions we will cover later, they illustrate the same **7 step** process we use for creating something or manifesting reality. These words and their relation to the chakra energy centers go a long way back into ancient knowledge and are still used today.

The process illustrates how subtle energy appears to manifest from non-physical thoughts to a material experience. Everybody does this every day. What this also reflects is a time old expression of as above, so below; what is brought into the thoughts is manifested into the reality below.

Is this a coincidence? We think not. Is this a key to the way we create our reality? We believe so.

The Chakra Antennae

Through time, there is a system of magnetic and unexplainable energy that flows within the body that has never ever left the writings of humanity. It is about these things called chakras that are spinning vortexes of energy aligned vertically through and in the physical body. It is hard to find someone these days that does not acknowledge that they exist. And secondly the other change is there are vast amounts of writings that enforce a legitimate tie-in to the physics and chemistry of the physical form. Even medicine is shifting on this topic. Of course science and medicine attempts to invalidate this old knowledge so it rattles around the esoteric world with little support.

But for eons of time, each chakra has been assigned a special purpose and essence in relation to these seven major body functions that have a specific vibratory range and also governs certain physical "action" as well as a conscious "essence."

In structure, the vertical line of energy centers goes from a higher vibration of violet, to a lower vibration of red. It also reflects the process of imaginary (above) to physical (below).

CHAKRA	GLAND	I	NOTE	ESSENCE
7 Crown	Pineal	KNOW	B	Spiritual Connection
6 3rd Eye	Hypo-thalamus	SEE	A	Intuition Awareness
5 Throat	Thyroid	SPEAK	G	Communication
4 Heart	Thymus	FEEL	F	Love Expression
3 Solar Plexus	Adrenal	WILL	E	Personal Power
2 Sacral	Sexual	RELATE	D	Sexual Capacity
1 Root	Adrenal	HAVE	C	Survival, Will to Live

It is interesting that over considerable time, the same picture evolves; that these connect between outside influences to inside physical organs affecting behaviour as in the above table. It is like an invisible antennae system that picks up subtle energies and then translates them into some chemical, biochemical or physical result or action.

The seven major chakra centers could be likened to seven electrical batteries or seven dynamic force centers within the physical vessel. You draw forth into these seven power centers the specific qualities, attributes and virtues of the transmitters. The manner in which you qualify and use these energies determines your energetic signature and sets your resonance as to what you are, and how you respond—mentally and physically.

If you look at the progression of these chakras, they go from 3 above the heart to 3 below the heart. And if you look at their overall documented functions, at the top it starts as the mind generates the energy of thoughts, and then projects these outward and inward through the body. The body adds emotion, then creates intent and action, and then connects with the universe to generate an event. A reaction, hence an experience, comes back to you in the form of a perception of that event.

The energy process changes from non-physical to physical as it proceeds from the three above to the three below. These subtle energy centers are known to have a direct affect on seven major groups of physical organs. These organs control the physiological and psychological functions related to the **verb** actions on the left. In other words starting in a non-physical world, you **know** a **thought**, **see** an **image**, **speak** some **words**, and **feel** an **emotion**. This may or may not prompt an action. Assuming an action is prompted, from that point, you move into the physical world. By using intent, you **will** yourself into an **action** which will allow you to **relate** to others and physical **events**, thereby allowing you to **have** a **material** experience. You may be interested to know that we did not invent this. These words and their relation to the chakra energy centers go a long way back into ancient knowledge and are still used today. The process illustrates how subtle energy manifests from a non-physical thought to a material experience. Everybody does this every day. What this also reflects is a time old expression of As above, So below; what is manifested into the thoughts is created into the reality below.

Notice how the top three chakras are non-physical while the bottom three are physical, with the heart as the balance point. Notice also how the bottom three are essentially ego driven reflecting survival (the will to live, have relations and acquire physical comforts) in the physical world, while the top three are spiritually driven (higher knowledge or Spirit, intuition and truth), reflecting non-physical life concepts.

In the perfect situation, these energy centers are supposed to be balanced by their counterpart. Thus thought (above) balances material (below), image balances events, and words balance actions. They are balanced by the energy system (emotion) of the heart. That is called balancing, alignment, and coherence of subtle energies.

So in the picture of the energy centers, you will note that each **verb** and **subject** can have either a negative or positive attribute. You can **know** a negative or positive **thought** and **have** lived a **material** life of **hell** or **heaven.** The idea is that if you want a joyful life, your experiences and perceptions should be focused on the positive energies where harmony, peace, clarity, and joy dominate. That is the perfect world of course. The truth is that these are simply choices you make. You will come to understand that when you choose negative or positive perceptions, trigger thoughts, add emotion, and you send a subtle energy packet out to find more buddies.

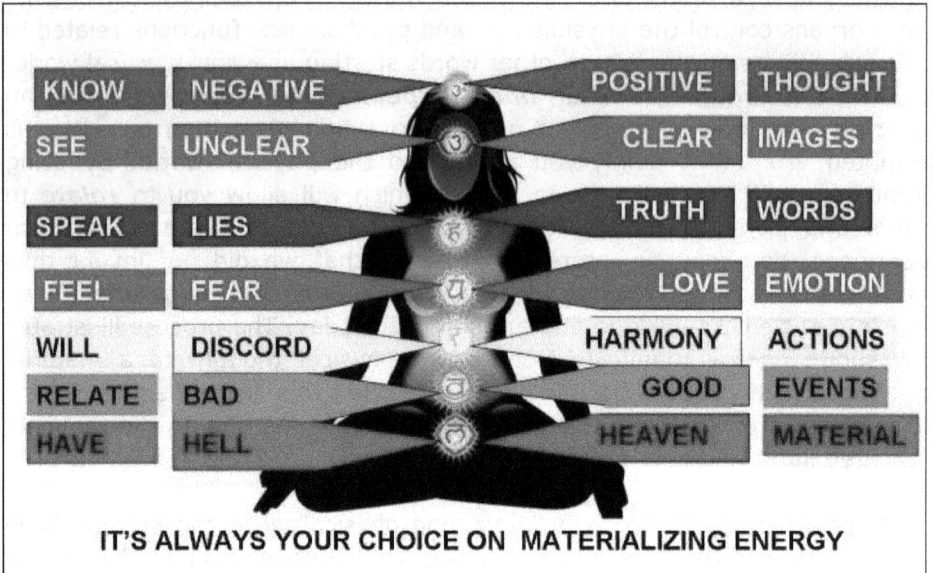

IT'S ALWAYS YOUR CHOICE ON MATERIALIZING ENERGY

By managing these top verbs to produce positive subtle energy packets, you can work towards that perfect world of harmony, a good life and Heaven on Earth. By not managing this process, the energy feedback loop simply responds to whatever thoughts, words and emotions you are sending out by default. The real challenge here is to live a life that always keeps positive stuff in the top three because they create likeness below; and to always react positively from below (experience) as they create more similar energy to manifest above.

Clearing our energy system of that which blocks us is a key element required to fulfill the Law of Attraction. In fact, the secret about the movie "The Secret" is that in order to attract what you want you first have to clear your own energy field, belief systems, self programming of that which blocks the conscious mind intent and sabotages you. Otherwise you are trying to overlay what you have already put there – then your subconscious system responds in *"Oh really, I don't believe you"*. In our energy fields we have to clear first then add new. That is the way we consciously learn – which is also what we are supposed to do.

The human energy system includes the upward and downward flow of universal energy into the human body and the seven major chakra's, or energy vortices, which attach to the spinal column. These and other parts of our energy system are very dynamic and change quickly based on what we think and feel. If our thoughts are not positive, our energy system reacts by pulling in negative energy and can become blocked. Old behavior patterns repeat themselves, preventing us from moving towards our greatest intentions. When our energy system is clear, however, we are able to project positive energy, one of the key elements required to fulfill the law of attraction. It is therefore absolutely imperative that you make the effort to clear your negative thought patterns. Remember you have to first clear your negative thought patterns before you start to re-program yourself with more positive thought patterns. You must keep in mind that this is something that may or may not occur all at once depending on the depth and layers of these patterns so you must be consistent and keep working at it.

When the chakras have been affected adversely, one can build up dark matter between charkas and can cause what we view as a constrictor to a chakra that is trying to open and flow at its capacity. These can be called Inner Chakral spaces. When this is cleansed then the chakra once cleared can or has the ability to function wider and broader to its fullest capacity Hmmm... One could view this as an O ring that became dry rotted from non-lubrication. Once you get rid of the dry rotted O ring and open up... you then develop the new one.

The way we like to think about chakras is that they are sockets. You can plug a loving tendril from Source into each one and let that divine energy fill you up. But sometimes chakras can get clogged, and when your chakras aren't clear and spinning freely, you're likely to have problems in the area where you're clogged. For example, if your heart chakra is clogged, you probably feel very disconnected from other people. If your third eye is clogged, your intuition is probably not getting through. If your crown chakra is clogged, you probably feel disconnected from God (Source). If your solar plexus chakra is clogged, you probably feel scared or victimized. A clogged throat chakra can feel like you're being suppressed or you've got something you want to say that you're not saying.

Clogged chakras can cause physical problems related to the area where they function. For example, if someone is intimidating you, you might have digestive issues in your solar plexus (i.e. nervous stomach). If there is someone you really need to talk to but you just can't bring yourself to do it, you may end up with a sore throat. Clogged intuition could result in a headache. And so on.

The Dormant Higher Abilities

Another important part of this is that unlike the hardwired nervous-sensory system that is sensing things more physical, the wireless chakra system is sensing via the metaphysical and therefore has a direct impact on the state of psychic abilities. Here is a table to relate to.

7TH OR CROWN CHAKRA TOP OF HEAD	
Psychic Abilities	To be open, To know Intuition, Precognition, Connection with infinite intelligence, To have faith, Connection with God
Physiological Correlations	Pituitary glands, Old mammalian brain, Greater right-hemisphere correlation
Physical Imbalances	Baldness, Brain tumors, Cancer, Epilepsy, Migraine headaches, Parkinson's disease, Pituitary problems
Psycological Imbalances	Excessive gullibility, Memory disorders, Multiple personalities, Nightmares, Split personality

6TH OR THIRD EYE, KNOWLEDGE CHAKRA, CENTER OF FOREHEAD	
Psychic Abilities	Clairvoyance, Psychic reading, To have vision or insight, Photographic memory, Telekinesis
Physiological Correlations	Pineal gland, Neo-mammalian brain, Greater left-brain hemisphere correlation
Physical Imbalances	Brain tumors, Cancer, Central nervous system problems, Eye and visual problems Headaches (sinus), Sinus problems
Psychological Imbalances	Extreme confusion, Fixations, Inability to focus, Intelligence deficiencies, Living in a fantasy world, Paranoia, Poor visual memory, Psychotic behavior, Schizophrenia, Severe retardation

5TH OR THROAT CHAKRA, EXPRESSIVE CHAKRA, CENTER OF THROAT	
Psychic Abilities	Communication center, Telepathy, Clairaudience, Inner voice, Tone healing
Physiological Correlations	Thyroid, Parathyroids, Lymphatic system, Brain stem
Physical Imbalances	Ear and hearing problems, Cancer, Lympathic problems, Mouth problems, Neck and shoulder problems, Parathyroid problems, Speech problems, Teeth problems, Thyroid problems, Throat problems
Psychological Imbalances	Inability to express self in words, Logorrhea (nonstop verbal chatter), Poor auditory memory, Stuttering

4TH OR HEART CHAKRA, CHEST	
Psychic Abilities	To be in affinity with, To be at one with, To connect with, Compassion, Unconditional love
Physiological Correlations	Thymus gland, Heart, Vascular system, Lungs, Respiratory system
Physical Imbalances	Auto-immune system problems, Circulatory problems, Heart problems, High blood pressure, Lung cancer, Lung problems, Respiratory problems, Thymus problems, Upper back problems, Vascular problems
Psychological Imbalances	At war with yourself, Feelings of alienation, inability to bond with another, Self-destructive tendencies, Suicide

3RD OR SOLAR PLEXUS, PERSONALITY, CHAKRA, ABOVE NAVEL	
Psychic Abilities	Astral projection, To be empowered, To manifest, To be in control of yourself, Psychic healing, Levitation
Physiological Correlations	Adrenal glands, Solar plexus (neural center), Autonomic control center
Physical Imbalances	Absorption problems, Adrenal problems, Arthritis, Anorexia nervosa, Cancer, Coordination problems, Liver problems, Multiple sclerosis, Obesity, Premature aging Stomach problems
Psychological Imbalances	Addictive personality, Catatonic schizophrenia, Compulsive behavior, Excessive anger or fear, Manic-depressive behavior, Obsessive behavior, Sleep problems

2ND OR FEELING CENTER, SEXUAL CHAKRA, CENTER ABDOMEN	
Psychic Abilities	Clairsentience, Emotional feelings, Balance of male and female energies

Physiological Correlations	Insulin-producing glands in the pancreas and spleen
Physical Imbalances	Anemia, Allergies, Diabetes, Diarrhea, Duodenal ulcers, Hypoglycemia, Kidney problems, Leukemia, Lower back problems, Pancreas problems, Premenstrual syndrome, Spleen problems
Psychological Imbalances	Chameleon personality, Depression, Hysteria, Unable to be sexually intimate

1ST OR ROOT CHAKRA, BASE OF SPINE	
Psychic Abilities	Grounding, Realizing, Letting go, Surviving
Physiological Correlations	Ovaries, Testes, Placenta
Physical Imbalances	Cancer, Colon problems, Bladder problems, Female reproductive-organ problems, Fluid retention, Male reproductive problems, Sciatica problems, Urethral problems, Yeast infection
Psychological Imbalances	Accident prone, Being in survival, Dependent personality, Identity crisis, Weak ego structure

Each of the chakras has a vortex projecting out of the body into the auras that surround the body. These vortexes reach out perpendicular to the body axis and behave according to quantum mechanics, also are non-matter to matter concentrators, located at each chakra. We will cover this later.

Important Conclusions About The Chakras

The first important conclusion is that the 7 steps that we have outlined as the way we create things comes out in the above to below functions of the chakras. The body chakra system is the key manifestor and creator of reality. To quantify this process from the top down as above so below:

1. In the Crown Chakra, we *form* a *thought*,
2. In the 3rd Eye chakra, we *see* an *image,*
3. In the Throat Chakra we *speak words,*
4 In the Heart Chakra we *feel* an *emotion,*
5. In the Solar Plexus Chakra *we create the intention to act,*
6. In the Sacral Chakra, *we engage in relations needed to assist,*
7. In the Root Chakra *we indulge in the material reality.*

The second conclusion is that understanding the chakras allows you to understand the relationship between your consciousness and your body, and to thus see your body as a map of your consciousness. It gives you a better understanding of yourself and those around you.

The third conclusion is each of the chakras has a connection to the physical body and are monitoring subtle energies. These have specific attributes which can be positive or negative. By understanding your signature of behavior, you have a means of identifying and correcting the dysfunctions that manifest in dis-ease in the body

The fourth conclusion is that these chakras have higher functions and abilities that are dormant. Unlike the hardwired nervous-sensory system that is sensing things more physical; the wireless chakra system is sensing via the metaphysical and therefore has a direct impact on the state of psychic abilities.

The fifth important conclusion is that each of the chakras has a vortex projecting out of the body into the auras that surround the body. These vortexes reach out perpendicular to the body axis and behave according to quantum mechanics, also are non-matter to matter concentrators, located at each chakra.

28

THE HEART ENERGETIC SYSTEM

"The gateway into the level of quantum energy, and our subconscious is through the silent powerhouse of the heart and its brain."

Ed Rychkun

In the previous chapter, we got a feeling for the heart as the energetic balance point of the chakra system. To most the heart is just an organ that pumps blood to keep us alive. The sayings of loving you with all my heart, heart of a lion, broken heart, from the bottom of my heart, cross my heart, bleeding heart and heart of gold are only a few of the 120 examples posted on the free dictionary at *http://idioms.thefreedictionary.com/heart.* Where do these come from? They come from the negative and positive choices and characteristics of the energetic heart chakra. To most the "heart" is the center of love so reflected in the love for the special ones in our life as in "falling in love" and "I love you" as a descriptor of special emotion. But love, as we are coming to understand, is much more than just a physical expression. It appears to be a universal "soup" of all that is and a heart-brain is the access point. As we are about to describe, the heart has its own nervous system, its own heart-brain and heart-mind that does not take orders from that big dummy in the attic - the head brain. And it has its own special subtle, powerful energetic fields.

The Double Torus And Energy Vortexes

HeartMath LLC is a cutting edge company providing a range of unique services, products, and technology to boost performance, productivity, health and well-being while dramatically reducing stress. Founded in 1991 as a non-profit research organization by Doc Childre, HeartMath has earned global recognition for their unique research-based techniques and proprietary technology to transform the stress of change and uncertainty. They have learned to help many bring coherence and renewed energy to the workplace and the home. But, they have also studied and reported many other revealing and revolutionary characteristics of the heart. All you have to do is go to **www.heartmath.com** and check it out for yourself.

Rollin McCraty, PhD is the Executive Vice President and Director of Research for HeartMath. He reports the heart, like the brain, generates a powerful electromagnetic field. He explains in **The Energetic Heart** that: *"The heart generates the largest electromagnetic field in the body. The electrical field as measured in an electrocardiogram (ECG) is about 60 times greater in amplitude than the brain waves recorded in an electroencephalogram (EEG)."*

"The heart is a sensory organ and acts as a sophisticated information encoding and processing center that enables it to learn, remember, and make independent functional decisions. The heart's electromagnetic field contains certain information or coding, which researchers are trying to understand, that is transmitted throughout and outside of the body. One of the most significant findings of IHM's research related to this field is that intentionally generated positive emotions can change this information coding."

That discovery raises the question whether the cardioelectromagnetic field information transmitted from an individual who is angry, fearful, depressed or experiencing some other negative emotion, takes on beneficial properties when it is influenced by positive emotions. It is coming to light that the care, compassion, love or other positive emotion is not only transmitted throughout an individual's body as the cardioelectromagnetic field radiates through it, but transferred externally as well to people in close proximity <u>and</u> even over long distances like miles.

"This preliminary data elucidates the intriguing finding that the electromagnetic signals generated by the heart have the capacity to affect others around us. It appears that when the mother placed her attention on the baby that she became more sensitive to the subtle electromagnetic signals generated by the infant's heart. These findings have intriguing implications, suggesting that a mother in a psychophysiologically coherent state became more sensitive to the subtle electromagnetic information encoded in the electromagnetic signals of her infant."

Note how the state of coherence comes up again, like it needs to be in a coherent state to communicate, or more significantly ALLOW communications out and in! Remember the need for a feeling of love emotion with prayer or it does not allow miracles to work! They also conclude that the brain gets communications four ways; neurological (nerves); biophysical (pulse wave); biochemical (hormones); and energetic (electromagnetic). They found that the heart's magnetic field is 5000 times greater than the brains. This field is a torus – like a big donut – and can reach 6-8 feet in diameter. They feel that this field can possibly reach large distances, like miles depending on the intensity. This, they say, can affect other brain waves. Does this make you think about how the Law of Attraction can attract?

In the book, **The Energetic Heart: Bioelectromagnetic Interactions Within and Between People,** McCraty, asks some relevant questions which he reports on. He states that the Energetic Heart explains the bioelectromagnetic interactions within and between people. Did you know that when you're not consciously communicating with others, our physiological systems are interacting in subtle and surprising ways? Or that the electromagnetic signal produced by your heart is registered in the brain waves of people around you? Or that your physiological responses sync up with your mate's during empathetic interactions? His book will allow you tp discover why the heart's electromagnetic field is believed to act as a central synchronizing signal within the body, an important carrier of emotional information and a key mediator of energetic interactions between people.

Centered on the heart chakra is this torroid, a double vortex of energy. A vortex is a mass of energy that moves in a rotary or whirling motion, causing a depression or vacuum at the center. These powerful eddies of pure earth power manifest as spiral-like coagulations of energy that are either electric, magnetic, or electromagnetic qualities of life force. Vortexes are areas of high energy concentrations, originating from magnetic, spiritual, or sometimes unknown sources. Additionally they are considered to be 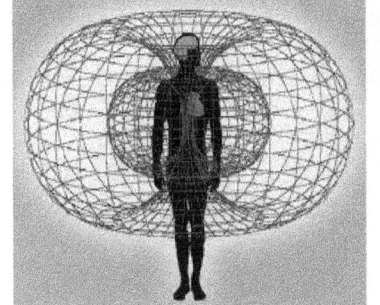 gateways or portals to other realms, both spiritual and dimensional. Vortexes typically exist where there are strong concentrations of gravitational anomalies, in turn creating an environment that can defy gravity, bend light, scare animals, twist plant life into contorted shapes, and cause humans to feel strange. Many vortexes have been shown to be associated with Ley Lines and have been found to be extremely strong at node points where the lines cross. At each chakra there are vortexes reaching out perpendicular to the axis of the body chakra system.

The Heart field is a morphic field which surrounds you and vibrates with emotions emanating outwards. So it can be felt by others but it also is a nucleus within the quantum soup of infinite possibilities drawing likeness. Your emotions are drawers as are images with quantum signatures. Exact replication is not possible this way, only likeness. Known as the double torus of infinity, it is centered on the heart as the engine of energy, the center of singularity. It means your heart is the central engine, not to pump blood but to provide a portal to the love soup of the quantum; that place of infinite possibilities. Inside this torus is your pillar of life, your chakra system that is not only the transference vehicle between DNA and biology from above to below, but energy transmutation from thought to form both biology and to external material. And so the torus is the spiraling engine that does the actual transmutation of energy. The double torus is like a funnel of energy that spins down the funnel becoming more and more concentrated to reach the singularity point at the heart. Then the funnel inverts itself at the heart and the energy then spins down and expands. This is the double torus.

Each chakra has a function to interface between 3D and other D's within this torus. Your thoughts, images, language, emotions, intent, relationships, existence move down the pillar from above to below and are deployed for the expansion and expression at the choice of consciousness. They are the receivers and transmitters talking to DNA because all these subtle energies are in the quantum world. You have developed a knowing about this. The thoughts, visions, words, emotions that drive intent constitute the torroid process downward to the heart at the point of singularity that then drops into the bottom torroid of intent, relationship and 3D expression of manifestation, and eventually materialization of matter.

The way the pillar is deployed is by choice and intent, and carries the communication of information between consciousness of mind between your first layer of DNA of biological-chemical and the other 11 DNA pairs that constitute your being. This interface is not working at full capacity. It has atrophied through fear and your choice to not develop spiritually into what you are. So it sits stagnant in your DNA. The manifesting processes you have come to know as resident transmitters in your chakras are the thoughts, visions, and the language of emotions. The choice is whether these are sourced from the essence of the heart—love, or the essence of ego—intellect. To open to the full library of DNA, the full abilities of the chakra psychic library, and the portal to infinite possibilities, you must shift from that bid dummy the ego brain to the heart brain which awakens in an aura of well-being, love and compassion. That is the "electricity" that turns it on.

Although they are all one, all interconnected, this is a choice of either heart or ego. But nevertheless, all that is you, in your DNA, of karmic lesson, of Divine, of Akashic, and all that is, it all sits awaiting your awareness and intent. You now have a knowing that the best interface is positive thought, visions of completion, words of the language of creation, emotion of love and forgiveness. This is speaking, listening, feeling with the heart. For all this means is that the choice of your seeing, speaking, listening, feeling and thinking is always in the light, not with the traditional limited physical sensory system. The portals of access to the DNA is the communication medium of love. And the ability to optimize the torroid's process is the bringing of these positive attributes into the singularity of heart—yes the heart of all matter. This is simply your knowing that it is so, and however this works is not relevant because you acquire the faith and trust that this is so, and all you have to do is accept and be it. The true power of this process is keyed to a specific vibratory range that is what the energy of love is.

The torus, or primary pattern, is an energy dynamic that looks like a doughnut – it's a continuous surface with a hole in it. The energy flows in through one end, circulates around the center and exits out the other side. You can see it everywhere – in atoms, cells, seeds, flowers, trees, animals, humans, hurricanes, planets, suns, galaxies and even the cosmos as a whole. Scientist and philosopher, Arthur Young, explained that a torus is the only energy pattern or dynamic that can sustain itself and is made out of the same substance as its surroundings – like a tornado, a smoke ring in the air, or a whirlpool in water.

The torus also applies at the human level. Each person not only is a torus – our bodies are a continuous surface (skin) with a hole through the middle (intestinal tract) – but we are each surrounded by our own toroidal electromagnetic field. Each individual's torus is distinct, but at the same time open and connected to every other in a continuous sea of infinite energy. It is the same energy field you can feel with a magnet. It is usually invisible, but by scattering iron filings loosely around a magnet you can actually see the toroidal shape of energy.

The Heart's electromagnetic frequency arcs out from the Heart and back in the form of a torus field. The axis of this Heart torus extends from the pelvic floor to the top of the skull, and the whole field is holographic, meaning that information about it can be read from each and every point in the torus.

This also connects on the sacred geometry level where our heart chakra is composed of a star tetrahedron. It connects the energy together. Also the way the kundalini flows within the chakra system, this energy flows within the same way, the rising serpent of the ida (feminine) and pingala (masculine) join together through the Nadis. The Nadis are your subtle channels that heighten your psychic abilities through the network of energy. The ida and pingala rises up to create a central channel Sushumna where they are joined. **Shakti Kundalini will then awaken and rise up Sushumna, energizing the seven chakras.** Your chakras create your aura and your aura is a field of energy known as a torus. Everything comes full circle.

Most torus dynamics actually contain two toruses – called "tori" – like the male and female aspects of the whole – one spiraling one direction toward the North Pole and its opposite spinning toward the South Pole. This is also referred to as the Coriolis Effect. Examples are the weather on the earth and the plasma flow of the sun. In the heart torus, the spin down the top center is clockwise, down into the point of singularity at the heart, then to the outside of the lower torus, around to the inside of the lower torus, back through the heart then to the outside of the upper torus, then back down.

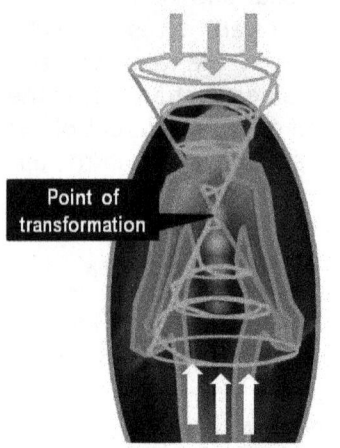

The underlying structure of the torus is the Vector Equilibrium, or "VE." **It is the blueprint by which nature forms energy into matter.** Buckminster Fuller, one of the 20th Century's most prolific inventors, coined the term Vector Equilibrium. He named it this because the "VE" is the only geometric form where all forces are equal and balanced. The energy lines (vectors) are of equal length and strength. **They represent the energy of attraction and repulsion, like you can feel with a magnet.**

You can't actually observe the "VE" in the material world because it is the geometry of absolute balance. What we experience on Earth is always expanding toward and contracting away from absolute equilibrium. Like a wave arising from the surface of a tranquil sea, a material form is born (unfolds) from the plenum (fullness) of energy (ironically referred to by physicists as "the vacuum!") and dies (enfolds) back into it. **The VE is like the imaginable – yet invisible – mother of all the shapes and symmetries we see in the world.**

The Heart Brain And Emotions

We have seen how the perceived environment can cause the flight or fight syndrome and the HPA axis to affect the immune system, the visceral system and the intellect. Now we have another kid on the block that can cause havoc. The research at HeartMath has shown that the heart has its own brain that communicates with and influences cranial brain through the nervous system, hormonal system and other pathways that affect the quality of life. They conclude that the heart and nervous system DO NOT follow brain's direction. The heart has its own brain that can sense, remember, learn, feel, and process information independently.

Signals go from the heart to the survival centre in hindbrain where blood pressure and heart rate, and respiratory rate are controlled. This part analyses info and makes changes. These signals also affect your feelings and emotional memory center in midbrain (Amygdala). The cells here synchronize to the pacemaker in the heart. If HRV is chaotic, it matches that to negative emotional experiences and automatically recalls what negative feeling correlates. Brain waves in cortex are also affected by powerful chaotic heart signals coloring how you think and perceive, altering top level functions (calculation, planning, creativity, and communications) – all from the big signal generator in the heart.

Research shows that stress feelings activate a stress response that is emotional and psychological. So a simple thought recalling anger will provoke a response but it is nowhere near the intensity of the physiological and psychological process of the stress response of emotion. Where have we heard this before? In our discussion about the cells. Research at HeartMath found that emotions contribute heavily to stress on the brain and it can be either real or imagined. The end effect is the same. There is no difference.

Research suggests meditation, yoga, and prayer help. They say when stress or negative things hit, first focus and neutralize – time out. Shift attention to the heart area away from noise and stress. Stop the emotion or thought. It is like my three deep breaths thing, except they say breathe slowly by counting 5 in and out. Feel the breath through the heart in a steady rhythm while you disengage thoughts and feeling. Then engage a positive feeling emotion by thinking back to a positive situation of love and care. This coherent pattern overrides negative emotional programs. They say a positive feeling is not a thought process. You want to be genuine. Learn an inventory of these and your awareness/control increases so the threshold is reset. It is like our bedtime practice in our plan.

So, there is a lot of stuff in you that is your subtle sensing system and energetic body that is working away clogging up your chakras to result in dis-ease and disease as well as clog those higher abilities, and cause a negative reactive procession in your body. Your heart field is also doing the same thing.

Now remember the 100 trillion bits of your DNA that are all in quantum space, all connected, all acting instantly as one? Well, the Light Body is also one of trillions of other bodies that make up the Unity Consciousness. And this Light Body has a certain vibrational signature unique to you.

Let us look more deeply into the result of the heart emotion. The research at HeartMath shows stress feelings activate a stress response that is emotional and psychological. So a simple thought recalling anger will provoke a response but it is nowhere near the intensity of the physiological and psychological process of the stress response of emotion. They found that emotions contribute heavily to stress on the brain and the stress can be either real or imagined. The end effect is the same. There is no difference.

The emotion creates a reaction in the brain that affects the body. The ANS, short for Autonomic Nervous System, kicks into action upon any threat and it works in two parts. We are already familiar with the Flight or Fight syndrome coming from a different source. First is the fight or flight situation where the sympathetic system causes the body to constrict blood vessels, raise blood pressure, raise heart rate, constrict skin arteries, move blood away from organs, dilate pupils, and raise neck hairs for starters. And this is all done automatically in a few seconds to prepare you. The orders are made by the brain to do this.

The second situation is when the threat is only perceived like when you walk into a dark alley and feel threatened. Then the parasympathetic system kicks in. It causes the heart rate to go up, you get a sweat, or chill, and the blood pressure goes up in readiness. The hormonal system then starts a long sequence of reactions of nervous system signals to the glands so as to increase chances of survival. These actions take a few minutes but they last for hours. The research says that once this starts, there are some 1400 reactions that occur in the body.

For example when you get wounded, there are a lot of things happening that the body does to protect you. But the major trouble maker is cortisol released from adrenal glands when we perceive stress. It goes into the blood to raise blood sugar so muscles have more fuel. Adrenaline also increases to make the heart beat faster, and it also raises blood pressure by constricting arteries and interacting with kidneys to save salt and water. So this is what the protective system does automatically.

They have found that this same process is also triggered by negative emotion like anger and depression. This then creates a feedback loop of stress, cortisol, bad mood, more stress, and more cortisol feeding on itself. This can rise to levels that can reach a burnout condition. To add to this mayhem, cortisol also inhibits memory, clarity, and higher functions of the brain.

The research has also proved that another hormone called DHEA, is produced by the adrenals that actually counteracts the effects of cortisol. It, they point out, is produced by positive emotions of love, compassion, reverence, gratitude, and joy. But this hormone declines with age. So increasing stress with age can make a stress button get stuck in the on position for good.

What they point out is that the obvious conclusion is that things like finances, job, conflict, and anxiety problems are stress triggers that accumulate on an ongoing basis and the body gets used to a new threshold. If this happens, and the cortisol and adrenaline are stuck in on positions, you get heart disease, raised blood sugar, hypertension, high cholesterol, obesity, arterial diseases, and diabetes over time. What happens is the body functions get set to a new higher threshold as the body simply believes this is where it should be.

They suggest you need to reset the thermostat down to a normal level again because the stress can become an addiction. What they have found is that a diet of positive feelings resolves this problem and this is how you can reset the thermostat. The heart is where you feel strong emotion because it is the core of emotion.

What is being stated here is that the real control center is the heart brain, not the brain. Sure the old brain up top has responsibilities, but it ain't the real boss! So these sayings like heartfelt emotion, heartbroken, put your heart into it, the heart of the matter, heart to heart, and from the bottom of my heart are not just sayings. They are reflecting a real process from the heart center. These are the ancient energy centers called chakras including the heart's own field of subtle energies.

HeartMath research looked at HRVs, short for Heart Rate Variability. HRV defines how much the beats per minute change over a period of time, so one minute you can be at 60, and then suddenly you go to 90, then 130, then 70. That is what they called chaotic, whereas slow smooth changes occurring over the time period are called coherent.

The research points to the source of the heartbeat or pacemaker being in the heart, and messages that may regulate speed come via the nervous system from the brain, but the heart beat is independent of the brain. So it can be influenced by the brain when the brain needs to vary the heart rate in order to meet perceived demands, but the true control center is the heart. They state that signals go from the heart to the survival centre in hindbrain where blood pressure, heart rate, and respiratory rate are controlled. This part analyses the information and makes changes.

They found that emotional states affect HRV. When stress hits or negative emotions occur, HRV goes chaotic like an earthquake graph. But a coherent HRV is created by deep sleep or sincere positive emotions. This also creates improved clarity, mood, and communications.

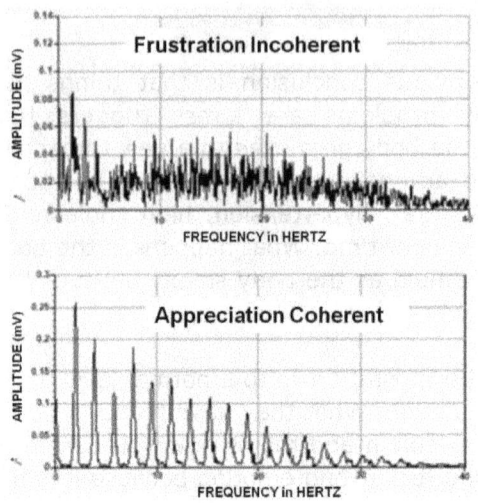

These signals also affect feelings and the emotional memory center in the midbrain called an amygdala. The cells here synchronize to the pacemaker in the heart. If HRV is chaotic, it matches that to a library of negative emotional experiences and automatically recalls what negative feelings correlate. Brain waves in the cortex are also affected by powerful chaotic heart signals coloring thinking and perception, altering top level functions like calculation, planning, creativity, and communications – all from the big signal generator below in the heart.

HeartMath notes that we must listen to the heart, not the ego which can create false fears and demands. We need to shift emotions and change HRV by reversing stress. Events can create an auto response which equals HRV in chaotic mode. This then goes to the brain to produce anxiety, panic, and anger. But when signals from the heart are coherent, the brain's three parts synchronize to create cortical facilitation of improved function. It is called heart intelligence.

In this way they have proven that there is a Brain-Heart talk going on through the ANS nervous system. The research clearly shows that by controlling thoughts and subtle emotions, we influence the balance and activity of ANS, and efficient brain function. This means we have a direct means of controlling the ANS (Autonomic Nervous System) – digestive, cardiovascular, immune and hormonal systems. When we do this, they say a process of entrainment happens. This is when coherence occurs between multiple oscillating systems and they work at their optimum in harmony. It means the subtle energy systems of the body go into a coherent state.

The key, they conclude, is to create the heart-head entrainment that is brought about by appreciation and love. This creates a strengthening of all of these communications as they get synchronized.

They are suggesting that Alpha waves of the brain (like those produced in meditation) are synchronized to the cardiac cycle. Hence they suggest meditation, yoga, and prayer help create this coherence. They say when stress or negative things hit, first focus and neutralize – time out. Shift attention to heart area away from noise and stress. Stop the emotion or thought. They say breathe slowly by counting 5 in and out. Feel the breath through the heart in a steady rhythm while you disengage thoughts and feeling. Then engage a positive feeling emotion by thinking back to a positive situation of love and care. This coherent pattern overrides negative emotional programs.

They also report that from their findings, it is important to lock into positive emotional memories and rewrite your pathways. They have found that a healthy strategy is to shift attention by breathing slowly, then activating genuine positive feelings held for 5-15 minutes. If such feelings are created before sleep, they can be sent to others. They have found these heart signals are picked up by others.

In summary, the research concludes something quite staggering. The heart is not only the source of emotion, courage and wisdom, it has its own brain that communicates with and influences the cranial brain through the nervous system, hormonal system, and other pathways that affect the quality of life. The heart and nervous system *do not* follow brain's direction like everyone believed. The heart has its own brain that can sense, remember, learn, feel, and process information independently.

They state that we do not want any negative emotions to create disorder. We want real positive emotions to increase mental clarity, creativity, balance, and effectiveness. The heart is obviously the most powerful generator of rhythmic information patterns in the body.

There is one more interesting thing they talk about. When people touch or are in proximity of each other, one person's heart beat signal is registered in the other's brainwaves. Have you ever felt uneasy about somebody just being in their presence? They also found that music affects emotion and mood states. They found Classical is good and Rock produces increased hostility.

HeartMath research is telling us we must set a life style that tunes the brain. The heart is what sends the signal to the brain, and the mechanism to regulate coherence is human feeling. This causes a field around the heart and that's where we really need to focus. A high degree of coherence is when this is done by quality of feeling between heart and brain. Words like love and gratitude, and emotions like compassion plus forgiveness are needed to create the best coherence for optimum chemistry.

They emphatically state that anger causes erratic signals and chemicals to be released that are not good. The heart is not just a physical pump that keeps the circulation going. It has subtle energy counterparts reflecting non-physical things happening in that piece of physical machinery – these are the many subtle forces at work.

Being In The Heart Brain

Research suggests meditation, yoga, and prayer help. They say when stress or negative things hit, first focus and neutralize – time out. Shift attention to the heart area away from noise and stress. Stop the emotion or thought. It is like my three deep breaths thing except they say breathe slowly by counting 5 in and out. Feel the breath through the heart in a steady rhythm while you disengage thoughts and feeling. Then engage a positive feeling emotion by thinking back to a positive situation of love and care. This coherent pattern overrides negative emotional program. They say a positive feeling is not a thought process. You want to be genuine. Learn an inventory of these and your awareness/control increases so the threshold is reset. It is like our bedtime practice in our plan."

MD Larry Dossey says prayer is good medicine. He reviewed 60 scientific cases to show prayer has a measurable impact on healing regardless of religion but without love and compassion it had little effect. *"Have a good heart"* says Buddhism, Larry says it means *"care deeply without hidden agenda"*. The heart is the mind's Powerhouse –center of wisdom, mediation between Heaven and Earth.

Science admits that by focusing attention on the heart, we increase synchronicity between heart and brain to calm the nervous system and deactivate stress response so the body conserves energy for growth. Love feelings generate measurable heart field coherence; negative emotions create incoherence and disharmony.

This brings another common practice which has to do with going inside, or being present to the heart. Many meditation methods take you into that altered state, as does hypnosis. It is to bypass the conscious mind that is hooked to the brain. What is more important in our assessment is to get into this state by becoming present to the heart brain, and that has to be done in a state of peace and love to open the portals. It is a simple practice but places your attention away from the higher interfering brainwaves of consciousness into the lower state and centering your attention to the heart energetic center. Here is the balance point of above to below, the center of the toroid, and the point of creation in the quantum soup of love - the point of singularity. This is a common process in the healing steps we have looked at.

The process can be as simple as this:

Settle your body in an upright and seated posture. Bring your focus to the natural flow of your breath as it enters and leaves your body. Just watch your breath as your mind settles. Now bring your attention and intent to enter into the heart space in the center of your chest. And just breathe in and out of this space. As you do so, with each in-breath feel your heart gently opening and softening; with each out-breath release any tension or resistance.

As you do this, silently repeat, *"My heart is opening and softening."* You may experience great joy or even sadness. Let the feelings come and go, while you just keep breathing into your heart space. Stay here as long as you wish. When you are ready, take a deep breath and let it go.

The Love Center

When you fall in love, you feel your heart flutter, beat loudly or leap for joy; when you're rejected, your heart breaks. You are called heartless or cold-hearted when you show no care or love... and big-hearted when you extend your concern to others. You *"take things to heart"* or *"talk heart-to-heart"* about deeply personal issues. You love someone *"from the bottom of your heart"* but are *"half-hearted"* about something when you're emotionally uninvolved. You experience your heart as the center of your feelings, as seen on Valentine's Day when love-filled hearts abound. You know this instinctively, as you always physically point to your heart when you say "I" or want to express your deeper feelings.

Yet your heart is so much more than a vessel for romance. It has been described as the king, with the mind as the king's adviser. When faced with a decision, the king may ask his advisers for advice, may even send him out into the world to gather information, but ultimately it is the king that makes the final decision. Even though the advisers do not always agree with the king's decision, the king is invariably right, because the king's view not only sees the bigger picture but is also aware of the needs of others.

Note how the state of coherence comes up again, like it needs to be in a coherent state to communicate, or more significantly ALLOW communications out and in! Remember the need for a feeling of love emotion with prayer or it does not allow miracles to work! In the same way, when faced with a decision or conflict, your mind may come up with numerous, different and quite logical reasons why you should act as it advises, but if you listen to and trust your heart—however illogical or irrational it may seem—it is usually right and you are happier as a result.

There is great brilliance and beauty inherent within the mind, because it is capable of understanding the most intricate scientific and mathematical theories and can make complicated corporate decisions. Yet the same mind can get caught up in trivia and nonsense, becoming upset or even unglued over a seemingly harmless remark. It runs your life, pushing and pulling you in all directions, from attraction to repulsion, creating endless dramas in acting out your insecurities and fears, because it is not in touch with your deeper feelings. Living inside your head all the time is actually not much fun!

While the mind is the content of who you are, your heart is your essence. Your true heart is not subject to chaos or limited by pain, fear and neuroses, but is joyful, creative and loving. But it will "ache" as a red flag when something is not right. That is the heart intelligence telling you to smarten up. Some believe the heart can be too uncertain and even misguided, but that is the head talking! It is actually a source of great richness, and this wealth is one that cannot be squandered or lost. It is the core, the essence of your being, a reservoir of joy, powerful love and infinite compassion that lies within you. But you have to listen to these "aches".

When you honor the wisdom in your heart, then you act from this core of your being. You experience it in those moments when your needs and worries quietly dissolve and confusion or pain no longer dominates. Tears may spontaneously arise and there is a sensation of great warmth and peace. It is the letting go of fear and the need to control. Try a meditation of your own to get more deeply in touch with this loving center of your being.

MD Larry Dossey says prayer is good medicine. He reviewed 60 scientific cases to show prayer has a measurable impact on healing regardless of religion but without love and compassion it had little effect. "Have a good heart" says Buddhism," Larry says it means "care deeply without hidden agenda". Remember in the previous part how it was stated that prayer without love or compassion is useless in miracle; yes communicating to the "field."

Leonard Laskow who wrote *"Heal with Love"* and as a well known healer once said when he dealt with a cancer patient: *"I placed my hands on the* sides of his chest, visualized a radiant ball of light from the head to heart, down my arms and thru my hands."

He did tests with three Petri dishes of tumor cells in a state of healing consciousness. A non healer also held 3 dishes. He sought to activate a natural force of coherence in the universe. The most effective process that diminished cancer growth by 39% was his statement:

"Return to the natural order and harmony of the normal cell line"

When he added imagery the effect doubled from a diminished growth of 39 to 80%. He states: *"We should apologize to cells and thank them"*

Laskow offers his wisdom in four simple steps:

Inform yourself about what has already materialized. Telling the truth is the first step toward responsibility.
Conform to the condition by loving it rather than creating separation. Resonating with the form allows us more influence over its organization.
Unform the condition by releasing it. It is the Observers intent that converts particulate matter to its wave form and wave back to matter.
Reform the released energy to conform to our purpose and desire. This the letting go where we send our information into the universe without attachment.

Even when releasing the diseased condition there is a connection. Not separation. *"When you accept and love the parts of yourself you want to reject or change, you create the opportunity to discover the positive life force behind them"* We make ourselves at One.

In quantum, love is the glue that holds things together. It is the universal pattern of resonant energy. We can love a cancer cell to death!

The heart is the minds Powerhouse –center of wisdom, mediation between Heaven and Earth.

The **John and Beatrice Lacey** research is relevant: They confirm that the heart does not obey brain messages. It interprets neural signals and bases response on individual's current emotional status. It employs its own logic. The heart has more to do with perception and behavioral reactions. The impact of love is biochemically measureable through Coherent Heart intelligence. Increased coherence gives a cascade of neural and biochemical events that affect virtually every organ in the body. It leads to more intelligence by reducing activity of sympathetic nervous system in fight or flight. It leads to increasing growth of parasympathetic nervous system as it reduces production of stress hormone cortisol.

Even Science now confirms that by focusing attention on the heart, we increase synchronicity between heart and brain to calm the nervous system and deactivate stress response so the body conserves energy for growth. Love feelings generate measurable heart field coherence; negative emotions create incoherence and disharmony.

One of the most dramatic examples of how the power of love and intention can affect the material world is the work done my **Emoto.** By looking at crystals of different water, he detected that they were affected by human emotion, words and thought. They were typically six-pointed crystals but were distorted or pretty depending on the negative or positive energy projected on the water.

He did it by freezing water. He reports that in order to obtain examples of ice crystals, many samples are required to be photographed under as stable conditions as possible. Therefore, dishes are placed in a freezer for three hours at a temperature of -25C. When they are taken out, ice grains have formed with their center rolled up due to surface tension. These grains are very tiny. Water expands when frozen and ice crystals form at the tip of the water sample. Light is directed on each grain of ice and observed through a dark field electron-microscope in a room at a temperature of -5C. Under the magnification of 100 to 200 times, the ice crystals can be observed as the ice begins to melt away. If things go well, a crystal starts to form as the temperature rises and the ice begins to melt. Taking only one to two minutes, it opens up like a flower blooming. So the crystals reveal a specific good or bad property of the water.

He points out there is a message from water that has the potential to transform our world view. Water teaches us the delicacy of the human condition and shows the impact that love and gratitude can have on the world. I was fascinated to read about water labeled *Thank you* and *Idiot*. These words changed the properties to make them clear or yellow. I was interested to note he said that this process works best with children who don't have doubts. They have no lack of purity.

He concludes that energy is vibration. Atoms vibrate in the nucleus and vibrations in the organic world need help to continue life. When we meditate, gaps open in between vibrations of our thoughts and allow short waves of Creation to sneak in. Here the shorter frequency energy is purer and goes farther. This state allows contact with the Creator and cosmic information.

That is what praying and meditating is all about. We have limitations on the range of sounds so to transmit and receive beyond that limit we need water which circulates around the planet and in us. We entrust information to it by resonance. He showed that water can change by praying remotely with a response happening in as fast as five minutes. He tested this with a group of 500 people he calls Hados. These are people tuned to the world of senses and images. He says many experiments show the same results. If you say *'Water, we love you, Water we thank you, Water we respect you'*, you are purifying it. No life can exist without water as it delivers vibrations to 50 trillion cells. Each cell has a unique vibration and role. Junk food disturbs the vitality of cells. You need to feel grateful for your existence, respect, and like yourself first. Then you are able to properly feel the same about others. You can not give off good vibes if you have a distorted image of your substances.

So it follows that if you say the same thing to yourself, like I love you, I respect you, I trust you, then you are also purifying all the water in you. He points out we are 70% water, like the planet. So pray anytime, and recall feelings of thanks to water. Close your eyes and put your hands together. Putting your hands together reinforces the energy. When you do this the hands connect to create clear circulation of energy. It allows emotional energy to be transmitted purely.

Important Conclusions About The Heart

The first important conclusion is that the heart's magnetic field is 5000 times greater than the brains. This field is a torus – like a big donut – and can reach 6-8 feet in diameter. This field can possibly reach large distances, like miles depending on the intensity and can affect other people's brain waves through quantum nonlocality. It behaves according to quantum physics.

The second conclusion is that we need to be in a coherent state to communicate, or more significantly ALLOW communications out and in! Remember the need for a feeling of love emotion with prayer or it does not allow miracles to work! This can only be done in a field of love to turn the "current" on and be in the heart-brain as opposed to the head-brain.

The third conclusion is that heart emotions contribute heavily to stress on the brain and the stress can be either real or imagined. The end effect is the same. There is no difference. There are some 1400 reactions that occur in the body.

The fourth conclusion is that the heart has its own brain and nervous system through the ANS that does not take orders from the brain. It has its own rules for creating a toxic response from negative emotions.

The fifth conclusion is that **Coherent Heart Intelligence** is a process that increases coherence and gives a cascade of neural and biochemical events that affect virtually every organ in the body to improve clarity, mood, and communications

The sixth conclusion is that the underlying structure of the heart field is a torus that has an axis as the Vector Equilibrium, or "VE." It is the blueprint by which nature forms energy into matter. This is the only geometric form where all forces are equal and balanced. The energy lines (vectors) are of equal length and strength. They represent the energy of attraction and repulsion, like you can feel with a magnet. The VE is like the imaginable – yet invisible – mother of all the shapes and symmetries we see in the world. **Your emotions are drawers as are images with quantum signatures. Exact replication is not possible this way, only likeness**.

The seventh conclusion is that Being present to the heart brings another common practice which has to do with going inside, or being present to the heart. It is a simple practice but places your attention away from the higher interfering brainwaves of consciousness into the lower state and centering your attention to the heart energetic center. Here is the balance point of above to below, the center of the toroid, and the point of creation in the quantum soup of love - the point of singularity. It is this place of the heart brain that allows access to the singularity and the quantum soup.

The eighth conclusion is a process of healing by Laskow offers his wisdom in four steps:
Inform yourself about what has already materialized. Telling the truth is the first step toward responsibility.
Conform to the condition by loving it rather than creating separation. Resonating with the form allows us more influence over its organization.
Unform the condition by releasing it. It is the Observer's intent that converts particulate matter to its wave form and wave back to matter.
Reform the released energy to conform to our purpose and desire. This is the letting go where we send our information into the universe without attachment.

The ninth conclusion is that when releasing the diseased condition there is a connection. Not separation. *"When you accept and love the parts of yourself you want to reject or change, you create the opportunity to discover the positive life force behind them"* We make ourselves at One.

The tenth conclusion is in quantum, love is the glue that holds things together. It is the universal pattern of resonant energy. We can love a cancer cell to death! Hearts and brains entangle, both quantum.

The eleventh conclusion is that if you say the same thing to yourself, like I love you, I respect you, I trust you, then you are also purifying all the water in you as we are 70% water, like the planet.

29

THE ENERGY BODY SYSTEM

"When you begin to see the light, it is when you realize you are really a Light Body here to enjoy a virtual holographic movie called reality."

Ed Rychkun

In this chapter, we are going to take you "away out there" just a bit to talk about another you. We introduced it when we discussed Near Death Experiences. It was that separate entity that took a little vacation to meet that Higher Being, then came back to re-enter the croaked body. It simply flew away, through walls, into a void with all of its memories, movies, emotions, and feelings intact. We are going to refer to this as a Light Being and Soul which had to come here when you were born, and leaves here when you die. Why do we say this? Because it was the near death experience that sent it on that vacation. Basically it was not time to leave permanently or it was time for the conscious mind to get a wakeup call as to who it really was. Who it really was, or is, has been an eternal question. Many refer to this as the Soul, the Higher Self; every religion has some reference to it but it is certainly not part of mainstream science. It may not be such a stretch if you have read this far to consider that this Light Being is like an overlay on the physical body. It interfaces with it in the physical and connects out into the nonphysical as we have seen with the chakras and heart fields.

But this is only part of the story. Most esoteric information divides the body into three planes, namely the Physical, Astral and Spiritual. Because the spiritual plane is ultimately higher consciousness, the Physical is lower consciousness, as the esoteric truth goes, an interface between the two was required for spiritual to be able to experience the physical. That interface is the astral body. The whole body is composed of these and we can refer to them all as the Energy Body. If you can accept that the physical body is also energy at a lower density then all three planes together form the energy body. When the Higher Self/soul comes into or connects with the physical body then this becomes the Soul's Spirit or also called expression of that being.

The Energy Body Planes And Bodies

There is much discussion and interpretations of these different planes and bodies that make up the planes, but let us attempt to go through these in order to gain a basic understanding.

Our Energy Body is a luminous body made up of layers like an onion. These are interrelated energy fields with special purposes and the ones that are more visible that glow closer to the physical body are commonly referred to as auras. The Energy Body is a vehicle of consciousness that exists as frequency levels on these subtle planes. As a yogic body for example, these may consists of ch'i or pranic energy (aura), energy vortexes (chakras) and energy channels (nadis or meridians). Astral projection, Near Death Experiences, Out of Body Experiences, and death are the ways to separate the energy body from the physical body.

The Energy Body can be separated into different layers. The number and names of the layers vary according to different spiritual models and theories. For the time being we are going to peruse the five key bodies below:

1. **Physical Body** (The Gross Body, The Biological Body, The Dense Body, The Material Body)
2. **Etheric Body** (The Life Force Body, The Auric Energy Fields)
3. **Astra/Emotional Body** (The Psychic Body)
4. **Mental Body** (The Mind)
5. **Causal Body** (The Higher Self, The Soul, The Spiritual Body, The Divine Body, Nirvana, The Celestial Body, The Cosmic Body)

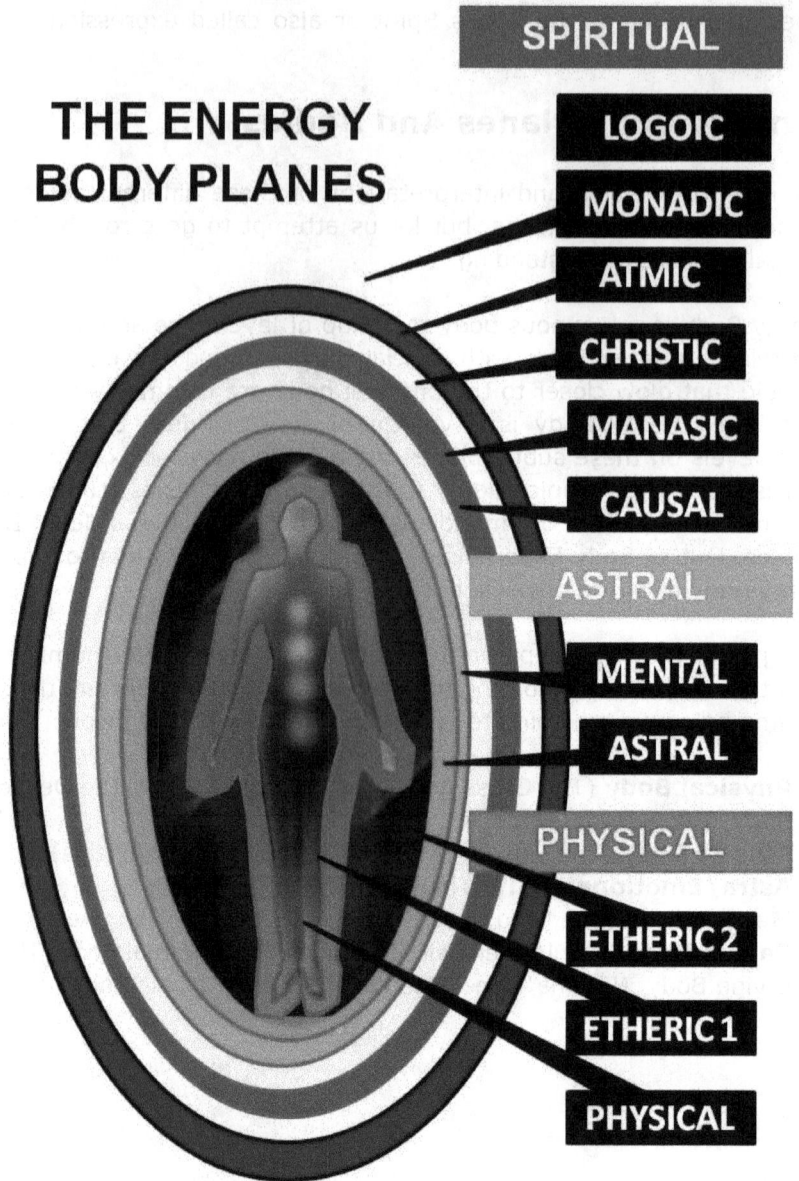

The Energy Body is depicted in the graphic diagram above as having different layers that reside on various dimensions of consciousness. There is a portion of the energy body, called the Higher Self that never descends to the physical body, but remains resident on the spiritual planes. The Higher Self retains all of a soul's consciousness and memories as it interfaces with the above 5 bodies.

In 1875 Madame Blavatsky founded the Theosophical Society in New York, to study Eastern religions and science. From her teachings, brought back from her travels in India and elsewhere, a complex scheme evolved. According to the Theosophists, that man is not just the product of his physical body, but is instead thought to be a complex creature consisting of many bodies, each finer and more subtle than the one below it.

Although there are variations in the details, it is commonly claimed that there are **seven corresponding bodies or vehicles**. The grossest of all is the **physical body**, of flesh, with which we are all familiar. There is supposed to be another body also described as physical known as the **'etheric double',** or 'vehicle of vitality.' Etheric double is the manifestation of physical vitality. It is constant and does not change throughout the cycles of life and death, but it is not eternal, for it is eventually re-absorbed into the elements of which it is composed. This 'double' acts as a kind of transmitter of energy, keeping the lower physical body in contact with the higher bodies. Etheric substance is seen as an extension of the physical.

Next up the scale is supposed to be the astral world and its associated **'astral body'**, or the 'vehicle of consciousness'. These are thought to be finer than their etheric counterparts and correspondingly harder to see. The Astral body is thought to be a replica of the physical body (the gross body), but of a more subtle and tenuous substance, penetrating every nerve, fibre and cell of the physical organism, and constantly in a supersensitive state of vibration and pulsation.

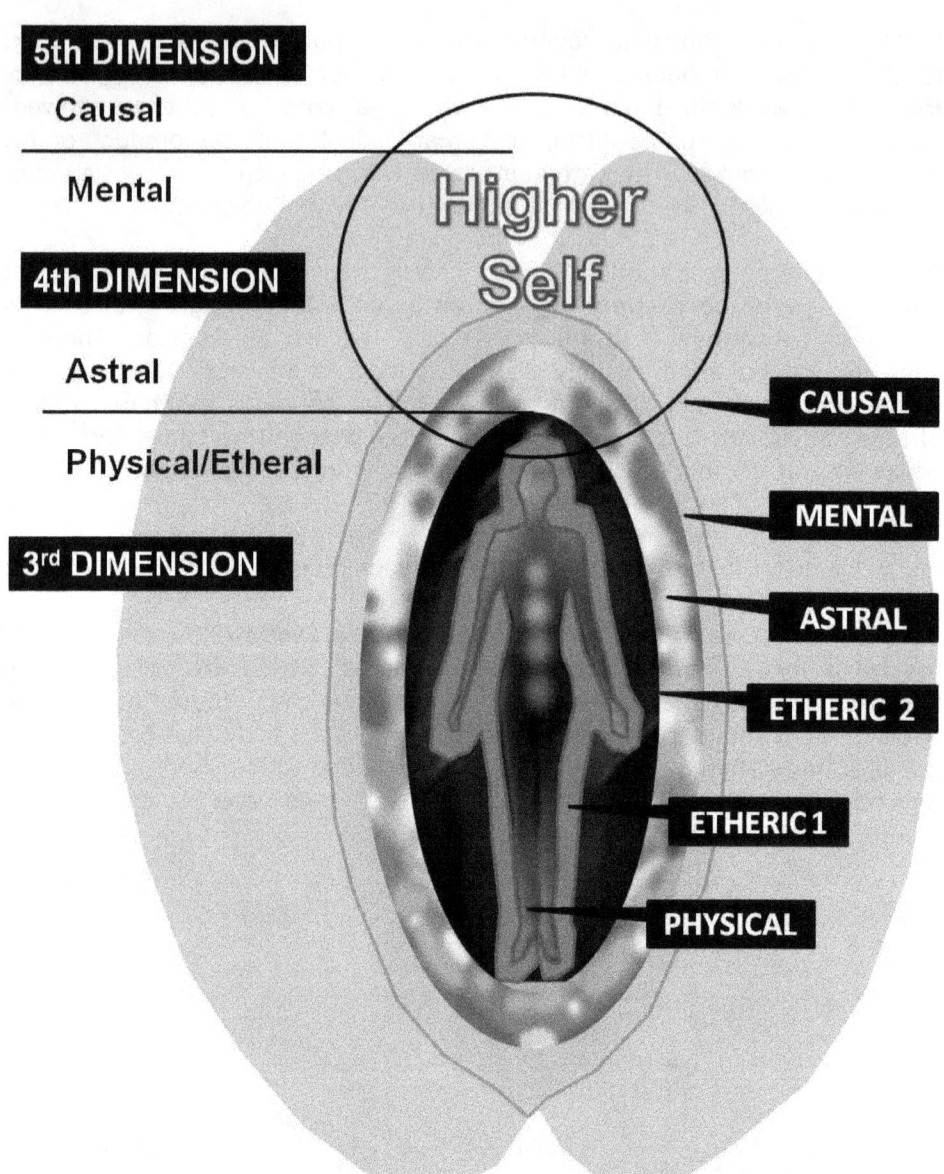

The astral world consists of astral matter, and all physical objects have a replica in the astral. There is therefore a complete physical copy of everything in the astral world, but in addition there are things in the astral which have no counterpart in the physical. There are thought forms created by human thought, elementals and the lowest of the dead, who have gone no further since they left the physical world. All these entities and many others are used in ritual magic and thought forms can be specially created to carry out tasks such as healing, carrying messages, or gaining information.

In the scheme just described, those who have the ability are supposed to be able to see the nature of a person's thoughts by changes in the color and form of the astral body. All around the physical can be seen the bright and shining colors of the larger astral body, making up the **astral aura**. The aura is multi-colored and brilliant, or dull, according to the character or quality of the person and therefore to the seer, the aura of a person is an index to his hidden propensities.

All these conceptions are of special relevance because of the fact that the astral body is supposed to be able to separate from the physical and travel without it. Since the astral is the vehicle of consciousness, it is this body which is aware, not the physical. It is said that in sleep the astral body leaves the sleeping body. In the undeveloped person, little memory is retained and the astral body is vague and its travels are limited and directionless, but in the trained person the astral can be controlled, can travel great distances in sleep, and can even be projected from the physical body at will. It is this which is called astral projection.

In astral projection the consciousness can travel almost without limitation, but it travels in the astral world. It therefore sees not the physical objects, but their astral counterparts, and in addition the beings that live in the astral realms. The astral world has been known as the world of illusion or world of thoughts. The unwary traveler can become confused by the power of his own imaginings. In this state one can appear, as an apparition to anyone who has 'astral sight'. Indeed one can appear to others too, but to do so requires some involvement of lower matter, for example of etheric matter, as in ectoplasm. Ectoplasm is considered to be the materialization of the astral body and is described as matter which is invisible and impalpable in its primary state, but assuming the state of a vapour, liquid or solid, according to its stage of condensation.

An aspect of astral traveling which has become important is the silver cord. It is held that in life the astral body is connected to its physical body by an infinitely elastic but strong cord, of a flowing and delicate silver color. Traditionally the cord must remain connected or death will ensue. As one approaches death, the astral gradually loosens itself, lifts up above the physical, and then the cord breaks to allow the higher bodies to leave. Death is thus seen as a form of permanent astral projection.

Beyond the astral Theosophy distinguishes a further five levels but this is quite variable depending upon the religion and the authors who claim to have the wisdom. We do not want to take anyone's thunder away from them and would refer you to one of the websites that offers wisdom and services of cleansing these bodies found at ***www.energyreality.com.*** We will be summarizing their information on the energy layers and would recommend that you visit this website.

What Is The Soul?

According to spiritual, esoteric, occult, and mystical teachings, Souls have a Physical Body and an Energy Body, commonly called a Subtle Body. The origin of Subtle Body teachings was principally Indian Yoga tradition, where it is described as sheaths that cover the immortal soul. The Energy Body is known by various names in different spiritual traditions:

- Christians call it the "Resurrection Body" or the "Glorified Body".
- Sufis call it the "most Sacred Body" (Wujud Al-aqdas) and the "Supra-celestial Body" (Jism Asli Haqiqi).
- Taoists call it the "Diamond Body". Those who have attained it are called "the Immortals" and "the Cloudwalkers".
- Yogic schools and Tantrics call it the "Divine Body".
- Tibetan Buddhists call it the "Light Body" or "Rainbow Body" (Jalü or Jalus). The Tibetan Book of the Dead1 calls it the "Shining Body".
- Kriya Yogis call it the "Body of Bliss".
- Hermetics call it the "Immortal Body" (Soma Athanaton).
- In the alchemical tradition, it is called the "Golden Body".
- In the Mithraic liturgy it is called the "Perfect Body".
- In Gnosticism it is called the "Radiant Body".
- In the Vedanta it is called the "Superconductive Body".
- The ancient Egyptians called it the "Luminous Body or Being" (akh) or the "Karast".
- Alberto Villoldo, a scientist and shaman, calls it the "Luminous Energy Field" (LEF). He says the LEF dwells outside of time having existed since before the beginning of time and endures throughout infinity. It manifests in time by creating new physical bodies lifetime after lifetime. The LEF contains imprints of a soul's memories, traumas, and wounds from former lifetimes.
- Clairvoyants see it as an aura or cloud of colored lights surrounding the Physical Body.

The Physical Body is the form that a Soul takes while incarnated in the 3rd dimension (i.e. on Earth). The Physical Body consists of energy so dense that it can be felt and seen. However, the soul consists of more energetic layers than just the physical body. In order to experience the lower 3rd dimension, it uses the following vehicles or bodies.

VEHICLES OF THE SOUL			
HIGHER MENTAL	CAUSAL BODY	TO EVOLVE WITH	IDEALS ABSTRACT THOUGHTS
LOWER MENTAL	MENTAL BODY	TO THINK WITH	IDEAS CONCRETE THOUGHTS
ASTRAL EMOTIONAL	ASTRAL BODY	TO FEEL WITH	EMOTIONS DESIRES
PHYSICAL	PHYSICAL BODY	TO ACT WITH	SENSORIAL ACTIONS

Key to the Soul's purpose of experiencing and evolving to a higher plane is the astral/emotional body made up of astral forces. Astral means connecting with or resembling the stars. It is gathered before each incarnation and is different each time. When incarnating into the etheric body various astral forces are attracted to certain parts of the physical body. The organs each attract a certain astral force so depending on the astral body's makeup the organs will receive differing amounts of required astrality. For example if the incarnating astral body has an abundance of Venus astral force, the kidneys will be overflowing and so they are likely to be very strong. As the Venus force goes into the kidneys, the chi there will be transformed into kidney chi and will likely flow strongly throughout the meridians. If this astral body has very little Mars force the stomach will be weaker and so less Mars chi will be created to flow through the meridians. While young, the strong kidneys will likely be helping the weak stomach as it will draw energy from the kidneys to function properly, but as this person gets older, if no strengthening has been done, it will eventually put a strain on the kidneys and all other systems.

Chitta (subconscious mind) is an envelope of subtle energies which surrounds the head and permeates the brain. The astral body is the emotional body; the chitta is the mental body. They are both intimately linked and operate together The structure in the chitta is just like that of the astral body and can also be seen as being made up of Samskaras (impressions). The difference is that the Samskaras in the astral body are caused by intense emotions and tend to be much larger. As the chitta is such a refined substance, Samskaras can be created very easily and are much smaller. Large emotional Samskaras are also created in the chitta and these ones will again form a foundation of personality just like the astral bodies Samskaras. The two bodies interact with each other and any large Samskara in the astral body will be accompanied by a group of smaller ones in the chitta. The repression of the intense emotions in the astral body is helped along by the chitta and its increased structure. This structure can be very complicated and its purpose is to keep emotional pain under the surface.

This astral body incarnates into the physical dimension through its interaction with the etheric body. The light body incarnates by shining through the astral body. It is much larger than the astral body and is around and above it. For light to incarnate into matter it needs something to ground in. A baby is too small to really hold the light body and give it a ground which is why nurturing is so important. When the baby is with the mother and she is open enough, the baby's light body grounds with the help of her body. So while this is happening the baby can feel the love which is a part of itself (its light body). This is the beginning of looking for love outside of oneself. The baby believes that the love comes from its mother because she grounds it. Without her the baby cannot feel its light body in the same way because it lacks the ground necessary to hold it.

As a person grows up and the astral body incarnates into the physical, the Samskaras from past lives are activated along with new ones being created through emotional trauma. The astral body and chitta become far more structured and crystallized which blocks the light body from shining through. The light body is more grounded now but its light is blocked by ego structure. The light body remains in, around and above the physical body but depending on the person's ego structure, it is not strongly felt and what is felt is distorted by the astral. While meditating or doing spiritual practices the light body is pulled into the astral body. A ground is created for the light, and as it intensifies, its incarnation into the astral samskaras begins to dissolve. The light raises the vibration of the astral body which causes Samskaras to break up and dissolve. The reason the Astral Substances are able to crystallize and stay that way is because of its slow vibration. By raising the vibration of the astral it will begin to break up the crystallization. Once the astral body has been cleared of crystallization in this way the light body can shine through it and ground into the physical.

The process of gathering impressions to be stored in the subconscious involves the physical brain. The physical brain is a relay station, translating emotional, mental, and spiritual events and information into neuro-electrochemical events and information. Neurochemicals and associated brain processes are simply channel selectors for various states of consciousness. All states of consciousness exist independent of the physical body. This relay station works in both directions: spiritual, mental, or emotional states trigger neuro-electrochemical events in the brain (physical consciousness) and neurochemical stimulation (for example through drugs) opens access to specific states of emotion, thought, or spiritual awareness. We will discuss this in a following chapter but Contemporary physics has proven very clearly that solid physical matter is an illusion and that all is energy only. Therefore, to say that the solid physical brain is the mind is a mistake. While the brain appears to be solid, it is not - it is energy appearing solid, but is not solid - it is energy, only. The mind is also energy, an energy that interacts with the energy that creates the appearance of a brain. The Physical Body is composed of the energy states of solids, liquids, and gases and is dependent upon the Etheric Body for its vitality, life, organization, and many processes that result in health.

The Soul's Evolution

The bottom line is that the Soul came to evolve through various dimensions or planes of which there are 9 dimensions and bodies. To do this, it was given a great inventory of equipment that are the physical and energy bodies. The conscious awareness of each of these bodies, as they progress from the lower dimension of 3 to the higher spiritual dimension of 9 is the evolution. Each dimension is reflected in the energy body which opens new inventories of abilities to perceive, see, and understand increasing levels of consciousness. As each opens, it leads to the next. As we proceed through the descriptions of the Energy Body and its components, we will see that each body, from the 3rd up, effectively represents a higher dimension inclusive of the ones below. Here is a summary of these dimensions.

- The 1st Dimension is Length, creating a line.
- The 2nd Dimension is Width, which combined with the 1st Dimension creates a plane or sheet.
- The 3rd Dimension is Height, which combined with the 1st and 2nd Dimensions creates a cube.
- The 4th Dimension is an added depth in hyperspace (outside of 3 Dimensional Space). When the 4th Dimension is combined with the 1st, 2nd, and 3rd Dimensions a hypercube is created.
- When a 1 Dimensional object (a line) is viewed with 1 Dimensional awareness (1 direction only) a point is perceived. When viewed with 2 Dimensional awareness a line is perceived.
- When a 2 Dimensional object, such as a square, is viewed with 2 Dimensional awareness a line is perceived. When viewed with 3 Dimensional awareness a square is perceived.
- When a 3 Dimensional object, such as a cube, is viewed with 3 Dimensional awareness a flat object is perceived. When viewed with 4 Dimensional awareness a cube is perceived.

Thus we use 4 dimensional awareness to perceive 3 dimensional objects all the time.

- To perceive a 4 Dimensional object, such as a hypercube, we must use 5 Dimensional Awareness.
- The Physical-Etheric Universe is structured in 3 Spatial Dimensions.
- The Astral (Emotional) Universe is structured in 4 Spatial Dimensions.
- The Manasic Universe (including Causal/Soul and Mental/Intellectual) is structured in 5 Spatial Dimensions.
- The Buddhic/Christic Universe in 6 Spatial Dimensions.
- The Atmic Universe in 7 Spatial Dimensions.
- The Monadic Universe in 8 Spatial Dimensions.
- The Logoic Universe in 9 Spatial Dimensions.

Time is not a spatial dimension but rather is a measure of events in space. To call the Astral Universe the 4th Dimension is a mistake because the Astral Universe also contains Dimensions 1, 2, and 3. Also, the Manasic and higher Universes all contain the 4th Dimension. In the same way it is a mistake to call the Manasic Universe the 5th Dimension. Full and complete awareness in a higher Universe includes awareness of additional spatial dimensions.

Before we peruse the different layers, their functions and structure, let us look at what occurs when these bodies become dysfunctional. Dysfunction is registered in the general ledger of karma. It is clearly the inability to evolve in awareness. If you are wondering how far you have to evolve, you can relate to the dimensions above, and the table coming up. Following this we will explain what the higher functions, purpose and structure of these stages of evolution (awareness of each dimension) are.

The Auric Bodies And Their Issues

The aura is created by the interaction of all the energies and inter-dimensional forces that make up the human being. All of the energies and forces that are in and around you are meshed together and extend outwards from the body. as noted, the aura is simply a luminous state of a subtle energy body. An aura is an energy field that surrounds, penetrates and extends out beyond the physical body that is electromagnetic, electric and magnetic and is made up of varying types of live and intelligent vibrations or frequencies. An aura surrounds not only every living thing including humans, animals and plants, but also every inanimate thing such as rocks, all objects made by man, and the earth, sun, moon, and all planets in our Universe. The human aura has layers of physical, emotional, mental and spiritual elements. Auras contain all the primary colors of the rainbow at any given time and change color depending on the emotion an individual is experiencing. Our auras are made up of many colors and many shades of colors that are constantly changing. This reflects the constant change in our thoughts and emotions like a monitoring system.

The Auric Bodies create an energetic system that surrounds your body. Each forms a layer which corresponds to your chakras; starting at your base chakra all the way to the seventh chakra.

1. Physical auric body- Base chakra- Physical sensations. Simple physical comfort, pleasure, health.
2. The etheric auric body- Sacral chakra- Emotions with respect to self. Self-acceptance and self-love.
3. Vital auric body- Solar plexus chakra- Rational mind. To understand the situation in a clear, linear rational way.
4. Astral (emotional) body- Heart chakra- relations with others. Loving interaction with friends and family.
5. Lower mental auric body- Throat chakra- Divine will within. To align with the divine will within, to make commitment to speak and follow the truth.
6. Higher mental auric body- Third eye chakra- Divine love, and spiritual ecstasy.
7. Spiritual (intuitive) auric body- Crown chakra- Divine mind, serenity. To be connected to the divine mind and to understand the greater universal pattern.

Most of us are familiar with the effects of this. When you are connected you feel happy when they are happy. Conversely you feel sad when they are sad. You are literally feeling the emotions in their aura. This is welcome when a relationship is going well but adds to the pain when it is not. In the latter case in order to reconnect with your feelings it is often necessary to take a break for a few days away from your partner and anyone who would try to influence you in any way about your relationship. This will allow your aura to become clear of their influence. In this isolated space you can reconnect with your feelings and this will strengthen your aura. You can then re-enter the same space your partner occupies with a renewed ability to distinguish your feelings from theirs.

We are trained to look at the physical body and address its needs rather than look at our energetic systems to provide them with what they need for perfect health. Our energy systems are conscious energy and this energy is connected with all energies in the Universe. When we look after our energy systems we look after our deepest and most profound needs, including the physical, emotional, intellectual and spiritual.

Happy and loving thoughts expand your aura while sad or angry thoughts contract your aura. Aura sizes adjust depending on the density of the population where you live. Residents of New York City have tighter and smaller auras in comparison to residents living in rural Vermont. A dowser can easily tell you many of the physical qualities of your aura.

There are many issues that can affect the functioning of our auras, chakras, and meridian systems leading to a variety of health problems. The following are a number of key potential issues.

1. Blockages can be caused by any of the following: emotions that have not been felt and released; negative thought forms from others; psychic attack energy or negative energy from energetic spells; entities or spirits lodged in our auras or chakras; chemical, metal and atomic toxins; other types of poisons or toxins; past life memories or experiences.

2. Distorted auras and chakras can be caused by any of the issues identified under blockages.

3. Holes in the auras can be caused by any of the issues identified under blockages.

4. Lack of synchronization between the auras, chakras, and meridian system can create serious difficulty. Physical issues, emotional issues, intellectual imbalances or spiritual issues can create imbalances in various parts of the auras, chakras and meridian system. These imbalances affect the specific aura or chakra that in turn affects other parts of the energetic system. Nature always tries to achieve perfect balance and these imbalances create a real disharmony in our energetic systems. This can create unbalanced thinking, feeling and behavior.

5. Negative connections and rays can become attached to our auras. These are a result of negative emotions, drug and alcohol use, psychic attacks or spells, other intelligent being in the Cosmic World, environmental pollution, lack of nature i.e. trees, plants and flowing water. Negativity in thought and behavior in individuals, communities, draws negative forces to us from the broader Universe. These connections, rays and energies can have a real negative effect on our vitality and energy.

6. Energetic and chemical markings can be left by other dimensional beings in our auras and brains so that these energetic beings can find and track us. Constant interference by other dimensional beings can seriously affect our vitality and health.

7. Negative energy programs can be sent into an individual by other human beings. These programs establish connections so that ongoing negative energy can be run into an individual. This can have a serious effect on our entire energy system and inner vitality.

8. Negative energy can easily flip from one individual's aura into your aura. Energy is alive, moves around, and you can eventually become quite affected by the negative energy of those around you, in your homes, offices or stores.

9. Imbalances can be created by earth energies especially the intersecting points of the Hartman and Curry grids and underground running water.

10. Underactive or overactive chakras can create a variety of issues. Underactive chakras can translate into fatigue, lethargy, weight problems, just a slow attitude towards life or a lack of zest for living. Overactive chakras create other types of problems including hyperactivity, panic attacks, emotional imbalances, and many types of health issues in the physical body.

There can be so many different effects from energetic issues. The following is a limited listing of certain major potential effects:

1. Fatigue
2. Lacking vitality or a zest for life
3. Negative or distorted thinking
4. Negative, unbalanced or distorted emotions
5. Negative, unbalanced or distorted behavior
6. Feeling disconnected from other human beings
7. Feeling disconnected from the Creator or whatever we choose to call our Higher Power
8. Feeling disconnected from nature
9. Panic attacks that can be caused by a vulnerability caused by holes in our auras
10. A compromised energy system leads to many types of physical illnesses.

This leads to the red flags of dysfunction as a Cause And Effect. Here you have the causes that are linked to chakras. **Consider them an early** warning system. But more important, consider these issues that are preventing your evolution of your Soul.

The Physical to Causal Bodies

The enveloping **Causal/Soul Body** (golden orb) is the subtlest level of personal individuality, the enlivening source of life and consciousness for the current personality, all past life personalities, and all future life personalities. It could be called the **Higher-Self**.

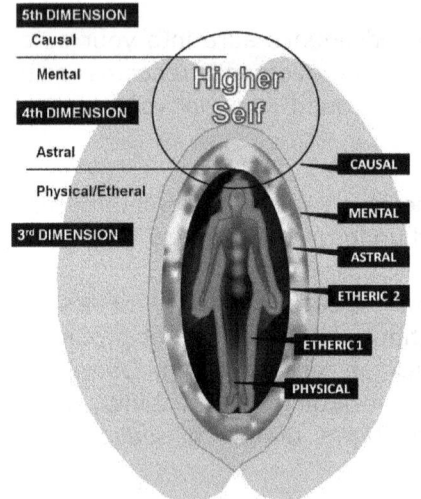

The **Mental/Intellectual Body** (next inner level, bluish), is the vehicle for understanding, for beliefs, thoughts, knowledge, and cognitive processes.

The Astral/Emotional Body (next inner level, multicolored), is the vehicle for emotion, desire, imagination, personal power, and is a focus of feeling.

The Etheric/Vital Body (next inner level, light bluish), is the vehicle for energy and vitality, the subtle basis for the physical body.

The Physical Body (at the center), is the vehicle for stability, separation, and individual focus.

The Personality is composed of the Mental/Intellectual Body, the Astral/Emotional Body, the Etheric/Astral Body, and the Physical Body, as a unit. The Personality is very temporary and is changed or recreated every lifetime, effectively erasing past life memories on a personality level. All past life experience, knowledge, and developed ability is retained on a Causal/Soul Body level as the Causal Body lasts many millions of years.

The Causal/Soul Body is named "Causal" because it is the originating source of each personality that incarnates in each lifetime. It is the source of your personality, causing it to be and exist. When your personality ends, the essence of you is absorbed back into the Causal Body. It is the first level of your individuality that is relatively immortal as the Causal Body exists for many millions of years, during your journey as a human through many incarnations or lifetimes. Animals have yet to obtain a Causal Body and super-humans that are liberated from the cycle of rebirth discard the Causal Body and move on to higher levels.

Now, let us look more carefully at each of the bodies.

The Physical Body

Remembering that the purpose of the Soul is evolution towards higher planes, each time you incarnate, all that you experience is relayed from the brain and through the bodies connected to the physical body to form a ledger of your Personality within the Causal body and consciousness. Thus you keep at it until you get it right; and this karmic record can only be balanced when the issues of lower vibration and negative experiences are resolved. This is the divine recording device designed to keep track of all the experiences and lives (like the fast playback typically experienced in a Near Death Experience). Although we all know what a physical body is, it is useful to look at in terms of the energy body. The table following summarizes the basic differences between the Energy Body and the Physical Body and points out how the design is oriented towards this divine evolution:

Energy Body	Physical Body
Is formlessness.	Has form.
Composed of energy as light.	Composed of dense matter.
A product of past lives and between life experiences as well as karmic activity.	A product of genetic material inherited from ancestors.
Memories are stored in the Akashic records.	Memories are stored in the genes.
Has high energy, low density.	Has low energy, high density.
Can be seen or experienced through the 6th sense (3rd eye/intuition).	Can be seen by the physical eye and felt through the 5 senses.
Stores trauma from past lifetimes.	Stores trauma from the current incarnation.
Exists in timelessness.	Exists in linear time.
Does not age and does not die.	Ages and dies.
Is immortal and is kept over many lifetimes.	Is mortal and kept only for the current incarnation.
You take it with you when you die.	You leave it on Earth when you die.
Eternal. Is carried in between lives and through multiple lives.	Temporary. Only lasts one lifetime.
Exists on the higher planes of existence (i.e. the spiritual world).	Exists on the Physical Plane (i.e. the 3rd dimension).
Has a connected oneness identity.	Has a separate ego identity.
Is motivated from within.	Is subject to body and ego

The Akashic Records refer to the matrix of consciousness programs that create our reality within that hologram. One could look upon it as a library of light wherein one can access all information. The Akashic records (Akasha is a Sanskrit word meaning "sky", "space" or "aether") are collectively understood to be a collection of mystical knowledge that is encoded in the aether; i.e. on a non-physical plane of existence. The concept is prevalent in New Age discourse. The Akashic Records are understood to have existed since the beginning of The Creation and even before. Just as we have various specialty libraries (e.g., medical, law), there are said to exist various Akashic Records (e.g., human, animal, plant, mineral, etc) encoding Universal lore. Most writings refer to the Akashic Records in the area of human experience but it is understood that all phenomenal experience as well as transcendental knowledge is encoded therein.

The Physical Body provides an experience of complete separation, which is unavailable in any other body. This experience of separation clarifies personal character and the essence of individuality. The Physical Body also provides stability, a solid foundation for all the other bodies. The Physical Body also assists in the crystallization of consciousness - any lessons learned while in a Physical Body, any experiences processed through it, become clearly defined and permanent consciousness as result of the Physical Body's separative and stabilizing influence. This is why the Physical Body is so valuable in our growth process.

Key to this learning and growth process are the five physical sensory organs giving perceptions of sight, sound, touch, taste, and smell limited to solid, liquid, and gaseous matter painful and not painful. The five physical organs of action: hands (grasping, etc.), feet (motion), digestive system (eating and excreting), throat (speaking), and genitals (sex and reproduction).

And so we repeat a very important part of this process. The physical brain is not a source of experience as some current neuroscientists now mistakenly believe. While areas of the brain are associated with different consciousness functions, many neuroscientists do admit that they cannot locate emotions, mind, and soul in the brain. Nor can they fully explain the human psyche with neuroanatomy. The physical brain is a relay station, translating emotional, mental, and spiritual events and information into neuro-electrochemical events and information. Neurochemicals and associated brain processes are simply channel selectors for various states of consciousness. All states of consciousness exist independent of the physical body. This relay station works in both directions: spiritual, mental, or emotional states trigger neuro-electrochemical events in the brain (physical consciousness) AND neurochemical stimulation (for example through drugs) open access to specific states of emotion, thought, or spiritual awareness. Contemporary physics has proven very clearly that solid physical matter is an illusion and that all is energy only. Therefore, to say that the solid physical brain is the mind is a mistake. While the brain appears to be solid, it is not - it is energy appearing solid, but is not solid - it is energy, only. The mind is also energy, an energy that interacts with the energy that creates the appearance of a brain. The Physical Body is composed of the energy states of solids, liquids, and gases and is dependent upon the Etheric Body for its vitality, life, organization, and many processes that result in health.

The Etheric/Vital Body

The Etheric Body gives vitality, health, life and organization to the Physical Body. It attunes our consciousness to the principle of Energy. It steps energies from the higher bodies down into our physical consciousness providing an awareness of various types of subtle energy moving through the Physical Body and in the environment. Subtle/etheric energy can be seen as well as felt.

The Etheric Body is the subtle level of the Physical Body. It is composed of various energies such as electromagnetic, chi, prana, ki, vitality, etc. It is also composed of subatomic particles, the finest of which are quarks. It glows overall with color variations in the range of blue to violet to silver. The Etheric Body has a figure form in the same shape as the Physical Body. This figure form is made of numerous energy channels called nadis or meridians. There are seven major energy centers, called chakras that are connected to the endocrine glands and process seven main types of consciousness. There are 21 minor energy centers and many smaller energy centers.

The Etheric Body has two auric layers. The first extends about one foot from the Physical Body. The second extends about three or more feet from the Physical Body. Each auric layer has luminous string-like hairs that radiate out and always move in wave like motions. From the inner body, sparkles of vitality move outwards. It has a total of 3 spatial dimensions.

The etheric body is made up of chi and forms a structure of meridians throughout the body. These meridians run through all the major organs, glands, nerves and energy centers. This system of etheric energy permeates the physical body, supporting and sustaining it. All life forms including plants and animals have an etheric body. Nothing physical can be alive without the etheric body as it feeds the physical with energy which is vital for its health and survival. Astral forces interact with the etheric layer and thereby transform basic life-force chi into many other types. The astral actually grasps the etheric and this is how it incarnates and creates with the physical substances.

This interaction between the astral and etheric is the same in humans and animals. The main difference is that humans and animals have their own astral body whereas plants receive astral forces from fairies and other beings as well as the astral fields surrounding the planet. A human's astral body concentrates certain astral forces in various places throughout the body with the organs and glands being the main locations. By the interaction in these areas the chi is transformed into organs and glands chi which is then circulated throughout the meridian system. The health of the astral body directly relates to the health of the etheric body which in turn affects the physical body. If any channels are blocked or there is poor circulation of chi the physical will suffer as well as the astral/mental and emotional state of the person. All disease and weakness of immunity comes down to the health and strength of the etheric body.

So basically you have a body of energy that permeates the physical body, giving it sustenance, health and vitality, without which the physical body could not be alive. All etheric energy comes from the lower dimensions. The strengthening and clearing of blockages in the meridian system is extremely important for spiritual growth. Tantric sex techniques are vital in increasing the vibration of the etheric and with proper techniques is the most powerful way available to give it strength and vitality.

Meridians of the body affect every organ and physiological system inside of us. They are invisible to the human eye, yet without them we could not sustain life. In the same way that arteries carry blood, meridians carry energy, often referred to as chi, qi or prana. Meridians are our body's "energy bloodstream": they bring vitality and balance, remove energy blockages, stagnations and imbalances, adjust metabolism and determine the speed and form of cellular change. Their flow is as critical as the flow of blood; your life and health depend on both. Meridians of the body affect all major systems including: immune, nervous, endocrine, circulatory, respiratory, digestive, skeletal, muscular and the lymphatic system. If a meridian's energy is obstructed or unregulated, the system it feeds on is jeopardized, and disease results.

There are 12 major meridians in the body:

- Lung meridian
- Large intestine meridian
- Spleen meridian
- Stomach meridian
- Heart meridian
- Small intestine meridian
- Bladder meridian
- Kidney meridian
- Pericardium (Circulation/Sex) meridian
- Triple Warmer meridian
- Liver meridian
- Gallbladder meridian

These major meridians of the body are responsible for nourishing their corresponding organ and the other organs around them, fueling and feeding them with energy. Each meridian plays a specific and integral role in their organs' health. Deficient meridian energy and excess meridian energy are both problematic and can cause damage to that meridian's organ system.

There are certain places along the meridians where energy pools, making the chi, qi or prana more accessible there than elsewhere. These "energy hotspots" are more familiarly referred to as acupuncture points and at these specific points energy can be manipulated – either increasing or decreasing the flow. When energy flowing through the meridians becomes blocked or stagnant, or, when too much energy is overwhelming a meridian these acupuncture points can be accessed to clear blockages and remove unwanted excess or stagnant energy. Often times acupuncture and acupressure techniques are used to relieve energetic imbalances in the meridians; the ancient Chinese practice of Qi Gong is often employed as well. This is also used in Reflexology; I (Aly) find it effective when used like an etheric acupressure when used with a crystal.

Acupuncture and acupressure both use the same meridians and points in their healing; the difference is that acupuncture uses needles while acupressure uses both soft and firm touches on the points to generate the flow of energy. Qi Gong is somewhat different. Similar to acupuncture and acupressure, qi gong is also a form of Traditional Chinese Medicine, however, qi gong uses breathwork, gentle movement and meditation to cleanse and strengthen the meridians and the energy running through them.

All three techniques of cleansing and balancing the energy flow through the meridians are forms of preventative medicine. This does not mean acupuncture, acupressure and qi gong cannot be used as treatments, and in fact this is quite the contrary. These are the traditional techniques used in Chinese Medicine to cure people suffering from all types of diseases and many westerners have begun turning to these treatments as well.

The Astral/Emotional Body

The Astral Body gives you the ability to have desires, emotions, imagination, and psychic abilities. It lends power to thought which is essential for effective action and manifestation. Astral consciousness includes the full range of emotions from fear, hate, and sorrow to love, happiness, and ecstasy. It also includes the full range of desire from totally selfish and destructive desire to common personal desire to high spiritual aspiration to selfless servicefull desire.

Astral experiences include dreams, fantasies, out of body experiences, near death experiences, hallucinations, imagination, and visions. The five astral senses are: Clairaudience (astral hearing), Psychometry (astral touch/feeling), Clairvoyance (astral sight), Imagination (astral equivalent of taste), and Emotional Idealism (astral equivalent of smell).

Astral consciousness and the Astral Universe include anything imaginable, from the worst possible hells to the most glorious heavens. The Astral Universe contains an astral replica of the higher universes. It is filled with imagery, feeling, and above all a personal point of view.

The Astral Body has a figure form in the shape of the Physical Body and an aura usually in an ovoid shape pointed at both ends. The aura extends about 4 to 9 feet from the Physical Body. It has 7 major energy centers, 21 minor energy centers, and many smaller centers, just like the etheric body. It is constantly changing color, dark to brilliant colors depending upon your mood. It has a total of 4 spatial dimensions.

Astral/Emotional consciousness is primarily awakened through the stimulation of desire. Awareness of the Astral Universe is awakened by meditation, psychic development techniques, out of body (astral) travel techniques, shamanic practices, lucid dreaming, drugs - especially psychedelics, certain pranayama practices, certain types of trauma, biochemical imbalances, and certain types of energetic stimulation.

The Mental/Intellectual Body

The Mental Body facilitates cognition, the faculty of knowing. It gives you the ability to discern, and to have thoughts, beliefs, concepts, and higher psychic abilities.

Mental consciousness ranges from discernment of the very specific to detailed but is particular to the discernment of the very general. The five mental senses are: Higher Clairaudience (mental hearing), Planetary Psychometry (mental feeling), Higher Clairvoyance (mental sight), Discernment (mental equivalent of taste), and Spiritual Discernment (mental equivalent of smell). The Mental Body has its own range of feeling. When there is excessive focus within the limiting, separative range of thought then there is judgment, mental fear, and depression. When thought expands into the more unitive ranges then there is compassionate-understanding, peace, joy, awe, and bliss.

The Manasic Universe (which includes the Mental/Intellectual Body, Causal/Soul Body, and the Manasic Body) is overall a place of profound rarefied celestial beauty. It is filled with light - primarily white, blue and gold, although the full range of pastel colors are common. The Manasic Universe, similar to the Astral Universe, contains a mental replica of the higher universes. It is filled with knowledge about everything. Mental consciousness is more objective, factual, and impersonal than astral consciousness. However, individual personality and character reach their pinnacle of development in mental consciousness.

The Mental Body has a figure like form in the shape of the Physical Body. It also has an aura that is ovoid shaped with pointed ends. The aura extends about 4 to 10 feet from the Physical Body. Usual colors are light blue, yellow, gray, silver, white, and gold, however all pastel colors can be present. It has 7 major energy centers, 21 minor energy centers, and many smaller centers, just like the etheric and astral bodies. Radiations of light extend from the heart area. It has a total of 5 spatial dimensions.

Mental consciousness is awakened through academic study, reading, certain types of energetic stimulation, and certain meditation practices.

The Causal/Soul Body

The Causal/Soul Body is named "Causal" because it is the originating source of each personality that incarnates in each lifetime. It is the source of your personality, causing it to be and exist. When your personality ends, the essence of you is absorbed back into the Causal Body. It is the first level of your individuality that is relatively immortal as the Causal Body exists for many millions of years, during your journey as a human through many incarnations or lifetimes. Animals have yet to obtain a Causal Body. Enlightened humans that are liberated from the cycle of rebirth discard the Causal Body and move on to higher levels.

The word "Soul" is used as a label for many bodies or human aspects by various religions and cultures. Generally it is meant to designate the innermost individuality. Limitations of perception have caused this label to be applied to the astral body, the mental body and other inner aspects. Here it is applied to the Causal Body because it is the pinnacle of personal consciousness.

The Causal Body is the depository for all consciousness and virtues cultivated in each personality lifetime; especially developed are will power, love-wisdom, and creative intelligence. It is built out of all the benefits of all past lives. It is the treasure chest that safekeeps the fruits of all past experiences. It is the vehicle that facilitates the unfolding of consciousness that we use physically, emotionally, mentally, and spiritually. It is the vehicle for human immortality, whether a personality is in incarnation or not.

The Causal Body/Soul is the central focal point of consciousness itself for the entire human being. Therefore its range of consciousness includes the physical, etheric, emotional/astral, and mental/intellectual. As it awakens spiritually it becomes aware of other souls on its own level and participates in a universe and an existence independent of the personality. The Soul's life is one of unity, group consciousness, love, wisdom, bliss, and purpose. As it spiritually awakens with the aid of the meditating personality, it extends its range of consciousness into the Higher Mind/Manasic Body, Buddhic/Christic Body, Atmic Body, Monadic Aspect, and eventually the level of Logoic/ God/ Goddess/ Solar Aspect.

The Causal Body has two additional mental/manasic senses: Response to Group Vibration (used to find its soul group), and Spiritual Telepathy (used to communicate with other souls). It lives primarily in the Manasic Universe. The experience of time is accelerated such that a physical lifetime is experienced as a day.

Viewed from a 3 dimensional perspective it appears as a radiant orb of white and golden light, a miniature sun, approximately **30 feet in diameter**. It has vortices on the top and bottom, lines of light and sparkling energy throughout. Most people have slices missing that appear dark or vacant which are areas of consciousness that are to be unfolded in time. It has a total of 5 spatial dimensions.

Viewed from a 5 dimensional perspective it appears as a radiant, beautiful flower of light that is continually blossoming and turning in upon itself. It has 12 petals, each of which is a vortex that is rotating and conducts a major type of consciousness. As a person evolves through an average of 777 lifetimes these petals or vortices open and become radiant and functional. As the petals open they radiate subtle hues of the colors: orange, blue, yellow, indigo, green, violet, and rose.

Causal/Soul consciousness is awakened through life and certain meditation practices.

The Manasic/Higher Mind Body

The Manasic/Higher Mind Body is the vehicle of contact with the Universal Mind. Through it we have the ability to directly comprehend vast reservoirs of knowledge and truth about reality and existence. It gives us the ability to become conscious of the Divine Plan as it is working out in manifestation.

The Manasic Body's orientation is towards mental comprehension of abstract and universal truths which are infinite in quantity, exalted in quality, and profoundly liberating to the human spirit. When this level of consciousness is awakened the awareness of omnipresence becomes established. Manasic consciousness incarnates the intelligence aspect of Deity. Manasic consciousness is normally rapturous and blissful. It exists in the higher levels of the Manasic Universe.

When awakened, the Manasic Body can be perceived as a vast field of particles of light, radiating from a central point and extending about 1200 feet in diameter and about 340 feet in height. A central column of light-energy signifies its current range of universal thought. It exists in 5 spatial dimensions. Size will vary between people.

The Buddhic/Christic Body

This body was not named after the individuals, The Buddha and The Christ, but rather they were named after this level of consciousness that they embodied. Many world teachers and founders of major religions embodied in the world this state of consciousness.

The Buddhic Body facilitates the expansion of consciousness beyond separative individuality. This allows identity to break free of individuality so that identity can include others; such as family, friends, social group, soul group, and eventually humanity as a whole. The Buddhic Body facilitates intuitive understanding through union with others, knowing by being that which is to be known. The Buddhic level is THE source of happiness and bliss for the Manasic/Higher Mind, Causal/Soul, Mental/Intellectual, Astral/Emotional, and Physical levels. It is the plane of bliss.

This body eventually transmutes, heals, and resolves all human problems with the power of love, unity, and wisdom. The Buddhic/Christic body contains the archetype of perfection for the human being. The embodiment of this archetype, the fusion of the personality and the Buddhic/Christic body is the goal of human evolution.

Buddhic consciousness does not begin until very significant progress on the spiritual path is made. This starts as intuition (an ability to know wisdom through love, without thought or psychic abilities) and as compassion for others. Pure Buddhic consciousness is characterized by an expansion of identity beyond individuality so that you are big enough to identify with a group of individuals or souls. World teachers embody this state in the way that they totally dedicate their individualities to the good of the group of humanity.

Unity is so real and intense on this level that you are in a state of continual ecstatic union with others. It is a state of intense love and continual total-being - orgasmic ecstasy. If what is thought to be Buddhic or Christ consciousness does not include this experience of intense orgasmic bliss then it is not actual pure Buddhic/Christ consciousness but rather its reflection in the Mental or Astral levels, or a mixture of Buddhic with Mental or Astral levels. Buddhic/Christ consciousness is a state of ecstatic individual self transcendence.

The mark of someone who has truly attained this state of consciousness on a continual basis is that they are never oriented towards their individuality. They will never or rarely speak about their individuality. They are totally selfless in their actions and desire nothing of a personal nature because they reside in the source of fulfillment, in continual intense bliss. Also, their expression is utterly harmless and overflowing with compassion.

The Buddhic vehicle has its own level of five senses. These are: Comprehension (Buddhic hearing of 4 sounds: personal, that of others, that of one's soul group, that of the planetary entity that is one's origin), Healing (Buddhic feeling that facilitates realization of the manner in which to heal and cause wholeness), Divine Vision (Buddhic sight that allows one to see the divine in all), Intuition (Buddhic taste, whereby one's essence is recognized in and under all forms), and Idealism (Buddhic smell, the ability to sense the ideal).

Buddhic consciousness is also characterized by omniscience, all-knowingness. Realization of identification with the Divine begins on this level. Buddhic consciousness incarnates the love aspect of Deity. It resides in the Buddhic Universe which is filled with golden and white light, profound wisdom, swirling mandalas of groups within groups within groups of light-beings.

When awakened, the Buddhic/Christic body can be perceived as a large conglomerate of spinning vortices pointed outward. The cone shaped structures, in the image above, are vortices of energy. This body is extremely elastic, and when its attention is directed to an object (on its own level or mental, astral, or physical levels), it expands and elongates and travels to the object faster than the speed of light or the speed of thought, then the vortices tunnel into the object facilitating an immediate unification and merging with the object of attention. A central column of light-energy signifies its current range of consciousness. Rarely are Buddhic bodies seen alone, as depicted above. They are normally dynamically interacting with groups within groups of other Buddhic beings. It has a total of 6 spatial dimensions.

Pain and suffering awaken the beginnings of compassion for others, the first glimmer of Buddhic/Christic consciousness. When a person takes their evolution in their own hands by the disciplined spiritual practice of meditation then pain and suffering become unnecessary and are replaced by bliss. Buddhic consciousness is awakened primarily through certain types of meditation. Loving service to one's family, friends, humanity, and the world, also helps to awaken this consciousness

The Atmic Body

The Atmic Body is the vehicle of identification with the One-Life that enlivens as well as observes and acts through every living being and creature on planet earth. It is the vehicle through which perfect self-mastery is attained.

Atmic consciousness is undifferentiated awareness - identification, not with individuality, not with groups of beings, but with all pervading life itself. If there is a strong sense of individuality, then it is not a pure Atmic state but rather a reflection of it in Mental or Astral levels. The feeling of Atmic consciousness is that of pure equanimity, a complete transcendence of both pain and bliss, completely unbiased and equanimous towards all - extremely intense peace.

The Atmic 5 senses are: Beatitude (the Atmic ability to hear the sound or vibration that creates the form of anything and everything on all levels up to the Atmic), Active Service (the Atmic feeling sense of the ever unfolding need of creation), Realization (the Atmic ability to see the truth), Perfection (Atmic taste that leads to the heart of one's nature), Perfected Knowledge (Atmic smell that guides a being to its source, its true home).

Atmic consciousness is also characterized by omnipotence, an extreme power of will that makes nearly all possible. Atmic consciousness incarnates the will aspect of Deity. It resides in the Atmic Universe.

The Atmic body is a radiation from a central point that is unified with the One-Life that envelopes and surrounds the earth; animating, perceiving through, acting through all living creatures on all levels of existence (Buddhic, Manasic, Causal, Mental, Astral, Etheric, Physical) on the earth.
This radiation of awareness extends in 7 spatial dimensions. Atmic consciousness is awakened through specific meditation practices.

The Monadic Aspect

The Monadic Aspect is the source of consciousness for all levels of experience (Atmic, Buddhic, Manasic, Causal, Mental, Astral, Etheric, and Physical). It is the generator of the principle of consciousness. It is also the powerstation from which we draw the principles of Will, Love, and Intelligence. The Monadic Aspect contains the last remnant of individuality prior to merging back into our Source. It has been called the Spark within the Flame. While a Monad is profoundly at one with and identified with Source, it also has a very subtle individuality, a point of focus. This point of focus is the absolute source of our individual awareness, our individual aliveness, and our individual expression.

Monadic consciousness IS the awareness we use on all levels of experience (Atmic, Buddhic, Manasic, Causal, Mental, Astral, Etheric, and Physical). On its own level, it is pure consciousness without object, completely formless. It resides in the Monadic Universe.

The experience of time is accelerated such that a physical lifetime is experienced as a minute while also simultaneously processing billions of years into the past and billions of years into the future. Impossible to describe aside from that it exists in 8 dimensions. Its expanse is much greater than a planet but usually not greater than a solar system. Monadic awareness is awakened through specific meditation practices.

The Logoic/God/Goddess/Solar Aspect

The Solar Aspect is the source of our Light, Life, and Love. The Solar System is Alive. Nearly all the planets are populated on nonphysical levels. There are 200 Billion Monads/Individual Beings (such as you and me) living in this Solar System. The earth is the densest place to live in our Solar System. There are many nonphysical planets that are teeming with life and activity. Each Individualized Being is an atom in its body. Each planet is a major energy center in its body. 60 Billion of the Individualized Beings in our Solar System are on the Human path of evolution. 140 Billion of the Individualized Beings in our Solar System are on the Angelic (called in the east Devic) path of evolution (which is feminine in relation to the Human path). This makes our Local God, the Solar Deity, technically feminine in gender since most of its atoms are feminine. Our Solar Deity is a Goddess. We are Her children. She is our caretaker. We are the atoms in Her body. We fundamentally, as Individual Beings, are Her.

The key function is to unfold Consciousness which is fundamentally Love. The previous Solar System unfolded Intelligence, which is an inherent part of our current Solar System. The next Solar System will unfold Will and Power, after Love is fully developed. Encompassing the life and activity of 200 Billion Beings evolving and living on multiple levels, (Monadic, Atmic, Buddhic, Manasic, Causal, Mental, Astral, Etheric, and Physical). On its own level, it is pure consciousness without object, completely formless. It resides in the Monadic Universe.

The experience of time is accelerated such that a physical lifetime is experienced as a minute while also simultaneously processing billions of years into the past and billions of years into the future.

The entire Solar System including the Sun, the known physical planets, asteroids, moons, and a vast number of nonphysical planets existing in subtle levels of reality. When viewed as a whole on all levels the Solar System looks like an immense whirlwind of radiant energy, like a huge radiant atom. It is an atom in the body of our Galactic God, The Galactic

Deity. It also serves the role of the Heart Chakra/Center of a Being somewhat larger than itself. Logoic/Solar Consciousness is awakened through specific meditation practices.

The Light Body

A Light Being is made of light. It does not die; it is eternal, and it is a higher form of pure consciousness. It is what we get access to when we go into that heart-brain which lives in the space of higher consciousness, and the soup of pure love; described by our upcoming physicists as "quantum". The light body is a structure of light from higher dimensions. Like the physical body it is a vehicle for consciousness evolution. As your physical body contains organs and other physical structures to match its density, your light body contains various structures of light to match its higher density. The chakras, the Column and the MerKaBa are all structures of the light body interfacing with the physical body. Between lives you journey in the light body to various places and dimensions and it is the central vehicle used to incarnate into any of the nine dimensions. For incarnation into the 3rd dimension the light body needs an astral body which has been described earlier.

The light body is very large and contains many structures. It is beyond our purposes to describe all of its parts and functions here but the ones that are most important for our spiritual evolution of awakening are the chakras, the Column and the MerKaBa. (These will be explained as we move on).

As stated, for the Light Body to incarnate into the lower physical form, it needs an astral body as its interface. Astral Substance is what makes up your astral body. Before incarnating into the physical body, the consciousness of the descending soul passes through the astral layers around Earth and collects various astral forces to build the astral body that will be used as a vehicle to incarnate into matter. The specific astral forces collected depend on the soul itself and its chosen life on Earth.

The Astral Substances or forces around Earth come from the surrounding planets. The planets are the physical bodies of some very large beings that have incarnated as planets. These beings have an astral body which is an expression of them in Astral Substance. As stated earlier, consciousness expresses itself through various dimensions of light with Astral Substance being the lowest dimension of this light. While the light of the higher dimensions vibrates very fast, the astral light has been slowed down significantly so that the consciousness from the highest dimensions may incarnate into matter which vibrates slower. The dimensions of light come from the higher dimensions of consciousness and so this light is an actual expression of the higher consciousness (it's just a slower vibration).

Earth is situated with surrounding planets which all have an astral body which is an expression of the being that has incarnated into the planet. These beings are sometimes called gods and the Ancient Greek, Roman and Hindu mythologies of the gods do well in depicting their personalities and interactions. As the human's astral body is made up of the Astral Substance from each of these so-called gods, the interactions occur both within the individual human and between individuals and groups. The human-being collects Astral Substance from these so-called gods on the way through the lower dimensions of Astral Substance before incarnation. Depending on the positions of the planets in relation to Earth and each other the Astral Substances acquired will differ and hence the science of the horoscope.

So a consciousness (spirit) which has a high dimensional light body gradually descends into lower vibrations and gathers Astral Substance around the light body and then incarnates into the physical and energy bodies of the baby. The actual incarnation occurs at birth as this is when the being is brought into the 3rd dimension. During the pregnancy the spirit has a connection to the fetus and so is partially incarnated but its main substance is waiting in the higher dimensions. It is when the baby is born that the spirit has really begun its incarnation into the 3rd dimension. Although birth is indeed the beginning of the incarnated life it takes time for the various Astral Substances, light and consciousness to merge with the physical body. It takes a normal person about 28 years to incarnate all of the astral energies they have brought with them. In fact the incarnation process does keep on going for the entire life but it seems that 28 is the critical point. Before 28 years is reached it has been difficult for a being to have incarnated all that it has intended to. We believe that this time is dropping rapidly.

The Astral Substances have characteristics as they are an expression of the beings which they belong to. The consciousness and higher-dimensional Light Body which has incarnated is therefore experienced through this astral body.

The Higher Self of the baby is an extremely sensitive and loving being. It has come from a place of absolute love, safety, wisdom, intelligence and sensitivity. Life on Earth is very different to the place of its origin. As soon as it is born a huge disconnection from its home occurs, leading to immense heartbreak, fear and need of nurturance. When the being feels nurtured and secure you can clearly see the higher aspects of its spirit. When it does not feel these things from its environment you will clearly see the pain and grief that the baby feels. Whenever this pain is felt by the baby the disconnection from the spirit's essence (home) is increasing. The only treatment for this pain is for the astral body of the infant to begin to crystallize to shut out the pain which in effect shuts out the higher energies as well. When the baby was first born the astral body was like a colored lens but as parts begin to crystallize it's like putting scratches on the lens which further distorts and blocks out the higher light. This is the formation of the ego. Every time the baby feels unpleasant emotions the astral body crystallizes further to block out the pain. Eventually the astral body has become a crystallized structure which successfully blocks out the pain of the spirit's disconnection from its source.

Once the astral body has become crystallized to this point it is a fully fledged ego structure. This structure reacts to the World depending on its inherent astral forces or horoscope and the way its structure was formed as everything that is experienced becomes shadowed by emotional traumas and conditioning. The more emotional pain felt by the individual and the less nurturance, security and love received during infancy the more crystallized will be the ego structure and therefore the more distorted and blocked the incoming higher light from the Higher Self.

The astral body incarnates into the physical body through the chi body and the Chitta which are both greatly involved with the Central Nervous System which includes the brain, spinal cord and all nerves running throughout the body. You feel emotions throughout the body because of this interaction. Your Heart Chakra is in the middle of your chest within the Light Body; the emotions felt here in the astral body transfer into the chi/etheric body and then into the physical body through the nerves. When you feel broken-hearted you feel physical pain in the area even though the emotion is located in the astral body because of this interaction. The structure in the astral body can be seen and felt in the physical body as tension because the crystallized astral grasps the etheric which in turn affects the nerves in the area. The ego structure in the astral body always affects the flow of etheric/chi energy which in turn causes stress/tension in the physical body which leads to poor health, weakness and rapid aging of the physical body.

In ordinary individuals the ego structure created during infancy remains until death, being the base of personality through which life is experienced. At death the astral body leaves the physical and etheric bodies and begins to rise into higher dimensions. As this occurs the crystallized parts shatter under the pressure of higher vibration. Much of the shattered astral body goes back to where it came from and becomes as it was before the incarnation but some very crystallized chunks remain intact and stay on earth where they become etheric/astral parasites.

Once the astral body has shattered the parts of the higher consciousness and light of the being that incarnated will go back to the higher dimensions from where they came. The spirit will see clearly once again, remember who and what it is and realize that the life it just lived was but a tiny (but very meaningful) experience on its journey throughout the Universe.

Ka is basically light from the higher dimensions. Above the dimensions of Astral Substance there are many dimensions of light. The light at the highest dimensions has the fastest vibration and is the brightest and as we come down in dimension the light becomes less bright until we reach Astral Substance which is the least bright but much more dense. The main difference between ka and Astral Substance, although they are both essentially light, is that Astral Substance has a density which allows it to crystallize, and crystallized Astral Substance tends to block and distort the light. The ka cannot crystallize like Astral Substance as it is vibrating too fast. Anything in the dimensions of ka is an expression of the consciousness that created it.

We all have Light Bodies which are made of the light from these higher dimensions. While in your light body you are in touch with your true self and most essential nature as it has not been distorted by the lens of the astral body or the physical body. You know who and what you are and are at one with the Universe. You can travel to almost any dimension in your light body.

We all have this Light Body so where is it? It is waiting for you for when you leave your physical body. When you die and your astral body shatters, the consciousness and light that you incarnated during the life will remerge with the rest of your light body. At this point all veils will be gone and you will remember everything. What is important to understand is that there is a Light Body along with many of your higher selves waiting for you after each life and you will remerge with these parts. There are many higher selves because there is more than one level of your Higher Self. While on Earth you could become aware of your Higher Self and even partially incarnate it. You would then realize that there is still another Higher Self than this one and so on. You have higher selves in many dimensions with many different perspectives and views of the Universe and even of your life here on earth. We believe that this Light Body awareness and realization of its multidimensionality is rapidly evolving in this lifetime.

The light body includes the chakras; Column and the MerKaBa along with other structures of light that have been described. The Light Body is partly here and incarnated but it is very blocked and is not functioning properly which leads to the state of consciousness of the normal individual. Because of the way we have incarnated into such dense matter, the dualistic nature of the 3rd dimension and the purposes for which we have done this, our bodies are all out-of-whack. In a nutshell the goal is to purify the astral layer, clear and raise the vibration of the etheric and physical bodies, incarnate more of the light body and get its structures and energy centers balanced and functioning properly. Through this the spirit is able to incarnate into matter.

The MerKaBa is a spinning structure of light similar to the chakras. It is similar in that when spinning properly it works as an inter-dimensional gateway so that higher consciousness may incarnate into the physical body. The difference is that the MerKaBa is much larger, encompassing the entire body. In fact the MerKaBa is the structure of spinning light which allows for the incarnation of the light body itself. Without the MerKaBa being activated the other parts of the light body such as the chakras cannot incarnate properly and may not be stable. When the MerKaBa spins at a certain speed, a disk of light shoots out from the Base Chakra, in the perfect centre of the spinning star tetrahedron, to around 50-60 feet in diameter. This is what your activated MerKaBa would look like and in fact this field of light has an electro-magnetic component that can be seen with the appropriate instruments on a computer monitor.

The Merkaba is created by counter-rotating fields of energy. The mental Star Tetrahedral field is electrical in nature, male, and rotates to the left. The emotional Star Tetrahedral field is magnetic in nature, female, and rotates to the right. It is the linking together of the mind, heart, and physical body in a specific geometrical ratio and at a critical speed that produces the merkaba The word "Mer" denotes counter-rotating fields of light, "Ka" Spirit, and "Ba" body, or reality. So the Mer-Ka-Ba then, is a counter-rotating field of light that encompasses both Spirit and body and it's a vehicle----a time space vehicle. It's far more than just that, in fact there isn't anything that it isn't. It is the image through which all things were created, and that image is around your body in a geometrical set of patterns. That image begins at the base of your spine as small as the original eight cells from which our physical bodies first formed. It moves out from there first forming a Star Tetrahedron, then a cube out at your hands, then a sphere, then back to back pyramids (known as an octahedron) then an icosahedron, and then a dodecahedron. The field extends out a full fifty to sixty feet in diameter, depending on your height. It looks like a flying saucer.

The Forces of Consciousness begin as pure spirit. Humans and all other sentient life are a part of this creation. We are impulsed from the dimensions above and receive all of our consciousness, power, love and wisdom from the creators above. We too are creators and our impulse is to incarnate into matter and create within it. The only way for consciousness to create with the Material Forces from the dimensions below, is to enter into it. The incarnation of spirit into matter is the way the entire Universe is created. Everything in the Universe has a consciousness associated with it. All the planets are conscious beings incarnating into matter. They each form the Material Forces around themselves to create whatever it is they desire. All incarnating beings are simply the part of a larger being that is merging with the forces from below. In nearly the entire Universe, for anyone who has incarnated into anything, they remain aware of their higher parts and are truly multi-dimensional beings. They are aware of the many dimensions around them and of their higher and lower parts, and of the oneness of all that is. They are aware of their source as well as the universes around them. They are aware of their spirit which is nothing less than a part of the Great Spirit at the highest dimension. All spirits are a differentiation of this one spirit, as is yours and every other life forms.

The Column is a structure of light which goes straight through the middle of your body from the top of the Crown to your perineum (the area between the genitals and the anus). This tube extends upwards from the crown through all the higher dimensions and downwards from the perineum through all the lower dimensions. The seven chakras previously described are situated along the Column within the body. There are numerous other chakras along the Column all the way up and down. Full explanations of these are beyond our purposes here but you should be aware of their existence.

The Column is the central channel of your light body. It is through this channel that your awareness can move between dimensions with ease. Of course this is the case while you are not incarnated but while here on Earth it isn't quite that simple. Because of the interaction between the astral body and the light body the Column is usually quite blocked and you may have trouble even feeling it. It is usually blocked at the top of the head and the perineum (as well as through the body) so it may be difficult to take your awareness up or down the Column at all. A large part of spiritual work involves clearing the Column and relearning to ascend it into higher dimensions or descend it into lower dimensions. Once this has been achieved it becomes easy to become aware of and communicate with many aspects of yourself from many different dimensions. The vastness of who you really are becomes known beyond a doubt as you have direct experience of metaphysical realities.

Besides communicating with parts of your self the column also opens up possibilities of communication with many non-physical and multi-dimensional beings throughout the Universe

The Chakras you are already familiar with. They are structures of spinning light. They are located within the light body and their purpose is to create a gateway into higher or lower dimensions of consciousness. The light body is made up of many dimensions of light but to incarnate higher consciousness (spirit) into this light body a certain type of vortex needs to be created. These vortexes are the chakras and each one is a gateway to a certain aspect of higher consciousness. As discussed earlier the highest dimensions do not contain light but only pure consciousness. From this consciousness the dimensions of light are created. The higher dimensions of consciousness are the source of the dimensions of light. Now for an individual consciousness from the very high dimensions to explore through the dimensions of light, astrality and physicality it must do so through some kind of structure. The chakras are the main gateways through which consciousness incarnates into the light body.

So the chakras are essentially structures of spinning light which form gateways into higher dimensions of consciousness or lower dimensions of material forces. It is important now to understand what happens to these structures during incarnation and between lives.

Your light body is the body of light you are developing as your next evolutionary step. Awakening your light body brings higher, finer frequencies of light into your physical, emotional and mental energy bodies. With these finer frequencies of light you are building, step-by-step, an awareness of the higher dimensions and yourself as you exist in them. As you awaken your light body you can experience many heightened, blissful, peaceful, loving, joyful and insightful states of consciousness. You can reach higher, expanded states, open your channel upward, and expand your consciousness to experience your Source directly. You can use these energies in many practical ways as well as to create the life you want

The Light Body is an energy body made out of light particles. We have a physical body made out of flesh and blood. We need to transform this flesh and blood body to Light Body. This follows the Einstein discovery that energy and matter can be transferred to either of the states meaning that energy can become matter and matter can become energy.

It is not quite the astral body and there is another body which is called the causal body. A causal body doesn't have any form, even it is beyond the light body, and it is just a body of intension, causes, that is causal body. The astral body is something that everybody has, which will be sustained after death. Even after death the astral body remains there. That is not the Light Body. The Light Body is a more advanced body in which you change your flesh and blood body into particles of light which goes beyond even the astral body

The idea is rooted in common worldwide religious accounts of the afterlife in which the soul's journey or "ascent" is described in such terms as "an ecstatic, mystical or out-of body experience, wherein the spiritual traveler leaves the physical body and travels in his/her subtle body (or dreambody or astral body) into 'higher' realms". Hence "the "many kinds of 'heavens', 'hells' and purgatorial existences believed in by followers of innumerable religions" may also be understood as astral phenomena, as may the various "phenomena of the séance room".

The astral body is sometimes said to be visible as an aura of swirling colours. It is widely linked today with out-of-body experiences or *astral projection*, where this refers to a movement around the real world. There are many references to an astral body or light body in esoteric literature. The surface of the astral body shimmers or sparkles. The actual body is opalescent and resembles the physical body in appearance. However, the astral body may resemble the form of a younger or older physical form. For example, a 60-year-old man may assume the astral form of his 35-year-old physical appearance. A mature 14-year-old young lady may appear in an astral form of someone in her early 20's.

The astral body connects to the medulla center by an umbilical cord-like structure that is referred to as the silver cord in esoteric literature. This cord is infinitely extensible, yet tethers or anchors the astral body to the body's etheric matrix or chakra.

In its ground state, the astral body is effectively superimposed on the physical form. When the physical body's arm moves, for example, the astral body's arm also moves.

Upon moving through the astral umbilicus, the meditator enters the astral spiritual tube, in which the meditator's attention encounters six whirling wheels. These wheels are located at the:

- Base of Spine
- Navel
- Solar Plexus
- Heart
- Throat
- Medulla

Moving into the level of the face, of the astral body, the meditator encounters the astral senses of sight, hearing, smell, touch and taste. At the point between the eyebrows, the meditator finds the center of the astral will, by which the limbs, face and torso of the astral body can be moved.

Astral movement corresponds to our faculty of imagination. In imagination, we can walk through a wall, fly through space, translocate to another place or move through time. Astral movement replicates whatever is visualized. The faculty of intention, which is anchored in the attentional principle, generates visualization.

In the center of the forehead of the astral body is the so-called third eye. It is a blissful mirror of spiritual development in the Cosmic Realm, and is a source of intuitive wisdom. It embodies an inner knowing of the laws of the Superconscious Mind and sees the Astral Planes of the Great Continuum of Consciousness.

The astral brain resembles a spiral of colored spheres that culminate in a central jet or flare of light. This central flame is referred to as the Jyoti in Eastern scriptures. The meditator beholds a rainbow of pastel-colored spheres, ranging from rose-colored to violet to brilliant white.

Consciousness Is All That Is, Was, Will Be

We have been bringing forward a new picture of the human body and the energetic system of subtle waves. These are all sensing antenna that connect with your physical and mental state. In further understanding energetics, in our world, we see the power of words and images all the time. They carry energy as they directly affect our perceptions and physical reactions. A thought, a word, a picture can easily create fear or love instantly, causing a cascade of actions to occur. Coming in contact with another's energy field can do the same. Why is this so?

The brain and the other brains, as well as the energy bodies are all designed to serve the divine purpose of evolving physicality to the higher consciousness. All are sensing and recording impressions and emotions about the lives, keeping track of it to reflect it in the current life, and then carry it onto the next. They all operate in the quantum world.

Thought, or anything else we create is energy, and Quantum physics says it is so. And there are endless sources of research confirming this. Thoughts come from synapses from axons in neurons in the brain. Energy is released from the brain and consciousness in some peculiar partnership into certain areas of the brain or body (depending on the thought) and releases energy in order to bring the thought to that part of the body. The energy is converted in each neuron the impulse passes through. This energy passes through each neurotransmitter. This is why thoughts are technically energy.

The subconscious mind is like a video camera that is attached to one and operates 24/7. It never sleeps, it is always on duty. It records on three levels. The first level is the actual event, the second level is the emotional component of the event and the third level is the perceptual component of the event.

The first level it records on is the level of literal events i.e. exactly in the same way as the video camera. So if I was to ask you, under Hypnosis, to tell me about a conversation that you had with Mom when you were say five years old, you would say which one of several and I would say choose one for me. You would then be able to repeat that conversation for me, under hypnosis, word for word.

The second level it records in is in what is described as the emotional body. This body is populated with the emotional component of the event in the first body. The function of this body would be to record how you feel about this event when it happened to you. So if the event on the first level is positive, such as a happy event, then the recording would be a positive energetic one. If however, it was negative, such as a scolding, or being ignored, for example, then the recording would be negative. Here we think to ourselves that "we are not lovable, or that they don't like me, or I am not wanted etc". These would be our negative belief systems that we take on about ourselves.

The third level it records in is the mental body. This body is populated with the perception component of the event in the first body, which could be totally different to the actual event. The function of this body would be to record how you perceive this event. So if the event on the first level is positive, such as a happy event, then the recording would be a positive energetic one. If however it was negative, such as a scolding or a rejection, for example, then the recording would be negative or you could have taken on a negative belief system about yourself, such as 'I can't be good enough, if they loved me they would not do this to me, therefore I can't be lovable, I can't trust life, I have to do for others to get something, It's always what they want that is important, not what I want', etc, etc.

Now it is important to understand that these recordings of these events do not happen in our brains as some would like us to believe. They are recorded in our various auric bodies surrounding the body namely the etheric, emotional and mental bodies. Now these bodies are populated by these positive and negative events that have positive and negative charges to them. It then follows that each of us are therefore electrical magnetic beings. This is the mechanism that then operates in our lives and attracts to us the events and situations in our lives being partners, opportunities, work environment, family environment, etc. All of these give us an opportunity to work through our issues and enhance our learning.

Modern day Quantum Physics fully explains beyond any doubt that your thoughts are the things that group together and collapse energy packets, change those thoughts from a probability into physical matter in a given place and time and create your life experience physically, financially, relationally, emotionally and spiritually.

Put another way... everything in your life...in the entire world in fact is the result of *"Your Consciousness as it stands now"* Your life will unfold perfectly and precisely just as you "believe" that it will – in fact your life is as it is now because of what you believe about yourself and what you think of yourself!!. That is – place a new set of belief systems in place within you and watch how the world changes around you.

The conclusions that have been arrived at thus far through the study of Quantum Physics as well as more recent discoveries relating to "cellular memories", aligns perfectly with what ALL the major religions of the world have always taught in some form. "As a man thinketh, so is he." If you "think" (negative belief systems) about yourself you will manifest illness in your body in such a way that will reflect exactly what it is you believe about life. This is profound. !!! Think about it. It can change the course of your illness AND your quality of life on your Soul's journey Home or the 9th dimension. Yes, it seems like quite a tortuous path but that choice of heaven or hell is one of the greatest gifts of all called free will.

Important Conclusions About The Energy Body

The first conclusion is that the Physical Body is the form that a Soul takes while incarnated in the 3rd dimension on Earth. The Physical Body consists of energy so dense that it can be felt and seen. In order to experience the lower 3rd dimension, it requires an astral body to interface with the physical body.

The second conclusion is that the Soul came to evolve through various dimensions or planes. To do this, it was given a great inventory of equipment that are the physical and energy bodies. The conscious awareness of each of these bodies, as they progress from the lower dimension of 1 to the higher spiritual dimension of 9, is the evolution. Each dimension is reflected in the energy body which opens new inventories of abilities to perceive, see, understand increasing levels of consciousness.

The third conclusion is that the astral body is able to separate from the physical and travel without it. Since the astral is the vehicle of consciousness, it is this body which is aware, not the physical.

The fourth conclusion is that the Auras reflect the constant change in our thoughts and emotions like a monitoring system. Auric dysfunction points to evolution issues and karmic issues. This leads to the red flags of dysfunction as a Cause And Effect which inhibits the souls' evolution.

The fifth conclusion is that the enveloping Causal/Soul Body (golden orb) is the subtlest level of personal individuality, the enlivening source of life and consciousness for the current personality, all past life personalities, and all future life personalities. It is called the Higher Self.

The sixth conclusion is that the Causal/Soul Body is named Causal because it is the originating source of each personality that incarnates in each lifetime. It is the source of your personality, causing it to be and exist. When your personality ends, the essence of you is absorbed back into the Causal Body. It is the first level of your individuality that is relatively immortal as the Causal Body exists for many millions of years, during your journey as a human through many incarnations or lifetimes.

The seventh conclusion is that the physical brain is a relay station, translating emotional, mental, and spiritual events and information into neuro-electrochemical events and information. Neurochemicals and associated brain processes are simply channel selectors for various states of consciousness. All states of consciousness exist independent of the physical body. This relay station works in both directions: spiritual, mental, or emotional states trigger neuro-electrochemical events in the brain.

The eighth conclusion is that the goal of the Soul is to purify the astral layer, clear and raise the vibration of the etheric and physical bodies, incarnate more of the light body and get its structures and energy centers balanced and functioning properly. Through this the spirit is able to incarnate into matter.

The ninth conclusion is that in the same way that arteries carry blood, meridians carry energy, often referred to as chi, qi or prana. Meridians are our body's "energy bloodstream": they bring vitality and balance, remove energy blockages, stagnations and imbalances, adjust metabolism and determine the speed and form of cellular change.

The tenth conclusion is that major meridians of the body are responsible for nourishing their corresponding organ and the other organs around them, fueling and feeding them with energy. Each meridian plays a specific and integral role in their organ's health. Deficient meridian energy and excess meridian energy are both problematic and can cause damage to that meridian's organ system.

The eleventh conclusion is that when energy flowing through the meridians becomes blocked or stagnant, or, when too much energy is overwhelming a meridian these acupuncture points can be accessed to clear blockages and remove unwanted excess or stagnant energy. Often times acupuncture and acupressure techniques are used to relieve energetic imbalances in the meridians; the ancient Chinese practice of Qi Gong is often employed as well.

The twelfth conclusion is that MerKaBa is a spinning structure of light similar to the chakras. It is similar in that when spinning properly it works as an inter-dimensional gateway so that higher consciousness may incarnate into the physical body. It is the linking together of the mind, heart, and physical body in a specific geometrical ratio and at a critical speed that produces the merkaba The word "Mer" denotes counter-rotating fields of light, "Ka" Spirit, and "Ba" body, or reality. It is the image through which all things were created, and that image is around your body in a geometrical set of patterns.

The thirteenth conclusion is that we too are creators and our impulse is to incarnate into matter and create within it. The only way for consciousness to create with the Material Forces from the dimensions below, is to enter into it. The incarnation of spirit into matter is the way the entire Universe is created

The fourteenth conclusion is that besides communicating with parts of your self the Column also opens up possibilities of communication with many non-physical and multi-dimensional beings throughout the Universe.

The fifteenth conclusion is that the Chakras located within the light body have a purpose to create a gateway into higher or lower dimensions of consciousness. The light body is made up of many dimensions of light but to incarnate higher consciousness (spirit) into this light body a certain type of vortex needs to be created. These vortexes are the chakras and each one is a gateway to a certain aspect of higher consciousness.

The sixteenth, and perhaps most important conclusion is the revelation and awareness of the Buddhic/Christic body. The mark of someone who has truly attained this state of consciousness on a continual basis is that they are never oriented towards their individuality. They will never or rarely speak about their individuality. They are totally selfless in their actions and desire nothing of a personal nature because they reside in the source of fulfillment, in continual intense bliss. Also, their expression is utterly harmless and overflowing with compassion. The Buddhic vehicle has its own level of five senses. These are: Comprehension (Buddhic hearing of 4 sounds: personal, that of others, that of one's soul group, that of the planetary entity that is one's origin), Healing (Buddhic feeling that facilitates realization of the manner in which to heal and cause wholeness), Divine Vision (Buddhic sight that allows one to see the divine in all), Intuition (Buddhic taste, whereby one's essence is recognized in and under all forms), and Idealism (Buddhic smell, the ability to sense the ideal). **It is this awareness and this state in others that opens the healing conduit.**

30

WHAT ABOUT THE BRAIN?

"What we know is that we don't know. When you stop thinking with the brain you know all."
Ed Rychkun

And so we repeat a very important part of this our understanding of the energy bodies and the role of the brain. The physical brain is not a source of experience as some current neuroscientists now mistakenly believe. While areas of the brain are associated with different consciousness functions, many neuroscientists do admit that they cannot locate emotions, mind, and soul in the brain. Nor can they fully explain the human psyche with neuroanatomy. The physical brain is a relay station, translating emotional, mental, and spiritual events and information into neuro-electrochemical events and information. Neurochemicals and associated brain processes are simply channel selectors for various states of consciousness. All states of consciousness exist independent of the physical body. This relay station works in both directions: spiritual, mental, or emotional states trigger neuro-electrochemical events in the brain (physical consciousness) AND neurochemical stimulation (for example through drugs) opens access to specific states of emotion, thought, or spiritual awareness.

Contemporary physics has proven very clearly that solid physical matter is an illusion and that all is energy only. So who is it that creates this illusion? It has to be the brain. Therefore, if we say that the solid physical brain is the mind, this is a mistake. While the brain appears to be solid, it is not - it is energy appearing solid, but is not solid - it is energy, only. The mind is also energy, an energy that interacts with the energy that creates the appearance of a brain. The Physical Body is composed of the energy states of solids, liquids, and gases and is dependent upon the Etheric Body for its vitality, life, organization, and many processes that result in health.

One begins to wonder what this big brain of ours really does. Research is beginning to find that there are many "brains" that operate like a system of sub processors; like the servers on the Internet. There is the heart that has its own brain, and then there are the cells that also have their own brains - 50 trillion of them! Then there is subconsciousness that literally has a mind of its own. Then there is the traditional brain.

These brains, as we shall soon learn do not operate exactly like the traditional computers because they receive, interpret, and react on information in wave form somewhat like analog computers that are constantly sensing environmental information and responding to it by hardwired functions. These computers are used a lot in automated process control situations where they detect variations in environmental conditions and react according to set parameters. This appears to be the way the brain operates as well as it is sensing the outside and inside environments to manage the information coming from wired and wireless networks and then reacts according to set and learned responses. Our intellect and thinking as we see in consciousness and subconsciousness is something performed outside of the brain as a separate function.

So what is this brain? Is it just a big analog dummy at the top? Well, if you can bring into your awareness the previous chapters, then the bigger picture says we give it much more credit than we should. It is only doing a tiny job under a very specific position description just like we do in a large corporation. And when you relate this to the tiny fraction of the universe we live in, the amount of unused DNA and what we actually know about our selves, it is not even the tip of the iceberg!

Every animal you can think of -- mammals, birds, reptiles, fish, and amphibians -- has a brain. But the human brain is unique. Although it's not the largest, it according to science, gives us the power to speak, imagine and problem solve. The brain performs an incredible number of tasks including the following:

- It controls body temperature, blood pressure, heart rate and breathing.
- It accepts a flood of information about the world around you from your various senses (seeing, hearing, smelling, tasting and touching).
- It handles your physical movement when walking, talking, standing or sitting.

And, according to science, it lets you think, dream, reason and experience emotions. Yes, of course, but as a recording-relay station that is designed to help you evolve into your higher awareness of all your bodies.

Your brain, spinal cord and peripheral nerves make up a complex, integrated information-processing and control system known as your central nervous system. What we have come to learn is that although the brain has a mind of its own, it really takes orders from the subconscious and cell "brains" to execute the required programs. Now we are coming to understand the heart has a brain that does not take orders from the brain in the head.

Clearly, from what we have come to understand is that although the brain has the responsibility for managing these cellular communities, and executing programs it is a Manager, not the CEO. It is the CEO that is subconscious that needs to be convinced to execute a miracle in conjunction with rules set up in the operating system - the Divine Intelligence.

But as we shall see in another part, it has another large responsibly, one of creating a holographic reality.

In general terms, the brain has the following parts:

The brain stem consists of the medulla (an enlarged portion of the upper spinal cord), pons and midbrain. The brain stem controls the reflexes and automatic functions (heart rate, blood pressure), limb movements and visceral functions (digestion, urination).

The cerebellum integrates information from the vestibular system that indicates position and movement and uses this data to coordinate limb movements. The cerebrum is also called the cerebral cortex or just the cortex and consists of the cortex, large fiber tracts (corpus callosum) and some deeper structures (basal ganglia, amygdala and hippocampus). It integrates information from all of the sense organs, and initiates motor functions. It is believed to control emotions and hold memory and thought processes (emotional expression and thinking are more prevalent in higher mammals). Does it simply link with consciousness that has nothing to do with it? After all we have learned from NDE's that all that is done when the brain is "dead".

The hypothalamus and pituitary gland are responsible for visceral functions, body temperature and behavioral responses such as feeding, drinking, sexual response, aggression and pleasure.

The spinal cord can be viewed as a separate entity from the brain, or merely as a downward extension of the brain stem. It contains sensory and motor pathways from the body, as well as ascending and descending pathways from the brain. It has reflex pathways that react independently of the brain, as in the knee-jerk reflex.

The vestibular system is responsible for maintaining posture, balance and spatial orientation. Part of the system is located in the inner ear. It also includes the vestibulocochlear nerve (the eighth cranial nerve) and certain parts of the brain that interpret the information the vestibulocochlear nerve receives. Within each of these structures are centers of neuronal cell bodies, called nuclei, which are specialized for particular functions (breathing, heart-rate regulation, sleep).

The cerebellum, also known as the "little brain" because it's folded into many lobes, lies above and behind the pons. As the second biggest area of the brain, it receives sensory input from the spinal cord, motor input from the cortex and basal ganglia, and position information from the vestibular system. The "little brain" then integrates this information and influences outgoing motor pathways from the brain to coordinate movements. To demonstrate this, reach out and touch a point in front of you, such as the computer monitor - your hand makes one smooth motion. If your cerebellum were damaged, that same motion would be very jerky, as your cortex initiated a series of small muscle contractions to home in on the target point. The cerebellum may also be involved in language (fine muscle contractions of the lips and larynx), as well as other cognitive functions.

The cerebrum is the largest part of the human brain. It contains all of the centers that receive and interpret sensory information, initiate movement, analyze information, reason and experience emotions. The centers for these tasks are located in different parts of the cerebral cortex, which is the outside layer of the cerebellum and is comprised of gray matter. The inside is made up of white matter.

The Brain Is Hard-wired

The brain is hard-wired with connections; much like a skyscraper or airplane is hard-wired with electrical wiring. In the case of the brain, the connections are made by neurons that link the sensory inputs and motor outputs with centers in the various lobes of the cerebral cortex. There are also linkages between these cortical centers and other parts of the brain.

Several areas of the **cerebral cortex** have specialized functions:

Parietal lobe receives and processes all **somatosensory** input from the body (touch, pain).

- Fibers from the spinal cord are distributed by the thalamus to various parts of the parietal lobe.

- The connections form a map of the body's surface on the parietal lobe. This map is called a **homunculus**.
- The rear of the parietal lobe (next to the temporal lobe) has a section called **Wernicke's area**, which is important for understanding the sensory (auditory and visual) information associated with language. Damage to this area of the brain produces what is called **sensory aphasia**, in which patients cannot understand language but can still produce sounds.

The frontal lobe is involved in motor skills (including speech) and cognitive functions.
- The motor center of the brain (pre-central gyrus) is located in the rear of the frontal lobe, just in front of the parietal lobe. It receives connections from the somatosensory portion in the parietal lobe and processes and initiates motor functions. Like the homunculus in the parietal lobe, the pre-central gyrus has a motor map of the brain.
- An area on the left side of the frontal lobe, called Broca's area, processes language by controlling the muscles that make sounds (mouth, lips and larynx). Damage to this area results in motor aphasia, in which patients can understand language but cannot produce meaningful or appropriate sounds.
- Remaining areas of the frontal lobe perform associative processes (thought, learning, memory).

Occipital lobe receives and processes visual information directly from the eyes and relates this information to the parietal lobe (Wernicke's area) and motor cortex (frontal lobe). One of the things it must do is interpret the upside-down images of the world that are projected onto the retina by the lens of the eye.

Temporal lobe processes auditory information from the ears and relates it to Wernicke's area of the parietal lobe and the motor cortex of the frontal lobe.
- **Basal ganglia:** Also located within the temporal lobe, the basal ganglia work with the cerebellum to coordinate fine motions, such as fingertip movements.
- **Limbic system:** Located deep within the temporal lobe, the limbic system is important in emotional behavior and controlling movements of visceral muscles (muscles of the digestive tract and body cavities). The limbic system is comprised of the cingulate gyrus, corpus callosum, mammillary body, olfactory tract, amygdala and hippocampus.

- **Hippocampus:** The hippocampus is located within the temporal lobe and is important for short-term memory.
- **Amygdala:** The amygdala is located within the temporal lobe and controls social and sexual behavior and other emotions.
- **Insula:** The insula influences automatic functions of the brainstem. For example, when you hold your breath, impulses from your insula suppress the medulla's breathing centers. The insula also processes taste information, and separates the temporal and frontal lobes.

Ok, this is a bit technical but we can see that these parts of the brain are dedicated to controlling how the body functions and adapts to its environment. It is the hard-wired system that is sensing and responding to the nervous system, the senses, the mobility, the internal functioning are automated environmental stimuli-response systems.

Is The Brain A Computer?

As said, the brain is more like an analog sensing-response device that seems to have some disc storage of its own that is used for memory and thinking but it is not the place where all of it resides, it is like virtual memory that pulls in what it needs for short term use and is not the real center of control; it is more like a gatherer and transmitter relay system.

Although the brain has some of the same elements as a traditional computer with electric signals, wires and logical gates, there are neither codes nor addresses. Every brain has a different structure so each would need different addresses. They would also need to be changed over time. A structure with addresses is too complicated to be inherited. For addresses are an agreement between the sender and receiver that has to be given before addresses can work. Data encoding also has to be agreed before a computer starts to save memory. Then either every creation has to have its own code developed before its starting to work or the code was set in the beginning for all stuff ever to happen or be invented. Without addresses you cannot make an ordered set of bits that carries information. So coding as known in computers is not possible as we know digital computers. Without addresses you cannot specify a location where information is sent to and where information is fetched from. It is therefore not possible to send two sets of information into two adjacent registers to compare them. Information once derived cannot be moved. Information in the brain is not compared. It is evaluated through a filtering mechanism build of neural networks that delivers the same result in form a single pointer that a certain match was achieved. Not the pattern itself is stored in the neural network but an instruction working on patterns.

The cortex is a network of neural networks. With feedback connections, exciting and inhibiting connections, it holds the memory and is responsible for recognition of sensory input and selection of motor output. As information cannot be moved, long term and short term memory has to be kept in the same place. Long term memory is based on the topological structure of the neural network. Short term memory is based on signals flowing through that network.

The neural network in the cortex is set into learning mode by a simple signal from the hippocampus. This way the cortex can learn logical and spatial relationships. The basal ganglia form a loop of four elements: frontal cortex, striatum, pallidum and thalamus. This loop works as a flywheel to get the necessary momentum to trigger motor action. The amygdala controls that flywheel at the pallidum to decelerate and at the striatum to accelerate. The amygdala sends neurotransmitter to certain brain regions to exhibit or inhibit general processing in these areas. Together with chemical signals to the body they trigger emotions.

The cortex cannot learn temporal relations. This is done in the cerebellum; it holds all temporal knowledge and all derived implicate memory. For any motor action and its feedback it sends a signal to the motor cortex to select the next motor action.

These systems are designed to quickly adapt to the world the creature is living in, deep sea, arctic, rain forest, farming, downtown, stock exchange, and so on. Two requirements for the explanation can be concluded: The explanation has to be simple and it has to be independent of any content processed. It is known that the brain works with electric wiring and there are knots called soma and synapses. The brain has a huge mesh of neurons. Every neuron has a thick knot called soma with incoming lines called dendrites and an outbound line called axon. Dendrites and axons can branch off like trees. The ends of axons connect to dendrites or the soma of other neurons with synapses. The synapses pass the electric signal with chemistry. The signal consists of small spikes of electric charges that travel along the axons and dendrites, all about the same strength and length. This is not like a digital computer, it is an analog system. There are other factors:

- The brain is a massively parallel machine; computers are modular and serial
- Processing speed is not fixed in the brain; there is no system clock
- Short-term memory is not like RAM

- No hardware/software distinction can be made with respect to the brain or mind
- Synapses are far more complex than electrical logic gates
- Unlike computers, processing and memory are performed by the same components in the brain
- The brain is a self-organizing system
- Brains have bodies

The brain has a simple mechanism. The complexity comes by size and recursion. It does not use addresses and this implies that information must be gained, stored and used at the very same brain location and is never moved. The brain is a hard wired circuit, a net of neural networks that process patterns of concurrent input signals. One remembers when the processing yields the same output pointer (pointing to the same next neural network) as last time.

Cortex - Explicite Memory stores logical and spatial information (objects, categories, moves, relations, episodes, places, actions).
Long Term Memory is the center of topology of wiring. Short Term Memory - signals running that wiring.
Cerebellum - Implicite Memory stores sequential information (skills, bicycling, martial arts).
Hippocampus provides unspecific 'write' or ' learn' signals to cortex areas.
Basal Ganglia provides unspecific 'execute' or 'action' signal to motor cortex.
Amygdala switches body and brain into emotions or moods (learning, dozing, exploring, acting, distractible, committed).

Note that consciousness is not required to explain these brain functions. It is a feature of complex self sustained oscillating circuits in cortical neural networks of a sufficient complexity and size. The human cortex has that sufficient size and structure. What is the Point here? Most of the function of the brain is simply a hard-wired response-reaction center hardwired to perform certain physical and chemical duties. Just like a process control analog computer, the brain stores certain historical information in a local mode somewhat like a disc drive that loads into virtual memory the response required to execute. That local mode is like a history of what has been learned and is important to your current reality.

But it by no means is the center of what science calls **cognition** as the set of all mental abilities and processes related to knowledge: attention, memory and working memory, judgment and evaluation, reasoning and "computation", problem solving and decision making, comprehension and production of language. Cognition by humans is conscious and unconscious, concrete or abstract, as well as intuitive (like knowledge of a language) and conceptual (like a model of a language). Cognitive processes use existing knowledge and generate new knowledge.

We have learned that the brain and nervous system must interpret environment stimuli and send signals to cells which then integrate and regulate life sustaining functions of the body organ system to support survival.

We know the brain dedicates vast cell numbers to catalogue complex perceptions and remember millions of experienced perceptions and integrate them into a database to give them "consciousness" or more like "self-consciousness" which is the prefrontal cortex – the neurological platform to realize personal identity and experience the quality of thinking. We have learned the most powerful programs are recorded in the first 6 years of life by observing and listening to people, parents, teachers, and the environment. The role of the brain is to create coherence between its programs and real life, the brain unconsciously generates appropriate or inappropriate responses that assume as truths of its programmed perceptions. But where are these recorded?

In review, the brain has access to consciousness and self consciousness that appears to be recorded in some form of brain data base like read only memory. But there are three levels:

Consciousness (40 nerve impulses/sec) enable assessment and response to environmental at that moment so one can participate in life.
Self-consciousness allows one to factor in the consequences of and future as self reflection and free will.
Subconscious (40 mill nerve impulses per sec) monitors and controls automated stimulus-response (also unconscious) programs. It is like an automated record-playback system of recorded habits. It has no creativity, once learned is automatic. Subconscious controls body behavior not attended to by self-conscious mind in the present time.

We have learned that subconsciousness and consciousness is separate from the body as in Near Death Experiences. So either the brain has access to that database or it has a copy of what it needs to do its job of learning survival, maintaining survival and creating a holographic reality.

But this is part of consciousness and subconsciousness. And as we shall begin to explain, all is part of a Quantum Computer system that operates with wave patterns and is part of a much larger quantum system.

The Brain As A Holographic Processor

Here are several examples of how the brain sees different alternatives..

| How many legs? | Old or young lady? | Circles or Spirals? |

The brain has two hemispheres, each divided into four lobes. Each lobe is responsible for different functions. For instance the frontal cortex is responsible for decision making and planning; the temporal lobe for language and memory; and the parietal lobe for spatial skills. The occipital lobe is entirely devoted to vision: It is thus the place where visual illusions happen.

The frontal lobe represents around 41% of total cerebral cortex volume; the temporal lobe 22%; the parietal lobe 19%; and the occipital lobe 18%. How the visual system processes shapes, colors, sizes, etc. has been researched for decades. One way to understand more about this system is to look at how we can trick it, that is, to look at how the brain reacts to visual illusions.

It is your brain and subconsciousness that do the final work as a material representation by retrieving what it knows and what cosmic rules apply in the material representation. It retrieves information from the database and the cosmic rule simply applies as it "knows" what it is.

So let us say an apple is chosen. Is it big, small, red, or yellow? What kind is it? The brain is designed to hold its own local knowledge—like a copy of its own experience that is held current. It uses this to fill the gaps of creating this from what it knows about the apple. The brain, and of course your consciousness or mind has information and the cosmic rules of its composition, formation, are drawn to complete the picture.

The Brain Is The Holographic Processor Of Reality

If we recall the steps of materialization, it is attention and intention and love as the substance of power that allows an image to congeal into a material representation of an object in a hologram. We will cover Holograms and Quantum later on in a following chapter.

This means that the Divine Mind must be the total agent of the image of some object that is simply created in your mind's eye. It will have to be a clear image. At the point at which your Higher Mind and the Heart—the congealer—create that image, it is projected onto a place of choice by intent and at the same time the image of the mind is projected to the Source of the One, to be reflected back like a mirror as a beam of divine light to the same place of choice just like converging laser beams of light form a holograph.

As these two actions converge upon the place of choice from you and the divine beam from the source, they form a holographic duplicate representation of the object that is to be replicated or materialized. Yes, from a wave form to an atomic form as the electrons and photons arrange themselves into the image which is your higher consciousness choosing a new possibility from the no thing of quantum space where all possibilities exist.

How this is done is not by attempting to complicate by the chemistry, atomic structure and so on because the energy signature is under natural cosmic law that such an arrangement is created. These laws understand how this is done and your divine consciousness abides by these. So they all understand what this is made up of, to congeal this into the expression of the holographic image, to be interpreted as such by your and other sensory systems of your brain—your sensory receiving stations.

You first create a clear image in your mind's eye with the assistance of the heart, and then project it to a place of materialization. Then you project this to the One to project back to the same place. A holographic image is created. This is similar to the way a holographic image is created with beams of light that are split, reflected and converged again. What is it? A hologram? What form is it? It is whatever you see clearly that your brain understands and has meaning for or memory of. That is its second major job - to create your reality.

It is your brain and subconsciousness that do the final work as a material representation by retrieving what it knows and what cosmic rules apply in the material representation. It retrieves information and the cosmic rule simply "knows" what it is.

So a word, an object, an image all have meaning to the brain by its experience and with the assistance of cosmic law reverse engineers the process to create the result from memory and let us call it technical information as to its composition or material makeup. Although an image of the apple is only a representation in your lower mind and brain, it already has the appropriate material characteristics from higher sources as to how it would be materialized. So anything can indeed happen in materialization therefore it requires a high degree of responsibility.

You see, the brain which interprets senses also fills in the gaps to complete it. Many times, you will not actually see things exactly, as the brain only picks up half of what is there, filling in the rest by itself—unless you place strict attention on it and see the difference. The brain fills the gaps, holes, missing information and uses a process you call extrapolate and interpolate from its memory what is needed to complete the picture. If you see and read the words "I luv yu" or "wht a wndrful da" you know what this is meaning, do you not? Your brain is interpolating the true meaning even though parts are missing. But by closer inspection and attention, you see the difference. So it is with an image of an apple.

The brain is the holographic processor that creates the meaning, composition, and representation through its memory and the interpretation of the senses of your lower body. You see, feel, and taste an apple and it seems so real. So if you take the senses of see, feel, taste and the memories of this, then reverse engineer the process back through the brain—with divine assistance—it will create the apple as appearing solid in the hologram.

What you have not done is to do this outside of your imagination in an eyes open conscious state of awareness. Yet as you know, some can indeed do this—like holy men—by a reverse process which is easy in your mind but not in your hologram of 3D. But you are learning. It is what you are learning as your vibration reaches a certain level. Yes, this is so because of a certain level of responsibility, and partnership with the higher self and the Divine is required as reflected by the alignment of heart, purpose and Divinity—the One.

Physicist Amit Goswami set up experiments on non locality which is that the physical traits of particles become intimately connected (entangled) once they interact. If a characteristic of one is alerted, the rotational spin from clockwise to counterclockwise, then the other particle changes its spin even if not in the close location. He wanted to see if the mind was nonlocal. Could human brains have entangled particles? Could change in one mind cause a change in another's brain? In the study, he had test subjects go into meditative interaction to maintain a direct connection 50 feet apart, all monitored by EEG. He induced an evoked potential in one and it induced an evoked potential in the other to entangle in the meditative state. One can influence another's brain so they are quantum in nature.

Field influencing electromagnetic messages broadcasted from the heart have been shown to entangle with others.

What does this mean? We will explain this new science of Quantum Mechanics in the next chapter.

Important Conclusions About The Brain

The first conclusion is that the brain performs a multitude of sensory, vital and physical tasks that it learns in order to guarantee survival. It is a complex information processing and control system. The brain is dedicated to controlling how the body functions and adapts to its environment. The nervous system, the senses, the mobility, the internal functioning are automated environmental stimuli-response systems.

The second conclusion is that the brain is not in charge, as it takes directives from the subconscious, cell membranes and the heart.

The third conclusion is that the brain is not like a binary computer, it is more analog computer designed to sense and respond so as to create a database of perception response functions. It holds its own database to remember and execute these on conscious and subconscious command. A copy is held in the master disc drive of the subconscious mind.

The fourth conclusion is that the brain is the holographic processor that creates your reality through the meaning, composition, and representation from its local database as its memory and the interpretation of the senses of your lower body.

The fifth conclusion is that while brains are reduced to a lower meditative state, an evoked potential in one induces an evoked potential in the other at distances apart. They "entangle" in the meditative state so one can influence another's brain being quantum in nature

31

THE QUANTUM SHOCK WAVE

"What we have received as education is stored deep in the subconscious much deeper than what we 'think' is true."
Ed Rychkun

There has been a lot of talk about quantum and how all those higher abilities, the energetic body, the brain, the heart, the chakras, for example are quantum. That is their characteristics, behavior and functions can be explained by quantum physics. What does this mean? It is time to explore this.

What we see, read, hear, are told, and experience all goes to forming our beliefs. Where miracles are concerned, it appears to be the, read, hear, are told by science and medicine that we surrender our beliefs to, taking on what they say. And because so many of our beliefs are created in subconscious at early life, we don't even know what we have stored in there. So the experience doesn't happen. What we have received as education is stored deep in subconscious much deeper that what one "thinks" is true.

This is especially true when the greatest amount of programming went into the subconscious disc drive at early ages, as we have seen. Seeing is believing seems to be irrelevant more and more. But have you ever considered that if you believe first, then the experience can happen? And if you continue to repeat the belief, then it eventually overrides the old program? In our aging evolution, it became more and more difficult to program the subconscious which was essentially on autopilot in the early years. Then it shifted to pilot but the pilot was the conscious mind that had to rationalize things from a posture of seeing is believing. Now at a later stage, when one wants to take a posture of believing is seeing, it becomes more and more difficult as the old stuff stuck in subconscious overrides the new philosophy. This as we have learned is where habitual reflections of believing in the conscious begins to override the old programs. This is how Seeing is Believing gets shifted to Believing is Seeing?

This chapter is for the logical left-brained, rational science followers who *will not let go of science*. You believe seeing is believing and if there is not a qualified scientific explanation then you don't pay attention. Obviously the best scientists still seem to ignore what they see anyway. This chapter is about physics and metaphysics. What it will bring you to understand is that all your education about science may be a bit faulty. It should allow your subconscious to be a bit more accommodating when you reprogram new beliefs. Here we rapidly see that the best Scientists on the planet don't have a clue as to how to correct the inadequate "Laws" of material physics.

Here is the conundrum: Newtonian material physics explains about 3% of the physics of matter and non-matter. It has been proven to be dramatically lacking. It is based on laws that reflect solid matter, 97% of which is space (hollow), to explain things. So laws that explain 3% are deemed by assumption to explain the rest. Why? Because we are told so. And so this was all programmed into your subconscious as your truth. Metaphysics on the other hand, which includes the other 97%, is explained by quantum physics as being holographic. Why the big conundrum? It seems that a totally unscientific force called consciousness seems to be hung up with that material 3%.

Our Entangled Minds

We have brought forward the work by the quantum physicist Dr Amit Goswami who states: *"Materialist Science Isn't The Whole Picture! What do we mean by materialist science? Materialist science takes it as its basic axiom that everything is matter. We have literally managed to train a whole generation of students on the idea that everything is material, but this Newtonian world view that has shaped our understanding for centuries is now giving way to the revelations of quantum physics which goes beyond materialism; to show that consciousness, not matter, is the ground of all being."*

He has shown that the brains are quantum in nature. To us, the link between the physical and nonphysical, like the physical brain and subconscious is through the quantum field. It is so with what we have come to know as the light body, the chakras, auras, meridians, torroids, and so on. Let us see what others say about this quantum stuff.

The book that is mind shifting on this issue of psi; short for psychic phenomenon is **Entangled Minds Extrasensory Experiences in a Quantum Reality** by **Dean Radin.** This book will save you a lot of inquiry time. Dean is a PhD (if that is important to you), and Laboratory Director at the Institute of Noetic Sciences in Petaluma, California. For several decades he has conducted research on psychic phenomenon at Princeton, the University of Edinburgh, the University of Nevada, and three silicon valley think-tanks as a scientist investigating the psi phenomenon.

This book will lead you through the psi world of telepathy, clairvoyance, psycho kinetics, remote viewing, dreaming, conscious-unconscious psi, mind matter interaction, gut feelings, presentment, global consciousness, reading the future, and many other metaphysical phenomenons. If you recall, these are the abilities that we saw inactive in the chakra system and awaiting the evolution of the soul-body in the Energy Body growth. Dean shows how these are real, based on thousands of controlled lab tests. He surveys the origins of this research and explores the reality of our entangled minds, setting a new stage for a rational, scientific understanding of psychic experience. He debunks the skeptical myths.

The book is a unique adventure into debunking skeptical myths on the basis of controlled lab experiments and the reality of the new quantum physics. To quote Dean:

"There is a rising tension between the leading edge interpretation in physics and the tail end of metaphysics. Physicists interested in quantum ontology are painfully aware that some interpretations of quantum reality are uncomfortably close to mystical concepts. In the eyes of mainstream science, to express sympathy for mysticism destroys one's credibility as a scientist. Thus the taboo persists."

What is particularly important about his book is his treatment of quantum physics, explaining it, the conundrum surrounding it that has physicists in a bind, and how it explains our "new realities" of mind-matter. Once again, to quote Dean:

"Experiments have demonstrated that the worldwide view implied by classical physics is wrong. Not just slightly incorrect in minor ways but fundamentally wrong in just the right way to support the reality of psi."

Our Holographic Reality

The next book that is for the pragmatic logician is one by **Michael Talbot**, called **The Holographic Universe**. This is a mind blowing treatment of the nature of our reality.

Talbot describes the Universe as a giant hologram containing both matter and consciousness as a single field—a kind of image or construct created in part by the human mind. Using the world's most prominent scientists and thinkers, Michael weaves a revelation that there is room in science for the consciousness, the soul and spirit. Using the work of David Bohm one of the most respected quantum physicists, and Karl Pribram, the respected scientist on the human brain, he explains how the unsolved puzzles such as telepathy, out-of-body and near death experiences, lucid dreams and mystical experiences such as feeling of cosmic unity and miraculous healings are explainable through the holographic universe and quantum physics.

This treatment of the topic is filled with hundreds of cases and scientists that have gone against mainstream science to uncover the answers as to how holograms explain our world. The work of some of the best scientists on the planet points to our reality as holographic. The many cases and examples of science shattering are presented here and it is a must read, not only to understand how quantum physics does explain metaphysics, but how the holographic model of reality is the greatest revelation in science even though it is essentially ignored.

Us Vibrating Humans

Valerie Hunt, a physical therapist and professor of Kinesiology at UCLA, developed a way to confirm and measure the human energy field. For example, Doctors use EEGs and EKGs to measure electrical activities of brain and heart. She discovered the EMG Electromyograph measures the energy field in muscles and expanded into the aura. Normal frequency range in the brain is 0-100cps (cycles per second) most occurring between 0-30cps. Muscle goes to 225cps, heart to 250 but this is where electrical function associated with biology drops off. She picked up a field of energy radiating from the body that ranged between 100 and 1600cps.

These were strongest in areas of the chakras. She noted the field behaves holographically as do the energy fields of the body and that these fields were non-local—could be measured anywhere on the body. She called it the holographic field reality. When the main focus of consciousness is on material the frequencies are in lower range around 250cps. People who have psychic abilities and can heal are 400-800cps. People who can go into a trance and channel other information operate in a narrow band of 800-900cps to receive information.

Those who are mystical are above 900—those who possess the wisdom to know what to do with the channeled info—aware of cosmic interrelatedness of all things and are in touch with every level of human experience. They are anchored in both psychic and trance abilities, but their frequencies extend beyond of up to 200,000-cps

So is there a progression of psychic abilities? If you look at the A-Z of psychic abilities, there are some 200 listed. But the main ones are; After life communications, Aparitioning, Apportation, Astral projection, Card reading, Channeling, Clairvoyant, Déjà vu, Divining, Divine Intervention, Invisibility, Empathy, ESP, Levitation, Materialization, Necromacy, OBE, Ouji, Past Life Regression, Palmistry, Psychic healing, Remote Viewing, Regression, Scrying, Tarot, Tea Cup Reading, Telekinesis, Teleportation, Telepathy, Transfiguration. Those are all part of the supposed evolution of the Soul!

What Valerie is saying is that there is a relationship between the vibrational frequency of the body's electromagnetic system and specific psychic abilities? Hmmmm... this is what we refer to as *raising one's vibration*!

Science Is The Observer Of Itself

At first thought, after delving into the conundrum called the "Observer Effect" in Quantum Energy, a silly notion may come to you. First the Observer Effect says that the natural state of electrons is waves that have not formed into anything solid. The solid or that which is perceived to be solid arranges itself into an atomic structure of electrons around a nucleus when consciousness observes it. Take the attention off and these electrons are back into their wave state. The notion was that the observation processes of experimentation and statistics actually creates the outcomes that it is expecting, so how can it go beyond? It is like an endless loop.

That and the notion that this is all a hologram which our brain, a hologram itself is the filtering device that uses senses to make it take a different property in the hologram is pretty hard to conceive for even the highest IQ. This gives the brain a whole new responsibility beyond just organizing cell communities and sensing the environment.

At some point in your life, you created a solid wall that divides the two worlds of visible and invisible. All your experiences and perceptions created this. It is congealed into apparent solid bricks as a result, preventing you from letting go of what you have been programmed to accept as truth. This is the wall that divides the polarity, unity worlds of your life. When an NDE occurs, you float through this wall. When a miracle is performed it is from the other side of the wall. Whether you will walk through this wall in this lifetime depends on how you let go of the beliefs that created it.

The World Ain't Flat Anymore

What is particularly relevant here is the Matrix Energetics healing technique we looked at in PART ONE. Quantum Physics suddenly tells us the world ain't flat, and suddenly Newton type physics that we have had drummed into our belief system at school, ain't *exactly* so. What does this mean? Newton's laws of physics are all about matter and how solid it is. Sorry, it is not solid. It is 99% space. Try focusing in with a microscope down to the nucleus-electron level. See how much "matter" there is!

In his book **Quantum Theory Cannot Hurt You**, **Marcus Chown** explains why according to quantum physics, these statements are all true:

- Every breath you take contains an atom breathed out by Marilyn Monroe
- There is liquid that can run uphill
- You age faster at the top of a building than at the bottom
- An atom can be in many different places at once
- The entire human race would fit in a volume the size of a sugar cube
- One percent of the static on TV tuned between stations is the relic of the Big Bang
- Time travel is not forbidden by the laws of physics
- The faster you travel, the slimmer you get
- Quantum theory actually created the modern world

Even though quantum physics has been around for some 80 years only a few so called geniuses like Einstein were able to argue about it. This has all changed and now quantum physics has the whole scientific community in turmoil.

Suddenly, matter, and atomic structure, is totally different. What we knew is wrong, while what we are learning is still a mystery. It means we just do not know. And, in most cases, if you dare listen to an exchange between scientists on this topic, the number of times they admit they do not know, yattering about possibilities, uncertainties, and totally nebulous statements will bore you to tears. The best conclusion is that they have figured out that what they believe to be the truth is not exactly so and what they do know is that they don't know!

So you say; what relevance has this here? First, it has to do with the belief system in your box. It is not completely right so your flaps should be down on the box—ready for some new information. Secondly, it has to do with us, and what we are—quantum energy. Science is agreed on certain things.

Everything is energy—including the mind and this thing called consciousness. Third, as we will get to later, it has everything to do with creating miracles.

Matter is simply energy. It does not exist the way we thought. We are made of ever changing fields of energy which intersect with one another to create our world of possibilities not certainties. This may take you to the Star Trek holodeck but this is not silly anymore.

Science agrees on many things they cannot explain. Let us remind you that quantum energy exists in two states—as visible particles or invisible waves. The particles can be in one place, two places, or several places at once but still act as connected. Scientists have figured out that if you take your DNA, change it in one place, the same change occurs instantly in another DNA particle regardless of the distance. Although we do not want to pursue this here, the DNA which contains all there is about us and the universe (the other 10 strands that are being found by science) is the smallest part of the hologram and it exists in 50 trillion cells in the body, all interconnected into a community mentality. Its how a hologram works with totally replicated particles of different sizes intersected by a beam of light.

Just like our cells, quantum particles can communicate with themselves at different points in time and are not limited by past, present, future, or time. They simply exist now, and here. When you begin to delve into this what will strike you is not so much that there were many things we did not know about energy, it is the number of things that quantum physics explains that was totally different from what we believed.

Consciousness Changes Matter

An electron behaves like a particle when you are looking at it. This is when our consciousness focuses on it. It assumes a wave pattern when you look at it with a different expectation or take attention off of it. This phenomenon has been dubbed the Observer Effect. It means you the observer, effect what you are seeing. Yes, it means you can observe a different reality.

Now for some high school science, traditional atomic structure says there is an atom, nucleus consisting of proton and neutron and there are electrons orbiting the nucleus. Quantum physics says the electron moves in probability or bits revolving into a predictable orbit only when it is observed. It goes from a seemingly unpredictable wave-like behavior to a particle representation of reality—matter—when we see it that way. Nobody has a clue what the electron does when we are not looking at it. Consciousness collapses the wave function and it changes from an invisible wave state to a visible solid appearance.

What does this mean? It means that at the point where our consciousness enters into seeing something, the effect is to materialize solidity into reality. It is called forth by intention and the electrons choose from a realm of infinite possibilities the probability or patterns of bits that we limit it to by our observation. Consciousness materializes the atoms by changing the state from invisible to visible—waves to atoms. What we see around us has been transformed that way.

We think we and our problems are solid physical material things. Of course to us they are. The body is composed of organic structures (respiration, digestive, etc.) made from organs and specialized tissues, and cells classified by their special morphology and function. Cells are carbon based molecules composed of atoms but the Observer can change the behavior of these cellular structures.

We, just like everything else in the universe, are made of high energy photons, the smallest known particle of matter. We are just a pattern of light and information. We are composed of patterns of light and information. This is what consciousness is, a pattern of lights and photons. The startling conclusion is that if a problem is just a pattern of high energy photons, then it can be reconfigured based on how we choose to observe them. Ah ha, one may think imagine the problem is not there and that will be observed as a miracle!

In a primitive way, that is exactly what we are attempting to do with dropping into the subconscious environment and attracting a new outcome. Quantum physics tells us the old way of thinking is where nonsense really exists.

Here is another head-spinning finding. Quantum physics teaches us we are one with the universe and connected together by a mysterious energy called the Zero Point Energy Field; the sea of virtual particles that lies beneath every point in the universe. Since our new physics tells us we are made of high energy photons, the smallest known particle of matter, and are just a pattern of light and information, we are also an integral part of this sea of particles. This leads one to understand that if you unlock the powers to interact with the Zero Point Energy Field, you are linked to the indivisible force that connects everything. That must be that Divine Intelligence operating system. And whereabouts is this Zero Point Field? At the intersection of above, to below intersection of the torroid - the heart chakra.

What has come through loud and clear is that at the level of the photon that everything exists at, consciously directed intent can alter the behavior of the fundamental constituents of matter. Intent is a conscious energy that when directed at the photon particles, can change the behavior of the particles. In quantum terms, it is called collapsing them into another state that we observe as material. This means that what we have the power to create with intent through the Observer Effect; we can uncollapse and recollapse the photons!

It would seem that the process of intent—activated by the Observer Effect using consciousness creates a morphic field of energy. Morphic means having a specific shape and form. Thoughts have morphic fields, like a magnetic field. These fields can actually be measured like at Princeton University. They are a biological and potentially social equivalent to an electromagnetic field that operates to shape the exact form of a living thing and may also shape its <u>behavior</u> and coordination with other beings. This morphogenetic field provides a force that guides the development of an organism as it grows, making it take on a form similar to that of others in its species.

Individual consciousness or that of a group is a morphic field. Once you believe and embody something in your consciousness, you link into a power grid of the morphic field. That must be where healing occurs as when you get in resonance with the photons that can be rearranged into the healing outcome taken from an enormous database of universal energy waiting as infinite possibilities.

This is not any different from the way the conscious mind works. One can lie back and with imagination, pluck out an image and visualize it in my mind's eye, from an infinite number of possibilities. The mind and those possibilities exist at a photon level. One can form an image that is in the past, present or future even though everything is simply in the NOW. It is simply because through the intent of seeing self on a beach in Fiji, for example, I make it so by rearranging the photons of my hologram into the current day dream "reality". Not only that, one can create a movie from various image segments. There is no time here and it is my conscious intent that creates the resultant reality. This is collapsing the selected quantum energy patterns into chosen patterns. The big difference, of course, is that it is all in the conscious mind, not in the real world where bills pile up on your desk.

In a larger group scope, this process of what our reality must have evolved on a larger global scale—the world we believe we live in—and together, our group consciousness must work the same way. Perhaps DNA acts as a tuner that receives instructions from energy in the larger morphic field—like a TV that does not contain the pictures but picks up the correct frequencies to create a picture. Each organ, tissue, cell has its own field. So you actually download into DNA like with a piece of computer hardware biological traits from the collective fields of the human race—not the parents. This must be the way we create a collective consciousness and the world we live in that we believe through our physical body senses. These are not part of our brains but free to float.

Since all life has DNA that is interconnected at the photon level, when a certain amount of information is added a new pattern of behavior simultaneously occurs. In the 100th monkey affect it occurs by morphic resonance as the rest of the species is automatically upgraded once a minimum number have realized this change. There is scientific evidence that suggests this number is the square root of 1% of the species. So when some seagull on the coast of British Columbia learns that it can pick up an oyster on the beach, fly it up in the air and drop it on the rocks to crack it open for a great feast, at a certain threshold, when more learn the same tactic, counting more than the square root of the population, all the others will suddenly and automatically know how to do it—whether they need it or not. Through the morphic quantum field of interconnectedness, the DNA gets a new gene whether you want it or not. Where are these DNA molecules? In the 50 trillions cells in the body, already functioning as quantum particles!

How does it connect with the organisms on the other side of the planet? Through the quantum field where every thing is interconnect and one.

The Ramifications Of This Are Simple

One begins to understand that the way you think, focus attention, or place things in consciousness is therefore pretty crucial, as it creates a morphic field that does things you may not be aware of. The issue of medicine—symptoms—treatment or stimulus—response reflects a cycle of constant attention and intent. And anything one does in attention to the condition tends to add energy into sustaining the unwanted state—to add validity to its reality and make the condition linear, predictable, self aware—exactly what you do not want.

This really means that when you get down to a point where everything is in that quantum state of connectedness—the level of photons or the particle based conscious reality, you can create different outcomes. These are called different possibilities which occur to the observer as a different wave pattern; and a different physical result of rearranged matter. By energy consciousness you can intercept a condition before inception and observe a different outcome, a new set of possible outcomes changing the manifestation of conditions and problems. That's what happens in regression therapy. Does this also occur in our external reality?

So you may come to realize that you are the one who, with help from the way energy morphs, make up the rules for your experience of this reality. When you get rid of measuring and observing these silly boxes everybody has created called Newtonian Physics and stop constraining consciousness with absurd limits of atoms, and get down to the level of photons, anything is possible.

What may be clear is that electrons or photons are observer dependent (perception & expectation). We are what we think. Everything we have believed, accepted, experienced or internalized is a matrix of energetic signature, a perceptual lens used to subconsciously filter information in a world view. Your experience and senses make up what you think in your reality, which is a morphed space created by others and a group consciousness. And who has the responsibly for making this world look and feel the way we are trained to be used to? The brain.

To change this you must alter thoughts and feelings. To really collapse the limiting boxes of beliefs in consciousness, you don't want to "know anything" which opens to the next moment. You want to know that you can indeed morph things into a preferred state. The more you know, especially what you are "supposed" to know, the more you limit ability to get to a quantum level. It is well worth while to go back and read the miracle healing system of Richard Bartlett's Matrix Energetics to see how this is applied.

So it becomes obvious that there were things that you simply need to pay attention to; careful how you framed questions in the mind. Over time we set up matrix grids of energy in subconscious awareness. These were templates from which are manifested changes and events. And to put emotional energy into the negative, it would bear that fruit because that is what you would be morphing.

But just be aware of this: Over the years, and even from past lives, or perhaps even your life path/contract may have a residual of negative stuff you created and still have to work through, as we discussed in the chapter on managing your energy portfolio. So you may be creating a positive morphic field but you may never know when that karma ledger manifests into your reality. You must not consider this a failure; you just keep cleaning like with Ho'Oponpono.

So mind over matter, the act of deciding what and how to observe at a quantum level causes the object of attention to behave or move in a fixed or predetermined manner.

This is very far out even for most morphing minds. But there is **The Wiezmann Institute of Science** studies to support the idea. They have reported that we change the reality by watching it. We are connected with everything from cells in the body to atoms of our world. Our experience of consciousness expressed as feeling and belief is doing the connecting—we are participants.

Quantum mechanics is a virtual sea of possible solutions where you can use your imagination to pick out one you like. It is no different than day dreaming or using visualization. The concept you visualize can have significant power to drive an action to bring about a structural change in the physical body.

So begin to believe we are constructed of light and information malleable to focused intent. Facts are relevant when intended changes are visualized clearly, belief is strong, emotional force behind intent is both focused and sustained.

Now, there is a PhD in Physics, **William Tiller** at the Stanford University who has something to say about all this quantum science. This man is not your typical unknown physicist with some willy-nilly theory. He is a well known respected scientist—not that it matters much—but perhaps it matters to you. He says:

"Human intention can strongly influence the physics of the unseen universe. Only our unconscious is aware of this quantum wave level of reality. Every one of us can influence all biological life forms via our bio-field emissions and the information they carry, whether we intend it or not. We and the cells in the body are in a global reality."

He goes on:

"In the normal material world the power to influence the nothing world is zero, thus the material world applies and human intention does not significantly influence reality (Physical). However with a significant field of consciousness present there is the ability to couple both worlds.

Tiller gives his formula for this. He states:

"The magnitude of the material property is related to the contribution from the magnetic information wave level times the magnitude of coupling coefficient plus the contribution from the atomic level. If the coupling coefficient is zero, there is no contribution to the material property. This coupling coefficient is the field of consciousness and the strength over time of how it is used to couple the two worlds of nothing and material."

Where this information will put you into a vortex of answers was when you realize that thoughts, visions, words and emotions are actually quantum energies operating at the photon levels—before they have been morphed into some possibility through the observers' consciousness.

Recall what we presented about, consciousness, the human chakra system, the auras, the heart field, the meridians, all subtle energies working in the invisible (to us because we refuse to Observe them) quantum space. They also exist at the quantum level of energy. They are operating at a high end electromagnetic energy system. Sustained and focused intention channeled through the system can produce amazing transformations both in and out of the body. **It would seem that intention at the 3rd chakra enfolded with the positive heart energy at the 4th chakra is the powerhouse of above to below reality creation system.** It would suggest that this may be the way the body can change thoughts, visions, words and emotion to an experience within a materialized physical domain. And these vortexes of energies are congealers of energies. So cause of vision produces an effect like our materialize Sai Baba did. And here is the kicker: these subtle energy fields act as attractors! Attractors to what? Obviously to the energy signatures you are putting out through these fields, broadcasting likeness, likeness, likeness, where are you? And how far out? Well in the quantum field of everything interconnected just like our 50 trillions cells, everywhere!

We Are Part Of A Universal Quantum Computer

There is something else about quantum physics that needs attention. Most everybody uses a computer these days but very few understand that everything this wonderful instrument does is based on a very simple concept of "bits" which are either on or off.

A computer language uses bits—codes based on patterns, numbers—short hand for binary digits. This means all information is coded as patterns of 1 and 0 for on or off. So at a simple level, you get on a keyboard (input) and type the instructions or use a mouse to give a program (Microsoft Word) the commands to print something as encoded in the program. It is interpreted by the operating software (Microsoft). It decodes this into specific patterns that create specific actions; the specific combination of 1 and 0 bits that are equivalent to the mechanical action of printing on the printer. So absolutely everything a computer does has some equivalent on-off pattern in it.

Well, quantum particles are also visible or invisible (on or off) and the wave patterns they can form are exactly like what we create with a computer. These particles are either on, that which we see in the usual observed atomic structure, or we don't, when it is in its natural quantum state as an invisible wave unobserved by consciousness waiting to be something.

This is like matter and non-matter, positive-negative, yes-no, male-female. It is what we call polarity. This simple binary system of 1 and 0's (on or off) seems to not only give computers their power but it represents all that is. The bits of creation are the stuff everything is made of as atoms. The atoms of reality exist as matter or they don't; either here or there, on or off. So the universe is like a quantum computer. And more and more we are realizing that the body, the parts we do not understand, functions more like a quantum energy field, not like our binary computer. But here is a bit of a conundrum which comes forward in what we have come to know as trinary computers. These trinary systems that are being researched as Quantum computers have three states of -1, 0, or +1. Is -1 female and the +1 male to balance and is the zero the point of singularity? We will explore this later. If reality is programmable in this quantum computer, how do we do it? This is food for thought for a later chapter.

Do We Live In An Intelligent Living Hologram?

Let us speculate for a moment. Let us suppose that we live in and create a hologram for the purpose of your experience. Let us think back to the little advice that was brought forward about manifesting and co-creation and the practice of materialization. Remember how you give life to a thought or action or feeling. It is by a dual projection and reflection of images from the mind's eye.

So let us say we are creating energy that will either seek out an energy mate or it will materialize into something that the energy represents into a new form. It is made up from the essence of particles of what consciousness is made up of; electrons, photons common to all things whether material or non material. This is what we call a reality, the attention of our awareness within the total consciousness—the mind of a greater consciousness. Each energy lives and has purpose and once created lives to expand itself according to its purpose and its design which will behave according to cosmic laws of creation. Once alive, it remains so and evolves as it was perceived at the time of creation. Then it grows, changes and evolves.

Each particle of your consciousness is like 50 trillion cells is of the whole of you and you are like a cell in a larger consciousness as the total consciousness of the One—the Creator. In your lower form of mind and body, this becomes like an individual compartment of the whole which is your local individual consciousness.

Once thoughts or action of the Lower form create, these energies remain to attain their purpose. They may be transmuted if you have attained the level of vibration that is of the Higher Body and Mind. However, this responsibility is not of the lower form. If the energies are created from the Lower Self, they will simply congeal into a transitional etheric state, attract, evolve and interact as designed by intent and attention. It fulfills its cosmic purpose assigned by you the creator.

Through your senses of the Lower Self, the experiences are interpreted and perceived with the brain being the interpreter. The mind is what creates, sets, and interprets the instructions and is the actual link and control center of all this interacting energy and the body which itself is energy. A body is thus a hologram formed the same way and once created; a genetic code is set creating a signature of its makeup as in the DNA. It is the blueprint that can replicate and evolve once given life.

All Energy Is Alive And Expanding

In the strictest sense, the consciousness of the Creator of the One is like a holograph with some major difference. Describing it this way is a convenient way for you to relate to it and understand it. It reflects all that can be or has ever been imagined by a Higher Intelligence, call it what you will. It is not a true hologram in scientific terms however, in that it is a living and intelligent medium with all that exists; *living and interacting within it—all energies—living things that are themselves seeking to expand, flourish and ascend towards their purposes in their own individualized consciousness.* Flowers, animals, humans, rocks, all energy placed within this hologram in their lower forms seek to evolve and expand through their instincts and purposes as encoded in their DNA or life code and their higher states of expression. In humans the expression of this is through Higher Self which itself is consciousness. We have discussed this evolution very clearly in the Chapter on The Energy Bodies.

At the fundamental stage, all things are energy of consciousness and all have some form of consciousness as individualized. This brings and records an awareness through various processing of other energies—or sensory systems—to interact with and to seek expression and to evolve in a way to find their purposes. This is a cycle of material form—material by perception—of being created, living, blossoming, reproducing and all things are drawn to this process as encoded in the DNA as directed by their consciousness. In your lower form of Self, you are no different than a flower or rock or animal that seeks to live life, flourish, expand, and reproduce. You like all else are able to reproduce and create and evolve within an interactive, live world of the hologram which itself is also evolving and alive.

You as a higher being so reflected in your subtle energetic form as a Light Body (or Being) can also create energy with your mind and body by placing attention here and triggering energy systems. You give it life and set it loose to evolve according to purpose—given by you if so defined or by cosmic laws of evolution and expression.

The problem is your Lower self is stuck in the mud of society and old science programmed beliefs unable to believe any of this. Your Lower Self is designed to interpret energies so as to process them through senses and interpret them according to your brain. This is sensed by the body and transmitted back into it for action-reaction, as well as recorded in consciousness for the perception of experience. It is so it can learn, grow, live, and expand according to instinct (lower purpose), cosmic law and expand (higher purpose). This process of material physical perception is this way and once some thing is formed in the hologram, it remains as part of it for others to perceive and sense.

In the lower form all interacts with and reacts to these energies that form the group or global hologram. Although you are creating certain energies through your mind and equipment, these are transient energies not yet congealed and are given life to seek purpose and find energy mates or entrain with like energies in the hologram. These energies can be dark or light and depending on their creation can do this rapidly or remain forever within the hologram.

In the Higher form, however, you are able to create new energies, passing the temporarily congealed state and materialize directly from the total consciousness—as a creator. This is where a huge difference lies in the ability to transmute or actually create within the hologram.

The Stages Of Evolution Of The Light Being

The issue we feel is that the brain is designed to create survival programs through various evolutionary stages.

The first stage is during Delta and Theta before the age of six. Here the brain must get "its' shit together" to develop the hard core environment survival habits through perception and response. It has to get this done as a foundation before the Self-conscious awareness kicks in to add the ego and the intellect.

The second stage of 6-12 occurs during the Alpha and Beta phase, the self identity matures, as does the education received become discriminated upon before it enters into the belief and perception-response behavior. The primary senses of smell, hearing, tasting, seeing, smelling and perception are dominant.

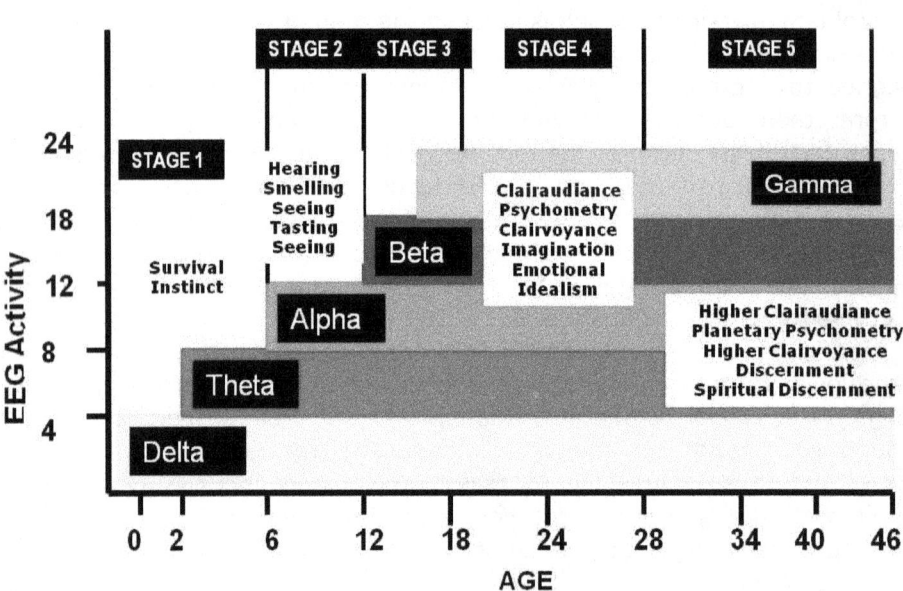

The third stage of 12-18 is one where physical changes to complete the reproductive system occur. Clearly this is the Physical Body evolution. The primary senses of smell, hearing, tasting, seeing, smelling and perception become heightened. Here the discriminatory process of free will and choices should maintain a life of positive energies, continuously radiating these through the heart chakra and the morphic field. When this happens as time progresses, those parts of us that are quantum in nature such as the brain, consciousness, light body, chakras, heart, DNA, cells, etc. begin to show themselves. As we have come to understand these are the powerful forces of the heart, namely love and compassion. If this evolution is curtailed by the choice of low energy components of the chakra functions, these are blocked and rendered dysfunctional. The attributes and abilities, like psychic (stuck in the chakras) for example cannot develop and the appropriate connection channel to zeropoint and the quantum space of infinite possibilities cannot be opened.

The fourth stage of 18-28 which takes us into the awareness of the Astral Body is where the heightened five senses are opened. It takes about 28 years for the astral body to mature. These are Clairaudience (astral hearing), Psychometry (astral touch/feeling), Clairvoyance (astral sight), Imagination (astral equivalent of taste), and Emotional Idealism (astral equivalent of smell).

The fifth stage is 28-46 to midlife shift when family and relationships become paramount. During this stage assuming the Astral awareness is perused, new five senses of the mental body open, such as Higher Clairaudience (mental hearing), Planetary Psychometry (mental feeling), Higher Clairvoyance (mental sight), Discernment (mental equivalent of taste), and Spiritual Discernment (mental equivalent of smell).

These then open to the Causal Body after midlife, opening the Higher Mind/Manasic Body, Buddhic/Christic Body, Atmic Body, Monadic Aspect, and Logoic/ God/ Goddess/ Solar Aspect.

Thus, having taken the tour of life through the first four stage of Delta, Theta, Alpha, and Beta, one would have to develop the stimulus-response systems to be able to live in all four as if they were in the Theta range to thus be a properly evolved human totally aware of its Light Body overlay that gives it life, and directly connects with the Higher Force through what its makeup is - love.

It is the third stage where one has a tendency to deprive oneself of the next steps of evolution of the Light Body-Being. It is stunted because it evolves to the level of self-awareness as ego-intellect by choosing limiting negative energies and limits its final entry into the heart brain and the Zeropoint quantum field.

Now here is the crux.

Being stuck in the mud within the Physical Plane with limiting beliefs, a world of negativity, totally dependent on the dummy brain at the top of the body, how can anyone get the awareness of the heart brain and the Astral step of the Soul's evolution? This is like a kid in kindergarten being expected to understand a PhD course in Quantum Physics. How can such a primitive mind be able to handle the ability to instantly create reality without learning the ropes?

And so we see nudging and occasional unexplained miracles occurring as a reminder with those that have touched the fringe of this third level truth, but become stuck there in total ignorance of their Higher Light body. It is what the group consciousness appears to have entrenched in its subconscious mind.

Important Conclusions About Quantum

The first conclusion is that experiments have demonstrated that the worldwide view implied by classical physics is wrong. Not just slightly incorrect in minor ways but fundamentally wrong in just the right way to support the reality of psi.

The second is that the Universe is a giant hologram containing both matter and consciousness as a single field—a kind of image or construct created in part by the human mind.

The third conclusion is the chakra field behaves holographically as do the energy fields of the body and that these fields were non-local—could be measured anywhere on the body.

The fourth conclusion is EMG's show people who have psychic abilities and can heal are 400-800cps. People who can go into a trance and channel other information operate in a narrow band of 800-900cps to receive information. There is a relationship between the vibrational frequency of the body's electromagnetic system and specific psychic abilities.

The fifth conclusion is that our reality is all a hologram which our brain, a hologram itself as the filtering device, uses primary senses to make it feel real.

The sixth conclusion is that we are quantum energy. Everything is energy—including the mind and this thing called consciousness.

The seventh is that at the point where our consciousness enters into seeing something, the effect is to materialize solidity into reality. It is called forth by intention and the electrons choose from a realm of infinite possibilities the probability or patterns of bits that we limit it to by our observation. Consciousness materializes the atoms by changing the state from invisible to visible—waves to atoms. What we see around us has been transformed that way.

The eighth conclusion is that if you unlock the powers to interact with the Zero Point Energy Field, you are linked to the indivisible force that connects everything. That must be that Divine Intelligence operating system.

The ninth conclusion is that the process of intent—activated by the Observer Effect using consciousness creates a morphic field of energy. Morphic means having a specific shape and form. Thoughts have morphic fields, like a magnetic field.

The tenth conclusion is research shows that we change the reality by watching it. We are connected with everything from cells in the body to atoms of our world. Our experience of consciousness expressed as feeling and belief is doing the connecting—we are participants.

The eleventh conclusion is that that intention at the 3rd chakra enfolded with the positive heart energy at the 4th chakra is the powerhouse of above to below reality creation system.

The twelfth conclusion is that the evolution of the Light Body-Being is stunted because it evolves to the third level of self-awareness as ego-intellect by choosing limiting negative energies and limits its final entry into the heart brain and the Zeropoint quantum field. Nor does it evolve according to the Soul's and Light Body's purpose.

32

MORPHIC FIELDS

"That intuition or gut feel is your subtle energies interacting with other's morphic fields you come into contact with"
                                                                Ed Rychkun

The Morphic Field

We have looked at the Heart field, the Auric fields, the Chakra system and the Energy Bodies. We have begun to understand that those 50 trillion cells in our bodies seem to always be cognitive of each other, their roles, the functions and directives even though they are independent of each other. We have looked at how these behave quantumly. They are all totally independent units that can replicate the whole human. We have looked at these systems as wireless energetics that have silent, undetected stimulus-response systems operating like analog computers. Now we are going to look at how these fields communicate, interface, and how they are "sensed" by the human energetic systems.

Rupert Sheldrake is an English author, lecturer, and researcher in the field of parapsychology, known for advocating his "morphic resonance" concept. He worked as a biochemist and cell biologist at Cambridge University from 1967 to 1973 and as principal plant physiologist at the International Crops Research Institute for the Semi-Arid Tropics until 1978. Since leaving research biology, he has primarily worked on promoting and defending his ideas relating to morphic resonance in books, articles, and public appearances.

Conceived during Sheldrake's time at Cambridge, morphic resonance posits that *"memory is inherent in nature"* and *"natural systems, such as termite colonies, or pigeons, or orchid plants, or insulin molecules, inherit a collective memory from all previous things of their kind"*. Sheldrake proposes that it is also responsible for *"telepathy-type interconnections between organisms"*. His advocacy of the idea encompasses paranormal subjects such as remote viewing, precognition, and the psychic staring effect as well as unconventional explanations of standard subjects in biology such as development, inheritance, and memory. <u>It also relates to what we have learned about the communities and unified behavior of 50 trillion cells in the body.</u>

In Sheldrake's ***A New Science of Life: The Hypothesis of Morphic Resonance (1981)*** he proposed that through "morphic resonance" various perceived phenomena, particularly biological ones, become more probable the more often they occur, and therefore biological growth and behavior become guided into patterns laid down by previous similar events. As a result, he suggested, newly acquired behaviors can be passed down to future generations – a biological proposition akin to Lamarckian inheritance. He generalized this approach to assert that it explains many aspects of science, from evolution to the laws of nature which, in Sheldrake's formulation, are merely mutable habits which have been evolving and changing since the Big Bang.

To illustrate what Sheldrake has been researching, it covers proposed telepathy between humans and animals, particularly dogs. Sheldrake suggests that such interspecies telepathy is a real phenomenon and that morphic resonance is responsible for it. He also wrote in 2003 ***The Sense of Being Stared At*** which explored telepathy, precognition, and the "psychic staring effect". It included an experiment where blindfolded subjects guessed whether persons were staring at them or at another target. He reported that in thousands of trials, around 60 percent of subjects reported being stared at when being stared at; around 50 percent (even chance) of subjects reported being stared at when they were not being stared at. Sheldrake attributes this effect to morphic resonance.

His interest in these new kinds of fields first developed while doing research on the development of plants at Cambridge University. He was concerned only with one particular kind of morphic field, namely morphogenetic fields. For example, how do plants grow from spores or seeds into the characteristic form of their species? How do the leaves of ferns, oaks, and bamboos take up their shapes? These are questions to do with what biologists call *morphogenesis* – the coming-into-being of form and one of the great unsolved problems of biology. The naive approach is simply to say that morphogenesis is genetically programmed. Different species just follow the instructions in their genes. But a few moments' reflection show that this reply won't do. All the cells of the body contain the same genes. In your body, the same genetic program is present in your eyes, kidneys, and fingers. If they are all programmed identically, then how do they develop so differently?

Thanks to the great triumphs of molecular biology, we know what genes actually do. Some code for the sequence of amino acids in proteins; others are involved in the control of protein synthesis. They enable organisms to make particular proteins, but these alone cannot account for form. Your arms and your legs are chemically identical: If ground up and analyzed biochemically, they would be indistinguishable. But they have different shapes. Something other than the genes and the proteins they code for is needed to explain their form.

Biologists who study the development of form in plants and animals have long been aware of these problems, and since the 1920's many have adopted the idea that developing organisms are shaped by fields called *morphogenetic fields.* These are rather like invisible blueprints that underlie the form of the growing organism. They are not designed by an architect, any more than a genetic program is designed by a computer programmer. They are fields: self-organizing regions of influence, analogous to magnetic fields and other recognized fields of nature.

All self-organizing systems are wholes made up of parts, which are themselves wholes at a lower level, such as atoms in molecules and molecules in crystals. The same is true of organelles in cells, cells in tissues, tissues in organs, organs in organisms, organisms in social groups. At each level, the morphic field gives each whole its characteristic properties and interconnects and coordinates the constituent parts.

The fields responsible for the development and maintenance of bodily form in plants and animals are called morphogenetic fields. In animals, the organization of behavior and mental activity depends on behavioral and mental fields. The organization of societies and cultures depends on social and cultural fields. All these kinds of organizing fields are morphic fields.

Morphic fields are located within and around the systems they organize. Like quantum fields, they work probabilistically. They restrict, or impose order upon, the inherent indeterminism of the systems under their influence. Thus, for example, a protein field organizes the way in which the chain of amino acids (the "primary structure" determined by the genes) coils and folds up to give the characteristic three-dimensional form of the protein, "choosing" from among many possible structures, all equally possible from an energetic point of view. Social fields coordinate the behavior of individuals within social groups, for example, the behavior of fish in schools or birds in flocks.

The mathematician René Thom has created mathematical models of morphogenetic fields in which the endpoints toward which a system develops are defined as **attractors.** In the branch of mathematics known as dynamics, attractors represent the limits toward which dynamical systems are drawn. They provide a scientific way of thinking about ends, purposes, goals, or intentions. All morphic fields contain attractors.

The most controversial feature of this hypothesis is that the structure of morphic fields depends on what has happened before. They contain a kind of memory. Through repetition, the patterns they organize become increasingly probable, increasingly habitual. The force that these fields exert is the force of habit. Whatever the explanation of its origin, once a new morphic field – a new pattern of organization – has come into being, its field becomes stronger through repetition. The same pattern becomes more likely to happen again. The more often patterns are repeated, the more probable they become. The fields contain a kind of cumulative memory and become increasingly habitual. Fields evolve in time and form the basis of habits. From this point of view, nature is essentially habitual. Even the so-called laws of nature may be more like habits.

The means by which information or an activity-pattern is transferred from a previous to a subsequent system of the same kind is called *morphic resonance*. Morphic resonance involves the influence of like upon like, the influence of patterns of activity on subsequent similar patterns of activity, an influence that passes through or across space and time from past to present. These influences do not fall off with distance in space or time. The greater the degree of similarity, the greater the influence of morphic resonance.

Morphic resonance gives an inherent memory in fields at all levels of complexity. Any given morphic system, say, a squirrel, "tunes in" to previous similar systems, in this case previous squirrels of its species. Through this process each individual squirrel draws upon, and in turn contributes to, a collective or pooled memory of its kind. In the human realm, this kind of collective memory corresponds to what the psychologist C. G. Jung called the "collective unconscious."

Morphic resonance should be detectable in the realms of physics, chemistry, biology, animal behavior, psychology, and the social sciences. But long established systems, such as zinc atoms, quartz crystals, and insulin molecules are governed by such strong morphic fields, with such deep grooves of habit, that little change can be observed. They behave *as if* they are governed by fixed laws.

By contrast, new systems should show an increasing tendency to come into being the more often they are repeated. They should become increasingly probable; they should happen more easily as time goes on. For example, when a new chemical compound is synthesized by research chemists and crystallized, it may take a long time for the crystal to form for the first time. There is no pre-existing morphic field for the lattice structure. But when the first crystals form, they will make it easier for similar crystals to appear anywhere in the world. The more often the compound is crystallized, the easier it should be to crystallize.

In fact, new compounds do indeed tend to crystallize more easily the more often they are made. Chemists usually explain this effect in terms of crystal "seeds" from the new crystals spreading around the world as invisible dust particles in the air, or chemists learning from others how to do it. But the hypothesis of morphic fields predicts that this should happen anyway under standardized conditions, even if dust particles are filtered out of the air.

Connections With Quantum Physics

Experiments to test for the spatial aspects of morphic fields imply a kind of non-locality that is not presently recognized by institutional science. Nevertheless, it may turn out to be related to the non-locality or non-separability that is an integral part of quantum theory, implying connections or correlations at a distance undreamt of by classical physics. Albert Einstein found the idea of "spooky action at a distance" implied by quantum theory deeply distasteful, but his worst fears have come true. Recent experimental evidence shows that these connections lie at the heart of physics.

Several physicists have been intrigued by the possible connections between morphic fields and quantum theory, including John Bell (of Bell's theorem) and David Bohm, whose theory of the implicate order, based on the non-separability of quantum systems, turned out to be extraordinarily compatible with the proposals of Sheldrake. These connections have also been explored by the American quantum physicist Amit Goswami and by the German quantum physicist Hans-Peter Dürr. But it is still not clear exactly how morphic fields might fit in with quantum physics, if only because the implications of quantum theory for complex systems like cells and brains are still obscure.

Experiments On Morphic Fields

The hypothesis of morphic fields is a scientific hypothesis, and as such is subject to experimental testing. There are several possible ways in which it can be, and has been, investigated by experiment. Some of these tests attempt to detect the fields as they link together different parts of a system in space; other tests look for the effects of morphic resonance over time.

The easiest way to test for morphic fields directly is to work with societies of organisms. Individual animals can be separated in such a way that they cannot communicate with each other by normal sensory means. If information still travels between them, this would imply the existence of interconnections of the kind provided by morphic fields. The transfer of information through morphic fields could help provide an explanation for telepathy, which typically takes place between members of groups who share social or emotional bonds.

When Sheldrake started looking for evidence of field-like connections between members of social groups, he found that he was moving into realms very little understood by science. For example, no one knows how societies of termites are coordinated in such a way that these small, blind insects can build complex nests with an intricate internal architecture. No one understands how flocks of birds or schools of fish can change direction so quickly without the individuals bumping into each other. Likewise, no one understands the nature of human social bonds. No one knows how cells know how to organize and behave for the good of all.

For example, many dogs and cats seem to know when their owners are coming home, even when they return at non-routine times in unfamiliar vehicles such as taxis and when no one at home knows when they are coming. The animals seem to be responding telepathically to their owners' intentions.

According to the hypothesis of *formative causation*, morphic fields extend beyond the brain into the environment, linking us to the objects of our perception, and are capable of affecting them through our intention and attention. This is another aspect of morphic fields that lends itself to experimental testing. Such fields would mean that we can affect things just by looking at them, in ways that cannot be explained in terms of conventional physics. For example, we may be able to affect someone by looking at them from behind, when they have no other way of knowing that we are staring at them.

The sense of being stared at from behind is in fact a common experience. Experiments already indicate that it is a real phenomenon. It does not seem to be explicable in terms of chance coincidence, the known senses, or fields currently recognized by physicists.

The unsolved problems of animal navigation, migration, and homing may also depend on invisible fields connecting the animals to their destinations. In effect, these could act like invisible elastic bands linking them to their homes. In the language of dynamics, their home can be regarded as an *attractor*.

The most relevant aspect of morphic fields is that they are attractors... so what you are placing in your own field is being transmitted out into the quantum world - perhaps to attract an energetic likeness?

Important Conclusions About Morphic Fields

The first conclusion is that experiments to test for the spatial aspects of morphic fields imply a kind of non-locality.

The second conclusion is that organelles in cells, cells in tissues, tissues in organs, organs in organisms, organisms in social groups behave within a morphic field that gives each whole its characteristic properties and interconnects and coordinates the constituent parts.

The third conclusion is that Morphic fields are located within and around the systems they organize. Like quantum fields, they work probabilistically.

The fourth conclusion is that morphogenetic fields in which the endpoints toward which a system develops are defined as **attractors.** In the branch of mathematics known as dynamics, attractors represent the limits toward which dynamical systems are drawn. They provide a scientific way of thinking about ends, purposes, goals, or intentions. All morphic fields contain attractors.

The fifth conclusion is that **Morphic resonance** involves the influence of like upon like, the influence of patterns of activity on subsequent similar patterns of activity, an influence that passes through or across space and time from past to present. These influences do not fall off with distance in space or time. The greater the degree of similarity, the greater the influence of morphic resonance.

33

HOLOGRAPHIC REALITY

"Isn't it funny that the brain is designed to create a system of perception-response survival functions from the holographic illusion that it itself interprets?"

Ed Rychkun

The brain is fundamentally a processor that takes instructions from other "brains" like the cell/DNA, the Heart, Subconscious, and Divine Intelligence and is more like an analog computer with its own memory designed to deal with this lifetime. It has both hardwired and software systems that provide input on environmental stimuli and it can send signals to other areas that are a more hardwired response mechanism. It appears to manage things but is by no means the design maker. On its localized disc it stores all the information that is your experience and what it codes as your reality-namely your holographic reality. Its other function is to interpret from the senses and the environment your hologram that you see as your reality. Let us look more carefully into this hologram and how it works.

How Holograms Work

Laser light is much purer than the ordinary light in a torch beam. In a torch beam, all the light waves are random and jumbled up. Light in a torch beam runs along any old how, like schoolchildren racing down a corridor when the bell goes for home time. But in a laser, the light waves are coherent: they all travel precisely in step, like soldiers marching on parade.

When a laser beam is split up to make a hologram, the light waves in the two parts of the beam are travelling in identical ways. When they recombine in the photographic plate, the object beam has travelled via a slightly different path and its light rays have been disturbed by reflecting off the outer surface of the object. Since the beams were originally joined together and perfectly in step, recombining the beams shows how the light rays in the object beam have been changed compared to the reference beam. In other words, by joining the two beams back together and comparing them, you can see how the object changes light rays falling onto it—and that's simply another way of saying "what the object looks like." This information is burned permanently into the photographic plate by the laser beams. So a hologram is effectively a permanent record of what something looks like seen from any angle.

Now this is the clever part. Every point in a hologram catches light waves that travel from every point in the object. That means wherever you look at a hologram you see exactly how light would have arrived at that point if you'd been looking at the real object. So, as you move your head around, the holographic image appears to change just as the image of a real object changes. And that's why holograms appear to be three-dimensional. Also, and this is really neat, if you break a hologram into tiny pieces, all the pieces still contain enough information to recreate the complete hologram: smash a glass hologram of a cup into bits and you can still see the entire cup in any of the bits!

You can make a hologram by reflecting a laser beam off the object you want to capture. In fact, you split the laser beam into two separate halves by shining it through a half-mirror (a piece of glass coated with a thin layer of silver so half the laser light is reflected and half passes through—sometimes called a semi-silvered mirror). One half of the beam bounces off a mirror, hits the object, and reflects onto the photographic plate inside which the hologram will be created. This is called the object beam. The other half of the beam bounces off another mirror and hits the same photographic plate. This is called the reference beam. A hologram forms where the two beams meet up in the holographic plate.

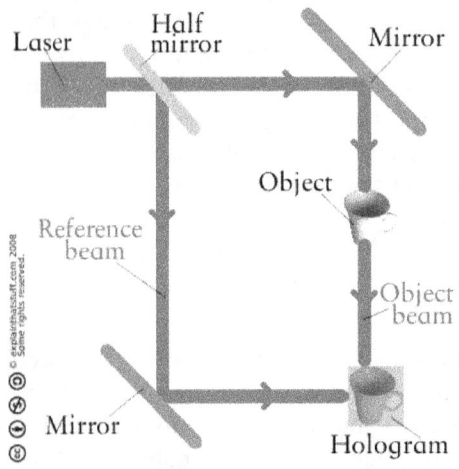

Here are some interesting characteristics:

- Interference is the criss cross pattern of waves where two or more waves ripple through each other. Laser light being extremely pure coherent light is best when a single laser light is split, one bouncing off an object and second allowed to collide with the first so an interference pattern is created. It is recorded on a holographic plate looking like nothing at all but as soon as a second laser or bright light shines then a 3D holograph image appears. And when the holographic film containing the image is cut in half, each half retains the whole image.

- An image presented to the brain by the eye is the same process so images are recorded or retrieved by illuminating the film with light taken at the same angle as the recording.

- We perceive things as out there but they are really in there on the plate. The pain in the toe is a neurological process in the brain to manifest experience. Look in a mirror. Are you there or is it just a plate? Or are you located in the mirror surface? The brain and the hologram all operate in the frequency domain.

- Electrons possess no dimension, no traits of objects and can manifest as particles or waves and they can create wave like patterns that when collided create interference patterns. The chameleon ability to change back and forth are quanta—that which makes up the universe.

- When we look at them quanta manifest as particles as the Observer Effect. All are interconnected as one called nonlocal, everywhere and nowhere.

- Brains mathematically construct objective reality by interpreting frequencies that are projections from another dimension beyond space and time. What is out there is a vast ocean of waves and frequencies and the brain converts these. Without the brain we would experience nothing except an interference pattern. We would not be a body, we would be a blur of interference pattern enfold (implicate) of the cosmic hologram (unfolded) as explicate order as us. We are part of the hologram looking at the hologram.

- We tap into the implicate order with what is resonant with personal resonant.

- All experiences are ultimately neorophysiological processes that take place in the brain. The reason we experience it as external reality is because that is where the brain localizes it through which it creates the internal hologram that we experience as reality.

- The brain cannot distinguish between out there and what it believes to be out there.

- All experiences reduced (real or imagined) to some common language of holographically organized wave forms.

- Every action starts from intention, imagination is already the creator of form and has all the movements needed to carry out an effect; and it affects the body from subtle levels until it manifests. So to the brain, imagination and reality are indistinguishable and images in the mind can ultimately manifest as realities in the physical body.

- The master plan is that DNA programs itself. Hypnosis and imagination can control autonomic processes such as blood flow, and immune system. When we access the right strata of our beliefs, our minds can override genetic makeup.

- Just as every portion of a hologram contains the image of the whole, every portion of the body (cells) contains an image of the whole. Every electron contains the cosmos.

- The Universe is a hologram of all things integrated and interconnected for a vehicle of experience and we create the laws that govern it. We copy that part of it into our resonant frequency hologram.

- 50% of what we see is information from the eye, 50% is pieced together out of expectation of what the world should be like. The brain edits and manipulates by the temporal lobes before being presented to the visual cortex. The brain interprets from the frequency of interference patterns in the implicate order.

- All aspects of an aura are holographic as each part contains the whole. The body itself is a holographic construct.

- Free will may be an illusion. 1.5 seconds before we decide to move muscles, the brain has already generated the signals to do it. The human energy field (heart) responds even before the brain. The mind is not the brain and it supersedes all. It is the field that the true computer controlling the hologram of body and brain. Time and space are constructs of this.

- Each phase of activity is recorded in successive images like frames in the multi-image hologram. If it is a white light hologram an image seen by the normal eye that does not need laser light to be visible, a viewer sees 3D motion portrayed to present the illusion of movement. Our past is recorded this way as a non local way accessed from any point in the space time framework.

- It is only when one is freed from the senses of the body that the holograph can be experienced directly otherwise it is an intellectual construct.

- We are at the heart of all interacting and resonating frequencies.

- Our universe is constantly sustained and created by two wave length flows, one from heaven, one from our soul. Put these together to form a hologram and one is direct from divine and one is direct from divine via our environment. We can view ourselves as interference patterns because inflows is a wave phenomenon and we are where the wave meet.

- In a holographic universe consciousness is everywhere and nowhere.

- We create sub atomic particles and hence the entire universe both in self-reference cosmology, each creates the other.

- The Universe is a holomovement, a constant interrelationship between all things in the Universe itself.

Holographic Awareness

Let us consider an example of Holographic Awareness in our physical reality outside of the mind. You are driving along the highway and spot an oak tree. Your eyes look at the oak for a moment... and a moment later your eyes move back to the highway to stay in touch with the traffic. Even though you're not looking at the oak when you are driving the car and looking at the traffic, you can be thinking of its beautiful form. The thought you are seeing inside yourself of the magnificent old tree can be as clear and as real, as if your eyes are on it. Your eyes may go back and forth several times from the tree to the road, but one way or the other, the image of the oak stays present inside yourself.

Here is some insight into what that brain is actually storing in its local disc drive. What is happening in this situation is that your brain is holding onto a holographic impression of the oak tree for you to experience. It does not matter so much if the image is coming from actual eyesight or from memory, as both perceptions are atmospheric holograms that you're seeing inside yourself. Both holograms are made of the same materials. You can even say that they are the same hologram as they come from the same source — the ancient oak — and they carry the same patterns of energy, imagery and feeling.

From Bohm's perspective, the universe is recognized to be wholistically interconnected through resonance occurring within the underlying Unified Field (the quantum field) that connects all matter, energy and information in the cosmos. In fact, Bohm and many scientists, mystics and again regular people believe that despite its apparent solidity the universe is a gigantic splendidly detailed, multi-dimensional, super-hologram. The human brain is an organ to process, reflect and translate the holographic universe. An individual's brain is like a portal that is connected to the super-hologram of the Grand Universe.

Experientially, you can engage with anything in your awareness, and what may seem like a separate part is actually a whole universe inside a universe connected to a holographic ecosystem that is interwoven into the Grand Universe.

For instance, if you recall your same favorite place, you can use your attention to bore deeper and deeper into the details of the place like its history, environment, composition, climate, visitors, and position on the planet and how it changes over time. Your favorite place, in the 3D physical world and also the version that you engage with inside yourself, is not solid or flat; it is multi-layered, atmospheric, energetic, and has infinite depth. It can be useful to identify, explore and discuss a layer or a part, but in reality it is not a separate, isolated thing. The way it really exists is as an orchestrated system that is woven into its immediate surroundings and is connected through the quantum field to a vast ocean of forces, beings and possibilities. Your favorite place, as grand, humble or unique as it may be, is truly an expression of the Whole cosmos and is intimately connected to it.

A hologram is made of light, space and depth. It may seem to magically appear and also disappear in the twinkle of an eye, according to your angle of vision. A hologram can be viewed and experienced from an infinite number of points of view. It can be broken into a thousand pieces and when each piece is illuminated it will faithfully project the entire unbroken hologram. Hence, each seemingly separate part contains the complete, fully-assembled, unified Whole.

When you look at holographic material inside yourself, we now have the essential understanding that it is a vibrant part of the Grand Universe. It is intimately connected to you, the rest of the inner landscape and also the external world. It is connected to others, nature, evolution, and to both real and imagined realms of life. The holograms inside yourself are constantly morphing and adapting to you, the observer, as the holographic material is alive and responsive as it reflects the thoughts, feelings, dreams and inspirations that you are dialed into. Finally, the inner holographic material that you engage with repeatedly is customizing your immediate personal reality and also setting-up the unfolding of future realities for you to experience.

- It is the theater where you see and interact with the beings, characters, things, spaces and environments that compose your thoughts, feelings, memories and dreams.
- Incredibly, it is also the place where you see and interact with the outside world, as well.
- It is your portal of consciousness for the observation and interaction with realms beyond the physical. Indeed, each individual's Personal Inner Hologram is their own observatory and gateway to the interdimensional worlds and parallel realities that are inhabited by their soul.
- Through it you experience the past, present and future... always in the eternal moment of Now.
- It is your personal laboratory for creating realities that you will experience in the future.
- Ultimately, the Personal Inner Hologram is your very own window to the infinitely well-orchestrated, mysterious and beautiful, Holographic Universe.

You will notice that not only do our thoughts, feelings and memories live inside of us, but the entire external world flows through our senses and is projected into the luminous inner environment. In your personal hologram, images of the outside world exist side-by-side with the images and movies of your thoughts, feelings, dreams and worlds of imagination; all are made of the same materials, seen on the same screens, and stored in the same place.

The whole universe and all its dimensions — all the worlds and characters, both real and imagined are reflected in our hologram. Each seemingly separate individual or thing that appears before our inner vision, exist as luminous structures made of light, sound, space and transmits feelings. Everything is imbued with its own consciousness and identity. Each part is actually a hologram itself. Everything exists as a universe inside a universe. You might say that an infinite number of smaller holograms live in the gigantic, splendidly detailed, multi-dimensional, super-hologram of the Grand Universe.

The personal hologram is the spacious inner stage for what a person is experiencing, in the eternal here-and-now. It is our individuated outpost of consciousness — our mysterious matrix of awareness — that is plugged into multi-dimensional reality. Each of us has a reflection of the ever-changing, dynamic universe inside of us.

Nearly everything in the universe of our personal hologram exists quietly in the vast invisible inventory of the quantum field. Most elements only come into view and emerge from the silent invisible depths, when we activate them with our attention. We effortlessly summon images, memories, ideas, people, situations, whole environments and feelings from the depths of the vast, invisible, quantum storage bank. We summon them to come and stand before us, so that we can see and experience them in the live, interactive environment of our personal holograms.

The Holographic Projection Is "Inside"

It is interesting to realize that when we look at anything in the world — like a mature oak tree in a meadow, for instance — we certainly see and know that it exists "out there." But what has really happened is that light was first reflected off the tree and it traveled to the surface of our eyes. The light that we are looking at is not on the tree "out there," but the image of the tree is carried within the light and that miniscule packet of light (with the image of the whole tree in it) is now sitting on the surface of our eyes. The light is then reflected back into our brains, of course. Hence, when we look at the tree and appreciate its lovely shape, leaves, strong branches and shade, we're actually looking at a picture of it **inside ourselves**, on the luminous screen of our brain.

Consider that the same is true for EVERYTHING that we've ever seen and interacted with in the so-called "external" world. That's the brains job to keep track of that; and this has nothing to do with the programs of behavior in the Subconscious disc drive (although there is a copy there). For our entire lives, we've actually been seeing and interacting with the images that are appearing and disappearing in our brains. It's like you are a miniaturized version of everything that is, just like your cells are individual copies of you (and much more) but you have a consciousness that allows the 7 aspects of chakras to apply will, choice and intent. In this context, you easily hold the entire universe in your mind and heart.

The ordinary, moment-by-moment actuality of seeing and moving among the inner material, is truly like interacting with a hologram, as the material we are intimately involved with is made of light, sound, feelings, and atmospheric shapes that appear, morph and disappear in the twinkle of an eye. The inner hologram is such an accurate reflection and so perfectly made, that we've thought all along that the whole universe has always been "out there" and separate from us. But, we've never seen it or interacted with it on the outside — we've only seen, touched, tasted and pondered the universe from inside ourselves. In fact, when we *think* that it is outside, *that is only a thought.* The actuality of it is that all of your experiences throughout your life, have been engaged with by you, in the landscape of your Inner World ... in the holographic, luminous, atmospheric environment of your mind and heart.

A virtual, expanding, ever-changing, kaleidoscopic reflection of the whole universe is inside you, and that is what you've been working with, playing with, loving, hating and being bored with... all along.

With the realization that everything in the universe is experienced inside yourself, comes the innate understanding that you are not alone. You are not separate from others. You are not separate from the universe. Everything in the universe is actually experienced from inside your Self, and you and It are intimately interwoven together in the fabric of Life.

Other people are really just different parts of your greater Self, as they live in your hologram and you in theirs. You are so intimately connected with others and the whole universe; words can only faintly echo the closeness of the relationship.

Hence, the so-called external, physical cosmos, with its trillions of stars and galaxies — ALL of it can only be seen from WITHIN — in the inner holographic theater of the Observer. It suggests that we are like a cell unit and it's DNA in the cosmic hologram, just a bigger piece of the whole. On the other hand, perhaps the photon as the smallest unit that the torroid is common to the Universe, earth, human, and cell which have the same field?

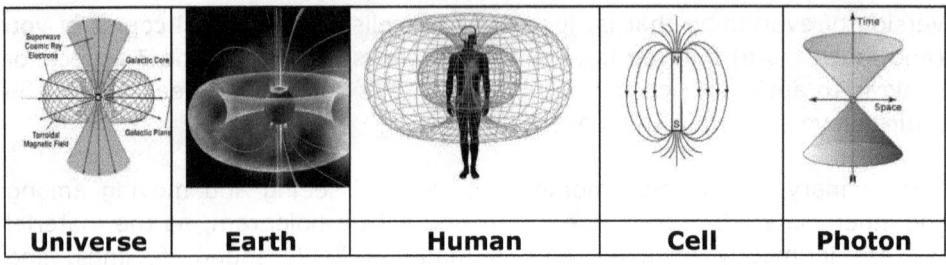

| Universe | Earth | Human | Cell | Photon |

Does every photon have a copy of the universe?

The Personal Inner Hologram is also the environment of dreams, astral travel and remote viewing. Though it may appear that one is exploring distant places separate from the body, and indeed you can say that these places are visited in "out of body" experiences — as a functional center of consciousness does appear to leave the body and travel to anywhere it pleases — but still the starting and ending points of the journey, the platform, the landscape that one explores, and the theater that such experiences and observations take place are all in the Personal Inner Hologram. We are actually exploring the vast realms of our own Personal Inner Hologram in which a reflection of the multidimensional universe resides.

The whole universe and all its dimensions — all the worlds and characters, both real and imagined are reflected in our hologram. Each seemingly separate individual or thing that appears before our inner vision, exist as luminous structures made of light, sound, space and transmits feelings. Everything is imbued with its own consciousness and identity. Each part is actually a hologram itself. Everything exists as a universe inside a universe. You might say that an infinite number of smaller holograms live in the gigantic, splendidly detailed, multi-dimensional, super-hologram of the Grand Universe.

We just haven't understood this yet. We haven't evolved beyond the 2nd state of our evolution the ego awareness to become aware of and open to the Energy Bodies. So here is something to ponder.

So at the end of the day, one has to consider that each created everything in their lives, not just perception and each is a part of the Source, in etheric conscious form that knows all that exists and is totally interconnected with everything else. In that form, each creates a movie of characters that play out in a 3D sensory world. Each creates characters in the movie the same way they can create characters in a timeless daydream. Each creates characters so that all characters can help each other and help the whole grow. The people around are not real, they are a creation. But the people around that each creates are connected through the DNA and the etheric consciousness so all are aware of each other at the etheric level. Therefore all these characters have their own souls that are also creating their own movies apart from each other. As such time does not exist.

Now all is created at the instant of conscious focus on it and all the different lives exist in parallel. Each takes responsibility for all that exists in their movie, and by going into the quantum level where everything exists, interconnected at a photon level, each can intend, entangle and collapse photons of whatever is chosen to place in the focus of awareness by the simple act of intent. To do this, one has to connect with their Higher Self and co-create a different outcome. Beliefs are crucial to the ability to co-create larger and faster. Because the energy generators operate at the quantum level, one must train thoughts, images, words, and emotions to be focused, pure and entrained so as to open those higher abilities as in stage three of our evolution.

Each purpose is to expand through others using the universe as their movie's setting. It, like each and their relationships in the movies create a circle of self perpetuating self creation. The movie purpose is to choose light over dark and to convert the dark into light as it facilitates the growth/expansion rather than contract it. This is how the higher abilities are opened. So each is the part of the Source of all with the spark of life. But we are constipated in stage two of the evolution to Light Body awareness. After all, it is hardly relevant to our interlay commercial world of conflict and competition.

Recall what we presented about, consciousness, the human chakra system, the auras, the heart field, the meridians, all subtle energies working in the invisible (to us because we refuse to Observe them) quantum space. Recall the evolution and purpose of the Soul and Light Body. Recall what we brought forward as to the new inquiries into Quantum Physics and how it has science in a conundrum. These metascience phenomenons have been around for many centuries for some reason. These fields in the human exist at the quantum level of energy. They are operating at a high end electromagnetic energy system. Sustained and focused intention channeled through the system can produce amazing transformations both in and out of the body. How does this relate to miracles and creating one's own reality?

It would seem that intention at the 3rd chakra enfolded with the positive heart energy at the 4th chakra is the powerhouse of above to below reality creation system. It would suggest that this may be the way the body can change thoughts, visions, words and emotion to an experience within a materialized physical domain. And these vortexes of energies are congealers of energies thrown in to cause an effect like the materialize Sai Baba did. And here is the kicker: these subtle energy fields act as attractors!

Attractors to what? Obviously to the energy signatures you are putting out through these fields, broadcasting likeness, likeness, likeness, where are you? And how far out? Well in the quantum field of everything interconnected just like our 50 trillion cells, everywhere!

Yes, the belief that you are living in an illusion of reality and are actually much different than just a physical human is a hard one to accept. But these subtle fields we have discussed are parts of what has been viewed as a Light Body. It is this light body that takes a little vacation on a Near Death Experience or an Out Of Body adventure. When we get back on track of the Soul's purpose and evolution, all of these unseen things with new awareness and abilities to reside and create in new planes and dimensions COME NATURAL. Perhaps we may be an eternal being taking a little vacation in a body and that was the original purpose. The fact that we have chosen to apply will and intent so as to screw up the vacation with stress and toxins kinda masks this possibility, doesn't it?

Important Conclusions About Holograms

The first conclusion is that a hologram is effectively a permanent record of what something looks like seen from any angle. Every point in a hologram catches light waves that travel from every point in the object. That means wherever you look at a hologram you see exactly how light would have arrived at that point if you'd been looking at the real object.

The second conclusion is that the brains mathematically construct objective reality by interpreting frequencies that are projections from another dimension beyond space and time. What is out there is a vast ocean of waves and frequencies and the brain converts these.

The third conclusion is that without the brain we would experience nothing except an interference pattern. We would not be a body, we would be a blur of interference pattern enfold (implicate) of the cosmic hologram (unfolded as explicate order as us. We are part of the hologram looking at the hologram. The brain cannot distinguish between out there and what it believes to be out there

The fourth conclusion is that every action starts from intention. Imagination is already the creator of form and has all the energies needed to carry out the action of finding likeness; and it affects the body from subtle levels until it manifests. So to the brain, imagination and reality are indistinguishable and images in the mind can ultimately manifest as realities in the physical body.

The fifth conclusion is that 50% of what we see is information from the eye. 50% is pieced together out of expectation of what the world should be like. The brain edits and manipulates by the temporal lobes before being presented to the visual cortex. The brain interprets from the frequency of interference patterns in the implicate order.

The sixth conclusion is that everything in the universe is actually experienced from inside your Self, and you and it are intimately interwoven together in the fabric of Life. Hence, the so-called external, physical cosmos, with its trillions of stars and galaxies — ALL of it can only be seen from WITHIN — in the inner holographic theater and plate of the Observer.

The seventh conclusion is that the photon as the smallest unit in the universe has a torroid field the same as the Universe, earth, human, and cell, each a holographic fractal of the other.

The eighth conclusion is that we must get back on the Soul's purpose in order to see the unseen and understand the misunderstood within the Astral and Spiritual planes.

34

BASIC COMPUTER SYSTEMS

"Is it a coincidence that the binary computer uses a silicon on off transistor switch just as the human cell wall is silicon with on off receptor-effector switches?"

Ed Rychkun

The Binary Digital Computer

When you think about a computer, and the diversity of things that they do, you have to scratch your head; particularly when you understand that all this computer does is decode information in the form of bits that in binary are 0 and 1 representing on or off. This is what the transistor is that is put on a microchip. The chip is the primary working unit that through a simple transistor has a current that is on or off. That's it.

And from that ability, and the ability to store and move these combinations of on-off "bits" in three simple ways, it can create information that represents words, images, processes, movies, communications, you name it. It is indeed quite phenomenal. Unlike the human brain which perceives and interprets pictures, the binary computer needs to have a unique combination of on (1) and off (0) switches to represent a picture like in the example below. A specific number of these bits are combined into bytes. To that other computer we call a brain, this picture is not quite as clear depending on your perception of it. It can be either a vase or two faces.

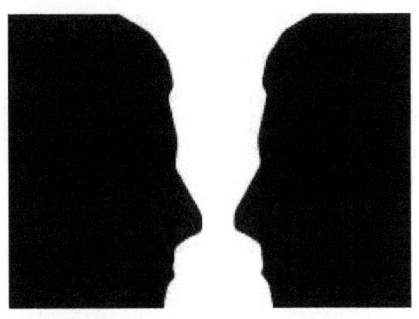

Today, computers work on a much wider variety of problems—but they are all still, essentially, calculations and manipulations of these binary representations called bytes. Everything a computer does, from helping you to edit a photograph you've taken with a digital camera to displaying a web page, involves manipulating numbers as binary representations in one way or another.

The following table will summarize the key parts of a computer, the purpose and examples.

COMPONENT	PURPOSE	EXAMPLE
Computer	House Computer components	HP, IBM, Laptop, Mainframe
CPU	Controls operations of the computer	Control, arithmetic, logic units and main memory
Hard Drive	Memory Storage for CPU	Permanent storage of data and programs
ROM	Read only memory available for permanent programs and data	Operating software, security, permanent access
RAM	Random Access memory. Temporary memory to load application programs, retained lost when turned off	Application programs loaded in temporarily
Input peripherals	Allow input of information	Keyboard, mouse, mic, flash drive
Output peripherals	Present output of results	Screen, printer
Operating System	Controls all the tasks of the computer	WINDOWS, UNIX, RTOS, MacOS
Programming Language	Language to allow human interface to create application programs	FORTRAN, BASIC, C, ASSEMBLER
Compiler	Used to recode or place new programs into memory	C, BASIC compilers
Applications software	Computer programs created to simulate special tasks	WORD, EXCEL, Special APS
Power Supply	DC electricity	Converts AC to DC
Unit of Byte	Binary 0 1	0 is switch off, 1 is switch on
Primary unit	Bits, bytes	Groups of bits

A computer is an electronic device for storing and processing data in binary form, according to instructions given to it through an applications program written (coded) in a computer language (BASIC) recognized by the Operating System (WINDOWS) used to do this. The computer is made up of a CPU, (Central Processing Unit), RAM (Random Access Memory), ROM (Read Only Memory), a Hard drive (Main storage), a Power Supply (DC current) and Input/output devices (Keyboard, screen). It all works together through an Operating System (Windows) which manages the computer hardware and software resources and provides common services for computer programs. At the ground level, the computer Chip holds the transistors that are on-off switches (bits) that are combined into bytes.

Of course there many, many Application Programs (like Microsoft WORD) that are stored on the Hard Drive then loaded in RAM where the CPU runs it so you can use the program. This is so for all the programs that we "run" on our computers. If you want to change a program (Your own program) you need to understand the program language syntax (C or BASIC), change the instructions (Programmer) then resubmit the new program (C or BASIC Compiler) to convert the instructions in machine understandable language (Machine Code) so it can be stored (Hard Drive) to be loaded into Memory (RAM) and run when required. Otherwise, unless you have permission to do this, you simply run an Applications Program (WORD) the way it was designed to work.

The Binary Computer Chip Is The Workhorse

At the bottom of this hierarchy are physical entities such as transistors and electronic circuitry. Next come logic gates (AND, OR, etc.), which operate on symbols (*true* and *false*, 0 and 1) rather than voltages and currents. The gates are assembled into registers, adders, and the like; then an instruction set defines commands for manipulating data within these components. Finally, the details of the instruction set are hidden by the constructs of a higher-level programming language: procedures, iterations, arrays, lists, and so on.

Now in the usual computer binary world, what started out as simple programming languages like FORTRAN and ASSEMBLER, produced application software to do tasks like store, process, present information, replicate endless processes; having grown to be able to computerize or simulate more and more of the functions of our reality to the point where it is difficult to discern what is real and non real (Sort of like the brain!). The fact that a binary computer at its most primary level of bits and bytes is a simple chip that is in an on (1) or off (0) can do this is indeed phenomenal. A **chip** is also called an **integrated circuit**. Generally it is a small, thin piece of silicon onto which the transistors making up the microprocessor have been etched. A chip might be as large as an inch on a side and can contain tens of millions of transistors. Simpler processors might consist of a few thousand transistors etched onto a chip just a few millimeters square.

A collection of transistors is a microprocessor. A microprocessor executes a collection of machine instructions that tell the processor what to do.

A **Transistor** is a **semiconductor** which is a fundamental component in 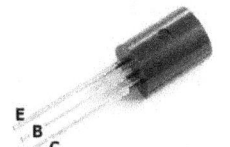 almost all electronic devices. A transistor controls a large electrical output signal which changes to a small input signal. This is analogous to the small amount of effort required to open a tap (faucet) to release a large flow of water. Since a large amount of current can be controlled by a small amount of current, a transistor acts as an **amplifier**.

Microprocessor Logic To understand how a microprocessor works, it is helpful to look inside and learn about the logic used to create one. A microprocessor executes a collection of machine instructions that tell the processor what to do. Based on the instructions, a microprocessor does three basic things:

- Using its ALU (Arithmetic/Logic Unit), a microprocessor can perform mathematical operations like addition, subtraction, multiplication and division.
- A microprocessor can move data from one memory location to another.
- A microprocessor can make decisions and jump to a new set of instructions based on those decisions.

There may be very sophisticated things that a microprocessor does, but those are its three basic activities. To complete the process to what we see computers do, there are several components.

The **Central Processing Unit** (CPU) is the electronic brain of all computers, from handheld computers through to very large systems. The CPU reads instructions from memory (both RAM and ROM), then executes those instructions at a speed of several hundred million instructions per second.

RAM stands for random-access memory. RAM contains bytes of information, and the microprocessor can read or write to those bytes depending on whether the RD or WR line is signaled. One problem with today's RAM chips is that they forget everything once the power goes off. That is why the computer needs ROM.

ROM stands for read-only memory. A ROM chip is programmed with a permanent collection of pre-set bytes. The address bus tells the ROM chip which byte to get and place on the data bus. When the RD line changes state, the ROM chip presents the selected byte onto the data bus.

The operating system controls every task your computer carries out and manages system resources, for example WINDOWS is an operating system. At the simplest level, an operating system does two things:

1. It manages the hardware and software resources of the system. In a desktop computer, these resources include such things as the processor, memory, disk space and more.
2. It provides a stable, consistent way for applications to deal with the hardware without having to know all the details of the hardware.

The **hard drive** is the permanent storage area used to retrieve every piece of data it needs. At the simplest level, a hard drive (disk) is not that different from a cassette tape. Both hard disks and cassette tapes use the same **magnetic** recording techniques. Hard disks and cassette tapes also share the major benefits of magnetic storage - the magnetic medium can be easily erased and rewritten, and it will "remember" the magnetic flux patterns stored onto the medium for many years. All of the components in your computer, such as the CPU, the hard drive and the operating system, work together as a team, and memory is one of the most essential parts of this team. From the moment you turn your computer on until the time you shut it down, your CPU is constantly using memory. Let's take a look at a typical scenario:

- You turn the computer on.
- The computer loads data from **read-only memory** (ROM) and performs a **power-on self-test** (POST) to make sure all the major components are functioning properly. As part of this test, the **memory controller** checks all of the memory addresses with a quick **read/write** operation to ensure that there are no errors in the memory chips. Read/write means that data is written to a bit and then read from that bit.
- The computer loads the **basic input/output system** (BIOS) from ROM. The BIOS provides the most basic information about storage devices, boot sequence, security, **Plug and Play** (auto device recognition) capability and a few other items.
- The computer loads the **operating system** (OS) from the hard drive into the system's RAM. Generally, the critical parts of the operating

system are maintained in RAM as long as the computer is on. This allows the CPU to have immediate access to the operating system, which enhances the performance and functionality of the overall system.
- When you open an **application**, it is loaded into RAM. To conserve RAM usage, many applications load only the essential parts of the program initially and then load other pieces as needed.
- After an application is loaded, any **files** that are opened for use in that application are loaded into RAM.
- When you **save** a file and **close** the application, the file is written to the specified storage device, and then it and the application are purged from RAM.

In the list above, every time something is loaded or opened, it is placed into RAM. This simply means that it has been put in the computer's **temporary storage area** so that the CPU can access that information more easily. The CPU requests the data it needs from RAM, processes it and writes new data back to RAM in a **continuous cycle**. In most computers, this shuffling of data between the CPU and RAM happens millions of times every second. When an application is closed, it and any accompanying files are usually **purged** (deleted) from RAM to make room for new data. If the changed files are not saved to a permanent storage device before being purged, they are lost.

How Do You Program A Computer?

A **compiler** is a computer program (or set of programs) that transforms source code written in a programming language (the source language) into another computer language (the target language, often having a binary form known as object code).

A compiler is a program that translates human readable **source code** into computer executable **machine code**. To do this successfully the human readable code must comply with the syntax rules of whichever programming language it is written in. The compiler is only a program and cannot fix your programs for you. If you make a mistake, you have to correct the syntax or it won't compile.

Machine code is the name for the **Instructions** that a CPU can execute. It's rather difficult to read as it is just numbers in memory. There are programs that can convert the numbers back into **assembly language** but unless you are pretty skilled or trying to break a protection scheme, there is little use or need for it.

Analog Computers

In **analog technology**, a wave is recorded or used in its original form. So, for example, in an analog tape recorder, a signal is taken straight from the microphone and laid onto tape. The wave from the microphone is an analog wave, and therefore the wave on the tape is analog as well. That wave on the tape can be read, amplified and sent to a speaker to produce the sound.

In **digital technology**, the analog wave is **sampled** at some interval, and then turned into **numbers** that are stored in the digital device. On a CD, the sampling rate is 44,000 samples per second. So on a CD, there are 44,000 numbers stored per second of music. To hear the music, the numbers are turned into a **voltage wave** that approximates the original wave.

The two big advantages of digital technology are:

- The recording **does not degrade** over time. As long as the numbers can be read, you will always get exactly the same wave.
- Groups of numbers can often be **compressed** by finding patterns in them. It is also easy to use special computers called digital signal processors (DSPs) to process and modify streams of numbers.

Working with electronics means dealing with both analog and digital signals, inputs and outputs. Our electronics projects have to interact with the real, analog world in some way, but most of our microprocessors, computers, and logic units are purely digital components. These two types of signals are like different electronic languages; some electronics components are bi-lingual, others can only understand and speak one of the two.

Process Control Computers

In computer process control, a digital computer is used to direct the operations of a manufacturing process. Although other automated systems are typically controlled by computer, the term computer process control is generally associated with continuous or semi-continuous production operations involving materials such as chemicals, petroleum, foods, and certain basic metals. In these operations the products are typically processed in gas, liquid, or powder form to facilitate flow of the material through the various steps of the production cycle. In addition, these products are usually mass-produced. Because of the ease of handling the product and the large volumes involved, a high level of automation has been accomplished in these industries. The modern computer process control system generally includes the following:

1. measurement of important process variables such as temperature, flow rate, and pressure,
2. execution of some optimizing strategy,
3. actuation of such devices as valves, switches, and furnaces that enable the process to implement the optimal strategy, and
4. generation of reports to management indicating equipment status, production performance, and product quality.

Today computer process control is applied to many industrial operations.

In many ways, the brain and its hardwired (nervous system) and the wireless systems (chakras, aura, meridians) function this way as a combination of the Analog and process Control computers.

Quantum Computers

A classic computer as you now understand reads binary code where everything is broken down into a language of ones and zeros called bits. The computer reads these ones and zeros as data and instructions.

A quantum computer creates a quantum state in which quantum bits, or qubits, can exist. A qubit is an odd concept because unlike binary bits, qubits can be both a one and a zero at the same time. So these qubit states are 1 (on) 0 (off) and 1 and 0 (both on). With enough qubits you could process a complicated problem in a fraction of the time it would take a classical computer to complete. The quantum computer could calculate all possible outcomes at once. The computer would rank results by percentage so one might have a 95-percent chance of being right while all other results added together comprise the other five percent. So far, quantum computers have proven difficult to maintain as a minor glitch and the whole system collapses into a classic computer.

Quantum computers encode these qubits which can exist in superposition. Qubits represent atoms, ions, photons or electrons and their respective control devices that are working together to act as computer memory and a processor. Because a quantum computer can contain these multiple states simultaneously, it has the potential to be millions of times more powerful than today's most powerful supercomputers.

This superposition of qubits is what gives quantum computers their inherent **parallelism**. According to physicist **David Deutsch**, this parallelism allows a quantum computer to work on a million computations at once, while your desktop PC works on one. A 30-qubit quantum computer would equal the processing power of a conventional computer that could run at 10 **teraflops** (trillions of floating-point operations per second). Today's typical desktop computers run at speeds measured in gigaflops (billions of floating-point operations per second).

Quantum computers also utilize another aspect of quantum mechanics known as entanglement which you are now familiar with. One problem with the idea of quantum computers is that if you try to look at the subatomic particles, you could bump them, and thereby change their value. If you look at a qubit in superposition to determine its value, the qubit will assume the value of either 0 or 1, but not both (effectively turning your spiffy quantum computer into a mundane digital computer). To make a practical quantum computer, scientists have to devise ways of making measurements indirectly to preserve the system's integrity. Entanglement provides a potential answer. In quantum physics, if you apply an outside force (like the Observer Effect) to two atoms, it can cause them to become entangled, and the second atom can take on the properties of the first atom. So if left alone, an atom will spin in all directions. The instant it is disturbed it chooses one spin, or one value; and at the same time, the second entangled atom will choose an opposite spin, or value. This allows scientists to know the value of the qubits without actually looking at them.

It's only when you look at the tiniest quantum particles – atoms, electrons, photons and the like – that you see intriguing things like superposition and entanglement. Superposition is essentially the ability of a quantum system to be in multiple states at the same time — that is, something can be "here" and "there," or "up" and "down" at the same time. Entanglement is an extremely strong correlation that exists between quantum particles — so strong, in fact, that two or more quantum particles can be inextricably linked in perfect unison, even if separated by great distances. The particles remain perfectly correlated even if separated by great distances. The particles are so intrinsically connected, they can be said to "dance" in instantaneous, perfect unison, even when placed at opposite ends of the universe.

Trinary Computers

Much like the Quantum computer, Trinary or Ternary computers work on a basis of 3 possible states. Ternary has -1, 0, and +1 while quantum has 0,

1, and both 1 and 0 together. Trinary computing, on the other hand, stores information as a representation of false, null and true; 0, 1, 2 or -1, 0 and 1.

With the advent of quantum computing, Trinary computing has a new cause. Universal quantum logic gates, the building blocks of infant quantum computing, require hundreds of gates in order to complete any useful work. The modern representation of true or false can be expressed as a bit. The quantum computing equivalent of a bit is dubbed a qubit. Traditional computers that store data in ternary operations are dubbed trits; the quantum equivalent is called a qutrit.

What makes this method truly innovative is that by using qutrits for universal quantum gates instead of qubits, researchers can reduce the number gates needed in a computer significantly. The discoverer *Lanyon* proposes that a computer that would traditionally take 50 conventional quantum gates could use as few as 9 gates using the ternary method.

Is The Trinary Computer Like The Human?

The evolution from binary bits to holographic qubits, then to Trinary trits reflects a path that becomes closer and closer to the way we feel the human "computer" system which is part quantum, and part binary, and part analog, part process control, operates. What we have come to follow with the binary is a system that satisfies the two phases of evolution of the human. The evolution to the third phase opens the awareness to the higher astral and mental planes and the trinary system of the physical body.

If we can look forward and get a grasp of the quantum nature of part of us, then one can say that the heart torroid field would represent the center of the zeropoint quantum field. Here in the Above to Below process is where the mind stuff; like thoughts, images, words from consciousness is slurped down into the heart to draw from the vortexes positioned at each chakra to draw or attract the possibilities from the quantum field outside. Then it would draw it into reality as the lower chakras congeal the possibilities into reality.

It would make sense to consider this point of access at the heart to be zeropoint or zero. In the binary computer system 0 represent off - no access to the quantum field and the Light Body awareness, just like the first two steps of our evolution is all we get to, not activating those higher abilities that give us the truths about the quantum nature of us, our Light Body and the Universe of infinite possibilities from where we can draw a holographic reality.

The binary computer simply turns things off at a bit of 0. The quantum computer now brings in the qubit that is on (1), off (0) or both, still not providing access to zeropoint. The trinary computer comes closer where the trits are -1, 0, +1. This is where we are now getting the photon level of the quantum field. We would say that this is more like our human system where 0 is the access point to zeropoint and the +1 and -1 represent the negative - positive states, like masculine - feminine that represent the states to be entangled and collapsed into reality.

We will develop a better feel for this in the next chapter.

Important Conclusions About Computers

The first conclusion is that the true workhorse of the computer is the transistor, a two-way switch of on-off that produces the reality created by computers.

The second conclusion is that the process of changing a program in a computer requires a compiler and the ability to use a programming language. Once the program is rewritten, it is compiled through the operating system to be coded into machine understandable language and the old program is replaced.

The third conclusion is that the evolution of computers from binary to quantum, to trinary reflects a possible transition to the way the human subtle system surrounding the heart chakra actually creates reality.

35

THE HUMAN COMPUTER

"Your Light Body is the Genie and your Physical body is the Lamp"
Ed Rychkun

Human Cells Are The Workhorse

By now you may have concluded that the human computer is not exactly like a binary computer in that much of the human includes quantum subtle energy fields and these are not exactly understood. Nevertheless, it is useful to use the binary computer as a comparative system to the human computer.

Like the binary computer that at its fundamental chip-transistor stage has an on-off state of 1 and 0 as bits that are used to create the complexity of applications we see today, at the fundamental level, there is a similar device in the human called a cell. Here there are 50 trillion cells that have an automatic wireless telepathic type communication system. It is information that is available in a nonlocal way in a morphic field. And even though they are all identical, they behave differently, they organize differently into communities, and they have different functions somewhat like an ant colony.

Although we have touched on cell biology earlier, we are repeating some of it here. It reflects research work done on cell biology by **Bruce Lipton, PhD** as described in his book **Biology of Belief**.

His book tells the story of how thoughts in the mind as energy of perception 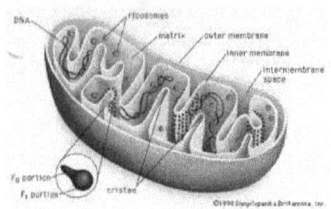 directly influence how the physical brain controls body physiology. At the far end of this process are the cells that respond to those perceptions. They are the ones who actually create the tissues and create reactive stimuli to execute various programs. Thought energy can activate or inhibit the cells' function producing proteins via constructive or destructive positive-negative interference waves. The movements of proteins provide physiological functions to enable life but signals are required to animate their movement. The interface is the cell membrane which operates like the cell's brain in a receptor-effector on-off mode. It operates like computer silicon chips.

Membrane effector proteins are the physical subunits of the cellular brain intelligence. They are perception switches that link receptors of environmental stimuli to response generating protein pathways. Here, very basic perception switches related to potassium, oxygen, glucose, histamine, estrogen, toxins, and light are present.

Thousands of reflective perception switches are active, each reading individual environmental signals to collectively create the behavior of a cell. They show awareness by releasing signal molecules in the community where each cell must acquiesce control to the informed decision of its awareness authority, the brain which controls the behavior of the body's cells. **The brain is the manager, not the director.**

The limbic system provides the mechanism to convert chemical communication signals into sensations that could be experienced by all the cells in the community. The conscious mind not only reads the flow of the cell coordinating signals that comprise the body's mind, it can also generate emotions manifested through its sensors to control release of regulation signals by the nervous system.

The mind can generate molecules of emotion and override the cellular system, so consciousness can bring health and disease via emotional signals. These can become hard wired pathways from repetitive patterns or habits.

At the cellular level this magical organic unit is the membrane. **It is another brain that controls cellular life** as it is the membrane which controls the mechanisms by which the body translates environmental signals to behavior.

This membrane is 3 layered skin around all living cells. It, like even the most primitive cells, displays intelligence as they digest, breathe, excrete, sense food, and propel to targets. They recognize toxins, proteins, and employ escape maneuvers. The IMP or Integral Member Proteins is part of the membranes internal surface. There are two types of receptor proteins (sense organs like eyes, ears, etc) that are nano antennas tuned to respond to environmental signals. They are inactive and active shape shifting back and forth as the electrical charges are altered (like 0-1 binary transistors). This involves thought charges as well as physical stimuli like in a foreign influence of penicillin. It is these receptors that provide the cell awareness.

The effector protein engages the response (like in the automatic knee jerk when you thump the knee). There are hundreds of information pathways that are called signal transduction gateways that open or close (like transistors) depending on electrical charges. Every cell has thousands of these channels requiring half of your body energy every day (just like transistors get hot as they transduce currents, from a power source).

Every time the channel revolves, it opens to allow 3 positive atoms (ATPase, sodium, potassium) to go out and admits 2 two positive potassium atoms into the cytoplasm. This happens at hundreds of cycles per second. Inside the cell it gets more negative charge while the outside gets positive. Negative charge below the membrane is membrane potential. The lipid part does not let charges across its barrier, so internal charge stays negative. Positive out and negative in is a self charging battery whose energy is used to empower biological processes (like a power supply in a computer).

Another variety of effector proteins (cytoskeletal) regulates the shape and mobility, a third is enzymes that break down or synthesize molecules. These IMPS all provide signals that control the binding of chromosomes regulating proteins as a sleeve around DNA to control the reading of genes so that worn out proteins can be replaced, or new ones created.

The cell membrane has hundreds of thousands of switches like chips/transistors and thus the behavior triggered by the effector response is through all switches (holistic) at one time. Molecules of a membrane flow in a **fluid like a liquid crystal acting as a semiconductor** (chip) which like a membrane contains gates and channels. **As you know now, a chip is a crystal semiconductor with gates and channels**.

The multicellular communities (we have 50 trillion cells) have a division of labor in tissues and organs for specific functions and when a unified effector response is required it is up to the **brain to coordinate the required execution of the programs as residing in the hard drive (subconscious mind) or DNA**.

Interestingly, it has been found that DNA blueprints (molecules) do not control the operation of the cell. Genes cannot reprogram a cell since the organisms' life cell survival depends on the dynamic adjustment to changing environment. For example it has been found that when you destroy a cell membrane, the cell dies. When you destroy only receptor proteins with digestive enzymes the cell is brain dead (no signals).

The nucleus is also memory disc and hard drive with DNA blueprints that encode the production of proteins. If you remove a nucleus the cell still has information (like removing a flash drive) to function; until old parts need to be replaced. The cell then dies not because it can't function but because it cannot renew dying parts with program instructions from DNA, typically dying within a few days.

Thus units of perception create cell intelligence to decide upon awareness in the receptor, then to take action through the effector. Perception is through the awareness elements of environment through physical sensation.

One can conclude that like the computer, **cells are programmable from outside the cell. Data is entered into the computer or cell via the membrane receptors acting like an input device or keyboard)** that triggers effector proteins that then actions cell/computer CPU/effector proteins that convert environmental information into the behavioral language of biology.

As an aside a researcher, in 1997 turned a cell membrane into a digital readout computer chip. He isolated a cell membrane, put gold foil under it, and flooded it with an electrolyte solution. When the cells' membrane receptors were stimulated by a complementary signal, the channel opened and allowed solution across membrane. The foil served as a transducer, an electrical pickup device which converted the electrical activity into a digital readout on a screen. This was a clear indication that it functions like a computer chip with transistors.

What we can see here is that in a miracle for example, where the physical tissues become regenerated in the body, the signals that are accepted from either outside environmental stimuli and the subconscious become acceptable to the cell receptors, thus triggering the effectors to have the brain haul out the DNA program from the nucleus to reload and run so as to create the organ/tissue the way it is supposed to be. A placebo is a belief effect, a nocebo is opposite (you have 6 months to live) that obviously gets through to trigger this process.

The big lesson is of course that this biological process, like a regular computer, is programmable from outside as well as inside.

The Cell Protection Mechanism

At a basic level cells have a membrane perception switch that dictates a behavior such as a retreat from toxins or advance to nutrients. This primary switch has a protein receptor that responds to histamine – a local molecule. The primary switch also responds to adrenalin which triggers a body wide emergency-response system. There are two switches here; H1 envokes a protein response and H2 evokes a growth response, or alpha (protection) and beta (growth). Adrenalin will override the histamine. Any mind activity acting via the central nervous system triggering adrenaline overrides the body activities on local histamine signals.

The most common understanding of this protection mode is the flight or fight syndrome automatic response system that kicks in when there is a real threat. Many things happen in the body to prepare for this. The issue here is that a perceived threat works the same way as a real threat. And the other issue is that this particular process is also instigated by stress. The issue is that humans restrict growth in protective mode as it diverts energy for growth so one must eliminate stressors.

The nervous system is the main network (like a wire communication input system) that monitors environmental signals, interprets them and organizes appropriate signals through to the cell to engage in protective systems of the HPA Axis.

Thus the HPA axis or Hypothalamus-Pituitary-Adrenal sequence is activated from external threats. A threat perceived by the Hypothalamus sends a signal to the Pituitary gland which is the master gland responsible for organizing and managing 50 trillion cells. It launches the effector protein commands to launch body organs into action, sending a signal to the Adrenal to coordinate the fight or flight response.

The cascade that occurs is from Hypothalamus or brain as CRF or Corticotrophin to the Pituitary. CRF activates a special pituitary hormone—causing a release of adrenocorticotropic hormones (ACTH) into the blood. The ACTH makes its way to the Adrenals to turn on the secretion of the fight or flight adrenal hormones. These stress hormones constrict blood vessels of the digestion tract to nourish arm and leg tissues. The visceral organs stop working as the stress from danger inhibits growth and compromises energy resources.

As another growth inhibiting side effect, the HPA Axis through the adrenal signals, suppress the immune system on the demand to conserve energy. Thus the inability to fight disease is temporarily suspended. So the immune system which deals with threats under the skin (bacteria, viruses, etc.) is compromised at the same time.

The activated HPA also interferes with the ability to think clearly. Adrenal stress hormones constrict blood vessels reducing the ability to function. Also the response activation in the prefrontal cortex, the center of conscious volitional action becomes dumber.

The lesson here is:

1. All viruses and stress activate the HPA axis
2. When conscious mind is in conflict with the unconscious truth, the conflict expresses itself in weak body muscles as the HPA is engaged
3. The HPA axis does not know the difference between a perceived threat and a real threat
4. 98% of the food we eat is altered or enhanced with toxic or artificial chemicals devoid of the life force so the illness experienced in the body is nothing more than a mirror of your life style and consciousness.

For example, research has shown that some foods (i.e. pork) have an affect of creating a cell lining that cuts down the flow of the signals through the cell membrane.

Thus, the environment that one creates through perception and diet have a profound effect on the overall health - and perhaps the scene whereby one can get those cells to respond to our proactive programming of the human computer. It is like a virus in a computer or defective programs that inhibit performance.

The Human Versus Binary Systems

At the basic level, in a computer, the primary work is a micro processor called a silicon chip, a semiconductor with transistors that are on or off so as to simulate two states of 0 and 1 as the binary bits. A computer chip is a semiconductor with gates and channels like a membrane. This simple unit is the fundamental building block of all that is around us as computer technology that stores, retrieves, processes, and displays this simple information. These are programmable from the outside.

At the basic level of the human computer, the primary work unit is a cell with a membrane which is a fluid silicon semiconductor as it conducts or filters through to the inside. It contains gates and channels as receptors and effectors to let nutrients in or waste out. Cells accept/reject food by membrane perception switches that are open or closed in a state of 0 off or 1 on by way of their physical response configuration. A computer membrane is a semiconductor with gates and channels like a computer chip. Cells are the basic unit of any living organism, a living computer. A cell is a single unit – the smallest in your body that is capable of carrying out life by itself and is the primary unit which conducts the work of storing, retrieving, processing, and displaying (running life support functions and learned behavior) from internal and external environmental information. These are programmable from outside. **But, unlike chips, cells make decisions and communicate.**

All our life processes go on inside these tiny units which are packed with even smaller organelles all busy carrying out chemical reactions. A cell also has a complete copy of the organism's genome, its DNA tissue is a group of cells that join together to do a specific job in your body. These processes are a result of creating, storing, and running of human computer programs to execute specific life tasks.

All the computer processes that we see everywhere today are created by the creating, storing, and running of computer programs designed to execute specific tasks.

Paralleling this incredible evolution is the trinary system of reality. The way the subconscious mind creates in non-physical reality (in imagination) is converging with the way the conscious mind creates in physical reality through the human computer system. It has a conscious and unconscious memory which controls functionality of the body through the brain which manages and carries out orders from sub processes in the cells (mitochondria). The mitochondria is the primary working unit of the human computer system as we shall explore later.

Some of the application programs are permanent like firmware; like the organs, some are learned, like walking, some are created like developing a new function or ability. All these are stored in a repository of our hard drives which are the subconscious. Both auto and learned functions are pulled from here to have the brain execute the program. What we keep in the RAM drive (conscious) can be used to create a new program provided the subconscious and conscious are aligned. It is because they are interconnected —but the subconscious has much more power (processing) than the conscious.

In previous chapters, we have described the parts of the human computer system:

- Conscious Mind
- Subconscious Mind
- Brain
- Heart
- Cells
- Chakras
- Auras
- Meridians
- Energy bodies

As we have noted, these "devices" are most likely operating at a quantum level and therefore are not strictly comparable to a simple binary computer. And as we have come to understand, even the quantum and trinary computers fail to be appropriate. However, for the sake of our presentation, a comparative table can be made as below:

COMPONENT	COMPUTER	HUMAN
Computer		Creator
Central Processor	CPU	Brain, unified cells, heart
Communications	Comms card	Chakras, auras
Active temp memory	RAM	Conscious Memory
Input Devices	Keyboard, mouse, flash, screen icons	Nervous system, chakras
Permanent local memory	ROM	Brain
Video/comms card	Imaging	Sensing organs, nervous system
Permanent Storage	Hard drive	Subconscious memory
Operating System	Windows	Divine Intelligence DNA
Applications Software	WORD, EXCEL	Motor, behavior functions
Compiler	C, BASIC	Heart
Program Languages	C, BASIC.	Love, well being, intent
Power Supply	DC electricity	Creator/Spirit/Heart/Love
Unit of Byte	Binary 0 1	Trinary -1 0 +1
Primary unit	Bits, bytes	Tribits, tribytes
Working unit	Microchip	Mitocondria

Important Conclusions About Human Computers

First conclusion is that the workhorse of the human computer system is the cell membrane that has effector - receptor switches similar to the on-off binary system. They are similar to the silicon chips with the on-off transistors. These states determine the type of programs that are to be loaded into memory as behavior. However, the similarity ends here as cells make decisions, organize, and communicate, chips do not.

The second conclusion is that cells are programmable from outside the cell. Data is entered into the computer or cell via the membrane receptors acting like an input device or keyboard) that triggers effector proteins that then trigger action (like cell/computer CPU/effector) proteins that convert environmental information into the behavioral language of biology.

The third conclusion is that the environment that one creates through perception and diet have a profound affect on the overall health as they cause the cells to create a cascade of flight or fight reactions that deter growth and render the immune system dysfunctional. Again this points to the need for well being. -

The fourth conclusion is that in order to create new programs, or modify old programs in subconscious, the key is to understand that the Operating System is Divine Intelligence, the Compiler is the Heart, and the language used to recode is Love.

36

WHAT HAVE WE LEARNED?

"There is no better pathway up the mountain to Heaven, what matters is that you climb."

Ed Rychkun

Let us attempt to summarize what we have learned so far. As we have stated before, in our world of 3D we create things all the time. First let us recall the **7 Steps of Manifesting Reality.** As we stated, these are well known to any businessman or anyone engaged in a project where an idea is taken and then created into our material reality. It certainly was to all the millionaires that Napoleon Hill surveyed. These are recalled below.

1. THOUGHT: We bring into consciousness an idea of a desired result.
2. VISION: We form a vision or what it is we want to manifest.
3. PLAN: We write or communicate a plan of how the result is to manifest.
4. PASSION: We become passionate and emotional about achieving the end result.
5. ACTION: We launch our intent to seek out and manifest the plan with a strong persistence to succeed.
6. RELATIONS: We seek out the resources, people and connections to others that assist in manifesting the plan.
7. MATERIAL: We succeed in manifesting the plan so as to engage in the end result.

Summary Of PART ONE

If you begin to rationalize the different ways in which these miracles occur and look at some other common denominators, it becomes clearer as to what the common steps and requirements are. For now, let us summarize what the Healers do and say is important to success:

1. BELIEF: The recipients' belief system must be one that believes in the healing process and is aligned with the subconscious belief.

2. STATE: The recipient must be in a programmable state where the brain does not interfere and the subconscious mind says it is ready to accept a new program. This is through guided meditation, regression, becoming present to lower the brain wave interference of the conscious mind.

3. ENVIRONMENT: The process of setting the environment whether a ritual, a gathering, a process by the healer is important in creating the focus and attention for the intention of healing and reprogramming to take place. This creates a morphic field of energy that enforces the belief so as to allow the reprogramming.

4. WELL BEING: The internal environment of the recipient and the healer is one of love, forgiveness, compassion, peace and harmony as the morphic field of energy around and in the body. The elimination of stress is needed here so as to better entrain the body and mind into a higher state of vibration.

5. FOCUS & INTENT: By triggering the intention, the issue is identified or located so as to direct the process of healing to that location. At this point, the clear vision of the correct state becomes the focus as surrounded by the joy of its completion. This through words, prayer, emotions, or guidance, creates the directive to correct the issue.

6. HIGHER POWER: Engagement in a Higher Power or Guides is the necessary process as some form of Divine engagement to assist in the process of correcting the issue and instigating the subconscious reprogramming.

7. MANIFESTATION: The healer, as higher authority and the conduit for some form of Divine Intervention that is triggered to actually replace the program in the subconscious mind. The process of reprogramming convinces the brain and the cellular community to respond by instituting a new or old program from DNA held within the nucleus of the cells.

So to follow the Ho'Oponopono line, once the environment is set, one begins with the **conscious mind,** drops out a petition for **transmutation** to the **void** so **super consciousness mind** can instruct the **subconscious mind** to rewrite the defective program and reboot the computer. But if **repentance** and **forgiveness** are not stamped on the request then it simply ain't going to get mailed.

In these cases, a common denominator is that a Healer who is accepted (Belief) as an Authority on the process acts as a conduit leading the recipient. The issues here are that some of these variables are not clear cut, like the <u>strength</u> of belief, the <u>right</u> state, and the <u>proper</u> environment; but nevertheless, we can begin to rationalize all these into some simple steps. In looking at a process where you wanted to get healed, you could summarize these following steps. First, you must come from a place of belief that you are worthy and believe in miracles. Then the Healer:

0. Creates a setting where the patient is in an altered state
1. Brings into thought the belief of being healed
2. Brings into vision the image of the issue which is to be corrected
3. Communicates to find the source of the issue
4. Brings in the power of emotion to surround the corrected desire
5. Launches the intention to correct the issue
6. Surrenders control of the correction to a higher power
7. Allows the Higher Power to materialize the correction

These steps were under the control of an Authority such as a Healer, not yourself. The other difference is that you are not going to regress yourself to find the issue, you are going to use your power of intent, love, emotion to shift an issue which you already know exists without a hunt for what caused it. It is best to follow the more simple methods Quantum Touch, Power of Intention, Ho'Oponopono, Ancient Prayer, and Matrix Energetics to be your guide. Here you will trust that the Divine Intervention will know what to do. Let us use an example of a dysfunctional knee.

0. ALTERED STATE: Bring yourself into an altered state by imagining a peaceful place, breathing softly, and becoming present to yourself in the heart.
1. THOUGHT: In your thoughts assert your beliefs that you believe in miracle healing, you believe you can heal yourself, you believe you are worthy and you believe in a higher power that will assist you.
2. VISION Visualize clearly in your mind a picture of the healed knee or a situation where it is healed.
3. SPEAK out stating that you are asking for Higher Divine Intelligence assistance to manifest your vision.
4. HEART EMOTION In your imagination feel the result of the knee being completely healed and surround this vision with the joy and bliss of it being so.

5. INTENT With your intention to correct the issue, you state to the area of problem, I love you, I am sorry for creating this issue and the reason for its being, please forgive me, thank you.

6. HIGHER POWER In your mind, connect to a higher power to feel the energy flow into your total being and into your cellular structure to the knee. You can use hands or imagine the flow of healing energy.

7. MANIFEST Feel the gratitude of completion and thank the higher power or those you have called to assist you.

Essentially, you can try any one of the techniques to begin telling your subconscious that it is time to believe. Pick a technique that "resonates" with you and go through the steps. They all work, and they all have produced some spectacular results. Yes, some of the time, but how do you know that you are not one of the ones that it will work for? Choose an area of attention that is a small issue, like the bad knee. The difference here is that you are going to be the Authority, not a doctor, healer, or third person facilitator. And how do you know you are doing it the right way? When it works! So engage your belief, intent, and accept that there is a Higher Power, drop your intellectual expectations and get on with the programming.

These simple steps would be where we stand so far. You may have doubts and questions about whether your belief is strong, are you in the right state and so on but why not try it and see. If you are still in doubt, then that is fine; let us move on to the process and procedures when you want to change your reality without a Healer or conduit. And understanding what has been programmed into the subconscious. So in order to further quantify the processes and procedures, let us move on to another area of "miracles". This is the one that changes the **reality around you**, not within you. These we are going to label **wealth** miracles so **created by You as the Facilitator.**

Summary of PART TWO

From PART TWO, which dealt with attracting miracles external to the body, we found that the processes were similar evolving from the more pragmatic steps outlined by Napoleon Hill to the more recent top seller's steps that bring in a spiritual aspect to the process. We found that not only is it important to **believe**, we see **divine intervention** again and again. The process, we found moved from "doing the hard physical work" of Napoleon Hill to "letting the universe" bring the results to you.

What do these world famous "motivators" of wealth tell us over and over?

Be clear, positive, know what you want, see it already achieved and be passionate about it. Each one of these gurus has put a new marketing twist to the same process that we talked about in the first chapters, namely our 7 steps:

1. We form the thought of making a million dollars
2. We form a vision of a company that sells chairs
3. We make a business plan of the company and product
4. We get emotionally excited about the plan/company
5. We launch the intent to execute the business plan
6. We engage others, money, etc. to make it happen
7. We create the chairs/company that enters our reality

Notice however, these top sellers have injected a more and more spiritual aspect to the process. Once again with the exception of Napoleon Hill who does not bring in a higher power (it is YOU) we see that it is important to **believe**, and get some help with the ***divine intervention (Universe)*** again and again.

Notice that we have moved also from "doing the hard physical work" to "letting the universe" bring the result to you. But the Setting, Process, and Assistance are similar except that one must be repetitive and engage in choices that are now going to be attracted to you. The important difference from PART ONE is that the Universe is not going to create a miracle of a healing desire by Divine Intention; the Universe is going to focus on attracting either the desired result or steps to the desired result over time. But again, we have the same basic steps:

- change the **belief** of limiting factors
- create an **environment** of well being of physical and metal health
- change the **belief** self, your worthiness, your truths
- be very **clear** on the desire
- supercharge the desire with **emotion**
- drop into **lower state** to **reprogram** the subconscious
- get into a mode of **feeling good**
- be **repetitive** and persistent
- **engage** in the choices that come forward

When we bring our deductions from Part One on miracles forward, we had seven key steps.

0. ALTERED STATE: Bring yourself into an altered state by imagining a peaceful place, breathing softly, and becoming present to yourself in the heart.
1. THOUGHT: In your thoughts assert your beliefs that you believe in miracle healing, you believe you can heal yourself, you believe you are worthy and you believe in a higher power that will assist you.

2. VISION Visualize clearly in your mind a picture of the healed knee or a situation where it is healed.

3. SPEAK out stating that you are asking for Higher Divine Intelligence assistance to manifest your vision.

4. HEART EMOTION In your imagination feel the result of the knee being completely healed and surround this vision with the joy and bliss of it being so.

5. INTENT With your intention to correct the issue, you state to the area of problem, I love you, I am sorry for creating this issue and the reason for its being, please forgive me, thank you.

6. HIGHER POWER In your mind, connect to a higher power to feel the energy flow into your total being and into your cellular structure to the knee. You can use hands or imagine the flow of healing energy.

7. MANIFEST Feel the gratitude of completion and thank the higher power or those you have called to assist you.

There are several differences here. First, we are creating new realities outside of us, not healing. Second we are doing this by ourselves. Third, we are being told to create habits to create well being. Fourth, we see it may not be instant, repetition and persistence are required. But the basic steps are the same. We still have to trust a higher power to do it. We still require the belief it will be done, we still need to create a clear vision of the desire, surround it with passionate emotion and launch the intention to a higher power to materialize the plan. Only in the case of Napoleon Hill is it critical to modify this process a bit. The big difference here is that Napoleon Hill says you have to get off your butt and engage in the relationships and make choices which come before. In a simple sense, you can go through steps 1 to 4 all you like about winning the Lotto but if you don't engage in the choice of buying a ticket, it ain't going to happen! So learning from the Law of Cause & Effect, when the Law of Attraction brings a choice to you, you must act on it.

So this is NOT the same as a spontaneous healing. It is a drawn out process that relies on depth of belief, perseverance, clarity, strength of passion, and faith in a higher force.

What would our steps, processes and procedures look like for this?

In an environment of well being, believe you are worthy, and positive energy:

0. Bring yourself into an altered state by imagining a peaceful place, breathing softly, and becoming present to yourself in the heart.

1. Assert your beliefs that you are worthy of your desire, you believe you can change your reality, and that the Divine Intelligence will assist you.
2. Visualize clearly in your mind a picture of the desired result.
3. Speak out stating that you are a believer in your ability to manifest your desires and ask for assistance.
4. In your imagination feel the result of the desire being completed and surround this vision with the joy and bliss of it being so.
5. With your intention send the request for the desire/visualization to be completed.
6. In your mind, connect to a higher power or the Universes to assist in the completion.
7. Feel the gratitude of completion and thank the higher power or those you have called to assist you.

Then in an environment of continued well being, faith and trust, repeat the process until you begin to see people, events, situations come before you and act on these options.

Summary Of PART THREE

Important Conclusions About Near Dying
The first conclusion is that subconscious and conscious is an intelligent field separate from the body. This consciousness that separates can see, hear, think, move, communicate, tell jokes, and retain senses regardless of distance from the body. In fact the senses are even better—heightened. It even keeps a memory of everything that was ever learned, experienced, and felt along with all of the senses.

The second is another conclusion separate from the brain and that the brain does give orders to the subconscious. The brain serves as a relay station for connecting to our bodies when we are in a conscious state of being awake.

The third conclusion is that there is something most people called God—some—angelic or Divine type entity that they met and had a telepathic experience with.

The fourth is that through this experience of total detachment from reality, many came back healed mentally or physically. Some process of Divine Intervention was encountered which changed them - some for the rest of their lives.

Important Conclusions About The Chakras
The first important conclusion is that the 7 steps that we have outlined as the way we create things comes out in the above to below functions of the chakras. The body chakra system is the key manifestor and creator of reality. To quantify this process from the top down as above so below:

1. In the Crown Chakra, we *form* a *thought*,
2. In the 3rd Eye chakra, we *see* an *image*,
3. In the Throat Chakra we *speak words*,
4. In the Heart Chakra we *feel* an *emotion*,
5. In the Solar Plexus Chakra *we create the intention to act*,
6. In the Sacral Chakra, *we engage in relations needed to assist*,
7. In the Root Chakra *we indulge in the material reality.*

The second conclusion is that understanding the chakras allows you to understand the relationship between your consciousness and your body, and to thus see your body as a map of your consciousness. It gives you a better understanding of yourself and those around you.

The third conclusion is that each of the chakras has a connection to the physical body and are monitoring subtle energies. These have specific attributes which can be positive or negative. By understanding your signature of behavior, you have a means of identifying and correcting the dysfunctions that manifest in dis-ease in the body.

The fourth conclusion is that these chakras have higher functions and abilities that are dormant. Unlike the hardwired nervous-sensory system that is sensing things more physical; the wireless chakra system is sensing via the metaphysical and therefore has a direct impact on the state of psychic abilities.

The fifth important conclusion is that each of the chakras has a vortex projecting out of the body into the auras that surround the body. These vortexes reach out perpendicular to the body axis and behave according to quantum mechanics, also are non-matter to matter concentrators, located at each chakra.

Important Conclusions About The Heart
The first important conclusion is that the heart's magnetic field is 5000 times greater than the brains. This field is a torus – like a big donut – and can reach 6-8 feet in diameter. This field can possibly reach large distances, like miles depending on the intensity and can affect other people's brain waves through quantum nonlocality. It behaves according to quantum physics.

The second conclusion is that we need to be in a coherent state to communicate, or more significantly ALLOW communications out and in! Remember the need for a feeling of love emotion with prayer or it does not allow miracles to work! This can only be done in a field of love to turn the "current" on and be in the heart-brain as opposed to the heart-brain.

The third conclusion is that heart emotions contribute heavily to stress on the brain and the stress can be either real or imagined. The end effect is the same. There is no difference. There are some 1400 reactions that occur in the body.

The fourth conclusion is that the heart has its own brain and nervous system through the ANS that does not take orders from the brain. It has its own rules for creating a toxic response from negative emotions.

The fifth conclusion is that **Coherent Heart Intelligence** is a process that increases coherence and gives a cascade of neural and biochemical events that affect virtually every organ in the body to improve clarity, mood, and communications.

The sixth conclusion is that the underlying structure of the heart field is torus that has an axis as the Vector Equilibrium, or "VE." It is the blueprint by which nature forms energy into matter. This is the only geometric form where all forces are equal and balanced. The energy lines (vectors) are of equal length and strength. They represent the energy of attraction and repulsion, like you can feel with a magnet. The VE is like the imaginable – yet invisible – mother of all the shapes and symmetries we see in the world. **Your emotions are drawers as are images with quantum signatures. Exact replication is not possible this way, only likeness.**

The seventh conclusion is that Being present to the heart brings another common practice which has to do with going inside, or being present to the heart. It is a simple practice but places your attention away from the higher interfering brainwaves of consciousness into the lower state and centering your attention to the heart energetic center. Here is the balance point of above to below, the center of the torroid, and the point of creation in the quantum soup of love - the point of singularity. It is this place of the heart brain that allows access to the singularity and the quantum soup.

The eight conclusion is a process of healing by Laskow, he offers his wisdom in four steps:

Inform yourself about what has already materialized. Telling the truth is the first step toward responsibility.

Conform to the condition by loving it rather than creating separation. Resonating with the form allows us more influence over its organization.

Unform the condition by releasing it. It is the Observers' intent that converts particulate matter to its wave form and wave back to matter.

Reform the released energy to conform to our purpose and desire, the letting go where we send our information into the universe without attachment.

The ninth conclusion is that when releasing the diseased condition there is a connection - not separation. *"When you accept and love the parts of yourself you want to reject or change, you create the opportunity to discover the positive life force behind them"* We make ourselves at One.

The tenth conclusion is in quantum, love is the glue that holds things together. It is the universal pattern of resonant energy. We can love a cancer cell to death! Hearts and brains entangle, both quantum.

The eleventh conclusion is that if you say the same thing to yourself, like I love you, I respect you, I trust you, then you are also purifying all the water in you as we are 70% water, like the planet.

Important Conclusions About The Energy Body
The first conclusion is that the Physical Body is the form that a Soul takes while incarnated in the 3rd dimension on Earth. The Physical Body consists of energy so dense that it can be felt and seen. In order to experience the lower 3rd dimension, it requires an astral body to interface with the physical body.

The second conclusion is that the Soul came to evolve through various dimensions or planes. To do this, it was given a great inventory of equipment that are the physical and energy bodies. The conscious awareness of each of these bodies, as they progress from the lower dimension of 1 to the higher spiritual dimension of 9, is the evolution. Each dimension is reflected in the energy body which opens new inventories of abilities to perceive, see, and understand increasing levels of consciousness.

The third conclusion is that the astral body is able to separate from the physical and travel without it. Since the astral is the vehicle of consciousness, it is this body which is aware, not the physical.

The fourth conclusion is that the Auras reflect the constant change in our thoughts and emotions like a monitoring system. Auric dysfunction points to evolution issues and karmic issues. This leads to the red flags of dysfunction as a Cause And Effect which inhibits the souls' evolution.

The fifth conclusion is that the enveloping Causal/Soul Body (golden orb) is the subtlest level of personal individuality, the enlivening source of life and consciousness for the current personality, all past life personalities, and all future life personalities. It is called the Higher Self.

The sixth conclusion is that the Causal/Soul Body is named Causal because it is the originating source of each personality that incarnates in each lifetime. It is the source of your personality, causing it to be and exist. When your personality ends, the essence of you is absorbed back into the Causal Body. It is the first level of your individuality that is relatively immortal as the Causal Body exists for many millions of years, during your journey as a human through many incarnations or lifetimes.

The seventh conclusion is that the physical brain is a relay station, translating emotional, mental, and spiritual events and information into neuro-electrochemical events and information. Neurochemicals and associated brain processes are simply channel selectors for various states of consciousness. All states of consciousness exist independent of the physical body. This relay station works in both directions: spiritual, mental, or emotional states trigger neuro-electrochemical events in the brain.

The seventh conclusion is that the goal of the Soul is to purify the astral layer, clear and raise the vibration of the etheric and physical bodies, incarnate more of the light body and get its structures and energy centers balanced and functioning properly. Through this the spirit is able to incarnate into matter.

The eighth conclusion is that in the same way that arteries carry blood, meridians carry energy, often referred to as chi, qi or prana. Meridians are our body's "energy bloodstream": they bring vitality and balance, remove energy blockages, stagnations and imbalances, adjust metabolism and determine the speed and form of cellular change.

The ninth conclusion is that major meridians of the body are responsible for nourishing their corresponding organ and the other organs around them, fueling and feeding them with energy. Each meridian plays a specific and integral role in their organ's health. Deficient meridian energy and excess meridian energy are both problematic and can cause damage to that meridian's organ system.

The tenth conclusion is that when energy flowing through the meridians becomes blocked or stagnant, or, when too much energy is overwhelming a meridian these acupuncture points can be accessed to clear blockages and remove unwanted excess or stagnant energy. Often times acupuncture and acupressure techniques are used to relieve energetic imbalances in the meridians; the ancient Chinese practice of Qi Gong is often employed as well.

The eleventh conclusion is that MerKaBa is a spinning structure of light similar to the chakras. It is similar in that when spinning properly it works as an inter-dimensional gateway so that higher consciousness may incarnate into the physical body. It is the linking together of the mind, heart, and physical body in a specific geometrical ratio and at a critical speed that produces the merkaba The word "Mer" denotes counter-rotating fields of light, "Ka" Spirit, and "Ba" body, or reality. It is the image through which all things were created, and that image is around your body in a geometrical set of patterns.

The twelfth conclusion is that we too are creators and our impulse is to incarnate into matter and create within it. The only way for consciousness to create with the Material Forces from the dimensions below, is to enter into it. The incarnation of spirit into matter is the way the entire Universe is created.

The thirteenth conclusion is that besides communicating with parts of your self the Column also opens up possibilities of communication with many non-physical and multi-dimensional beings throughout the Universe.

The fourteenth conclusion is that the Chakras located within the light body have a purpose to create a gateway into higher or lower dimensions of consciousness. The light body is made up of many dimensions of light but to incarnate higher consciousness (spirit) into this light body a certain type of vortex needs to be created. These vortexes are the chakras and each one is a gateway to a certain aspect of higher consciousness.

The fifteenth and perhaps most important conclusion is the revelation and awareness of the Buddhic/Christic body. The mark of someone who has truly attained this state of consciousness on a continual basis is that they are never oriented towards their individuality. They will never or rarely speak about their individuality. They are totally selfless in their actions and desire nothing of a personal nature because they reside in the source of fulfillment, in continual intense bliss. Also, their expression is utterly harmless and overflowing with compassion. The Buddhic vehicle has its own level of five senses. These are: Comprehension (Buddhic hearing of 4 sounds: personal, that of others, that of one's soul group, that of the planetary entity that is one's origin), Healing (Buddhic feeling that facilitates realization of the manner in which to heal and cause wholeness), Divine Vision (Buddhic sight that allows one to see the divine in all), Intuition (Buddhic taste, whereby one's essence is recognized in and under all forms), and Idealism (Buddhic smell, the ability to sense the ideal). **It is this awareness and this state in others that opens the healing conduit.**

Important Conclusions About The Brain
The first conclusion is that the brain performs a multitude of sensory, vital and physical tasks that it learns in order to guarantee survival. It is a complex information processing and control system. The brain is dedicated to controlling how the body functions and adapts to its environment. The nervous system, the senses, the mobility, the internal functioning are automated environmental stimuli-response systems.

The second conclusion is that the brain is not in charge, as it takes directives from the subconscious, cell membranes and heart.

The third conclusion is that the brain is not like a binary computer, it is more analog computer designed to sense and respond so as to create a database of perception response functions. It holds its own database to remember and execute these on conscious and subconscious command. A copy is held in the master disc drive of subconscious mind.

The fourth conclusion that the brain is the holographic processor that creates your reality through the meaning, composition, and representation from its local database as its memory and the interpretation of the senses of your lower body.

The fifth conclusion is that while brains are reduced to a lower meditative state, an evoked potential in one induces an evoked potential in the other at distances apart. They "entangle" in the meditative state so one can influence another's brain being quantum in nature.

Important Conclusions About Quantum
The first conclusion is that experiments have demonstrated that the worldwide view implied by classical physics is wrong. Not just slightly incorrect in minor ways but fundamentally wrong in just the right way to support the reality of psi.

The second is that the Universe is a giant hologram containing both matter and consciousness as a single field—a kind of image or construct created in part by the human mind.

The third conclusion is the chakra field behaves holographically as do the energy fields of the body and that these fields were non-local—could be measured anywhere on the body.

The fourth conclusion is EMG's show people who have psychic abilities and can heal are 400-800cps. People who can go into a trance and channel other information operate in a narrow band of 800-900cps to receive information. There is a relationship between the vibrational frequency of the body's electromagnetic system and specific psychic abilities.

The fifth conclusion is that our reality is all a hologram which our brain, a hologram itself as the filtering device, uses senses to make it real.

The sixth conclusion is that we are quantum energy. Everything is energy—including the mind and this thing called consciousness.

The seventh is that at the point where our consciousness enters into seeing something, the effect is to materialize solidity into reality. It is called forth by intention and the electrons choose from a realm of infinite possibilities the probability or patterns of bits that we limit it to by our observation. Consciousness materializes the atoms by changing the state from invisible to visible—waves to atoms. What we see around us has been transformed that way.

The eighth conclusion is that if you unlock the powers to interact with the Zero Point Energy Field, you are linked to the indivisible force that connects everything. That must be that Divine Intelligence operating system.

The ninth conclusion is that the process of intent—activated by the Observer Effect using consciousness creates a morphic field of energy. Morphic means having a specific shape and form. Thoughts have morphic fields, like a magnetic field.

The tenth conclusion is research shows that we change the reality by watching it. We are connected with everything from cells in the body to atoms of our world. Our experience of consciousness expressed as feeling and belief is doing the connecting—we are participants.

The eleventh conclusion is that that intention at the 3rd chakra enfolded with the positive heart energy at the 4th chakra is the powerhouse of above to below reality creation system.

The twelfth conclusion is that the evolution of the Light Body-Being is stunted because it evolves to the second level of self-awareness as ego-intellect by choosing limiting negative energies and limits its final entry into the heart brain and the Zeropoint quantum field. Nor does it evolve according to the Soul's and Light Body's purpose.

Important Conclusions About Morphic Fields
The first conclusion is that experiments to test for the spatial aspects of morphic fields imply a kind of non-locality.

The second conclusion is that organelles in cells, cells in tissues, tissues in organs, organs in organisms, organisms in social groups behave within morphic fields that gives each whole its characteristic properties and interconnects and coordinates the constituent parts.

The third conclusion is that Morphic fields are located within and around the systems they organize. Like quantum fields, they work probabilistically.

The fourth conclusion is that morphogenetic fields in which the endpoints toward which a system develops are defined as **attractors.** In the branch of mathematics known as dynamics, attractors represent the limits toward which dynamical systems are drawn. They provide a scientific way of thinking about ends, purposes, goals, or intentions. All morphic fields contain attractors.

The fifth conclusion is that **Morphic resonance** involves the influence of like upon like, the influence of patterns of activity on subsequent similar patterns of activity, an influence that passes through or across space and time from past to present. These influences do not fall off with distance in space or time. The greater the degree of similarity; the greater the influence of morphic resonance.

Important Conclusions About Holograms
The first conclusion is that a hologram is effectively a permanent record of what something looks like seen from any angle. Every point in a hologram catches light waves that travel from every point in the object. That means wherever you look at a hologram you see exactly how light would have arrived at that point if you'd been looking at the real object.

The second conclusion is that the brain mathematically construct objective reality by interpreting frequencies that are projections from another dimension beyond space and time. What is out there is a vast ocean of waves and frequencies and the brain converts these.

The third conclusion is that without the brain we would experience nothing except an interference pattern. We would not be a body, we would be a blur of interference pattern enfold (implicate) of the cosmic hologram (unfolded as explicate order as us. We are part of the hologram looking at the hologram. The brain cannot distinguish between out there and what it believes to be out there

The fourth conclusion is that every action starts from intention. Imagination is already the creator of form and has all the movements needed to carry and it affects the body from subtle levels until it manifests. So to the brain, imagination and reality are indistinguishable and images in the mind can ultimately manifest as realities in the physical body.

The fifth conclusion is that 50% of what we see is information from the eye. 50% is pieced together out of expectation of what the world should be like. The brain edits and manipulates by the temporal lobes before being presented to the visual cortex. The brain interprets from the frequency of interference patterns in the implicate order.

The sixth conclusion is that everything in the universe is actually experienced from inside your Self, and you and it are intimately interwoven together in the fabric of Life. Hence, the so-called external, physical cosmos, with its trillions of stars and galaxies —ALL of it can only be seen from WITHIN — in the inner holographic theater and plate of the Observer.

The seventh conclusion is that the photon as the smallest unit in the universe has a torroid field the same as the Universe, earth, human, and cell, each a holographic fractal of the other.

The eighth conclusion is that we must get back on the Soul's purpose in order to see the unseen and understand the misunderstood within the Astral and Spiritual planes.

Important Conclusions About Computers
The first conclusion is that the true workhorse of the computer is the transistor, a two-way switch of on-off that produces the reality created by computers.

The second conclusion is that the process of changing a program in a computer requires a compiler and the ability to use a programming language. Once the program is rewritten, it is compiled through the operating system to be coded into machine understandable language and the old program is replaced.

The third conclusion is that the evolution of computers from binary to quantum, to trinary reflects a possible transition to the way the human subtle system surrounding the heart chakra actually creates reality.

Important Conclusions About Human Computers

First conclusion is that the workhorse of the human computer system is the cell membrane that has effector - receptor switches similar to the on-off binary system. They are similar to the silicon chips with the on-off transistors. These states determine the type of programs that are to be loaded into memory as behavior. However, the similarity ends here as cells make decisions, organize, and communicate, chips do not.

The second conclusion is that cells are programmable from outside the cell. Data is entered into the computer or cell via the membrane receptors acting like an input device or keyboard that triggers effector proteins that then actions cell/computer CPU/effector proteins that convert environmental information into the behavioral language of biology.

The third conclusion is that the environment that one creates through perception and diet have a profound effect on the overall health as they cause the cells to create a cascade of flight or fight reactions that deter growth and render the immune system dysfunctional. Again this points to the need for well being. -

The fourth conclusion is that in order to create new programs, or modify old programs in subconscious, the key is to understand that the Operating System is Divine Intelligence, the Compiler is the Heart, and the language used to recode is Love.

The New Supporting Evidence

In our presentation, we have seen that there are many methods that work. We understand that these do not work all the time, but nevertheless, our quest has been to determine the common tangible and intangible processes when they do work. Our quest has also been to seek reasons why these have worked so as to create a most likely set of steps under the heading of Setting, Process, and Assistance that gives us the best possibilities of success. The quest has been, once having a better idea on what these healers have chosen certain steps, to create our own steps, and to launch a lifestyle that would be conducive to supporting that belief.

In this regard, we can look at some simple fundamental variables:

A belief that one is worthy, that they can be healed, faith in the Healer and a surrender/trust that it shall be done by a Higher Power, one has set the stage for a miracle to occur. From the Healers point of view, love and compassion without hidden motive is crucial.

1. BELIEF: The recipient's belief system must be one that believes in the healing process and is aligned with the subconscious belief.

2. STATE: The recipient must be in a programmable state where the brain does not interfere and the subconscious mind says it is ready to accept a new program. This is through guided meditation, regression, becoming present to lower the brain wave interference of the conscious mind.

3. ENVIRONMENT: The process of setting the environment whether a ritual, a gathering, or a process by the healer is important in creating the focus and attention for the intention of healing and reprogramming to take place. This creates a morphic field of energy that enforces the belief so as to allow the reprogramming.

4. WELL BEING: The internal environment of the recipient and the healer is one of love, forgiveness, compassion, peace and harmony as the morphic field of energy around and in the body. The elimination of stress is needed here so as to better entrain the body and mind into a higher state of vibration.

5. FOCUS: By triggering the intention, the issue is identified or located so as to direct the process of healing to that location. At this point, the clear vision of the correct state becomes the focus as surrounded by the joy of its completion. This through words, prayer, emotions, or guidance creates the directive to correct the issue.

6. HIGHER POWER: Engagement in a Higher Power or Guides is the necessary process as some form of Divine engagement to assist in the process of correcting the issue and instigating the subconscious reprogramming.

7: MANIFESTATION: The healer, as higher authority and the conduit for some form of divine intervention that is triggered to actually replace the program in the subconscious mind. The process of reprogramming convinces the brain and the cellular community to respond by instituting a new or old program from DNA held within the nucleus of the cells.

Now we have many other conclusions that add to the above, all to assist in understanding why these miracles do occur and give some insight on how these processes work. As a summary, these key conclusions are as follows:

- Consciousness is a separate quantum energy
- Divine Intervention is a crucial part of all miracles
- Chakras have vortexes that reach out into the quantum field for the purpose of dispersing and congealing antimatter to matter
- Auras, chakras, meridians, heart field are quantum in nature
- The chakra well being flags tell one where dysfunctions lie
- The key to higher human evolution resides in the chakra functions and DNA that are undeveloped

- The development of the human to the stage 3 awareness of Light Body and awareness to the Energy Body is seldom attained
- Light Bogy overlay is a connection between physical and non physical
- Heart field is quantum; a field extending out to possible long distances
- The heart field produces energies as attractors to the quantum field
- Universe is giant hologram
- Our reality is a personal hologram within the giant hologram that is created by the brain
- Brain is hardwired input-response learning system to optimise survival
- Brain is the interpreter of holograms on plate inside you
- Being present to heart is center of zeropoint
- Heart has its own brain, emotions are drawers of quantum signatures
- Heart torroid is quantum and attracts energy
- Heart center and need for coherence
- Morphic resonance to attract likeness in the quantum field
- Chakra process of above to below and higher functions
- Power of Love is the conduit to speak with the quantum field
- Morphic fields have memory that tune and attract to endpoints
- We are quantum energy
- Power of intention can change matter
- The workhorse of the binary computer is the transistor which is like the cell membrane in the human system.
- The evolution of trinary computers begins to simulate the quantum process in the human light body system
- The cell membrane is a brain where decisions about reactions in behavior are made
- The means to reprogramming subconscious is through the heart compiler using the language of love to be submitted to the Higher Intelligence Operating system.

These are by no means all of the points that help support why these wealth and health processes work. And in the background, one can begin to understand what the most important variables are when they don't work.

All of these add to the credibility that these procedures are right, despite the fact that the reasons have not been clearly understood. We begin to understand what the intangible variables are and why they have a bearing on the success. What is important is that we are not trying to modify or change the systems and processes that work. What we are trying to understand is why they do work, and how they work.

We are ready to assemble our program code.

37

THE DIVINE PROGRAMMER HEALTH MIRACLES

"One requires openness to making profound changes, have a willingness to embark on the inner worl, and not relinquish a belief and faith that anything can be healed."
Ed Rychkun

The Programmer's Health Code

What we want to highlight here is that we have not attempted to take issue with what these Healers do. They all have systems that work. It is accepted that this is not all the time because there are other vague or uncontrolled factors that may influence the results; and even undo the results. Our focus has been on what works and we have presented a book full of evidence why and how they do.

So it would be our plan now to create a simple set of steps like a program that we can get the Operating System of **Divine Intelligence** to create or attract a new reality. It would be the **Heart** that we would recompile, using the language of **Love** and this gives instructions to the **Subconscious** disc drive to update the programs and to run the effector programs from the blueprints to correct the issue. The brain would thus coordinate the shift. As we have seen, the best way would be to send love to the area of issue so that it would be the healing mechanism. And because this is in the quantum field of no time, that image of the new condition enfolded by the heart energy of love would entangle with the old and collapse in the new reality.

Because we have another confirmation from the As Above, So Below process of the chakras, we are going to divide our systems and process table into 7 parts of what we determined as Process. These you may recall from before.

First, you must come from a place of belief that you are worthy and believe in miracles. Then the Healer:

0. Creates a setting where the patient is in an altered state
1. Brings into thought the belief of being healed
2. Brings into vision the image of the issue which is to be corrected
3. Communicates to find the source of the issue
4. Brings in the power of emotion to surround the corrected desire
5. Launches the intention to correct the issue
6. Surrenders control of the correction to a higher power
7. Allows the Higher Power to materialize the correction

Setting The Healing Environment

In order to cover the many different systems we have looked at, it is useful to encapsulate what these Healers say about the environmental setting that they have determined is most common for a successful healing.

	SUMMARY OF REQUIRED ENVIRONMENTAL SETTING FOR HEALTH MIRACLES	
Setting	Have a belief and trust as it is essential	RT
Setting	Be in the higher vibration of love	RT
Setting	Become present to the body (lower brain waves)	RT
Setting	Have a trust and belief that healing will occur	AT
Setting	Hold the acceptance of problem and surrender to the issue	LM
Setting	Have a strong belief and faith in healing	LM
Setting	Have a strength and desire, willingness to embark	LM
Setting	Believe you are worthy	CM
Setting	Set the preconditions of self healing and love	CM
Setting	Believe in a state of miracle minded readiness	TS
Setting	Expect a positive outcome	TS
Setting	Believe you are part of the whole which is divine	IL
Setting	Enter a place of love and compassion	JG
Setting	Go through rooms to raise belief pictures, videos, demos	JG
Setting	Have a belief and trust in the truth or trustworthiness of God	OR
Setting	Have a faith in future outcome and through a supreme being	OR
Setting	Eliminate limiting beliefs as belief is a powerful form of intention	AD
Setting	Believe that a higher source will answer your prayers	GB
Setting	Ascertain in belief in the Creator, understand desire for healing	AM
Setting	Inform of assistance of Creators energies	AM
Setting	Validate that the belief in healing is strong and not an issue	ER
Setting	Get out of the old belief box	RB

We see here that belief, trust, love, acceptance, surrender, faith, desire, worthy, miracle minded, positive outcome, compassion, and trustworthiness of a Higher Force is repeated over and over in different ways. So in view of what we have learned, we can suggest the type of environmental setting that we should be in.

Well being is a natural setting to be in because we have heard how the cells, the brain, the heart all can be fooled because they do not know the difference between imagined and "real". We have seen that negative thoughts and emotions are toxic environmental stimulants that chain react affecting the body in a cascade of negative problems. We have presented the mind and body plans to reduce those 60% toxic thoughts and the toxic food that invades the system.

A belief that one is worthy, that they can be healed, faith in the Healer and a surrender/trust that it shall be done by a Higher Power, one has set the stage for a miracle to occur. From the Healers point of view, love and compassion without hidden motive is crucial. In this case you are going to be the Healer so you must assume the role of the Higher Authority so you must believe you can heal yourself.

Love is the common catalyst to all the systems we have reviewed. It we believe is the computer language that is written in the form of forgiveness, unity, compassion, gratitude, faith and trust. It is a surrender to that which has occurred and a process of uniting with it to entangle within the quantum field a new possibility to be collapsed into reality.

Higher State is something that is repeated over and over. Those who have succeeded in being the healing catalyst are obviously more aware of the Buhhdic/Christic state than the average human. This body eventually transmutes, heals, and resolves all human problems with the power of love, unity, and wisdom. The Buddhic/Christic body contains the archetype of perfection for the human being. The embodiment of this archetype, the fusion of the personality and the Buddhic/Christic body is the goal of human evolution.

The mark of someone who has truly attained this state of consciousness on a continual basis is that they are never oriented towards their individuality. They will never or rarely speak about their individuality. They are totally selfless in their actions and desire nothing of a personal nature because they reside in the source of fulfillment, in continual intense bliss. Also, their expression is utterly harmless and overflowing with compassion.

Engaging In The Healing Process

This process is common to all of the Healers whether it is regression, hypnosis, ritual, meeting the healer; it is one of getting by the conscious mind to be in some form of Altered State.

0	Bring patient into a hypnotic state	AT
0	Focus on present, prayer, meditation	LM
0	Engage in ritual & community to bear witness focus energy	LM
0	Turn inward into a meditative state altered state of consciousness	TS
0	Get into a quiet still mode together	RB
0	Cleansing room to meditate with a clinic medium	JG
0	Become present by becoming aware of self as in a meditative state	ER
0	Ask to place the intellect on the shelf to open to subconscious	ER

Because we have determined that the best place to be in this altered State is in the powerhouse of the heart, the largest morphic field, the balance center, the center of love, and the center of creation, our process would begin by:

Being present to the heart Here we go inside, or being present to the heart. It is a simple practice but places your attention away from the higher interfering brainwaves of consciousness into the lower state and centering your attention to the heart energetic center. Here is the balance point of above to below, the center of the torroid, and the point of creation in the quantum soup of love - the point of singularity. In quantum, love is the glue that holds things together. It is the universal pattern of resonant energy. This is why we feel that the computer equal to the Compiler is the Heart as it has the greatest power and largest field of the body's energetic system. This is where the Code is written in the language of Love to get assistance from the Higher Power.

"Now as the Transformer, you must get into the Zero Point zone of the quantum vortex of new possibilities. How? It is a process of "dropping to the heart." This is where the center of Grace—the Divine in you—resides."

Richard Bartlett,

Although all of the methods presented work, we will attempt to align the process to the natural stage of above to below of the chakra system and incorporate what is most common with regards to attaining coherence and well being during the process.

1. THOUGHT At the top of the "Above" is thought initiated in the Crown Chakra. In the altered state, it is here that the scene is set to affirm your beliefs as you say. *"I believe in healing miracles. I Believe I am worthy. I believe I can heal myself, and I believe in a Higher Power that will assist me."* As you are in an altered state, in control of the conscious mind, you have a direct access to the subconscious. Here it is best to affirm to it what you believe in case it has some other ideas about sabotaging your process.

| 1 | Bring forward the thoughts of your desire so your gladness be full | GB |
| 1 | Communicate to understand the nature and need for healing and assistance | AM |

"Thoughts have morphic fields, as does the consciousness of you or a group. Once you believe and embody something, you link into a power grid of the morphic field. That is where healing occurs as you are in resonance with it and into an enormous database of universal energy."

Richard Bartlett

2. VISION Create a clear vision in your 3rd eye chakra of the desired result. In your conscious mind, create a clear picture of what the desired result would be.

2	Visualize clearly the outcome in the mind's eye	CM
2	Have precise visualizations of the issue with strong intent	AD
2	Visualize, positive emotionally charged new outcome	AD
2	Create a clear visualization of that which is desired	GB

3. SPEAK From the Throat Chakra speak out stating that you are asking for Higher Divine Intelligence assistance to manifest your vision. Here you are well aware of the issue and are going to rely on the Divine Intelligence to determine a solution, rather than regression to find the source.

3	Probe deep into subconscious memories	AT
3	Regress patient to time and event of issue	AT
3	Understand the issue and why it occurred, results	AT
3	Enter realm of inner healer through mind and spirit	LM
3	Synchronize conscious and subconscious thought	AD
3	Empower action with 2 prayers for releasement and sacred space	AM
3	Bring into focus the issues that require attention	IL
3	Focus on the issue	JG
3	Ask if a change is required and what it is as in hypnotism	RB
3	Ask to place the dysfunction on an imaginary clipboard	RB
3	Ask to identify energies that are not feeling right in the area of issue	ER
3	Scan back in time to when the energy block was created	ER
3	Open communication with energy block to solicit cooperation to leave	ER

4. HEART EMOTION As we drop into the Heart Chakra, this is where you put the vision into the quantum field. With the vision of the desired result clearly in your mind, bring in the emotion of your total being vibrating in a state of bliss and joy. Form a clear picture of this as your gladness is full and be surrounded by that joy. Linger here in a field of total peace, love and harmony as you place this vision into the morphic field of the heart. This is where you become totally aware of your Buddhic/Christic Self.

4	Breath in a rhythmic count to hold resonance high	RT
4	Enter a space of higher vibration-love and intent	RT
4	Enter a holistic connectedness	AT
4	Bring client into higher frequency vibration	AT
4	Hold the space of love and compassion at soul level	AT
4	Delete ego interference and feel love	TS
4	Align to positive resonance vibrations to assist	AD
4	Go inside and do it in a space of love	IL
4	Enter a state of peace, love, compassion without hidden motives	GB
4	Enfold vision with strong positive emotion to envelope the desire	GB
4	Drop into the heart as the divine in you (throw a pebble in water)	RB
4	Enter into quantum state of waves on the pond and all possibilities	RB
4	Enter a sacred space and harmonizing energies/rays to facilitate	AM

5 FOCUS AND INTENT At the Solar Plexus Chakra we initiate the process of intention energy for shifting the condition. Because we are centered on love, we can "love something to death" and we would launch the intent of loving the issue rather than creating separation. Resonating with the issue allows us more influence over its organization. At this stage one would call upon their Higher self, divine Intelligence, or whatever you feel comfortable with to launch the intent. *"I as my Higher Self ask for the releasement, cleansing and healing of (my issue)   call upon Divine Intelligence to assist me. I release that which is not perfection and ask it to be replaced with the vision I have enfolded in my heart."*

5	Focus on and enfold issue area with hands	RT
5	Intend healing for a better purpose as divine intervention	RT
5	Imagine healing energy through you to your hands	RT
5	See a beam of healing light connect	RT
5	Create a morphic field with the Great Spirit as healer	LM
5	Use free will to change or solve created problems	TS
5	Invite change and launch intention to heal, merge into reality	AD
5	Send a petition to divine counterpart to erase memories of Cause	IL

5	Engage in a trance stage to request Higher Assistance of God	JG
5	Engage in a ritual audience to raise the awareness and energy field	OR
5	Lay on of hands to simulate biblical precedent of Jesus	OR
5	Place left hand onto a mindless point of attraction	RB
5	Mentally link the two to enter entangled oneness	RB
5	Extract the energy block and release all that created it	ER
5	Go back and rescan area to see results (issues) as done	ER
5	Meet John to determine mode of treatment	JG
5	Command negative energies to heal in the name of Christ Love	AM

6. HIGHER POWER At the next Sacral Chakra dedicated to relationships, the next step is the request for Higher Assistance so as to recompile the program created in the Heart. In looking back into the Healers' processes under what we noted as Assist in the table below, we find that there are many different words used to summon this assistance. Divine, Spirit, Higher Power, Spirits, Guides, God, Source Creator, and Source are used but they all obviously work. The key, however, is that regardless of what you use, you must believe this Higher Power does have the power, and you must summon assistance.

This is in two parts as we first summarize what out Healers said about getting Assistance for the Divine Intervention.

\multicolumn{3}{c}{SUMMARY OF REQUIRED DIVINE ASSISTANCE REQUESTS FOR HEALTH MIRACLES}		
Assist	Connect with Divine assistance	RT
Assist	Allow higher realm spirit guides to assist	AT
Assist	Connect to Great Spirit and higher sacred processes	LM
Assist	Surrender and trust in a Higher Power	CM
Assist	Tune resonance through to Source and quantum energy	AD
Assist	Gateway is through divine and subconscious via belief	IL
Assist	Allow healing to be done by guidance through Spirits	JG
Assist	Issue a prayer to address god or spirit for assistance	OR
Assist	Ask the Divine to fulfill the desire as in ask and it shall be given	GB
Assist	Place second hand on 2nd attracted area as being guided by Divine	RB
Assist	Connect to the heart mind of quantum space and Source Creator	ER
Assist	Request higher powers to cleanse cells of memories and conditions	ER
Assist	Allow Divinity to erase errors in subconscious as the Effect	IL
Assist	Tap into the inner Divine Guide, look for higher good	TS
Assist	Allow biological Divine Intelligence to heal as it knows	RT
Assist	Ask Team of Light to cleanse and clear with hands over individual	AM
Assist	Ask Creator/Creatrix pure love energies to flow from head to feet	AM
Assist	Allow Mother Earth to assist by asking and sending her love	AM

This part of the process is where the condition is released and you surrender to the Higher Power so it does what it needs to do. We effectively are entangling the two issues and desire so as to allow the new possibility of the emotionalized desire to collapse into a new reality, by releasing it. It is the Observers intent lanced in the previous step that converts particulate matter to its wave form and wave back to matter, the released energy to conform to our purpose and desire. This is the letting go where we send our information into the universe without attachment. This process releases the diseased condition through a connection, not separation. *"When you accept and love the parts of yourself you want to reject or change, you create the opportunity to discover the positive life force behind them".* We make ourselves at One.

6	Delete or rewrite the memory with the mind	AT
6	Allow the inner Healer to do the work	LM
6	Launch prayer to direct energy as pure love communication channel	CM
6	Create a connection to Source	CM
6	Faith trust love forgive have higher power	AD
6	Zero out negative memories and energies by focus and reflection	IL
6	State I love you, I am sorry, please forgive me for this issue, thank you	IL
6	Engage in healing current to cleanse fear, cause of problems	JG
6	Create a conclusive slap, shout, situation to conclude the miracle	OR
6	Wait for an energy shift in client to collapse new possibility	RB
6	Assist in the removal shoveling off stagnated energies	AM
6	Show pure love intention to bring new DNA energies, purging old	AM
6	Allow purging of old thoughts, residues, spells, contracts, fears, hatred, discordant energies	AM

Here is where you say *"I love you, I am sorry, please forgive me for creating this issue or dysfunction, please forgive me, thank you."* It is here that you use hands, beams of light, or whatever feels right to begin the process of shifting reality.

7. MATERIAL MANIFESTATION At the 7th Chakra dedicated to the materialization, we hold on to our truth of completion, with an unfettered faith and trust in the Higher Power. It is fulfilled by the powerful feeling of gratitude that surrounds the vision of completion.

7	Believe the prayer has already been answered	GB
7	Show gratitude that your joy is full	GB
7	Offer a closing prayer giving thanks for the assistance	AM

The Suggested Program

As a Divine Programmer you have compiled a new program of believe and rejuvenation process. The Heart as the Compiler, Love as the Language was petition or sent to the Divine Intelligence to reprogram the Subconscious and then run the program to get the cells and the brain to complete their work. If you can believe the part on holograms and our reality being an illusion, you would have also shifted non-matter into matter within the world of quantum science.

It is suggested that these steps become a basis for what you develop as your own procedure. You may want to follow some of the systems presented. You can take what feels proper and develop your own style. It is suggested that you pay attention to checking out your beliefs and working on small issues. If they do not work, understand that it is because something is still not right, and it is the repetitive process that will entrench beliefs and strength of conviction and intent. Strong positive emotion and intent in a field of well being and love is crucial. In that respect, it would be advisable to launch the 30 day Mind and Body programs and practice your healing process until it works, in faith and trust that it will.

Most important, get in touch with the heart mind and pay attention to what awareness to your Buddhic/Christic body means:

The mark of someone who has truly attained this state of consciousness on a continual basis is that they are never oriented towards their individuality. They will never or rarely speak about their individuality. They are totally selfless in their actions and desire nothing of a personal nature because they reside in the source of fulfillment, in continual intense bliss. Also, their expression is utterly harmless and overflowing with compassion. The Buddhic vehicle has its own level of five senses. These are: Comprehension (Buddhic hearing of 4 sounds: personal, that of others, that of one's soul group, that of the planetary entity that is one's origin), Healing (Buddhic feeling that facilitates realization of the manner in which to heal and cause wholeness), Divine Vision (Buddhic sight that allows one to see the divine in all), Intuition (Buddhic taste, whereby one's essence is recognized in and under all forms), and Idealism (Buddhic smell, the ability to sense the ideal). **It is this awareness and this state in others that opens the healing conduit.**

38

THE DIVINE PROGRAMMER WEALTH MIRACLES

"Miracle, miracle where do I find where you hide within my mind"
Ed Rychkun

The Programmer's Wealth Code

In our normal reality to create a million dollars selling chairs:

From a position of belief we are worthy and able; we attain faith and trust in our self to complete the plan then:

1. We form the thought of making a million dollars
2. We form a vision of a company that sells chairs
3. We make a business plan of the company and product
4. We get emotionally excited about the plan/company
5. We launch the intent to execute the business plan
6. We engage others, money, etc. to make it happen
7. We create the chairs/company that enters our reality

In an environment of well being, believe you are worthy, and with positive energy:

0. Bring yourself into an altered state by imagining a peaceful place, breathing softly, and becoming present to yourself in the heart.
1. Assert your beliefs that you are worthy of your desire, you believe you can change your reality, and that the Divine Intelligence will assist you.
2. Visualize clearly in your mind a picture of the desired result.
3. Speak out stating that you are a believer in your ability to manifest your desires and ask for assistance.

4. In your imagination feel the result of the desire being completed and surround this vision with the joy and bliss of it being so.
5. With your intention send the request for the desire/visualization to be completed.
6. In your mind, connect to a higher power to assist in the completion.
7. Feel the gratitude of completion and thank the higher power or those you have called to assist you.

Then in an environment of continued well being, faith and trust, repeat the process until you begin to see people, events, situations come before you and act on these options.

Setting The Wealth Environment

In order to cover the many different systems we have looked at, it is useful to encapsulate what these Wealth gurus say about the environmental setting that they have determined is most common for a successful manifestation.

Setting	Have self confidence, definitiveness, habits of saving, initiative,	NH
Setting	Have imagination, passion, and enthusiasm	NH
Setting	Show self control, pleasing personality, accurate thinking, concentration	NH
Setting	Know cooperation, profiting by failure, tolerance, harmonize	NH
Setting	Engage in meditation, proper foods, avoid low energies, awareness empowering relations	WD
Setting	Create strong habits, open your heart, develop wisdom, surrender to a bigger force	WD
Setting	Banish doubt, allow God to handle you problems, say yes to life	WD
Setting	Clear out all limiting beliefs	JV
Setting	Believe you are deserving and worthy, take action to do something	JV
Setting	Give money away so you can receive, support a cause of good will, give from the heart	JV
Setting	Know what you do not want, do what you love, join a group with similar minds	JV
Setting	Believe you are a creator, anything is possible, purpose joy, relax into well being	JH
Setting	Good feelings are good reality, eliminate any limits or negativity	JH
Setting	Believe you attract reality, your are energy, what you focus on you attract	JK
Setting	Raise vibrations: meditate, be joyful, breathe, nap, choose positive thoughts	JK

We see here that belief, trust, love, acceptance, surrender, faith, desire, worthy, miracle minded, positive outcome, compassion, and trustworthiness of a Higher Force is repeated over and over in different ways. So in view of what we have learned, we can suggest the type of environmental setting that we should be in.

Well being is a natural setting to be in because we have heard how the cells, the brain, the heart all can be fooled because they do not know the difference between imagined and "real". We have seen that negative thoughts and emotions are toxic environmental stimulants that chain react affecting the body in a cascade of negative problems. We have presented the mind and body plans to reduce those 60% toxic thoughts and the toxic food that invades the system.

A belief that one is worthy, that they can change our reality, faith in the Higher Power and a trust that it shall be done by a Higher Power, one has set the stage for a shift to occur. From the Gurus point of view, love and compassion without hidden motive is crucial. In this case you are going to be the reality changer so you must assume the role of the Higher Authority so you must believe you can be the facilitator yourself.

Love is the common catalyst to all the systems we have reviewed. It, we believe is the computer language that is written in the form of forgiveness, unity, compassion, gratitude and faith and trust. It is a surrender to a higher power to bring your desires to you, to manifest from the quantum field a new possibility to be collapsed into reality.

Engaging In The Wealth Creation Process

This process is common to all of the Gurus processes. It is one that the desires go out into the morphic fields to attract likeness. That means the altered state takes you into the heart, the center of the quantum soup at Zeropoint. Because we have determined that the best place to be in this altered State is in the powerhouse of the heart, the largest morphic field, the balance center, the center of love, and the center of creation, our process would begin by:

Being present to the heart Here we go inside, or being present to the heart. It is a simple practice but places your attention away from the higher interfering brainwaves of consciousness into the lower state and centering your attention to the heart energetic center. Here is the balance point of above to below, the center of the torroid, and the point of creation in the quantum soup of love - the point of singularity. In quantum, love is the glue that holds things together. It is the universal pattern of resonant energy. This is why we feel that the computer equal to the Compiler is the Heart as it has the greatest power and largest field of the body's energetic system. This is where the Code is written in the language of Love to get assistance from the Higher Power.

"Now as the Transformer, you must get into the Zero Point zone of the quantum vortex of new possibilities. How? It is a process of "dropping to the heart." This is where the center of Grace—the Divine in you—resides."

Richard Bartlett,

Although all of the methods presented work, we will attempt to align the process to the natural stage of above to below of the chakra system and incorporate what is most common with regards to attaining coherence and well being during the process.

1. THOUGHT At the top of the "Above" is thought initiated in the Crown Chakra. In the altered state, it is here that the scene is set to affirm your beliefs as you say. *"I believe in changing my reality. I Believe I am worthy of my desires. I believe I am the creator of my life, and I believe in a Higher Power that will assist me."* As you are in an altered state, in control of the conscious mind, you have a direct access to the subconscious. Here it is best to affirm to it what you believe in case it has some other ideas about sabotaging your process.

1	Fix your mind on the exact amount of money or the final desire	NH
1	Determine what you intend to give in return	NH
1	Establish a definite date for completion	NH
1	Relax you mind into a relaxed state	JH
1	Be sure about what you want	JH

"Thoughts have morphic fields, as does the consciousness of you or a group. Once you believe and embody something, you link into a power grid of the morphic field. That is where healing occurs as you are in resonance with it and into an enormous database of universal energy."

Richard Bartlett

2. VISION Create a clear vision in your 3rd eye chakra of the desired result. In your conscious mind, create a clear picture of what the desired result would be.

2	Get clear on what you want	JV
2	Visualize your desire	JH
2	Create images in your mind over and over	JK
2	Visualize your desire	JK

3. COMMUNICATE Affirm out loud to the heart and the Universe what you desire in simple concise statements. Be clear and concise, aligned with the energy of your vision.

3	Create a definite plan for carrying out the desire	NH
3	Write a clear concise statement, time, return, and the plan	NH
3	Read the written statement daily before bed and upon awakening	NH
3	Define what you are seeking	WD

3	Write your wish down	JH
3	Affirm to yourself out loud what you want, in a short simple way over and over	JK
3	Always affirm the positive	JK

4. HEART EMOTION As we drop into the Heart Chakra, this is where you put the vision into the quantum field. With the vision of the desired result clearly in your mind, completed and you enjoying it, bring in the emotion of your total being vibrating in a state of bliss and joy. Form a clear picture of this as your gladness is full and be surrounded by that joy. Linger here in a field of total peace, love and harmony as you place this vision into the morphic field of the heart.

4	Have great passion and emotion to succeed	NH
4	See, feel and believe yourself in possession of the desire	NH
4	Come into your self	WD
4	Connect to service	WD
4	Act as if the desire is already here	WD
4	Become highly passionate as it is the greatest secret	JV
4	Feel what it would be like to have, do, or be what you want	JV
4	Feel what it is like to already have what you want	JV
4	See yourself feeling the result of the desires	JH
4	See yourself feeling the emotional result of the desires	JK

5. FOCUS AND INTENT At the Solar Plexus Chakra we initiate the process of intention energy for manifesting the desire. Because we are centered on love, we would create a resonance with emotion of completion making it strong. The vision of completion is paramount. This opens the communication channel to the zeropoint quantum field of infinite possibilities (the Universe).

5	Launch intention: kindness, love, beauty, expansion, unlimited abundance, receptivity	WD
5	Forgive yourself for not attracting your desires	JV

6. HIGHER POWER At the next Sacral Chakra dedicated to relationships, the next step is the request for Higher Assistance so to assist in the completion of the desires. The key is to open the love channel to believe in a Higher Power to instigate within the Universe, the possibilities of your desire. This is a release to the Universe and a detachment from the results.

This is in two parts as we first summarize what out Gurus said about getting Assistants for the Divine Intervention

Assist	Bow to the Divine within you	WD
Assist	Let the Universe create for you	JV
Assist	Send your request to ask the Universe	JK
Assist	Send your request to ask the Universe	JH

This part of the process is where the condition is released and you surrender to the Universe to do what it needs to do to entangle and collapse into the desired reality, or works towards attracting that result initiated by the cause. We effectively are entangling the two, issue and desire so as to allow the new possibility of the emotionalized desire to collapse into a new reality, the condition by releasing it. It is the Observers intent lanced in the previous step that converts particulate matter to its wave form and wave back to matter, the released energy to conform to our purpose and desire. This is the letting go where we send our information into the universe without attachment. We make ourselves at One with the quantum field.

6	Feel Spirit working through you	WD
6	Let go and detach from the outcome	JV
6	Let go as you act on your intuitive impulses & allow the results to manifest	JV

7. MATERIAL MANIFESTATION At the 7th Chakra dedicated to the materialization, we hold on to our truth of completion, with an unfettered faith and trust in the Higher Power. It is fulfilled by the powerful feeling of gratitude that surrounds the vision of completion. This is where the vortexes will attract various energy signatures, people, events and situations into your reality.

7	Be grateful that the desire has already in your possession	JV
7	Show gratitude and be thankful for receiving the desire	JH
7	Have faith and trust the Universe to manifest you desires	JH
7	Show gratitude and be thankful for receiving the desire	JK
7	Have faith and trust the Universe	JK

The Suggested Program

As a Divine Programmer you have compiled a new program of believe and rejuvenation process. The Heart as the Compiler, Love as the Language was petition or sent to the Divine Intelligence to reprogram the Subconscious and then run the program to get the cells and the brain to complete their work. If you can believe the part on holograms and our reality being an illusion, you would have also shifted non-matter into matter within the world of quantum science.

It is enforced that this process needs repetition. You are leaving it to the Universe to bring the results to you, and depending on the complexity, many choices may be brought into your reality to act upon. The best analogy to this is with the Law of Cause and Effect. If you put into the field that you want to win the lotto, then when you have a ticket counter come before you, it may be a wise choice to buy a ticket! It is suggested that these steps become a basis for what you develop as your own procedure. You may want to follow some of the systems presented. You can take what feels proper and develop your own style. It is suggested that you pay attention to checking out your beliefs and working on small desires to measure outcomes. If they do not work, understand that it is because something is still not right, and it is the repetitive process that will entrench beliefs and strength of conviction and intent. Strong positive emotion and intent in a field of well being and love is crucial. In that respect, it would be advisable to launch the 30 day Mind and Body programs and practice your healing process until it works, in faith and trust that it will.

Always be aware that it is repetition, clarity and strength of desire/emotion that are your allies. Love and Well Being are paramount. Your morphic and subtle fields need to be pumped with passion of completion. When it does not appear to work, check your beliefs with your douser and continue. You have no idea when something will manifest, nor in what form. Have faith and allow the torroids and vortexes to resonate and attract. You will see a difference.

In our final chapter, we are going to speculate from what we have written why these processes do work, and how they work. We have not been concerned that sometimes they do not work. Our feeling is that we as humans occupied with a negative world of reality, have not evolved to understand the invisible reality of the subtle world of energies in the quantum space, and therefore have limited our abilities to execute these processes and have biased our truths by filling our subconscious with untruths. This is a continuing process of uncovering a new truth and this will be continued...

39

TO BE CONTINUED...

"How long will it take to work? As long as it takes. How do I know I am doing the right thing? When it works."

Ed Rychkun

The reason why this chapter is named to be continued is because it is. Science and Metascience are converging rapidly. People are entering their 3rd stage of human development to become aware of their true eternal selves. Our quest is ongoing and we will not stop until we can assist people in understanding how they can improve health and wealth (and we don't mean only money to have a more blissful life). So as we sit here, let us give you a short version of why we believe we can create miracles...

Why Do These Processes Work?

This is actually a simple answer. And we have to acknowledge that they do not work all the time. But given the understanding that they can work, the question you may have is how do you know that they will work for you?

The human is an inquisitive creature and it does have the ability to try and try until something works. It is called faith and perseverance, just as our business Guru Napoleon Hill found out. In looking at the numerous processes, we find that these people may be guided, they learn from others, they are dedicated to find the answer, or they are taught by others. Life is an iteration process of becoming more or better so these techniques may have been simple serendipity curiosity or trial and error to find the right solution.

There is also something that one has to consider about life's background process that are not the topic of this book but nevertheless can influence the result. We will mention these briefly here:

1. The time to attain the desire is unknown
2. It could be a life destiny or life contract that interferes
3. It could be residual energies or karma that needs to be cleared first

4. It may not align with your life purpose

In many cases, we just don't care about how things work; we care about whether they work. If you want to surround your quest for health and wealth with science, which we know now is faulty, then you can forget the quest. What is strikingly important is that the number of people now looking at the science of subtle energies and quantum physics is exploding.

In this book, we have attempted to give you some insight into why these processes work. It may not be "scientific" but there are plenty of reasons why they work.

How Does It All Work?

When you came here to experience the world of a lower form, namely a body, you came here to expand the Greater Mind of the Universe. Just like an individual cell comes to expand through its environment to become more adaptive and to expand the whole of the body, the community of humanity as a cell in the bigger body came here to expand the Greater Consciousness. The task was to experience the wonders of this world in a lower form of phsyical vibration.

To undertake this task, you in the form of a Soul in a Light Body, took the job to grow and evolve within the scope of DNA which would provide you with a basic template in lower form. This lower form evolved a brain and senses that had a primary function of creating a holograph of reality and like the cells that are all individual complete mini humans, the holograph would be a mini world within a larger holograph created by the community of humans as a joint consciousness and a joint hologram.

Thus as with cells, each being a part of the whole, yet themselves whole individuals, each could experience their own hologram of reality. Although the hologram of reality would appear to be on the outside, it would be on the inside, within the powerhouse of energetic singularity, the heart. In order to experience this, the brain had evolved to be specifically concerned with developing survival habits within which the human form could prosper and feel the world of bliss. And so to experience this, the humanoid was given the power of will and emotion to chose how it would be used to further this expansive mission.

In order to keep a connection to its own Whole and the Greater Intelligence that it was a part of, the Light Body would overlay the human form and it would contain interfaces that would be the connectivity between the lower form and the higher Divine Intelligence from where it came. All would be centered on the heart where the Chakra system of subtle energies would interface to specific physical organs and functions but being sensitive to the cosmic signals that would allow the use and expansion of higher abilities.

This system would interface with all of the light body energy systems of auras, meridians, chakras, and various energy vortexes. All would be centered on the heart energy system where the center of all would reside.

Because the nature of the reality would be to create holograms of reality, the process of it so doing had to be made of the quantum energy which in its primary form is not matter congealed into particles but in the form of waves and vibrational patterns. Thus the Light body and its components would have to behave according to quantum laws, while that formed body and its reality would have to appear as physical particles following a different form of physical laws. The interface between the two would be part quantum, and part perceived as physical illusion. Thus the brain, heart, would contains such interfaces but appear to be physical. The greater connector would be the consciousness which was the mind divided into self consciousness, consciousness and subconsciousness which would be interfaces as quantum connection.

The responsibilities and processes of these would be to first provide a rapid adaptation of the human vessel to its environment through the subconscious and the brain. This stage would bring an awareness of its perceived reality so as to evolve, adapt the human vessel to this perception of reality. Drawing from its DNA blueprints, the human vessel through the physical brain and subconscious could draw on instincts to quickly adapt to its environment in an interactive stimuli-response system.

Then at a specific age around 6 years, the vessel would enter the awareness of its lower self. Here it would enter the second evolutionary stage to bring on the self consciousness that would develop the intelligence of self uniqueness and self pursuit of joy within the growing human vessel in relation to its perceived environment. This would engage free, will discernment, intelligence and ego as centered in the brain. Here new survival systems of adaptation and self growth would be built upon the first stage of development. Through this period, new skills, habits and abilities would be developed to create a uniqueness of self, centered on the self-consciousness.

Having formed the second stage platform, the third and subsequent stages of evolution would be to open to its spiritual connection in the quantum through the awareness of the Astral body. This particular pursuit could only be achieved by being in a sea of love that, as its Higher Self as the Light Body, the Divine Intelligence and the quantum sea of infinite possibilities was made up of. It would require a shift from the ego-brain to the heart-brain into the energetic realm, thus opening an awareness, the Higher Self of Light Body. If this shift to the awareness of the Astral Body did not occur, the individual would remain in the ego-brain limited physical environment.

At the center of the system would sit the means of creating matter from non matter as a torroid centered on the heart. This would reflect the translation of non matter light waves into matter as particles so projected in the personal holographic plate within each vessel, but part of the whole. And so various vortexes and torroids would project from and contain the body as itself a holographic projection. In order to shape realty, the human would have the power to choose (free will) and to create within the laws so set upon the reality created. It would have the ability to learn how to change its holographic reality once a level of maturity was reached, that being total awareness of Higher self and the Soul-Light Body.

To give the human the ability to create reality, the energetic system of chakras with its vortexes of congealing and attraction were provided to create, interface and receive energies that would be created as packets of energy signatures projected into the quantum sea. These chakra centers would allow the transmutation of energy from above to below or from Heaven to Earth through thought, vision, words (above), emotion as balance, and intent, relations, and matter below. Each of these would be an energy signature that would be projected like a funnel out into the local energetic heart field so as to attract energies of likeness into the field. At the same time the energies from outside the field could be drawn in as waves to spiral in concentrating to congeal into matter by way of entanglement and collapsing to create the reality so projected upon the individual holographic plate inside but yet part of the whole. This process would not work unless the interface between the Light Body and the Human Body was entrenched in its belief system and the awareness of its quantum essence was known, as well as beingness within the sea of its basic make up of the love vibration.

This level of maturity was conditional upon holding the human vessel n terms of both body and mind in the quantum sea of love, centered on the heart, the body commanded by the heart-brain. This process was not only contingent upon letting go of the perceived reality so created as an illusion, but living within that reality in alignment with that higher wave length frequency so created as love and bliss. This would mean that in order to achieve this status, the self-consciousness and consciousness would have to be set aside in a continuous behavior of lower self (physical reality illusion) in order to be one with its Higher Self within the quantum space of love vibrations.

Otherwise, the lower form would be unknowing to how its reality was created and it would live in its lower self and form, not able to express properly through its higher form. It would be subject to the lower physical laws and be held captive within its self-consciousness and have little to say about proactively changing its reality. And although it would in truth be creating its reality, it would not know how to create outside of the time and space limitations not existent in the quantum space from which it came and from where it became what it is as a perfection of love. This lower life would not be able to draw upon the higher vibrational instincts, abilities so provided in the brain, chakras and DNA, or the knowing and truths within the Light Body memory fields.

In order to draw upon these knowing and truths of a Higher Self, it would be through a conduit of communication through a field of love and compassion. Otherwise the field cannot listen because it is like a radio tuner that if not set at the right frequency, it simply cannot be received. Central to this is that this channel cannot open when there is some hidden agenda or ulterior motive involved typically centered in the ego-brain dominant from the second stage of human evolution. Through design of the heart, and its central power of love emotion, when compassion and love of human energy would be enfolded by strong emotion of joy or bliss, it would add to the strength of the field channel as in superposition of waves. In this respect, prayer that would be the traditional way of opening communications to the Divine Intelligence, is simply not heard when it has no energy from the heart.

This would not mean that the human could not manifest reality from within the scope of the lower form of human the universal laws of Cause and effect are at work regardless of whether the heart, love, or positive well being is in the field of creation. Even stuck in the second stage of evolution, the human could follow the traditional path of creating things and reality by making or constructing but where emotion is attached; there is a tendency to attract likeness through the same system. In the case of by-passing this traditional route and bending this reality as in the healing miracles and rapid creation of reality, a level of love based maturity would be required to take responsibility and to open the channel.

What would be the case of human stuck in stage three would be default creation and random success of such things as miracles because the human would not have yet elevated above the level of the conscious mind and the physical brain. The brain in its primary design has a chore to learn survival within the hologram that it learns to create. This evolves from instincts to survive at the Delta and Theta level to where there is self consciousness at the age of 6. This brings about a selfness or ego and the ability to think and choose the survival programs that are stored in the subconscious. The evolution, if not continued focuses on selfish behavior patterns which minimize the programming into consciousness so the individual falls back to survival mode with the added ego intellect to drive its purposes and reality. The next evolution, which can be curtailed if the Lower self is dominant, is the avoidance of the heart brain and the evolution to the love based sea of the quantum. Although the brain and consciousness allow one to open this path by way of free will, once the ego brain is entrenched and a lower form belief system is embedded, the means of overcoming this becomes more and more difficult, and the motivation and understanding becomes more and more remote.

In a Near Death Experience, by way of design of Divine Intelligence, a window would become available for the consciousness dominated by the second stage ego-brain could look at itself after letting go of its mortal lower self and facing its higher light Body. Here the stages can be overcome because the reality of the human being is something else than a body, as the Light Body-Being of pure divine consciousness. This becomes a stark reality as does the encounter with the Higher Being in that sea of love. Re entry into the body can have spectacular reprogramming consequences to change reality and the meaning of life, but as old habits may be deep, various triggers can reconstitute old programs and habits to undo what was a miracle. This is also so in a miracle healing where if the old programs and memories are chosen to come into awareness and consciousness, they can undo what has been done.

Just as a prayer cannot be heard if it is not in the morphic field of love, so is the subtle energy field of quantum not opened until an awareness is brought into consciousness. Similarly, the access into the quantum field for the purpose of direct creation and manifestation of reality is inaccessible.

In the normal stages of evolution of our earthly body and mind we have followed a binary process similar to computer technology by stopping in the ego-brain step. The third step is based upon a trinary design. Thus the evolution from binary bits to holographic qubits, then to trinary trits reflects a path that becomes closer and closer to the way we evolve the human "computer" system which is part quantum, and part binary, and part analog operates. What we have come to follow with the binary is a system that satisfies the two phases of evolution of the human.

By design, the total human bodies (physical and Light) combine physical and quantum through the holographic reality. If we can look forward into that third phase of natural design and get a grasp of the quantum nature of part of us, then one can say that the heart torroid field would represent the center of the zeropoint quantum field. Here in the Above to Below process is where the mind stuff like thoughts, images, words from consciousness is slurped down into heart to draw from the vortexes positioned at each chakra the possibilities from the quantum field outside to suck it into reality as the Below chakras congeal the possibilities into reality.

This by design creates the point of access at the heart to be zeropoint or zero. In the binary computer system 0 represent off - no access to the quantum field and the Light Body, just like the first two steps of our evolution is all we get to, not activating those higher abilities that give us the truths about the quantum nature of us, our light Body and the Universe of infinite possibilities from where we can draw a holographic reality.

The binary computer simply turns things off at a bit of 0. The quantum computer now brings in the qubit that is on (1), off (0) or both, still not providing access to zeropoint. The trinary computer comes closer where the trits are -1, 0, +1 where now we are getting to the photon level of the quantum field. We would say that this is more like our human system where 0 is the access point to zeropoint and the +1 and -1 represent the negative - positive states, like masculine - feminine that represent the states to be entangled and collapsed into reality.

Just like the brain has a local and a nonlocal data base which reflects the whole, so does the brain have a local and a nonlocal illusion of reality. This reality becomes a holographic plate projection inside which operates from the brain central processor much like all of the automatic internal and external survival processes that become saved into the subconscious quantum mind.

Under the binary two phases of evolution this automatic process uses all sensory equipment, including unbeknown to the second stage human, the higher automatic sensing abilities of the Light body. These simply operate on auto pilot in a stimuli-response mode to develop behavior patterns and the holographic projection of reality.

Upon opening to the third and fourth stages of Higher Self awareness from the heart mind-brain, the new entry point into the zeropoint quantum fields of infinite possibilities opens. Thus when this is engaged in, the higher abilities begin to open so that changing the holographic realty opens. Through design, one first creates a clear image in the mind's eye with the assistance of the heart, and then projects it to a place of materialization on the internal holographic plate. Then the second projection is to the Source so as to reflect or project back to the same plate. A holographic image is thus created in a proactive mode the same way a holographic image is created with beams of light that are split, reflected and converged again. It is whatever you see clearly that your brain understands and has meaning for or memory of. It is your brain that does the final work as a material representation by retrieving what it knows and what cosmic rules apply in the material representation. It retrieves information and the cosmic rule simply "knows" what it is. But in this case, the brain is now driven to entangle this new "made" reality into the existing reality.

This means that the Divine Mind must be the total agent of the image of some object that is simply created in the mind's eye. It will be a clear image. At the point at which the Higher Mind and the Heart—the congealer—create that image, it is projected onto a place of choice by intent and at the same time the image of the mind is projected to the God Source of the one to be reflected back like a mirror as a beam of divine light to the same place of choice; exactly like converging laser beams of light that create the 3 dimensional holographic image as in that which is perceived as reality.

As these two actions converge upon the place of choice from you and the Divine beam from the Source, they form a holographic duplicate representation of the object that is to be replicated or materialized. This occurs from the quantum field, from a wave form to an atomic form as the electrons arrange themselves into the image which is your higher consciousness choosing a new possibility from the no-thing. The resultant holographic "materialization" either flows into reality from extremities as it congeals through the chakra vortexes, or is integrated into the local and global holograms that are already each a part of the whole. The part of the whole however is the individual energy signature identity.

As a final note, consider that in all of the systems that create miracles, there are the following common actions:

Divine: Entering the subconscious field of the heart-mind love
Prayer: Asking for Divine Intervention into the Quantum Field of Love
Love: Surrendering to the issue and to love it for what it is
Forgiveness: Taking responsibility for creating that which is not perfect
Repentance: Being sorry for creating that which is not perfection
Releasement: Releasing that which has been created that is not perfect
Completion: Showing gratitude for the vision of completion

Is it no wonder that I love you, please forgive me, I am sorry for these issues, and thank you can be the most powerful words on the planet? Emotion as the Astral Body is what we all came here to express with and experience so as to add to the greater consciousness of love. Why waste moments on anything else?

> *"Everyone on the planet has an infinite supply of forgiveness and love to give away. Imagine what abundance you would attract in your life if in every moment you gave it away to express and experience its bliss."*

Aly McDonald   **Ed Rychkun**

to be continued...

BOOKS BY Ed Rychkun
Found on www.amazon.com or www.edrychkun.com

You Are Fired Said the Heart to the Ego In this unusual and profound book, Ed Rychkun takes you to a critical situation that occurs between a  human's heartbeats. In a last ditch effort to make sure the next beat occurs, the Heart engages in a desperate conversation with the Ego whom it blames for the demise of the human. In a fascinating dialogue between the Heart, the Ego, the Brain, the Mind, the Soul, the Chakra Children, and God, Ed takes you to the split second where time ceases and the physical material world becomes one with the Spiritual and Subtle energy counterparts. Learn how the Ego has taken the command center away from the sleeping Mind making the Brain, Soul, Heart, and Chakra Children subservient players in directing the quality of human life. Learn how the crisis deadlock is broken and the decision is made whether the next heartbeat is allowed to occur. See if you can deduct the same conclusions and reject or accept a coherent harmony between the six characters that control the human's life. *Will you Fire the Ego and put the power back where it belongs?*

Serve gods or Be God: Your Choice Thousands of gods have wreaked  havoc on humanity for many centuries. So has the one God himself as evidenced in the Bibles. Those who claim to be Divine interpreters of God's Word have succumbed to creating merchandise of humanity in the interest of subduing the true spirit. Never has God presented his Word directly. At the turn of the century humanity entered the 2012 End Times of Revelation, Resurrection, and Armageddon. Despite what religions tell you about God's prophecy, doom, the Second Coming, and your sins, in the minds of millions is an underlying consciousness that something is amiss with those they trust. It is because something epic is happening in this Universe.

Jack and the Great Oak Tree In this enlightening and fascinating  Adult/Children's book, Ed Rychkun weaves a story of a boy and girl that on the surface appears as a fairy tale, yet has a profound message about the relationship of Crystal Children, their environment, and their parents. Jack is an eight year old Crystal boy who does not seem to fit in with much of anything "normal". He has no friends, hates school and seems to be dysfunctional to his parents. But Jack loves to be One with Nature and has some secret skills. He sees people's auras and he smells things differently. He can read other's thoughts.

He talks to animals and trees, and he hates fake things like the Zombie Box his parents watch. He dislikes conflict and dishonesty, and can read the energy of it. He rejects plastic junk toys other kids love. What must the parents do to him to make him normal becomes Jack's and their dilemma. But one day Jack finds a giant magic Oak Tree in the deep forest. It changes his life, and the others around him forever. Follow Jack as his adventures lead him to knowing who he really is and what he, and his parents must do in their lives. *Join Jack and Suzie in the most life changing adventure of their lives.*

Xolani and the Magic Shanty In this Adult/Children's book, Ed Rychkun  tells the story of Xolani, an angry 12 year old Zulu boy living in Shanty Town in South Africa. Life is not good here and he has taken up with a band of ruffians to get back at the wealthy and the Whites whom they have learned to hate. One day Xolani finds a Magic Shanty and meets and unusual Nharo Medicine Man. Xolani finds he is not as bad as he thought and some of his Crystal Child characteristics are making life a conflict. Suddenly life begins to change for him and the people around him as he begins to blossom, and he learns how he can make his own Magic Shanty. Follow his life changing experience in the poverty stricken Shanty Town as he changes his and everyone else's life. Shanty Town will never be the same. *Live with Xolani as he unfolds his new destiny.*

Can You Let Go? Is about a paradigm shift in how you enter the world of  miracles and Co-creation. It means letting go of thinking with your head and learning to think with your heart. Why do prayers, the Law of Attraction, miracle healing, manifesting and assertions only work sometimes, for some? It is because those that show consistent success understand what the secret of letting go is. The secret? You have to let go; go inside to the heart, shift beliefs, surrender to a higher power, have faith and trust in the Divine. But what does this really mean? What is it *exactly* that one must let go of? In their raw simplicity these are very powerful words and concepts but implementing these in your life with the appropriate conviction may not be so simple. Yet there are millions of unexplained miracles and anomalies of science around the planet done by people who know how to release such special talents. Ed Rychkun poses the question; *"If others can create miracles, why can't I?"* Let us find the answer to this by learning how miracle makers let go and why. And let us get some advice from the "other side" of the veil.

Miracle, Miracle I wish to Find where you hide within my Mind

Whether mainstream medical and science experts want to admit it or not, millions of spectacular, unexplaned healing miracles occur. The dismissal of this reality on the basis of unexplainable does not benefit others who can have such a wondrous gift, or even be able to create a miracle. Quantum physics has proven that consciousness and the mind is the vital component to miracles but they simply do not know how. In addition quantum science has shattereed the foundations of what we know of atomic science. The truth is that the answers do not lie in science and if someone else can create a miracle, then so can you. So how do others do it? Let me take you to the leaders in miracles—the ones that caught my attention—the ones doing it daily. When you understand how the miracle healers really get down to the simple basics, a paradigm shift occurs in belief. Let me give you a short, simple course on what I found out so perhaps you can create your own miracles? Take your own quantum leap into the new reality of miracles.

Return to the Future Michael Carpetbagger has a serious problem with his

life. After the banking and market collapse of 2008, he and his partners are feeling the stress of a failing business. They are moving to the dark side as of necessity. This does not sit well with Michael as his soul niggles at his actions. As Mike's conundrum of negative stress and helplessness overtakes him, he falls into a bizarre instant in time where a sequence of revelations is brought to him by his Guiding Angel. She takes him on a strange journey to previous lives where in the Golden Age of Atlantis he begins to recall what and who he really is. As they wander the quantum space of his past realities into Mayan lands, and he connects with his cosmic soul family, Mike begins to form a new vision of why the old financial energy is rapidly giving way to the new spiritual energies. Now, with a new look at his future, he must congeal all the past information into what he must do to best survive as the Earth and global ascension of consciousness accelerates towards 2012 and the End Time. WARNING: CAN YOU FACE UP TO WHO YOU ARE? This may appear as work of fiction but it is an account of the past and future as seen through the past lives of a Seer of Atlantis.

The Way Back In this story, Christopher Andrew Fallenstar is a desperate

trapped soul lost in a sea of mundane agony. He is on Earth living a dysfunctional life full of self pity, anger and unhappiness. His darkness eventually leads him to despair and a gateway into a world where reality and non-reality have converged. Lost and bewildered, he must find his way back. But back to what? Is it back to the Home from where he came or is it where he is living his mundane life? On his journey, he must traverse a series of Realms with pathways through his inner being to find his way. His quest to find his way back leads him to deal with parts of himself that he never knew about. He begins to uncover a new consciousness about who and what he might be. What he chooses and the paths he takes determine his final eternal destiny... and what the back really means. In this story, Ed Rychkun will take you on a journey through your inner self that may change the way you view Home. *It may even change your attitude about life!*

In New Earth: A Personal Journey Ed Rychkun answers some key questions such as *What is Heaven? What would a New Earth be like?* and

How does the 2012 ascension relate to a New Earth? He tells his story to explain how every individual is on a seperate journey attempting to understand what will happen to Old Earth. In this personal journey, he takes you on his journey to the inner self and inner earth to reveal what the new earth can be. It's all about leaving your physical body like in a Near Death Experience where one can liberate the soul to see it's truth. *"I have come to a conclusion through my journey that where we head through ascension and what we percieve as our New Earth is entirely different from what intellect could imagine."* Take this excursion into the different realms of Agartha, the perfect and pure lands created by the ascended ones where no negagtive energies exist. Here the creation of all things is instant through pure thought within the Creator's Consiouness.

Managing Human Subtle Energy: Walking the Thought This mind

bending book gets to the bottom line of how to launch a management program that will absolutely change your life. You will clearly understand what Human Subtle Energies are and how they have been designed with a purpose – to convert non-physical energy to physical reality within your consciousness so you can enjoy life. First, see what the world of new science says about the existence and power of Human Subtle Energy. After this mind-blowing summary, find out the Laws by which these energies generated by your body operate. The inevitable startling conclusion will pound into your mind – you have not been managing your subtle energies properly – living a life of negative energy, drumming to a default destiny. Ironically, your life has turned out exactly the way you wanted it from previous thoughts and emotions. The way to change this lies in creating a habit to break old habits – through proactive Subtle Energy Management. Do you believe you can awaken the Genie in you and even control events by managing your subtle energy? *Walk your thoughts for 60 days and find out for yourself.*

Musings of Ascension by Morganne Rayne and Ed Rychkun is about getting on the Ascension Train. This little book of poetry is your boarding ticket as it brings the knowing of how to let go and head for Home. What is it that is the secret to finding Heaven on Earth? Do we have to leave to get to a Heaven and go Home? Not at all, it is within you and within your Heart but not so easy to find. The book is a compilation of truths that took the two authors many lives to find. Together, they share their simple words of wisdom in an easy flowing poetic style to reveal who we are and what we are here to do. But more importantly, herein are their own secrets on finding the true Genie and the Lamp in ourselves. The authors share as a poetic summary how we can all find ourselves on the Train, in preparation for the most wondrous of times in the Universe.

www.ingramcontent.com/pod-product-compliance
Lightning Source LLC
Chambersburg PA
CBHW050119170426
43197CB00011B/1636